KU-353-894

Silencing the Opposition

How the U.S. Government Suppressed
Freedom of Expression During Major Crises

Second Edition

Edited by

Craig R. Smith

SUNY
PRESS

Published by State University of New York Press, Albany

© 2011 State University of New York

All rights reserved

Printed in the United States of America

No part of this book may be used or reproduced in any manner whatsoever
without written permission. No part of this book may be stored in a retrieval
system or transmitted in any form or by any means including electronic,
electrostatic, magnetic tape, mechanical, photocopying, recording, or otherwise
without the prior permission in writing of the publisher.

For information, contact State University of New York Press, Albany, NY
www.sunypress.edu

Production by Diane Ganeles
Marketing by Michael Campochiaro

QM LIBRARY
(MILE END)

Library of Congress Cataloging-in-Publication Data

Silencing the opposition : how the U.S. government suppressed freedom of
    expression during major crises, second edition / edited by Craig R. Smith.
        p. cm.
    Includes bibliographical references and index.
    ISBN 978-1-4384-3519-0 (hardcover : alk. paper)
    ISBN 978-1-4384-3520-6 (pbk. : alk. paper)
    1. Freedom of speech—United States—History.2. Political oratory—United
States—History.   I. Smith, Craig R.

    JC599.U5S542 2011
    323.44'30973—dc22   2010027440

10 9 8 7 6 5 4 3 2 1

We wish to thank Tim West,
a graduate fellow at the Center for First Amendment Studies,
for his research and technical assistance on this book.

Contents

Contents

Preface and Introduction

When all goes well, the free marketplace of ideas functions to provide participants with important information. That model works when freedom of expression has a high priority in the lexicon of the rights we cherish. If the free marketplace is properly protected by the First Amendment, the public should demonstrate its understanding of issues at the polls and in public discourse. That was the dream of the founders when they added the First Amendment to the Constitution on December 15, 1791. For more than two centuries the First Amendment has faced serious challenges that often impair the operation of the free marketplace of ideas. In this study, we examine those crises from the first one during the Alien and Sedition battle in the late 1790s to current challenges occurring after the attack of September 11, 2001.

In the course of this study, we contextualize these crises by reconstructing the background influences, external and internal threats, values, beliefs and attitudes that stimulated the participants. Along the way we examine the interpretation of the First Amendment in various Supreme Court decisions. We analyze the passage of new amendments particularly during the administrations of Abraham Lincoln, Andrew Johnson, and Ulysses S. Grant. We visit the holocaust visited on Native Americans, the labor crisis of the late nineteenth century and the struggle for women to obtain the vote. In those cases, freedom of expression is seen as intimately linked to freedom of assembly and the freedom of exercise of one's religious beliefs. Special attention is also given to the suppression of political expression through content controls placed on the broadcast media and limits placed on campaign contributions.

What the founders had to say about First Amendment rights at each crucial juncture on the road to its incorporation into the Constitution clearly revealed that they believed deeply in an expanded commitment to freedom of expression. Before the American Revolution, the common law of Blackstone focused almost exclusively on preventing prior restraint. By contrast the First Amendment protects citizens from intrusions by their federal government, specifically from the Congress, which was instructed to "make no law abridging" those rights. The fundamental nature of these rights was further endorsed when they were applied against the states in 1925. That is why the evolution of the First Amendment on its road to becoming our "first freedom" is central to this study. We hope to demonstrate that while certain First Amendment rights remain unsettled, these crises affected their development and changed their meaning for later generations.

The examination of the debates surrounding the ratification of the Constitution and the Bill of Rights revealed that the founders wished to preserve states' rights at the expense of federal power. The federal government was to be limited to delineated powers spelled out in the Constitution. This study demonstrates the ways in which erosion of that doctrine resulted in the renewed preeminence of the federal government as lawmaker and that to ensure civil liberties the doctrine of states rights had to be compromised.

Freedom of expression has been challenged and often suppressed during the 200-plus years following its incorporation into the Constitution. This volume examines that period by using illustrative case studies of the various forms of governmental suppression in our history because we believe that we can learn as much about our rights from our failures as from our successes. I will not at this juncture detail the forms of suppression to be examined, nor will I draw conclusions. My hope is that the reader will proceed through these chapters with an open and inductive mind, and then meet me at the conclusion where we can draw together the lessons of these studies. However, I do wish to raise some questions that will help the reader understand the story we are about to tell. In each case, there is a cycle of activity centering on the birth of a crisis, its growth during which opposing sides emerge, and its resolution. As we drive toward conclusions, we need to ask what are the similarities and differences in these cycles? A second question involves how much the public learned from these crises and how much of that learning was retained to be used to combat the next restriction on their freedoms? A third question follows from the second—in what ways did the First Amendment right of freedom of expression evolve during the course of America's history? Were freedoms stripped from it or added to it?

But before we begin, it is important to understand that while freedom of expression is seen as a primary and foundational right, it has been balanced against such other rights as privacy, fair trial, and national security. These very real tensions, which are in evidence as I write, are the reason the First Amendment continues to evolve and is sometimes restricted. This study focuses on various major crises the First Amendment has faced on the national level, paying particular attention to the strategic use of discourse to strengthen or weaken First Amendment rights.

This second edition of the book reinforces our thesis that governmental forces have used rhetorical strategies in simple and sophisticated ways to silence opponents. Although many of these strategies are not illegal, they should be surfaced because if we study which strategies are effective, how they evolve, and how they are unmasked, we will be better able to combat them in the future. Three sub-theses will also be examined. First, government suppression of opponents is an inevitable cycle in times of crisis. A new chapter on the crisis surrounding the attacks of September 11, 2001, points to the relevance of this issue in our own time.

Second, government methods of suppression have become more sophisticated as old methods are exposed and new technologies are developed. A new chapter on media and campaign reform reinforces the relevance of this development in our own time.

Third, the wider the gulf between the oppressed and the oppressors, the more militant and extra-legal the forms of suppression become. A new chapter on woman suffrage is particularly relevant to this thesis.

My fellow authors and I have selected the most important cases and they guarantee a comprehensive view of challenges to the First Amendment. They involve issues of free press, free speech, freedom of belief and assembly; each case involves the federal government or one of its agencies. Each of these events took place with the context of a war or the threat of civil violence. To further ensure the significance of each case study, it had to fall into one or more of the following categories: 1) those brought on by the action of the president of the United States as chief executive officer of the federal government; 2) those promulgated by Congress; 3) those created by radical party segments or movements momentarily seizing control of the legislative process; 4) those caused by conflict with a major international force; and 5) those that were the result of combinations of the first four.

Chapter 1 addresses the Alien and Sedition Acts, which were passed when war with France was imminent in the 1790s. Chapters 2 and 3 examine Lincoln's suppression of the Copperheads during the Civil War and Radical Republicans' revenge on Southerners' rights after it. Chapter 4 demonstrates that national and regional security was used to justify the holocaust perpetrated on Native Americans, whose cultural differences with Euro-Americans were significant. Chapter 5 considers how Presidents Harrison, Cleveland, and McKinley tried to prevent the formation of strong unions, perhaps the clearest violation of the right of assembly in our history. Chapter 6 examines the suffrage movement, which overlaps with the union movement but does not achieve its aim until 1920. Chapter 7 contextualizes Senator Joseph McCarthy's allegations that the administration suffered from communist subversion within the cold war inclusive of the collapse of National

China and the Korean War. Chapter 8 provides a lengthy study of how the Vietnam War was the impetus for Lyndon Johnson's and Richard Nixon's extra-constitutional actions and suppressive rhetoric. Chapter 9 demonstrates that even well-intentioned legislation can chill freedom of expression, in this case over the broadcast media and in political campaigns. Chapter 10 reviews how once again in the name of national security, certain rights were restricted during the crisis following the attacks of September 11, 2001.

More specifically, the authors examined Presidents Abraham Lincoln, Lyndon Johnson, and Richard Nixon because they provided clear cases that met the general criteria set out earlier. However, Presidents Jackson, Wilson, and Franklin Roosevelt could also be singled out for lesser transgressions as we shall see in the transitions between the studies. We selected the radical party segments, which included the Hamiltonians, the Radical Republicans, and the McCarthyists because they span our history and play on the double threat of external attack and internal subversion. These groups were particularly blatant and remarkably successful in stripping fellow citizens of their First Amendment rights in the name of national security. Finally, we examined the Native American, early Unionist, and feminist quest for recognition because they represent racial, gender, and class suppression. They provide clear cases of cultural and ideological suppression and thereby broaden the base of data from which we can draw conclusions about the uses of rhetoric in a free society.

The selection criteria worked to guarantee that in general these exigent situations embody major challenges to the principle of freedom of expression on the national scene and illustrate what happens to authority and radicalism in a nation that puts the right to expression at the top of its values. Challengers to such freedoms always do so by trying to elevate another *value* to prominence, and these cases give us a chance to look at other values in the American lexicon and in one case at the values of another culture that came in conflict with the Euro-American one. Sometimes the value is political power, sometimes it is national security, sometimes it is racial or gender equality, but whatever the value may be, it suffers the burden of trying to secure rank above the specially enshrined value of the First Amendment.

In the conclusion of this book, I hope to show that there are several unifying themes that emerge from these chapters. For example, we will learn that although history does not repeat itself exactly, some of these cases are remarkably similar and should give us pause when their tactics emerge anew in our own time. I would also note that the first use of the words "terrorist" and "terrorism" come from the French Revolution and were used widely in the American debate over the Alien and Sedition Laws. The English reaction to the "reign of terror" instigated by the Jacobin Clubs led to the popularization of the words. Those words show up again and again in our history during wars and domestic crisis. Even the unions were referred to as terrorist organizations when they were first formed and women for suffrage were jailed and tortured as if they were terrorists when they picketed the White House during World War I.

Obviously, we would not be writing this book unless attacks on freedom are consistently attenuated by counter appeals to freedom as the ultimate social right. Without the freedoms that flow from the First Amendment, Thomas Jefferson would have had great difficulty in overturning the suppression of liberty that occurred with passage of the Alien and Sedition Acts of 1798. Responsible members of the political system would have had great trouble checking the irresponsible actions of the Radical Republicans in 1868. Edward R. Murrow and those key in unmasking of Senator Joseph McCarthy in 1954 might easily have failed without freedom of press and speech. Television networks would have been unable to bring the tragedy of Vietnam into the living room of the American household. At least nationally, contests end in favor of freedom not only because ours is a constitutional republic in which freedom of expression is formally and sacredly asserted, but also because those who employ those freedoms understand how to use their freedom strategically. Thus, the cases examined attend to specific rhetorical tactics employed by the antagonists. These historic events furnish illustrations of threats to our institutions and preservation of them, all under the protection of freedom of expression.

Long Beach, California
2010

Chapter 1

The Alien and Sedition Crisis

Craig R. Smith

Less than seven years after the First Amendment was made part of the Constitution, it came under attack. This chapter demonstrates that the challenges to the First Amendment were politically motivated when the nation was perceived to be in serious danger. Facing a war with France and the potential of internal subversion, founders such as Alexander Hamilton and John Adams rationalized extra-constitutional activity on the part of the government. Despite protests from Democratic-Republicans, the Congress approved, and the executive branch carried out, legislation that muzzled freedom of expression. That action forced defenders of the Constitution to come forward and resolve the crisis in favor of the original, broader application of the First Amendment.[1]

Hamilton had been instrumental in the writing of the Constitution and in the monumental rhetorical effort to ensure its ratification. His essays in the *Federalist Papers* are among the most powerful. Like John Adams and for a long time James Madison, Hamilton did not believe that a bill of rights should be included in the Constitution. He believed that enumerating specific rights in the Constitution would imply that nonenumerated rights could be taken away from the states and their citizens by the Congress.[2] Hamilton argued in *Federalist* number 84 that if such a list of rights were included in the Constitution, then any rights left off the list would go unprotected by the Constitution. "Here, in strictness, the people surrender nothing, and as they retain every thing, they have no need of particular reservations." He went on to claim that the clause stating "We the people" guaranteed all natural rights to the people; not listing individual rights in the Constitution implied that these rights were the birthright of mankind. Furthermore, he believed that since the state constitutions that were written prior to the United States Constitution contained bills of rights, no such bill was necessary at the Federal level. For example, the Pennsylvania "Frame" of 1776 called for protection of free speech and a free press. The Virginia Declaration of Independence called the free press a "bulwark of democracy." Thus, when Hamilton defended the Constitution in the *Federalist Papers* and in the New York ratification convention, he did so as did most Federalists, without compromise.

This Federalist stratagem failed. By the time New York ratified the Constitution in July of 1788, it had already been ratified by enough states to form a union, New Hampshire providing the crucial 10th ratification in June of 1788, with Virginia following a few days later. The problem was that most states insisted that a bill of rights be added. Massachusetts and Virginia were adamant on the point. From Paris, Thomas Jefferson penned important letters to Madison urging him to support a bill of rights. And when he almost lost his House seat to James Monroe over the issue, Madison declared for a bill of rights. Patrick Henry, in league with George Clinton, Governor of New York, sought a second constitutional convention for the purpose of amending immediately. In order to head this effort off, Madison coaxed the Congress to take up the issue of amendments as soon as it could. By the summer of 1789, Madison had received 200 proposed amendments from the states. By September and led by Madison, the House reduced and consolidated the proposals into 26 amendments. Finally, a House–Senate conference agreed on 12 to submit to the states for ratification.

The nation then went through a second series of ratification debates that lent strength to the position that the Bill of Rights in general and the First Amendment in particular was meant to have broad application and not apply solely to political rhetoric and prior restraint.[3] Furthermore, analysis of these debates shows strong support for limiting federal powers and giving every benefit of the doubt to states' rights.[4] How then did the federal government come to a point where the Congress at the behest of Hamilton could pass legislation blatantly restricting the First Amendment rights of its citizens? The story is complicated.

This chapter begins by establishing the historical context of the Alien and Sedition crisis since the backdrop of events was used in the rhetorical appeals of both sides to justify their positions. That context reveals the twofold threat that the Federalists faced: national security was jeopardized by a foreign foe and internal agents; party supremacy was jeopardized by the growing ranks of Democratic-Republicans. Once the context is established, the chapter examines first Federalist and then anti-Federalist rhetorical strategies, concluding that even among Enlightenment thinkers, faulty logic, emotional appeals, and sophisms abound. At the outset, we should be clear on a crucial point of analysis for this chapter and those that follow. There is a difference between rhetorical strategies used to suppress the opinions of others, which may be immoral but legal, and legal actions taken by governmental agents, which may prove unconstitutional. Freedom of expression protects fallacious argument, but does not abide unconstitutional restrictions. That is why the crises that follow are difficult to deconstruct.

The Evolving Crisis

The Federalist Party held the majority in the U.S. Senate and House from 1791 to the end of John Adams' Administration in 1801. Comprised largely of men from the well-established merchant class and property owners of the North, the Federalist Party favored national, governmental protection for trade, strong defenses, and industrial expansion. The party had a wonderful record of nation building led by George Washington, John Adams, and Alexander Hamilton.[5] However, from the start Hamilton was intolerant of sedition, the criticism the government, in part because it was run by his party.[6]

Freedom of expression, however, was not challenged until a quasi-war developed with France. The royalist government of the Bourbons had made possible the American colonists' defeat of the British. The French Revolution, which began with the fall of the Bastille prison on July 14, 1789, had by 1792 become a bloodbath that even its instigators could not escape. In that year, Spain (ruled by Louis XVI's cousin) and Austria attacked France hoping to restore the monarchy. However, the allies lost a crucial battle at Valmy in September of 1792. Thus, they could not save King Louis XVI and his wife, Marie Antoinette, who were later beheaded. The leader of the radical Jacobin Club, Maximilian Robespierre, inspired a frightful struggle in the Paris Commune that led thousands to the guillotine. The paranoia reached its peak when Robespierre himself was finally put on trial. During his speech of self-defense, he paused to clear his throat and someone in the crowed yelled out, "He chokes on the blood of Danton!" Robespierre was executed the next day.

The victory at Valmy, witnessed and glorified by the romantic Goethe, inspired revolutionary leaders to claim that they would not relent until "all of Europe is ablaze."[7] The year ended with French forces seizing the Austrian-ruled section of the Netherlands. In February of 1793, the Directory declared war on England. Led by Edmund Burke, conservatives in England and Federalists in America feared that the terror would engulf the whole civilized world. This fear was not without cause given the excesses of the French Revolution. In the summer of 1794, however, Vice Admiral Horatio Nelson captured Corsica and his fleet blockaded French ports.

Britain's allies were less successful on land. By 1795 French successes led to a peace treaty with Spain. The British were alarmed. In that year, John Jay negotiated a treaty between the United States and Britain. France pointed out that such an agreement violated the U.S.–French treaties of 1778 and launched assaults on American commercial shipping.

Soon after, Napoleon Bonaparte launched a major offensive in the spring of 1796; he defeated the Duke of Savoy and forced the Austrians out of Northern Italy. In response in December of 1796, President Washington warned that his policy of neutrality might be compromised by the French; he recommended strengthening the navy. At the beginning of the next year, Washington warned of the activities of French war ships in the West Indies. In Europe, the British retreated from Corsica to Gibraltar and sued for peace. The Directory refused the offer and Napoleon went on to conquer the Italian peninsula by April of 1797. Austria quickly signed a peace treaty with France, further isolating the British.

John Adams, who had survived a close election, was inaugurated in March of 1797 and indicated his sensitivity to the possibility of war with France. In his rather partisan inaugural address, Adams warned the nation to be suspicious of sophistry and partisan intrigue along with the "pestilence of foreign influence, which is the angel of destruction."[8] Sounding warlike, Adams demanded reparations from the French for injuries to American maritime interests. Adams was referring to a practice of the French that had begun after the United States had signed the treaty with Great Britain negotiated by John Jay. The Directory of France resorted to seizing American ships trading with England because the Directory suspected an Anglo-American alliance. Many French leaders believed war with their former ally was imminent.

At the same time, America was having trouble with Ottoman pirates operating around Tripoli in Northern Africa. It became necessary for Adams to bribe these pirates to keep them from interfering with U.S. merchant marine fleets. In June 1797, a treaty with Tripoli was unanimously ratified by the Senate and proclaimed by Adams.[9]

In July of 1797, British Prime Minister William Pitt (the younger) again made peace overtures to the French, offering to recognize their hold over Netherlands. Word soon came that not only were the French not interested in peace, they had recalled Napoleon from Italy to mount an invasion of England. Napoleon soon realized that such a move could not succeed. Instead he recommended attacking the English alliances in the Middle East.

Adams sent a peace mission to France in October of 1797. Unfortunately, it was headed by the bellicose Charles Pinckney. After meeting with the French Foreign Minister, Charles Maurice de Talleyrand-Perigord, the envoys reported to Adams that Talleyrand was writing a report to the Directory on the cold war with America. Talleyrand had begged for more time since he had just been appointed to office, being called to the post from his position as Bishop of Autun. Furthermore, given his royalist past, Talleyrand needed time to build his credibility with the Directory.

Talleyrand was sympathetic to Adams because he had traveled in America from 1794 to 1796, just after he had been expelled from Great Britain where he had sought refuge from the French reign of terror. Nonetheless, the American envoys were suspicious of Talleyrand and believed he was stalling. The negotiations fell apart. Eventually, Talleyrand's report reflected American concerns about the French seizures of American ships. In fact, the report asked the Directory to reprimand French privateers in the West Indies. Nonetheless, in a message to Congress, Adams claimed the French had "inflicted a wound."[10] The Senate responded with a call for action.

At the same time, the United States was experiencing a steady influx of immigrants uprooted by the French Revolution. Most Federalists were alarmed by the arrival of these aliens. Reverend Jedidiah Morse claimed the "Illuminati" among the aliens were secular atheists loyal to Jefferson, even though many of them were actually displaced aristocrats.[11] The Federalists suspected that the influx was bringing a host of Jacobin[12] sympathizers to foment revolution and to act as French agents in the anticipated conflict. The President of Yale saw "our wives and daughters victims of legal prostitution; soberly dishonored; speciously polluted; . . . our sons become the disciples of Voltaire, and the dragoons of Marat."[13]

It is important to note that the words "terroriste" and "terrorisme" were first used in reference to the Jacobin Club, the father of the reign of terror. By 1794 the words were carried into the English language in denunciations of the French excesses instigated by Robespierre, who was executed in that year. The English extended the words to the Directory and eventually to Napoleon, even though they had ended the reign of terror and restored order in France. By 1798, even *La Dictionnaire de l'Academie* referred to terrorism as a system or regime of terror.[14]

Allegedly, the Jacobin revolutionaries were prepared to spread their brand of anarchy from nation to nation. These fears were given a philosophical justification in many treatises, most notably Burke's *Reflections on the Revolution in France*, which became a primer for those rallying to stem the radical tide. Later Burke wrote about the "Thousands of those Hell-hounds called Terrorists . . ."[15] and included the Directory in this category. In response, Thomas Paine had written his *Rights of Man*, which Jefferson endorsed. Paine's two-part tome was thought to have inspired an uprising in Ireland and discontent in England, which distracted that nation from its problems with the French. At the height of the Alien and Sedition crisis in America, the English faced a revolt in County Wexford in Ireland in May of 1798. The destruction of the rebel force led to another wave of Irish immigration into America, which would eventually strengthen Jefferson's Party's ranks.

In fact, Hamilton was quick to realize that the new immigrants almost unanimously supported his political opponents, the Democratic-Republican

Party of Thomas Jefferson, James Madison, and James Monroe. As ambassador to France from 1784 to 1789, Jefferson made no secret of his admiration for Enlightenment thinking. He was taken with its combination of scientific discovery and reliance on reason. He became a fan of Joseph Priestly, the man who discovered oxygen and invented sparkling water. At times, Jefferson had been an apologist for the French Revolution, especially in its less extreme modes.

Unlike Hamilton, the primary author of the Declaration of Independence had premised his support for the Constitution on the condition that a bill of rights be added. He wrote to David Humphries on March 18, 1789:

> I am one of those who think it a defect that the important rights, not placed in security by the frame of the constitution itself, were not explicitly secured by a supplementary declaration. There are rights which it is useless to surrender to the government, and which yet, governments have always been fond to invade. These are the rights of thinking, and publishing our thoughts by speaking or writing.[16]

Jefferson's concern for the passage of the Bill of Rights was understandable given his long involvement in its evolution. He had written to Madison on December 20, 1787, "A bill of rights is what the people are entitled to against every government on earth, general or particular."[17] Jefferson also wrote to Washington from Paris on November 4, 1788, "I am in hopes that the annexation of a bill of rights to the constitution will alone draw over so great a proportion of the minorities, as to leave little danger in the opposition of the residue...."[18] On December 21, 1788, he wrote to Francis Hopkins the same sentiment—that those opposed to the ratification so recently would now come over to support it once a bill of rights was passed.

Jefferson urged Madison to serve as his surrogate in the debate over the new constitution. For example, Jefferson wrote "To Madison" from Paris on November 18, 1788, "As to the bill of rights however I still think it should be added." Madison's conversion to this position came in February of 1789 when he almost lost a House race to James Monroe, then a protégé of Patrick Henry.

A month later in another letter to Madison, Jefferson made an important point that has direct bearing on the doctrine of original intent. He said he supported a bill of rights because of the power it gave to the judicial branch. The legislative branch achieved its power through the legislation it passed; the executive branch had wide-ranging powers to enforce laws, draft treaties, and administer the government. However, Jefferson wisely and prophetically noted that the judicial branch's power rested on sand. Thus, a clearly stated bill of rights was essential if the court system, and particularly the Supreme Court, was to arbitrate the rights of citizens. Even with a bill of rights, it would later take John Marshall's brilliant decision in *Marbury v. Madison* of 1803 to establish the Supreme Court's power to review legislation to determine if it passed constitutional muster. However, that ruling would have to wait until after the Alien and Sedition crisis in which Jefferson's motives would be called into question.

The Federalists perceived a threat to the sovereignty of the United States in the all-but-certain war with France. After all, by June of 1797, the French had seized or sunk more than 300 American ships in the Atlantic and the Gulf of Mexico. It was not difficult for the Federalists to make this case and sell it to the public especially when the French seemed in no mood to compromise. In December 1797, new French decrees against neutral vessels went into effect. In February of 1798, while they rested at anchor, a slew of United States ships were set ablaze in Charleston Harbor by a clandestine French marauder. In March 1798, the president called for zeal in defense of the nation.[19] In April 1798, the French added insult to injury by demanding tribute through their agents X, Y, and Z. The American representative replied, "Millions for defense; not one cent for tribute!" The sentence became a war cry in the American press. Hamilton demanded that the president order an attack on New Orleans, then held by the French. In response and over the objections of Vice President Jefferson, Adams persuaded Congress to approve the building of the frigate *United States*, which could carry up to 44 large guns.

Throughout this period, Federalist leaders met, often in secret, to find ways to enhance the chances of their party retaining control of all branches of the government. They carefully monitored the press and encouraged their friends to publish supportive articles. Unfriendly papers were scrutinized and enemy lists were drawn up. It was a moment in history when freedom of political expression in America could be called into question on theoretical and practical grounds. The value of freedom had, in fact, not been historically tested for it had been only seven years since the First Amendment had been added to the Constitution. During this undeclared war with France, Federalists not unnaturally feared disaffected aliens would try to destabilize the national government, and those aliens seemed certain to swell the ranks of the Democratic-Republican Party—who now called themselves simply "Republicans"—in opposition to Federalist political power. No doubt the Hamiltonians wanted to *preserve* a Federalist America. Thus, an ulterior motive emerged that put the spur to the Federalist propaganda horse: they wanted to keep their party in power.

They began by identifying the threat in vivid terms. Federalists linked internal subversion by Jacobins to weakening America's resolve for an external war with France. Even Adams became suspect when he countered Hamilton's call for a strike against New Orleans with a call for calm. Then they enhanced the threat with legal, but heavy-handed rhetorical strategies that turned the public in their favor.

For example, *unproven assertions* often enhanced the perception of the foreign threat. Public pronouncements couched in extreme terms proved effective in gathering support to confront it. Jonathan Dayton, Federalist Speaker of the House of Representatives, caused consternation in 1798 by asserting that armies were massing in France, preparing to conquer the United States:

> As to the means of invasion, it was known that there were already collected upon the coasts of France, bordering upon the English Channel, a numerous army which, in gasconading style, was called the Army of England. It was known that there were also collected and collecting at various ports in that quarter, ships of war and transports of all descriptions.[20]

The Speaker described what could be a possible scenario. It was not difficult to imagine particularly in a world of conspiracy and intrigue. Nonetheless, it was simply not true.

Hamiltonians also relied on the stratagem of *false cause* to make their cases. One of the Hamiltonian contentions was that the French Directory, which had taken over in 1794 after the fall of the Jacobins, was sending its army to the United States because the army would overthrow the Directory if left unemployed in France. Given the events of the time, the Federalists had plenty of ammunition to support such an assertion. Armies of Revolutionary France did, in fact, invade neighboring European states to spread the Revolution. French Territory in North America could serve as a launching pad for an invasion of the United States. Those "XYZ" dispatches of April 1798 gave the assertions credibility with the mass of voters.

This context also allowed the Federalist to *exaggerate a minimal threat* so that it assumed the proportions of a significant crisis. For the Hamiltonians, the example of the Republican newspaper *Aurora* "proved" that sedition was rampant throughout the country. The *Aurora* was a Philadelphia paper that supported the Jeffersonians and was highly critical of the Adams Administration. This paper often portrayed President Adams as imperious. It also called the motives of Hamilton into question not only on its editorial page but in regular reporting. In congressional debate Representative Long John Allen remarked that "liberty of the press and of opinion is calculated to destroy all confidence between man and man; it leads to a dissolution of every bond of union."[21] Other Federalists accused the *Aurora* of sedition and claimed that the press in general frequently instigated disloyalty toward the government.

Once the rhetorical context was established, some Federalists had little difficulty employing *guilt by association* when replying to challenges during the debate over Alien and Sedition legislation.[22] One such attack was watched closely by members of the House and by citizens in a packed gallery. Speaker Dayton rebutted a speech by Albert Gallatin, a Republican leader who had originally come to the United States from Switzerland. Dayton himself was known to be a moderate Federalist so his insinuations concerning Gallatin's foreign origin and his presumed friendliness to European radicalism were all the more striking. Said Dayton:

> And why should that gentleman [Gallatin] be under no apprehension? Was it that secure in the perfect coincidence of the principles he avowed with those which actuated the furious hordes of democrats, which threatened the country with subjugation, he felt a confidence of his own safety, even if they should overrun . . . the states? He might indeed contemplate an invasion without alarm . . . he might see with calmness . . . our dwellings burning.[23]

When Congressman Jonathan Livingston objected that the new laws required "no indictment; no jury; no trial . . . no statement of accusation," he was answered with the claim that the insidiousness of French intrigue made these objections irrelevant. Using a tactic that would resurface often in our history, most prominently in the McCarthy era (see chapter 7 of this book), Federalist Congressman H. G. Otis claimed the laws were necessary because the French had "pushed their intrigues into some of the first offices of government." Once again, a Federalist successfully magnified a perceived threat by casting aspersions on the trustworthiness of objectors.

Using these fallacious but effective rhetorical tactics, the Hamiltonians redoubled their efforts to preserve their party from the growing numbers of Republicans and to mitigate the prospect of losing the White House in the election of 1800. These appeals set off more fears among common citizens. The Federalists increased the sense of danger from infiltration by pointing to the outspoken sedition of certain Republicans, who were growing in number. Federalist Congressman Otis, later to head the ill-fated Hartford Convention of 1812, which called on New England to secede, said in reply to a Republican colleague, "The gentleman . . . vociferates for the evidence of plots and conspiracies against the government. . . . If the gentleman insisted upon evidence of seditious dispositions in our country, *I would refer him to his own speech.*"[24] The synergy between the Hamiltonians and the media should not be overlooked. The Federalist press supplied the accepted facts for the Hamiltonians' faulty logic. Then the Federalist press reported the Hamiltonian claims to the public further reinforcing fears and planting premises that Federalists could use in building persuasive arguments on which to campaign.

Moving Beyond Rhetorical Strategies

These rhetorical attacks gave the Hamiltonians the ability to initiate activities including restrictive and unconstitutional legislation. By 1798 the Federalists had already raised a large standing army and gained control of it by pushing Hamilton to the position of acting commander. With the endorsement of Washington and President Adams in tow, they set up a Department of the Navy and armed merchant ships; eventually 14 American war ships were commissioned and 200 other vessels took out letters of marque for reprisals against the French. The culmination of the Federalist campaign came with the passage of the Alien and Sedition Acts in July of 1798. Debate on the Acts in the House of Representatives was marred by both physical violence and slander.

The Federalist agenda comprised an extreme threat to personal freedoms. Congressman Robert Harper of South Carolina, speaking to this issue, justified a restriction on freedom in the face of internal subversion. As the author of the Sedition Bill and former Chairman of the House Ways and Means Committee, he brought considerable credibility to the debate. He developed a scenario of collapse, which revealed the essence of Federalist fears: philosophers of the French Revolution, who were in every country, were paving the way for Jacobins who followed closely in their wake, bent on seizing power by violent means—means that had been used during the reign of terror in France. Harper put it this way:

> Philosophers of [the French] revolution exist in all countries. . . . They advance always in front and prepare the way by preaching infidelity, and weakening the respect of the people for ancient institutions. . . . The Jacobins follow close in the train of philosophers, and profit by their labors. This class is composed of that daring, ambitious, and unprincipled set of men, who possessing much courage, considerable talent, but no character, are unable to obtain power, the object of all their designs, by regular means, and therefore, perpetually attempt to seize it by violence.[25]

These themes were developed by the press and the pamphleteers so that in a few months the entire country was exposed to expressions of fear of French Jacobins.

The Republicans coaxed a few Federalists to their side of the aisle on a few emendations to the bills. The most important of these was securing March 3, 1801, for an end to the Acts. This date was the day before the next presidential inauguration and Republicans hoped to have a president in place who would allow the acts to sunset. Another modification occurred, which relied on the case of publisher John Peter Zenger, who almost 70 years earlier had used truth as a defense in libel case. The moderates now included language assuring that the truth could be used as a defense in sedition trials. That is, true criticism of the government could not be categorized as sedition. Furthermore, the moderates excluded federal judges from coming under the sedition law so they could not be penalized for issuing opinions that were critical of the government.

After these concessions, the bills were passed usually on straight party votes. The first roll call in the House was on a motion to prevent a second reading; it failed 47–36 with some Republicans throwing in the towel.[26] On the important vote, the House passed the bills by only three votes, 44–41. Thomas Tillinghast became the only Republican to vote for the measures.[27] The votes in the Senate were more lopsided given the Federalist majority there. President Adams promptly signed the legislation and it became law.

The Acts were clearly violations of the First Amendment, though they were never reviewed by the Supreme Court.[28] The "Naturalization Act" extended from 5 to 14 the number of years of residence required before full U.S. citizenship could be granted. The "Act Concerning Alien Enemies" authorized President Adams to order the expulsion of "dangerous" aliens during peace time. The "Act Respecting Alien Enemies" authorized the president to apprehend, restrain, secure, and remove enemy aliens during time of war *or undeclared hostilities*.[29] The "Sedition Act" prohibited conspiracy against the U.S. Government and also prohibited writing, printing, uttering, or publishing false, scandalous, and malicious writings against the U.S. Government.[30]

In no time, the Federalists used the new laws to go after their enemies. Editors and publishers of Republican newspapers, which had ridiculed members of Congress or the administration were arrested, as were several leading figures of the Republican Party. However, the Federalists often found judges to be more moderate than they expected. Of those arrested, only about 15 were ever indicted and only 11 of those were brought to trial.[31] However, 10 of them were convicted of violating the law.

The poster child for these trials was Congressman Matthew Lyon of Kentucky, who, in October, 1798, was convicted under the provisions of the Sedition Act.[32] Not only was he the first member of Congress to be convicted of a crime while in office, he was the first to be put in jail for criticizing the political system and its leaders. His arrest, trial, and conviction set a dangerous precedent for the new nation. Here was the point at which partisanship overpowered legitimate uses of the government. Lyon's constituents seemed to understand this. They reelected the Congressman while he sat in his jail cell,[33] and when Federalist tried to vote to expel him from the House, the Republicans were successful in blocking the move.

Another law closing down free speech was prompted by a Philadelphia Quaker named George Logan. With no authority or backing from the government, he traveled to Paris to try to end the quasi-war. Though he failed in his idealistic quest, the Federalists rammed a new law through Congress, which the president signed as the Logan Act, and which prohibited private citizens from initiating diplomacy with foreign governments. It is still in force today though often ignored by such unofficial diplomats as Jesse Jackson, Jimmy Carter, and Ramsey Clark.

The Federalists rode rough shod over the helpless Republicans. In 1798 alone they created more than 20 new laws, which Adams signed. The most important abrogated all treaties with France, expanded the army, armed sea vessels, authorized attacks on French vessels on sight, and nominated former President George Washington as Commander of the Army with Hamilton second in command. Washington's acceptance of the command was dramatic because it contradicted some of the recommendations he made in his famous "Farewell Address." Washington did not believe in international neutrality any more than he believed in nonpartisanship. In his acceptance of this latest assignment, the Father of the Country referred to the "insidious hostility" of France and their "agents" in America. He attacked their "disregard for solemn treaties" and our ministers. He took aim at their "war upon our defenseless commerce."[34]

Adams was losing control over the situation. However, Hamilton's modesty fooled few in Congress; most members understood him to be the real commander with the aging Washington serving only as a figurehead. Party leaders knew that Hamilton had managed to talk Washington into openly supporting the Sedition Law, while Hamilton personally demurred on the issue. The American public was another matter. Because they were less vigilant and less in the know than members of Congress, the public fell for Hamilton's political strategy in the election of 1798; they provided large majorities that kept the Federalists in power. Jeffersonians were identified with the hated French.

The Republican Response

As we have seen, the British were distracted from their war with France due to a rebellion in Ireland; but the French had their troubles, too. Napoleon had decided to slip past the British fleet of Admiral Nelson and landed in Egypt in July 1798. Napoleon scored an immediate victory over the local rulers only to turn around and see Nelson destroy the French fleet anchored in Abukir Bay. Nonetheless, Napoleon scored several more victories on land, slaughtering the citizens of Jaffa along the way. When the Ottoman allies of the English held Acre, on the Palestinian coast, Napoleon retreated to Cairo and then decided in August 1799 to leave his army behind and return to France proclaiming that he was the hero of the Middle East. In November 1799, he seized power from the Directory. This was not difficult to do because the Directory had attempted to colonize parts of Italy, including the Island of Malta, thereby offending the Russian czar, a member of the Knights of Malta. The czar led a coalition against the French that was successful in chasing them from their Italian enclaves.

This defeat opened the door in the fall of 1799 for Napoleon's rise to power. He cut a deal with two members of the Directory, removed those who opposed him, and then marched to the Council of Five Hundred to make a plea for their support. However, his rhetorical skills suddenly failed him and he fainted, forcing his brother Lucien to save the day with troops who expelled the Council. Just as Edmund Burke had predicted, France collapsed from the inside and turned to a general who became its dictator.[35]

Although the failure of democracy in France was a disappointment to Jefferson, he realized that it presented an opportunity in the fight to overturn the Alien and Sedition Act. He could portray Hamilton and his party as the men of oppression trying to undo the rights so dearly won in the American Revolution just as Bonaparte was undoing the rights won in the French Revolution. Jefferson was careful not to reveal his correspondence with Talleyrand, still the French Minister of Foreign Affairs. Nor did the vice president admit to writing a series of resolves that were approved by the Virginia and Kentucky legislatures in 1799. The Kentucky Resolutions read as follows:

> *Resolved*, that the several States composing the United States of America are not united on the principle of unlimited submission to their general government; but that by compact under the style and title of a Constitution for the United States and of amendments thereto, they constituted a general government for special purposes, delegating to that government certain definite powers, reserving each State to itself the residuary mass of rights to their own self-government; and that whensoever the general government assumes undelegated powers, its acts are unauthoratative, void, and of no force: That to this compact each State acceded as a State, and is an integral party, its co-States forming, as

to itself, the other party: That the government created by this compact was not made the exclusive or final judge of the extent of the powers delegated to itself; since that would have made its discretion, and not the Constitution, the measure of its powers; but that as in all other cases of compact among parties having no common Judge, *each party has an equal right to judge for itself, as well of infractions as of the mode and measure of redress.*

The Virginia Resolves appealed for the preservation of the free marketplace of ideas as well as constitutional freedoms. Adams believed that the resolves were fomenting revolution because they argued that states could resist federal law if they believed it was unconstitutional. He became particularly concerned when Jefferson spoke of the danger of increased presidential power. The vice president also argued for free speech and press, a sure sign as far as Adams was concerned that Jefferson wanted to use popular appeals to bring the federal government to a halt. Much to Adams' distress petitions were arriving from around the country demanding the repeal of the laws. Nonetheless, the House voted 52 to 48 to reinforce the Alien and Sedition Acts early in 1799. Adams also launched a shrewd diplomatic maneuver. He sent Rufus King to London to talk to England and Russia about a potential alliance. Talleyrand signaled that he might be ready to cool things down a bit in the quasi-war. Adams then assembled a new peace delegation, which included Patrick Henry, the former governor of Virginia and known states' rights advocate, to go to France. Henry's archenemy, Hamilton, protested vociferously.[36]

In the meantime, Madison supported Jefferson's view with a treatise of his own. It, too, supported states' rights and argued that the new laws gave the president too much power.[37] "The people not the government possess absolute power. . . . In the United States, the executive magistrates are not held to be infallible, nor the legislature to be omnipotent . . ." Despite the campaign of misinformation propagated by Federalist papers, he concluded that freedom of expression was essential to the workings of democracy: "The security of freedom of the press requires, that it should be exempt, not only from previous restraint by the executive, as in Great Britain, but from legislative restraint also; the Act will make us unfree because the people will be compelled to make their election between competitors, whose pretension they are not permitted, by the Act, equally to examine, to discuss, and to ascertain." Madison's treatise would play an important role during the next administrative challenge to a free press (see conclusion of this chapter). For now we need only note that these three pillars—states' rights, limited presidential power, and free speech—supported the Republican counterattack on the Federalists. It proved effective. In the off-year elections of 1799, the Republicans did well.

Even before political leaders emerged to attack the Hamiltonians, newspapers had laid the groundwork for such an attack. One of the strongest arguments that can be made for a free press can be drawn from the role that opposition papers played in rousing the public against the Alien and Sedition Acts. *Greenleaf's New Daily Advertiser* published an attack on the Sedition Bill while the ink from the president's signature was still wet. On Wednesday, June 13, 1798, it carried these words:

> If the constitution of the United States was not considered by the majority of the house of representatives as a mere dead letter, or a piece of musty parchment, they would never have ventured to bring in a bill so directly contravening one of the most essential articles of freedom, and as clearly defined as any other clause in the bill of rights, namely, liberty of speech, printing and writing, all of which will not merely be infringed, but wholly annihilated, should this nefarious bill pass into law.[38]

On July 3, 1798, the outspoken editor of the *Aurora* wrote, "What is meant by defaming a law is beyond my comprehension. To laugh at the cut of a coat of a member of Congress will soon be treason; as I find it will be to give a Frenchman a dinner or a bed, as soon as this bill passes."

The Boston *Gazette* came to the defense of the *Aurora* a few days later:

> The Editor of the Aurora was [recently] arrested, on a warrant from Judge Peters of the Federal Circuit Court, on a charge of libeling the President, and the Executive Government in a manner tending to excite Sedition, and opposition to the laws, by sundry publications and re-publications. . . . The period is now at hand when it will be a question difficult to determine *whether there is more safety and liberty to be enjoyed at Constantinople or Philadelphia.*

Southern papers took up the call for repeal. The Norfolk *Herald* of September 1, 1798, not only opposed the bills, but applauded mass action against them:

> The real friends to the liberties and happiness of America will rejoice at the decided part which the people of Virginia have taken against the Alien and Sedition bills. In the large and respectable county of Goochland, the people met on Monday last to consult on the present crisis of American affairs, and adopted

by almost an unanimous vote, Resolutions, expressive of their strongest disapprobation of the late acts of Congress and the President. There was a very full meeting consisting of about four hundred, of these not more than twenty or thirty were against the Resolutions. They also voted instructions to their delegates in the state legislature, requesting them to move, in the next session of the Assembly, a Remonstrance to Congress, against the late obnoxious acts of government, or to support any other constitutional measure which may be deemed more effectual, to vindicate the liberties of Speech and the Press, and to restore the trial by jury.—BRAVO!

The leading advocate of the Acts, Congressman Harper, reacted to the protests in South Carolina by introducing legislation to distribute Alien and Sedition Acts nationwide. For Republicans, this action was roughly akin to the Sheriff of Nottingham posting notices on trees that those who aided Robin Hood would be arrested.

Over the past 50 years, Americans have become accustomed to artists protesting against government policies whether they result in wars or infringements on rights. It was no different in 1798, 1799, and 1800. Poets and songwriters knew that the Alien and Sedition Acts could portend of censorship in the near future. They used their crafts to stir the public against the new restrictions. On September 17, 1798, one of the most devastating attacks on the Federalists' repressive policies came in a poem placed in the Boston *Gazette* and attributed to "Americanus." It was followed by the announcement of the resignation of the paper's editor, Benjamin Edes:

Since we are forbid to speak, or write
A word that may our BETTERS bite,
I'll sit mum-chance from morn to night;
But pay it off with THINKING.
One word they ne'er shall fish from me
For Master Rawle, or Charley Lee;
Yet, if they'll let my thoughts be free
I'll pay them off with THINKING.
When George began his tyrant tricks,
And Ropes about our neck would fix,
We boldly kicked against the Pricks
Nor sat mum-chance, a THINKING.
We freely spoke, and freely thought,
And freely told him what we sought.
Then freely seiz'd our swords, and fought
Nor dreamed of silent THINKING.

If Hancock and great Washington,
    Had nothing said, and nothing done,
His race the tyrant would have run,
    Whilst we were mum a THINKING.
Had Dickenson not dar'd to write,
    Had common sense not spit his spite,
Our soldiers had not dar'd to fight,
    But set down mum, a THINKING.
We swore that thought and swords were free,
    And so the Press should ever be,
And that we fought for Liberty,
    Not Liberty of THINKING,
But Liberty to write or speak,
    And vengeance on our foes to wreak;
And not like mice, in cheese, to squeak,
    Or, sit down mum, a THINKING.
Again on Constitution Hill,
    We swore the sovereign people's will
Should never want a press or quill,
    Or tongue to speak as THINKING.
That still we're sovereign who'll deny?
    For though I dare not speak, Yet I
ONE SOVEREIGN RIGHT, will still enjoy
    The SOVEREIGN RIGHT OF THINKING.
    AMERICANUS.

In fact, the election of 1800 was the first in which campaign songs were used to ask citizens to vote for a specific candidate. The Federalists had appropriated "Yankee Doodle" as their campaign song. Using the same tune, the Jeffersonians sang of attacking "men in pow'r [who] cry 'sedition.'" Other lyrics praised Jefferson and the action he would take if he were elected:

If you peace and freedom love,
Act with circumspection,
Ev'ry foe to these remove,
At your next election,
Choose for chief Columbia's son,
The immortal Jefferson.
He will ever-ever-ever-ever stand,
Watching o'er your freedom.

After Jefferson's Inaugural, a lyricist wrote:

Acting in a noble cause,
He abolished cruel laws,
Set the mind and body free,
He's the son of liberty.

The Defeat of Hamilton

The poems, editorials, and resolves had an effect as did the less bellicose nature of the French. In desperation, the hard-core Federalists responded with a counteroffensive. Hamilton expanded the army when the Federalists put Hamilton in command when Washington stepped down.[39] Hamilton used his authority the next month to crush John Fries' Rebellion in Pennsylvania.[40] He then worked to replace the conciliatory Adams with the more hawkish Charles Pinckney as nominee of the party for the elections of 1800. Jefferson could see that the Federalists were disintegrating, but he knew that they were likely to be ever more dangerous in that state.

A measure of the desperation of Hamiltonians can be seen in their attempt to convict Thomas Cooper, an anti-Federalist newspaper publisher, of sedition.[41] Once editor of the Republican leaning *Gazette*, which was distributed in Sunbury and Northumberland, Pennsylvania, Cooper had been outspoken in his opposition to the Sedition Act.[42] When Cooper was criticized for his views, he responded by printing a handbill for which he was charged with seditious libel. Specifically, Cooper accused President Adams of "a stretch of authority which the Monarch of Great Britain would have shrunk from; and interference without precedent, against law and mercy!"[43] At the trial Cooper hoped that his First Amendment rights and the truth he spoke would be an adequate defense. Associate Justice Samuel Chase of the Supreme Court presided over the federal trial. The prosecution tried to overcome Cooper's arguments by claiming that he had made false statements that insulted the president and thereby the citizens of the country.[44] The prosecution suggested that if such libels were allowed to go unchecked they might foment revolution.

Cooper responded that the political system was based on free and open debate and that the public had a right to know about the conduct of political officials. After all, many of the founders had attacked King George III by revealing his abuses of power and claiming he was insane.[45] The prosecution responded that Cooper's testimony was damning and that the Sedition Law was written precisely to take care of problems like Cooper. Judge Chase, a Federalist, fined Cooper $400 and sent him to jail for six months.

Then there was case of James Callendar. He had written for the *Aurora* in Philadelphia, issued the standard Republican arguments and attacked

Adams and Hamilton. When it became clear he was going to be arrested, Callendar moved to Virginia, where he began another series of attacks during the election of 1800.[46] He put out a pamphlet favoring Jefferson and attacking President Adams, for which he was brought to trial in May of 1800 in Richmond. The most serious claims made by Callendar seem to be that Adams was trying to close the frontier, that he was an "aristocrat" who "proved faithful and serviceable to the British interest."[47] Not surprisingly, Associate Justice Chase relished the chance to come to Richmond to hear the case. Callendar was defended by prominent Virginia Republicans including William Wirt and Philip Nicholas, who at the time was the attorney general of Virginia. They argued that what Callendar had written in his pamphlet was true and therefore exempt under the Sedition law. Furthermore, they claimed that the Sedition Law was unconstitutional. When Judge Chase disallowed these arguments, the defense team refused to continue. Following instructions from Chase, the jury found Callendar guilty.

As public outrage grew, many people demanded that their representative in Congress repeal the Acts. The Republicans made a valiant effort but the Federalists held firm in early 1800. However, the growth of the standing army and the direct tax on citizens provided Republicans with more ammunition to attack the Federalists. American naval vessels won victories at sea providing Adams with needed credibility and calming fears of an invasion. When he fired Hamiltonians McHenry and Pickering from the Cabinet, the split with Hamilton was complete. During the election campaign of 1800, Jefferson, Burr, Monroe, and Madison enjoyed watching the internecine fighting in the Federalist Party. Those loyal to Adams claimed that Hamilton had fathered a creole bastard.[48] In October, Hamilton accused Adams of "vanity without bounds," "disgusting egotism," "distempered jealousy," and "desultriness of mind."[49] When Hamilton's missive somehow got into the hands of Aaron Burr, he passed it on to Republican newspapers. The public began to see in the Alien and Sedition Acts what Congressman Jonathan Livingston had predicted early in the debates over the Sedition Bill: "The President alone is empowered to make the law, to fix in his mind what acts, what words, what thoughts or looks, shall constitute the crime contemplated by the bill. . . . He is not only authorized to make this law for his own conduct, but to vary it at pleasure, as every gust of passion, every cloud of suspicion, shall agitate or darken his mind."[50] Luckily for Adams, Napoleon set his sights on other nations. In May 1800, he crossed the Alps into Italy to retake the territories the Directory had lost in their war with the coalition forces headed by the Russians. After taking Milan, Napoleon defeated the Austrians at Marengo, one of his most impressive strategic victories.

The signing of the Franco-American Convention relieved the external pressure and revealed that Hamilton was at best mistaken, for an agreement *could* be reached with the French after all. The Jefferson-Burr ticket was elected in 1800, ending Hamilton's dreams of power and striking a blow from which the Federalist Party would not recover. In February of 1801, just days before Jefferson's Inaugural, Adams concluded a treaty with France ending all pretense of a crisis. The Sedition Act expired by its own terms on March 3, 1801, just before Jefferson's inauguration. In the election of 1802, only 39 Federalists survived in the House against 103 Republicans. Only nine Federalists survived in the Senate as against 25 Republicans.

Conclusion

The free press and such articulate writers as Jefferson and Madison defeated the Federalists in part by revealing how their actions, like those of Judge Chase, contradicted their rhetoric and constitutional principles. Federalist suppression of free speech was clearly in conflict with the goals of liberty and internal tranquillity. Worse, their corruption of freedom of expression by using it to advance faulty claims came back to haunt them. Jefferson, in his first Inaugural Address in March 1801, expressed the sentiments of what was by then the majority of the nation and the spirit of later responses to radicalism:

> Let us, then, fellow citizens, unite with one heart and one mind. Let us restore to social intercourse that harmony and affection without which liberty and life itself are but dreary things. And let us reflect that, having banished from our land that religious intolerance under which mankind so long bled and suffered, we have yet gained little if we countenance a political intolerance as despotic, as wicked, and capable of as bitter and bloody persecutions. . . . Every difference of opinion is not a difference of principle. We have called by different names brethren of the same principle. We are all Republicans, we are all Federalists. If there be any among us who would wish to dissolve this union or change its republican form, let them stand undisturbed as monuments of the safety with which error of opinion may be tolerated where reason is left free to combat it.

Jefferson immediately pardoned all who had been convicted or who were awaiting trial under the Acts.[51]

And so the first assault on the First Amendment ended with one of its strongest proponents becoming president.[52] This assault, like those that we examine in the following chapters, was motivated by perceived threats, be they the possibility of war, internal subversion, and/or loss of political power. When the threats become real for the public, the radical segment can seize the moment and advance its legislative agenda. But unless the perception of the threats is sustained, the agenda will eventually fall victim to a resurgence among the defenders of constitutional rights. In this case, several rhetorical tactics ranging from logical fallacies to synergy with the media were used to enhance the public's perception of a threat from a foreign foe. Eventually, those employing rhetoric on behalf of the constitutional principles prevailed, but only because the historic context changed. That should give us pause, for had the context not changed, one wonders what would have become of our liberties.

Notes

1. For an examination of the original intent of the founders with regard to the First Amendment, see Craig R. Smith, *To Form a More Perfect Union* (Lanham, MD: University Press of America, 1993).

2. This was also the initial position of James Madison who was later persuaded by his constituents and Thomas Jefferson that a Bill of Rights was essential. See Smith, 152–156.

3. The belief that the First Amendment's free speech and press clauses were meant only to protect political speech and to protect from prior restraint gained some currency with the publication of Leonard Levy's 1960 study, *Legacy of Suppression: Freedom of Speech and Press in Early America* (Cambridge: Harvard University Press). However, even Levy recanted this position in his 1985 book on the *Emergence of a Free Press* (New York: Oxford University Press) particularly on pages vii–xix. By then the thesis that the First Amendment was strengthened at almost every turn in the legislative drafting process had been thoroughly supported. See for example, David Anderson, "The Origins of the Press Claus," *U.C.L.A. Law Review* 30 (1983): 533–537.

4. See Craig R. Smith and Scott Lybarger, *The Ratification of the Bill of Rights, 1789–91* (Long Beach: Center for First Amendment Studies, 1991).

5. For an analysis of the roots of Federalist thinking see Smith, *The Ratification*, chapter 2.

6. Thomas Fleming cites Hamilton's fears in *Duel: Alexander Hamilton, Aaron Burr and the Future of America* (New York: Basic Books, 1999), 71.

7. Derek Jarrett, *Britain 1688–1815* (New York: St. Martin's Press, 1965), 408.

8. John Adams, "Inaugural Address," *Inaugural Addresses of the Presidents of the United States* (Washington, DC: GPO, 1974), 10.

9. One of the most interesting phrases of the treaty is its claim that the United States is "in no sense a Christian nation." The phrase was essential to assuaging the fears of the Ottomans regarding religious retaliation. But since the treaty

was carefully reviewed and unanimously approved, the phrase is revealing about the sense of religion in Enlightenment America.

10. John Adams, "Special Session Message," in James D. Richardson, ed. *Messages and Papers of the Presidents*, vol. 1 (Washington, DC: Bureau of National Literature and Art, 1907), 235–236.

11. Samuel Elliot Morrison and Henry Steele Commager, *The Growth of the American Republic*, vol. 1 (New York: Oxford University Press, 1962), 359.

12. Gerald Malcolm Howat, general ed., *Dictionary of World History* (London: Thomas Nelson, 1973), 757.

13. Morrison, *The Growth of the American Republic*, 359.

14. It is worth noting that the wave in France was also referred to as a "Red Terror," probably because of the blood that flowed from the guillotine. Thousands were executed.

15. Edmund Burke, *Select Works of Edmund Burke: Volume 3, Letters on a Regicide Peace* (Indianapolis, IN: Liberty Fund, 1999), 359.

16. Thomas Jefferson, *The Papers of Thomas Jefferson*, Julian Boyd ed., vol. 14 (Princeton, NJ: Princeton University Press), 678.

17. *Thomas Jefferson Papers, University of Virginia* http://wyllie.lib.virginia.edu:8086 or http://etext.virginia.edu/toc/modern/public/JeffLett.html:1787122.

18. *Jefferson Papers*, 1788120 or Jefferson, *The Papers of*, vol. 14, 328.

19. Richardson, *Messages and Papers*, 264.

20. Leonard W. Levy and Merrill D. Peterson, eds., *Major Crises in American History*, vol. 1 (New York: Harcourt, Brace and World, 1962), 200. Quotations that follow from the House debate over the Alien and Sedition Acts are from this source unless otherwise noted.

21. Levy and Peterson, *Major Crises in American History*, 28. Long John Allen was one of those involved in the fisticuffs that broke out during this debate.

22. See T. F. Carroll, "Freedom of Speech and of the Press in the Federalist Period: The Sedition Act," *Michigan Law Review* 18 (1920): 615.

23. Levy and Peterson, *Major Crises in American History*, 199. By 1807 Dayton would become so frustrated at the ascendance of the Democratic-Republicans that he would join Burr in an attempt to overthrow the government.

24. Levy and Peterson, *Major Crises in American History*, 207; from *Annals of Congress*, 5th Congress, 2nd Session, June 21, 1798.

25. Levy and Peterson, *Major Crises in American History*, 197; from *Annals of Congress*, 5th Congress, 2nd Session, March 29, 1798.

26. Robert Williams, a Democratic-Republican, voted with the Federalists.

27. The legislation was revisited by the Congress the next year when an attempt to repeal failed. When the Federalists found themselves in a lame duck Congress near the end of 1800, they tried to write an extension into the laws, but that failed.

28. These acts were directed primarily against anti-Federalist editors of French and English heritage, such as Thomas Cooper, Joseph Priestly, James Callendar, Benjamin Bache, Count de Volney, and others. For further information on the Alien and Sedition Acts, see Frank Maloy Anderson, "The Enforcement of the Alien and Sedition Laws," *American Historical Association Reports*, Annual Report for the Year 1912 (Washington, DC: American Historical Association, 1914) 113–126; Claude Gernade

Bowers, *Jefferson and Hamilton* (St. Clair Shores, MI: Scholarly Press, 1925), chapters 16 and 17. These Acts are reprinted in Henry S. Commager, *Documents of American History*, 9th edition (Englewood Cliffs, NJ: Prentice-Hall, 1973), 175–178.

29. This Act is in force (50 U.S.C. Sec. 21–24, 1982) with only one substantive change: states no longer have the jurisdiction to deal with enemy aliens.

30. The Alien and Sedition Acts were never reviewed by the Supreme Court. Justice William J. Brennan Jr., observed in *New York Times Co. v. Sullivan*: "Although the Sedition Act was never tested in this Court, the attack upon its validity has carried the day in the court of history . . . Jefferson, as President, pardoned those who had been convicted and sentenced under the Act . . . stating: 'I discharged every person under punishment or prosecution under the sedition law, because I considered, and now consider, that law to be nullity . . . ' The invalidity of the Act has also been assumed by Justices of the Court. Their views reflect a broad consensus that the Act, because of the constraint it imposed upon criticism of government and public officials, was inconsistent with the First Amendment" 376 U.S. 245, 276 (1962). See John Chester Miller, *Crises in Freedom: The Alien and Sedition Acts* (Boston: Little, Brown & Co., 1951), 193; William M. Malloy, "Annual Report for 1912" of the American Historical Association *reprinted in* House Document No. 933, 63rd Congress, 2nd Session, 115–116.

31. See Frank M. Anderson, "The Enforcement of the Alien and Sedition Laws," "Annual Report for 1912" of the American Historical Association *reprinted in* House Document No. 933, 63rd Congress, 2nd Session, 120.

32. For a study of similar measures used during World War I, see Clark Kimball, "Patriots versus Defenders: The Rhetoric of Intimidation in Indiana During the First World War," in Thomas L. Tedford, John J. Makay, and David L. Jamison, eds., *Perspectives on Freedom of Speech* (Carbondale: Southern Illinois University Press, 1987), 53–65.

33. In 1840 the fine imposed on Lyon was returned to his heirs. The fact that Federalists would actually jail a political opponent shows how strongly they acted when they felt threatened. Hamilton's grasp at control of the army was an example of the extra-legal maneuvering that can occur. See Smith, *Freedom's Fetters* (Ithaca, NY: Cornell University Press, 1963), 2nd edition, 185–186; Frank Luther Mott, *American Journalism: A History of Newspapers in the United States through 250 Years: 1690–1940* (New York: Macmillan, 1949), 149.

34. Washington to John Adams, July 13, 1798, in Richardson, *Messages and Papers*, 268.

35. Napoleon became Emperor of France in December 1804 summoning the Pope to come to bless the ceremony. A Pope had crowned Charlemagne Holy Roman Emperor in 800, and Napoleon wanted to imitative that event. However, he took the gold laurel crown and put it on his head himself. In May 1805 in Milan, he was declared King of Italy.

36. The parallel between Adams' levelheaded approach to the French crisis and Eisenhower's approach to the Korean crisis in uncanny. Both men suffered severe criticism from the radicals in their own ranks. See chapter 6 of this book.

37. For more on Jefferson and Madison's resolves see Adrienne Koch and Henry Ammon, "The Virginia and Kentucky Resolves: An Episode in Jefferson's

and Madison's Defense of Civil Liberties," *William and Mary Quarterly* 5 (1948): 149–150.

38. Early American newspapers can be obtained through Readex on microfilm. They can be retrieved online at www.readex.com. The list of offerings used here was updated on February 28, 2003.

39. In a letter to Theodore Sedgwick, Hamilton wrote that the militia of loyal states could not be counted on to restrain "a refractory and powerful state. . . . When a force has been collected, let them be drawn toward Virginia, for which there is an obvious pretext [that of strengthening border defenses in the Mississippi Valley], then let measures be taken to act upon the laws and put Virginia to the test of resistance." Hamilton to Theodore Sedgwick, February 2, 1799, Henry Cabot Lodge, ed., *The Works of Alexander Hamilton* (New York: G. Putnam's Sons, 1903), 340–342, quoted in Stephen G. Kurtz, *The Presidency of John Adams: The Collapse of Federalism, 1795–1800* (Philadelphia: University of Pennsylvania Press, 1957), 356.

40. In March 1799, a group of angry Pennsylvania Germans led by Fries, a militia officer, organized an attempt to rescue some of their outspoken allies who had openly defied the direct tax imposed by the Federalists. Federal marshals were prevented from incarcerating the men, skirmishes broke out, and General McPherson's Pennsylvania army was rushed to the scene. Kurtz, *The Presidency of John Adams*, 358.

41. Cooper defended himself when he came to trial on April 19, 1800. Judge Chase's handling of the case was prejudiced against Cooper. In his speech to the jury, Cooper said, "We have advanced so far on the road to despotism in this republican country that we dare not say our President is mistaken." Thomas Cooper, *An Account of the Trial of Thomas Cooper, of Northumberland: On a Charge of Libel Against the President of the United States* (Philadelphia: Printed by J. Bioren, 1800), 25. Cooper was convicted but eventually pardoned by Jefferson.

42. Thomas W. Benson, "Rhetorical Impasse: The Sedition Trials of 1800," *Southern Speech Communication Journal*, 31 (1966): 198.

43. As quoted in Benson, "Rhetorical Impasse . . . ," 198.

44. Benson, "Rhetorical Impasse . . . ," 199.

45. The founders knew that there was great animosity between the Whigs, who often favored the American cause, and their king, who hated them.

46. Benson, "Rhetorical Impasse," 202.

47. As quoted in Benson, "Rhetorical Impasse . . . ," 202.

48. Richard B. Morris, *Great Presidential Debates and Decisions: State Papers that Changed the Course of History* (New York: Harper & Row, 1973), 5.

49. John D. Stevens, "Congressional History of the 1798 Sedition Law," *Journalism Quarterly* 43 (1966): 253.

50. Levy and Peterson, *Major Crises in American History*, 204; from *Annals of Congress*, 5th Congress, 2nd Session, June 21, 1798.

51. See Eduard Gerard Hudon, *Freedom of Speech and Press in America* (Washington, DC: Public Affairs Press, 1963), 48.

52. Jefferson's election was a difficult one. He did not win the popular vote, nor would he and his running mate Aaron Burr have achieved their electoral vote without slaves counting as three-fifths of person in Southern states thereby increasing Southern clout in the college. In the end, it was Hamilton who came forward and

threw his support behind Jefferson fearing that Burr was the worse evil. Hamilton was repaid for this sensible act on the bluffs of New Jersey where he was shot to death in a duel with Burr.

Chapter 2

Lincoln and Habeas Corpus

Craig R. Smith and Stephanie J. Hurst

The purpose of this chapter is to explore ways in which the Lincoln Administration suppressed certain freedoms during the Civil War.[1] This was a time when many tensions developed and civilians demanded protection from arbitrary arrest and the right to protest the conduct of the war. These demands ran headlong into the suspension of habeas corpus,[2] which the government often deemed necessary to keep the peace and to protect it's military operations. At the same time, the president was often conflicted by these competing claims. His anxiety was expressed in letters to friends and in his reluctance to apply the full powers of the presidency on behalf of suppression. Lincoln recognized that an individual's protection from arbitrary arrest is closely tied to his or her right to free speech. He knew that the suspension of habeas corpus made it easier to enforce restrictions. And he knew that the court of jurisdiction plays a large part in determining how and what expression will be curtailed. Military tribunals tend to be much more severe than civilian tribunals. Thus, tension would be exacerbated by jurisdictional disputes throughout this crisis. We hope by this juncture that the reader understands that Lincoln's dilemma is not some remote, isolated moment in American jurisprudence. It is a moment that recurs and one that we are facing at the time of this writing. (See chapter 10 in this book.)

The Road to Abolition

However, before we can understand the dilemma facing Lincoln, we need to understand how it evolved. The call for abolition was an outgrowth of the second great religious awakening in America. Perhaps the most influential of the moralists was William Lloyd Garrison, whose attack on slavery was so strident that it often led to violence. His first attack came on January 1, 1831, from Boston, when he was only 26 and writing in *The Liberator*'s founding issue:

> [After a tour of the South] I determined . . . to lift up the standard of emancipation in the eyes of the nation, *within sight of Bunker Hill and in the birth place of liberty.* That standard is now unfurled; and long may it float, unhurt by the spoliations of time or the missiles of a desperate foe—yea, till every chain be broken, and every bondman set free!

When threatened with censorship and even lynching in 1835, Garrison became a strong defender of the First Amendment in terms of his speaking rights and his right to mail the inflammatory *The Liberator* across state lines. He called for slaves to rise up and throw off their chains. These calls led to grave fears and even riots in the South. In September 1835, vigilante groups were formed in South Carolina to deal with supporters of abolition; their first acts included impounding a press in Charleston and seizing a load of abolitionist tracts that had been mailed from the North. The local postmaster wrote Postmaster General Amos Kendall that he would no longer deliver such tracts.

Led by John C. Calhoun, Congress voted to imposed a "gag rule" on abolitionist petitions to the Congress. A clear violation of the right to redress grievances, the rule required that all such petitions be sidetracked to a committee where they were left to gather dust. Former President John Quincy Adams, then a member of the House, regularly attacked this procedure and defended the right to petition Congress. He made these speeches over the protests of the majority in Congress who refused to accept the petitions of abolitionists. In response, Adams said, "The right of petition . . . is essential to the very existence of the government; it is the right of the people over the Government; it is their right, and they may not be deprived of it."[3] Adams read them aloud day after day and was eventually censured for his behavior.

Next, Calhoun and his Southern cohorts demanded that the administration intervene to prevent further violence. On December 7, 1835, in his "Seventh Annual Message to Congress," President Jackson sent a message to Congress which condemned "various sorts of publications calculated to stimulate . . . insurrection." In order to maintain peace "within our borders," he asked for authority to instruct the Post Office not to accept or transmit such documents. Jackson did not want the Post Office "used as an instrument of" insurrection. He "respectfully suggest[ed] the propriety of passing such a law as will prohibit, under severe penalties, the circulation in the Southern

States, through the mail, of incendiary publications intended to instigate the slaves to insurrection."[4] In the Senate, the bill was to be drafted by a committee headed by Calhoun and containing only one Northerner, John Davis. On February 4, 1836, however, Calhoun failed to gain a consensus from his hand picked committee. Calhoun was caught in a bind. If he accepted the government's right to suppressed literature through the Post Office, he supported violating one his strongest principles, states' rights. If he allowed the mail to go through, he opened the South to arguments in favor of abolition of slavery. Calhoun tried to avoid the horns of this dilemma by arguing that the federal government could work to support state laws that attempted to quell the dangerous rhetoric of abolitionists. His bill forbade postmasters from receiving, forwarding, or delivering mail, which the *states* prohibited. Calhoun thus invented yet another one his many constitutional dodges with the phrase "federal reinforcement." But the precedent of the Alien and Sedition crisis was not far from senators' thoughts. On February 4, 1836, the Report on Senate Bill 122 concluded:

> It is the ground taken, and so ably sustained by Mr. Madison, in his celebrated report to the Virginia Legislature in 1799, against the Alien and Sedition Law, and which conclusively settled the principle that Congress has no right in any form or in any manner to interfere with the freedom of the press. The establishment of this principle not only overthrew the Sedition Act, but was the leading cause of the great political revolution which, in 1801, brought the Republican Party, with Mr. Jefferson as its leader, into power.[5]

In April the debate over Calhoun's bill was intense. Some argued that it would create martyrs of the abolitionists; others claimed it violated the spirit and the letter of the First Amendment. Senator Daniel Webster of Massachusetts said the bill was worse than the Sedition Act since it used prior restraint against the press. Still others argued that the bill put the government on the side of slavery. Would Calhoun produce such a bill to suppress newspapers distributed in the North by Southerners who supported slavery? The Senate voted the bill down.

On the grounds that the First Amendment applied to the federal government not to the states, Amos Kendall ordered the Post Office not to deliver insurrectionist literature where it might cause trouble and states had asked that it be kept out. Thus, where states like Virginia passed laws forbidding the tracts, the Post Office would not deliver them. By fiat and with the cooperation of Southern states, Kendall accomplished what Calhoun had failed to achieve.

President Jackson referred to the issue in his "Farewell":

[T]he signs of evil are sufficiently apparent to awaken the deep-
est anxiety in the bosom of the patriot [George Washington].
We behold systematic efforts publicly made to sow the seeds of
discord . . . to excite the South against the North and the North
against the South, and to force into the controversy the most
delicate and exciting topics—topics upon which it is impossible
that a large portion of the Union can ever speak without strong
emotion. . . . Mutual suspicions and reproaches may in time create mutual hostility, and artful and designing men will always be
found who are ready to foment these fatal divisions and to inflame
natural jealousies of different sections of the country. . . . [States]
should frown upon any proceedings within their own borders
likely to disturb the tranquility of their political brethren in other
portions of the Union.[6]

Soon the president's worst fears were realized. Having been forced to
leave St. Louis to protect himself and his family, Elijah Lovejoy was killed
by a pro-slavery mob in Alton, Missouri. Lovejoy, a preacher and briefly a
publisher of the religious newspaper *The Observer*, printed anti-slavery editorials and spoke against slavery at every opportunity. His printing presses were
destroyed on three separate occasions. When the city of Alton demanded
that he close down his press, Lovejoy defended himself in a famous ora-
tion filled with religious imagery. In the speech, he assumed the posture of
a martyr, seeming to realize that the speech would cost him his life. Soon
his fourth printing press arrived. A gang set fire to the building in which it
was housed and killed Lovejoy.

The martyrdom of Lovejoy reinforced the linkage Jackson had created
between the First Amendment and the controversy over slavery. As we shall
see, those issues would haunt the administration of Abraham Lincoln.

Lincoln and War Powers

This chapter provides an opportunity to examine the development of
presidential war powers, particularly the suspension of habeas corpus, as they
affected free speech, press, and assembly. It also supplies examples of rhetoric
bordering on a clear and present danger in wartime and a look at military
and civil tribunals as they functioned to diminish and/or protect free speech
during this crisis. It establishes a theme of this book: The Supreme Court is
more likely to uphold restrictive actions, orders, and legislation in war than

in time of peace. In short, this chapter lays the precedential groundwork for crises that followed, including the one surrounding the treatment of enemy combatants from the war in Afghanistan.

The Writ of Habeas Corpus

Providing defendants with their rights in courts of law, habeas corpus is the right of a citizen to obtain protection against unlawful detention and deprivation of such basic rights as freedom of speech. In a letter to Erastus Corning on June 12, 1863, with his usual eloquence, Lincoln drew a clear picture of the dilemma he faced:

> Must I shoot a simple-minded soldier boy who deserts, while I must not touch a hair of a wily agitator who induces him to desert? . . . I think that in such a case, to silence the agitator, and save the boy, is not only constitutional, but, withal, a great mercy.[7]

Lincoln's conundrum had a significant impact on First Amendment issues.[8] The United States Constitution specifies that, "the privilege of the writ of habeas corpus shall not be suspended, unless when in cases of rebellion or invasion, the pubic safety may require it."[9] The Constitution is clear in indicating that suspension is a possibility in specific cases, but vague as to who determines when public safety is in danger.[10] Clearly, it is the president's duty to invoke the suspension, but is it also his duty to determine when an invasion or rebellion threatens the public safety? Or is that decision assigned to the Congress, which already has the power to declare war?

In *Ex parte Milligan*, decided *after* the war was over in April 1866, David Dudley Field wrote the following opinion, which has been cited in several of the contemporary cases regarding "enemy combatants:"

> Has the President in time of war by his own mere will and judgement of the exigency, the power to bring before the military officers any man or woman in the land, to be there subject to trial and punishment, even to death? If the President has this awful power, whence does he derive it? From the Constitution? He can exercise no authority whatever, but that which the Constitution of the country gives him. Beyond it, he has no more power than any other citizen. Our system knows no authority beyond and above the law.[11]

Two issues emerge: first, does Congress or the president decide when rebellion or invasion are substantiated? Second, does Congress or the president delegate the power in such an instance?[12]

During the Civil War, President Lincoln suspended the writ of habeas corpus three times and in each case freedom of expression was restricted: first, on April 27, 1861, again on September 24, 1862, which was only a few days after signing the Emancipation Proclamation, and finally on September 15, 1863. Although there is no exact record of the total number arrested during the Civil War, the Commissary General of prisoners lists 13,535 citizens arrested from February 1862 to April 1865. It should come as no surprise then that freedom from arbitrary arrest became the most important constitutional issue in the early part of the Civil War. This freedom was limited by the fact that the majority of the loyal North, both Democrats and Republicans, believed that secession was not a constitutional right and that a rebellion was underway. A clear threat to the Union resulted in extraordinary actions to save it. Those actions elevated constitutional issues to paramount concern. Thus, these suspensions of rights enhanced the controversy regarding the constitutionality and amount of power allotted to the president. They also encouraged such government agencies as the Post Office to restrict free press by confiscating controversial issues of newspapers and other publications. Newspapers and speakers who were critical of the war and Lincoln's conduct of it, were harassed and often jailed. Union soldiers continued to close down Copperhead papers into 1864 as antiwar editorials and messages of despair in these newspapers caused morale problems in Union Armies. Subsequently, many Union regiments established their own camp newspapers.[13] These suspensions of newspapers fed into anti-Southern sentiment that encouraged citizens to take the law into their own hands such as in the cases where they destroyed Copperhead presses or roughed up speakers, thereby suppressing their ideas.

Such cases also occurred against groups advocating for peace in the South. In North Carolina the state's largest newspaper, the *Standard* became an outspoken peace advocate. On September 9 and 10, 1863, several Confederate soldiers from General Benning's brigade of Georgia, broke into the paper's office and devastated it.

Suspension of the Writ

On April 14, 1861, Fort Sumpter fell to the Confederacy. In Maryland, the public had forced the pro-Union governor Thomas Hicks to call the legislature controlled by Southern-Right Democrats into session to vote on secession. Hicks warned the president that the legislature was filled with Confederate sympathizers.[14] Lincoln was reluctant to act as a letter to General Winfield Scott dated April 25, 1861 indicates. In it Lincoln discouraged ordering the arrest of members of the Maryland legislature:

The Maryland Legislature assembles tomorrow at Annapolis; and, not improbably, will take action to arm the people of that State against the United States ... they have a clearly legal right to assemble; and, we can not know in advance, that their action will not be lawful, and peaceful ... we can not permanently prevent their action ... we can not long hold them as prisoners ... I therefore conclude that it is only left to the commanding General to watch, and await their action, which, if it shall be to arm their people against the United States, he is to adopt the most prompt, and efficient means to counteract, even, if necessary, to the bombardment of their cities—and in the extremist necessity, the suspension of the writ of *habeas corpus*.[15]

However, the crisis quickly took a turn for the worst and the president filled Maryland's capital with federal troops and military authorities to prevent a debate over whether Maryland should secede. On April 27, 1861, Lincoln gave General Scott the following instructions ostensibly to prevent secession-minded Marylanders from interfering with the Capital's communication with the North:

You are engaged in repressing an insurrection against the laws of the United States. If at any point on or in the vicinity of the military line, which is now used between the City of Philadelphia and the City of Washington, via Perryville, Annapolis City, and Annapolis Junction, you find resistance which renders it necessary to suspend the writ of Habeas Corpus for the public safety, you, personally or through the officer in command at the point where the resistance occurs, are authorized to suspend that writ.[16]

A declaration of martial law was implemented in the city of Baltimore on May 13. By June 13 Maryland had organized four Union regiments and Unionists candidates won six seats in a special congressional election. Union officials, however, continued an air of distrust regarding underground Confederate activities in Baltimore.[17] Union soldiers made several arrests including the Baltimore marshal of police George Kane, Baltimore Mayor William Brown, and, on September 17, nine members of the Maryland legislature and the chief clerk of the Maryland Senate. In short, suspension of basic rights was used to close down political debate in such legitimate forums as the city council and the state legislature. There is perhaps no worse example of the restriction of free speech in the entire Civil War than this one. Duly elected members of a state legislature were prevented from assembling and speaking on a critical issue. Along with free speech and assembly, states' rights were crushed in this effort to preserve the Union. Lincoln's hierarchy of values was clear. Like John Adams during the sedition crisis, Lincoln would save the Union even if that meant trampling on the rights of elected officials. For all of his hand wringing, Lincoln believed it was better to save the Union than live up to its guarantees.[18] In 1862 in a public letter to Horace Greely, he went so far as to say, "If I could save the Union without freeing any slave I would do it; and if I could save it by freeing all the slaves I would do it."[19]

Ex parte Merryman

Less than a month after his suspension of the writ, a case began wending its way through the courts. The *Merryman* case was brought to bar to determine whether the president or the Congress had the power to suspend the writ of habeas corpus. It began on May 25, 1861, when John Merryman, a Southern sympathizer and secessionist from Maryland, was taken into military custody. Merryman was a wealthy landowner and lieutenant in a secessionist cavalry unit that, during the April troubles, had burned bridges and torn down telegraph wires.[20] He immediately asked to be released under a writ of habeas corpus and tried in a civilian court.

In one of the oddities of history, the Chief Justice of the Supreme Court Roger B. Taney, a Democrat appointed by President Jackson, sat in judgment on the case as the circuit judge. Taney had penned the infamous *Dred Scott* decision of 1857,[21] which Lincoln had consistently attacked in his campaign for a senate in Illinois and in his presidential run. In fact, Lincoln had alleged that Taney was part of Democratic Party conspiracy to maintain the slave states. Now Taney and Lincoln crossed swords again.

In arguing for the president's power to suspend the writ, Attorney General Bates contended that the three great branches of the government are coordinate, separate, and equal; the executive cannot rightly be subjected to the judiciary. The president, he maintained, is in a peculiar manner their preserver and protector as the defender of the Constitution.[22] Moreover, it is the president's duty to put down a rebellion because the courts are too weak to do so. Bates pointed out that the power of the presidency does open the way for possible abuse; however, it is just as true that a legislature may be factious or a court corrupt. The president cannot be required to appear before a judge to answer for his official acts because the court would be usurping the authority of Executive Branch.[23] Bates contended that for any breach of trust the president is answerable before the high court of impeachment by the House and trial in Senate and no other tribunals.

In filing his opinion, Taney responded that the president had no lawful power to issue such an order and that a writ of habeas corpus should be restored. In *Ex parte Merryman*, Taney claimed that only Congress could suspend the writ and that the president, though sworn to "take care that the laws be faithfully executed," had broken the laws himself. In a clever rhetorical ploy, Taney interpreted the constitution by constructing it according to its context. He pointed out that the provision regarding habeas corpus appears in that portion of the Constitution, which pertains to *legislative powers*, not in the section on executive powers; therefore, it was safe to assume that suspension of habeas corpus was a legislative, not executive prerogative. Taney argued further that the military authorities should reveal the day and cause of the capture of Merryman and explain the reasons for the detention of Merryman.[24] Such requirements were, of course, mandated in civilian courts, but not in military ones, where combatants could be held without a time limit and initially need not be informed of charges against them.

In a message to Congress on July 4, 1861, Lincoln answered Taney. He began by pointing out that he was reluctant to suspend the writ, but that dire threats to the nation in general and the military in particular required such action:

> Soon after the first call for militia it was considered a duty to authorize the Commanding General in proper cases, according to his discretion, to suspend the privilege of the writ of habeas corpus . . . This authority has purposely been exercised but very sparingly. Nevertheless, . . . the attention of the country has been called to the proposition that one who is sworn to "take care that the laws be faithfully executed" should not himself violate them. Of course some consideration was given to the questions of power and propriety before this matter was acted upon. The whole of the laws which were required to be faithfully executed were being resisted . . . in nearly one-third of the States. Must they be allowed to finally fail of execution even had it been perfectly clear that by the use of the means necessary to their execution some single law, are in such extreme tenderness of the citizens liberty that practically it relieves more of the guilty than of the innocent, should to a very limited extent be violated? To state the question more directly, are all the laws *but one* to go unexecuted, and the Government itself go to pieces, lest that one be violated? . . . But it was not believed that this question was presented. It was not believed that any law was violated. The provision of the Constitution . . . is equivalent to a provision—is a provision—that such privilege may be suspended when, in cases of rebellion or invasion, the public safety does require it. It was decided that we have a case of rebellion.[25]

Lincoln further stated that the attack on Fort Sumter left him with no choice but to, "call out the war power of the Government; and so to resist force, employment for its destruction, by force for its preservation."[26] As with his *Dred Scott* majority opinion, Taney stuck to the letter of the law and read the Constitution strictly. Lincoln sought refuge in a higher law: the law of survival.[27] He gave his defenders grist for their propaganda mills by claiming that his suspension of the privilege of the writ of habeas corpus did not violate any law. According to Lincoln, the Constitution was "silent as to . . . who, is to exercise the power" of suspension.[28] He would not release Merryman, even in the face of Taney's writ. Taney's attempt to convene the Supreme Court, which was in recess, failed and the matter went no further.

Horace Binney, a Philadelphia lawyer, came to the defense of the president through his widely circulated pamphlet, *The Privilege of the Writ of Habeas Corpus under the Constitution.*[29] In the pamphlet Binney attacked Judge Taney's arguments. The controversy excited lawyers and politicians, resulting in a paper war consisting of more than 40 published answers to Binney's pamphlet.

In the midst of this debate, Lincoln consistently argued that his paramount duty as chief executive was to preserve the integrity of the government.[30] On this depended the livelihood of the whole Constitution. In Lincoln's view, there had been no violation of the Constitution, since the Constitution permits suspension of habeas corpus in specific cases and does not specify what branch of the government is to exercise the suspending power.[31] As the provision was plainly made for an emergency, he argued, the natural inference is that the president should use his discretion. The president is always in charge, always commander-in-chief, while the legislature is often in recess. Lincoln believed that the danger should not be permitted to run its course until Congress could be called into session.[32]

This was not the first instance in which Lincoln would place the survival of the Union over the need to proceed in a constitutional manner. As early as May 4, 1861, the president enlarged the army by calling for volunteers without any congressional authorization. And yet, Lincoln's ambivalence on this issue emerged again in the earlier cited letter to Erastus Corning dated June 12, 1863. While the letter serves as a defense for his suspension of the privilege in the face of sharp Democratic criticism, speaking of "The Rebellion" Lincoln raises the issue of freedom of expression:

> Their sympathizers pervaded all departments of the Government and nearly all communities of the people . . . under the cover of "liberty of speech," "liberty of the press," and "habeas corpus," they hoped to keep on foot among us a most efficient corps of spies, informers, suppliers, and aiders and abettors of their cause

in a thousand ways ... Or, if as has happened, the Executive should suspend the writ, without ruinous waste of time, instances of arresting innocent persons might occur, as are always likely to occur in such cases; and then a clamor could be raised in regard to this, which might be, at least, of some service to the insurgent cause ... Yet, thoroughly imbued with a reverence for the guaranteed rights of individuals, I was slow to adopt the strong measures which by degrees I have been forced to regard as being within the exceptions of the Constitution, and as indispensable to the public safety ... the time [is] not unlikely to come when I shall be blamed for having made too few arrests rather than too many.[33]

Since Lincoln controlled the army for the most part, his position prevailed during the war. In fact some noted historians describe it as dictatorial.[34] It was not until the war was over that the courts undid the war rulings.

Military Commissions

Military commissions were often the arbiters of cases that came forward due to the suspension of the writ. Two important Supreme Court cases, *Vallandigham* and *Milligan*, illustrate the effect that war had on judicial decisions and free speech.[35] To understand them, we need to know that the general rule in common law is that in a section of enemy territory within military occupation, or in a region under martial law, the use of a military commission for the trial of nonmilitary persons who have committed offenses is allowed. Where there is no martial law, and where the ordinary civilian courts are unimpeded, military tribunals have no proper function to perform in the trial of civilians, especially for offenses outside the military code.[36] In explaining the use of military commissions during the Civil War, Judge Advocate General Holt stated that they originated in the necessities of the rebellion, and were indispensable for the punishment of crimes in regions where the courts ceased to exist and in cases of which the local criminal courts could not take cognizance. Such commissions were powerful, he claimed, because they were unencumbered by technicalities and because their process was executed by the military power of the United States.[37]

In Missouri, for example, martial law was in force along railroad and telegraph lines.[38] As a result, numerous cases arose in that state involving civilians who were tried for such offenses as bridge burning, destruction of railroad tracks, and cutting of telegraph lines. Military commissions tried civilians who engaged in such acts as furnishing information to the enemy, or sniping at Union troops.[39] The majority of cases brought before the commissions were of this sort.[40] And few caused any protest. This attitude drew a clear distinction between acts of destruction in war zones and speeches protesting the war in other areas. Widespread criticism arose when speakers were subjected to military tribunals in regions remote from military operations and not under martial law.[41] Much of the criticism was based on free speech suspensions stemming from Lincoln's decision in February 1862 to transfer control over internal security matters from Secretary of State Seward to Secretary of War Stanton. By order of August 8, 1862, United States marshals and local magistrates were authorized to imprison persons who discouraged enlistments or engaged in other disloyal practices. Immediate reports of such arrests were to be made to the Judge Advocate General so that the prisoners could be tried by military commission.[42] This policy change led to two contradictory Supreme Court cases: the *Vallandigham* case, decided by the Supreme Court in February 1864, and the *Milligan* case, which reversed *Vallandigham*, decided in 1866. The same Court that upheld the authority of a military commission in 1864 declared a similar commission's jurisdiction to be limited in an analogous case two years later. This difference was that at the time of *Milligan*, the country was no longer at war, and hence, national security was no longer in peril. The lesson is clear and will be repeated in subsequent chapters of this book: When national security is at risk, the Supreme Court is willing to tighten restrictions on basic civil rights; when national security is not at risk, the Supreme Court ends the restrictions and gives wider latitude to civil rights claims.

The Vallandigham Case

Northern confidence was slipping badly in 1862 as the army continued to prove ineffective against the rebels particularly in Virginia. The Union's continued misfortune not only undercut Lincoln's support but gave hope to a group that called itself the Peace Democrats. They sought a national convention including the South, which would negotiate an end to the war. Some formed secret societies such as the Sons of Liberty and the Knights of the Golden Circle, which engaged in "midnight raids and barn burnings."[43] They were quickly labeled the Copperheads, for the venomous snake that hid in unsuspecting places and struck without warning. These were mainly Northern Democrats who sympathized with the South and grew stronger with every Confederate victory. Many in the group were anti-Black and xenophobic and/or came from areas that bordered on the South such as congressmen from Southern Illinois, Indiana, and Ohio, not to mention the neutral states of Maryland, Kentucky, and Missouri.

Opposition to the Copperheads was strong but geographically spotty until it was discovered that members of the Knights of the Golden Circle were agitating for Midwesterners to join the confederacy or to form a confederacy of their own in the West. Suddenly, paranoia swept the North. The search for subversives rivaled the Federalist hunt for Jacobins during the Alien and Sedition crisis. Just as in that crisis, this one not had only the external threat of a militant South but an internal threat of Southern sympathizers within its borders.

The most prominent Copperhead was Congressman Clement L. Vallandigham of Ohio. He steadfastly opposed emancipation of slaves and argued that the war was needless. In fact, the division in the Congress in 1862 over war policy split almost perfectly along party lines and hurt Republicans in the 1862 elections. In January 1863, Vallandigham capitalized on the growing dissent when he said, "It is the desire of my heart to restore the Union, the Federal Union as it was forty years ago. . . . I see nothing before us but universal political and social revolution, anarchy and bloodshed compared with which the Reign of Terror in France was a merciful visitation."[44] By early 1863 Vallandigham had emerged as leader of the Peace Democrats professing himself a "better unionist than the Republicans whose fanaticism had provoked this ruinous war."[45]

On April 19, 1863, Major General Ambrose E. Burnside, in command of the "Department of the Ohio," issued "General Orders No. 38." These orders declared that persons committing acts for the benefit of the enemy would be executed as spies or traitors.[46] Any person committing an act deemed as expressed or implied treason would be subject to trial by a military court and punished by death or banishment. In a clear attempt to suppress freedom of expression, the order declared further that "the habit of declaring sympathies for the enemy will no longer be tolerated" and that, "Persons committing such offenses will be at once arrested, with a view to being tried or sent beyond our lines into the lines of their friends." "Declaring sympathies" included speeches, pamphlets, and editorials that supported the confederacy and/or opposed Lincoln's policies. Clearly free speech was chilled by such orders and large constitutional issues loomed. Would the courts uphold such a clear limitation on the First Amendment rights of its citizens who were not in a war zone? And would the courts deem a speech an act of treason?

In the spring of 1863, Vallandigham opened his campaign for governor of Ohio by challenging the new orders. In fact, he saw Burnside's order as an opportunity to secure the Democratic nomination.[47] So on May 1, 1863, he gave an address that was published throughout Ohio and well received particularly in Southern Ohio where loyalties to the South were high.[48] He specifically attacked the Emancipation Proclamation, signed by Lincoln only after the North had won the battle of Antietam, and warned of the collapse of American institutions.[49] He attacked the draft and Lincoln's suspension of habeas corpus. He said "King Lincoln" should be thrown from office and that the North should stop fighting the war. He called for a peace conference to restore the Old Union even if that meant excluding New England. The Cincinnati *Enquirer*, which had consistently warned of "negroes" migrating north under emancipation, supported Vallandigham's platform.

General Burnside ordered the arrest of Vallandigham for treason. In the early morning hours of May 5 in Dayton, federal troops broke into Vallandigham's home, arrested him and incarcerated him in Cincinnati.[50] Burnside brought Vallandigham to trial before a military commission charging him with "publicly expressing, in violation of General Orders, No. 38 ... his sympathies for those in arms against the ... United States, declaring disloyal ... opinions with the object ... of weakening the power of the Government ... to suppress an unlawful rebellion."[51] Vallandigham had a large group of supporters, particularly politicians from the Southern sections of Illinois, Missouri, Ohio, and Indiana. The trial was held against the backdrop of massive disdain for the Emancipation Proclamation. At the same time, Copperhead newspapers called for desertions from the army and navy. Lincoln learned of Burnside's arrest of Vallandigham via newspaper, and, to his credit, was "surprised and embarrassed"; however, Lincoln decided that more damage would be done if he renounced Burnside since the military commission that held Vallandigham had been established under his proclamation the previous September.

Vallandigham was convicted and ordered to be imprisoned in Boston for the duration of the war. He appealed to Judge Leavitt of the United States Circuit Court at Cincinnati for a writ of habeas corpus. The question as to a judicial review of the military proceedings arose. In his reply, Judge Leavitt refused the writ and the case was appealed to the Supreme Court of the United States.

At the trial, G. E. Pugh, arguing for Vallandigham, contended that the jurisdiction of a Military Commission does not extend to the case of a citizen, particularly one running for public office, and that the court had authority to issue a writ of *certiorari* in the present case. Pugh denied the jurisdiction of the Military Commission and Vallandigham refused to plead to the charge. After private consultation, the members of the Commission directed the Judge-Advocate to enter a plea of not guilty, and to proceed with the trial, with an allowance to the petitioner to call witnesses to rebut the evidence which might be introduced against him to establish the charge.[52]

At the conclusion of the proceedings Vallandigham read a statement to the Commission in which he declared that he had been arrested without due process of law, without a warrant from any judicial officer, that he was being held in a military prison and had been served with a charge and specification, as in court-martial or military commission, that he was not either a member of the land or naval forces of the United States, not in the militia in the actual service of the United States and, therefore, not triable for any cause by any such court. Vallandigham also alleged that the offense for which he was charged was "not known to the Constitution of the United States, nor to any law thereof;" that they were "*words spoken to the people of Ohio, in an open and public political meeting, lawfully and peaceably assembled under the Constitution, that they were words of criticism upon the policy and public servants of the people*, by which policy it was alleged that the welfare of the country was not promoted; that they were used as an appeal to the people to change that policy, not by force, but by free elections and the ballot box; that it is not pretended that he counseled disobedience to the Constitution or resistance to the law or lawful authority."

The Supreme Court refused to review the proceedings of the military commission. Among the many reasons provided by the Court for denying a writ of *certiorari* was that the case was not within the letter or spirit of the grants of appellate jurisdiction to the Supreme Court. The Court had no appellate jurisdiction to revise the proceedings of tribunals acting "under or by color of the authority of the United States," but which "do not exercise any part of the judicial power of the United States, except when the same is expressly given by special Act of Congress." As a result the Court contended that a military commission is not a court, within the meaning of the 14th section of the Judiciary Act of 1789. Therefore, there is, "no jurisdiction in this court to issue a writ of *habeas corpus ad subjiciendum*, to review or reverse, or the writ of *certiorari* to revise the proceedings of a military commission."

Vallandigham's supporters were infuriated. Governor Seymour of New York said the ruling "establishes military despotism.... If it is upheld our liberties are overthrown."[53] Democrats in Ohio immediately nominated Vallandigham for governor in absentia. In a letter to General Burnside, Lincoln explained that "all the Cabinet regretted the necessity of arresting ... Vallandigham ... but being done all are for seeing you through it."[54] On May 19, 1863, the president confounded his critics by commuting Vallandigham's sentence and exiling him to the South.

The candidate's supporters wrote a letter protesting Lincoln's orders. The letter considered Lincoln's "assumption of the right to suspend all the constitutional guarantees of personal liberty, and even of the freedom of speech and of the press" a "startling" thing, and declared that by such a claim to power would not only be "absolute over the rights of individuals, but equally so over the other departments of the Government." It added, "Surely it is not necessary to subvert free government in this country in order to put down the rebellion. . . . Indeed it is plain that your Administration has been . . . greatly weakened by the assumption of power not delegated in the Constitution."[55] The Democratic Party launched a major campaign against Lincoln claiming he had become a "military despot."[56] Governor Seymour claimed that the war was being fought to destroy democracy in the North as well as to put down rebellion in the South. Because Seymour was known as a man of character, his statement had wide impact damaging the president's hopes for reelection.

Thus, on June 12, Lincoln responded to Seymour's charges with a masterful public letter of his own. It was widely read and claimed in part:

> Vallandigham was, by a military commander, seized and tried 'for no other reason than words addressed to a public meeting, in criticism of the course of the Administration, and in condemnation of the Military orders of the General' . . . [Vallandigham] avows his hostility to the War on the part of the Union; and his arrest was made because he was laboring, with some effect, to prevent the raising of troops; to encourage desertions from the army; and to leave the Rebellion without an adequate military force to suppress it. He was not arrested because he was damaging the political prospects of the Administration, or the personal interests of the Commanding General, but because he was damaging the Army, upon the existence and vigor of which the life of the Nation depends. . . . I have learned that many people approve the course [I have] taken with Mr. Vallandigham, while I have not heard of a single one condemning it . . . And yet, let me say that, in my own discretion, I do not know whether I would have ordered the arrest of Mr. Vallandigham . . . I hold that, as a general rule, the commander in the field is the better judge of the necessity in any particular case. [I]t gave me pain when I learned that Mr. Vallandigham had been arrested. . . . [I]t will afford me great pleasure to discharge him so soon as I can, by any means, and believe the public safety will not suffer by it.[57]

Lincoln made the argument that Vallandigham wasn't arrested merely because of a speech that he made but because his words provoked resistance to the draft and desertion from the army. The fact that there was widespread desertion at the time solidified Lincoln's argument that Vallandigham, and others like him, created a resistance to the ability of the North to wage war on which the nation depended.

A delegation of important Ohio Democrats came to Washington in late June to implore the president to release Vallandigham from his sentence of exile.[58] Lincoln turned the tables on them by presenting them with clever dilemma. He said he would release Vallandigham if the delegation would agree to three propositions: 1) that a rebellion exists aimed at destroying the "National Union" and that in "your opinion" an army and navy are essential to suppressing it; 2) that no member of the delegation will do anything to hinder the military or encourage others to hinder it; 3) that members of the delegation will do all they can while the rebellion goes on to see the military is paid, fed, clad and supported.[59] If the delegation agreed to the propositions, they handed the president a justification for his actions and contradicted their own political followers. If they opposed, they would appear seditious. After an ineffectual response, the delegation returned to Ohio.

Vallandigham escaped his exile in the South on a blockade runner and made for Canada. In absentia, he encouraged his supporters to rally round his candidacy for governor of Ohio in 1863 but lost the election by 100,000 votes as Republicans staged a major comeback in that year's elections. Vallandigham then became a conduit for Confederate funds by organizing the Sons of Liberty, a group that was quickly infiltrated by government agents. The agents supplied Republicans with accounts of conspiratorial treason, which were repeated in speech after speech during the elections of 1864 by which time Vallandigham had not only returned to America, he had written the peace plank of the Democratic convention in Chicago and supported the candidacy of General McClellan for president. After the war, he ran unsuccessfully for several offices, his fame enhanced by the 1863 short story about him by Edward Hale "The Man without a Country." Having accepted the inevitability of the Fourteenth and Fifteenth Amendments, Vallandigham vowed never to mention the Civil War again. He died of an accidentally self-inflicted gunshot wound at the age 50 in 1871.

The Milligan Case

Lambdin Milligan was arrested on October 5, 1864, by order of General Hovey, in command at Indianapolis; he brought Milligan before a military commission on charges of 1) conspiring against the government of the United States, 2) affording aid and comfort to the Rebellion against the authorities of the United States, 3) inciting an insurrection, 4) disloyal practices, 5) violation of the laws of war.[60] Milligan, along with co-conspirators, was a suspected member of Vallandigham's secret antiwar society, the Sons of Liberty. Milligan's threat to the Union would appear on the surface to be much greater than Vallandigham's and border on unprotected speech. Since, even under these circumstances, the case would reverse *Vallandigham*, it is important that we consider it.

After several delays and the assassination of Lincoln, on May 19, 1865, a military commission sentenced Milligan to be hanged. Milligan petitioned the United States Circuit Court for a writ of habeas corpus. The controversy over Congressional versus Presidential power was reignited. Attorney General Stanbery and Benjamin F. Butler argued that:

> The Commander-in-Chief has full power to make an effectual use of his forces. He must . . . have the power to arrest and punish one who arms men to join the enemy in the field against him; one who holds correspondence with the enemy; one who is an officer in an armed force organized to oppose him; one who is preparing to seize arsenals and release prisoners of war taken in battle and confined within his military lines . . . During the war his powers must be without limit, because if defending, the means of offense may be nearly illimitable.[61]

Milligan insisted, however, that the Military Commission had no jurisdiction to try him upon the charges preferred, or upon any charge whatever, because he was a citizen of the United States and the state of Indiana and not in a war zone. The right of trial by jury was guaranteed to him by the Constitution of the United States.[62]

Milligan's case reached the Supreme Court and was decided in April 1866. Justice Davis announced the Court's ruling:

> During the late wicked Rebellion, the temper of the times did not allow that calmness in deliberation and discussion so necessary to a correct conclusion of a purely judicial question. Then, considerations of safety were mingled with the exercise of power; and feelings and interests prevailed which are happily terminated. Now that the public safety is assured, this question, as well as all others, can be discussed and decided without passion or the admixture of any element not required to form a legal judgement. . . . [T]he Constitution of the United States is a law for rulers and people, equally in war and in peace, and covers with the shield of its protection all classes of men, at all times and under all circumstances. . . . [O]ne of the plainest constitutional provisions was infringed when Milligan was tried by a court not ordained and established by Congress, and not composed of judges. . . . [A]nother guarantee of freedom was broken when Milligan was denied a trial by jury. . . . Martial law cannot arise from a threatened invasion. The necessity must be actual and present; the invasion real . . . It is difficult to see how the safety of the country required martial law in Indiana. . . . Martial rule can never exist where the courts are open, and in the proper and unobstructed exercise of their jurisdiction.

Chief Justice Salmon Chase concurred with an extension of the argument first used by his predecessor, Chief Justice Roger Taney in the *Merryman* case:

> The power to make the necessary laws is in Congress; the power to execute in the President.... But neither can the President, in war more than in peace, intrude upon the proper authority of Congress, nor Congress upon the proper authority of the President. Both are servants of the people ... nor can the President, or any commander under him, without the sanction of Congress, institute tribunals for the trial and punishment of offenses, either of soldiers or civilians, unless in cases of controlling necessity, which justifies what it compels, or at least insures acts of indemnity from the justice of the legislature.... What we do maintain is that when the nation is involved in war ... it is within the power of Congress to determine to what states or districts such great and imminent public danger exists as justifies the authorization of military tribunals for the trial of crimes and offenses against the discipline or security of the army or against the public safety.

The Court concluded that the laws and Constitution demand that any citizen not be tried by a military tribunal if there is a civilian court available and the alleged offense was not committed in a war zone. To do otherwise would mean that "republican government is a failure, and there is an end of liberty regulated by law."[63] In so doing, the Court declared that the guarantees of such freedoms as press and speech, the safeguard against arbitrary arrest, fair trial and Fifth Amendment privilege are not to be set aside during war if civilian rather than military courts can be convened to hear the charges. (As we shall see in chapter 10, this is the same position the Supreme Court eventually took with regard some detainees in the American naval base at Guantanamo, Cuba.) Milligan's trial and conviction by a military commission were overturned. The Court decided that there was no indictment against Milligan, since the Habeas Corpus Act of 1863 stated that political prisoners who could not be indicted by the grand jury should be released.

When the decision was announced, Republicans were infuriated. It fueled their drive for stronger laws to punish war criminals (see chapter 3). The ruling exemplifies one of the theses of this study that we mentioned early but bears repeating here: The Supreme Court is far more protective of basic liberties in peacetime than in wartime. This thesis will be reasserted when we study the Court's decisions in wartime and peace during and after various crises. However, at this juncture, it is important to finish the story of Lincoln's administration.

Habeas Corpus Act

Early in 1863, Congress took up the issue of an "Act relating to habeas corpus, and regulating judicial proceedings in certain cases." The purpose of the bill was to protect soldiers who followed the president's orders against future lawsuits and other legal action.[64] The Habeas Corpus Indemnity Act, passed on March 3, 1863, aimed at terminating the jurisdictional conflicts, such as those illustrated by the *Merryman* case. This act stated that "during the present rebellion, the President of the United States, whenever in his judgement the public safety may require it, is authorized to suspend the privilege of the writ of habeas corpus in any case throughout the United States or any part thereof."[65] The introduction of the bill led to heated debate in the House. The Republicans prevailed by sheer dint of numbers 75 to 41 but the Democrats entered a formal protest into the Journal of the House.[66] The bill easily passed in the Senate.

Under the act, the president's authority to "suspend" habeas corpus was recognized, military commanders were relieved from the obligation to answer the writ, and officers subjected to due process for arrests or imprisonments were given both immunity and the protection of Federal courts. The act did attempt to regulate and control arbitrary arrests by requiring the Secretaries of State and War to furnish lists of prisoners to federal judges. If grand juries found no indictments against them, prisoners were to be discharged by judicial order upon taking the oath of allegiance and entering into recognizance for good behavior. Where such lists were not furnished, a judge might discharge the prisoner if not satisfied as to the allegations of the petition. In the early part of the war, both arrests and releases were at the discretion of the president acting through the military officers. During this time the word of the president (or that of a Cabinet secretary whose power originated in the president) was enough to place a person in confinement. In some cases, Lincoln himself gave the order for arrest.[67]

The Habeas Corpus Act provided that, while the privilege is suspended, "no military or other officer [should] be compelled" to produce the prisoners in answer to the writ. Those not indicted were to be discharged by the Federal judge, and "every officer . . . having custody of [any] prisoner [was] directed immediately to obey and execute [the] judge's order."[68] The requirement that lists of political prisoners be furnished to the courts applied to future as well as previous arrests, and the speedy release of all citizens against whom no violation of federal law could be charged was to be expedited. Should the prisoners be detained beyond twenty days without the furnishing of such lists, on petition of the arrested person, he or she was to be discharged on the same terms as if the lists had been furnished.

Under the Act, the mandates of military officers concerning political prisoners were to come from Congress. The legislative branch of the government, in such an instance, should recover authority from the executive. A similar recovery was to be effected by the judicial branch, for prisoners were no longer to be detained by presidential authority, but were to be released by order of a federal judge unless indicted by a grand jury for offenses against the United States. Like other wartime statutes, however, the act seems to have had little practical effect.[69]

The Habeas Corpus Act offered no effective obstacle in the case of Vallandigham. In the *Milligan* decision, the Supreme Court held that the act should properly have applied to citizens subjected to such arrest and sentence, which was declared illegal in nonmilitary areas; but this decision did not come until after the war. Numerous arrests were made after March 3, 1863; releases were ordered, not by Federal judges, but by authority of the War Department. Since the Act confirmed the president's right to suspend the privilege of habeas corpus and afforded immunity to officers acting under the president's orders, legal sanction was given to a procedure for which Lincoln had been widely criticized. In practice the act strengthened Lincoln's hand while it weakened civil liberties.

Editors Under Attack

Given the turmoil surrounding the war and the fact that many of the factions involved sought and received support in the press, it is not surprising that censorship of the press became a tool of the Lincoln administration. As we have seen, restrictions on First Amendment rights led to arrests of newspaper editors by military authorities, the military suppression of such newspapers, and the prohibition of the circulation and sale of those newspapers by military authorities.[70] All of this despite an agreement that had been worked out early in the war to deal with press censorship. Representatives of newspapers had met with General George McClellan on August 2, 1861, and unanimously adopted resolutions that all "editors refrain from publishing . . . any matter that may furnish aid and comfort to the enemy. . . . That the government be respectfully requested to afford representatives of the press facilities for obtaining and transmitting all information suitable for publication, particularly touching engagements of the enemy."

Some of the military actions taken against newspapers and editors were based on the suspicion of their involvement in secret antiwar organizations. As we have seen, the Knights of the Golden Circle began to flourish during the Civil War and Copperhead editors often joined the club. Founded by Dr. George W. L. Bickley in 1854, the Knights of the Golden Circle had chapters as far north as Detroit, Michigan by April 1861.[71] It eventually transformed into the Sons of Liberty, partially funded by Vallandigham from Canada. It was groups like these that not only challenged the courts to uphold the free speech provision of the First Amendment, but its clause guaranteeing the right to assemble. Copperhead editors beat the drum for these rights.

Suppression of these editors began early in the war. For example, in August of 1861, the *Christian Observer* was closed by the U.S. marshal in Philadelphia.[72] At the same time, a federal grand jury in New York cited the *Journal of Commerce*, the *Daily News*, the *Day-Book*, the weekly *Freeman's Journal*, and the Brooklyn *Eagle* for the "frequent practice of encouraging the rebels now in arms against the Federal Government." This citation of misbehavior was followed by an order from the Postmaster General forbidding the mailing of these newspapers.[73]

Similarly, other newspapers were forbidden to circulate and sell. General Palmer temporarily prohibited the distribution of the Cincinnati *Enquirer* and Chicago *Times* within Kentucky. In New Haven, Connecticut the circulation of the New York *Daily News* was prohibited. From Ohio, General Burnside took similar action in excluding the New York *World* in his jurisdiction.

On February 23, 1863, the Davenport *Daily Gazette* in Iowa reported that some 75 convalescent soldiers from a nearby military hospital entered the office of the Keokuk, Iowa *Constitution*, wrecked the presses and dumped the type out the window.[74] In the spring of 1863, the *Crisis* and the Marietta, Ohio *Republican*, a Democratic paper, suffered damages at the hands of a mob of soldiers.[75] The next year a number of other newspapers in the Midwest, including the Mahoning, Ohio *Sentinel*, the Lancaster, Ohio *Eagle*, the Dayton *Empire*, the Fremont *Messenger*, and the Chester, Illinois *Picket Guard* experienced similar visitations.[76]

Along with suppression came the arrest of some editors. In October 1861 the editor of the Marion, Ohio *Mirror* was arrested on charges of membership in a secret antiwar organization. In Illinois, a number of men were taken into custody including the editors of the Paris *Democratic Standard*, M. Mehaffey and F. Odell. These men were imprisoned without trial in Fort Lafayette, Fort Delaware or the Old Capital Prison in Washington, D.C. In other Midwestern states, those arrested, usually on charges of interfering with enlistment or similar activities, included Dennis Mahoney, editor of the Dubuque *Herald*, and Dana Sheward, editor of the Fairfield *Constitution and Union*. In Philadelphia, the *Evening Journal* was suppressed by military order in January 1863, and Albert D. Boileau, its editor, confined to Fort McHenry for a few days until he wrote an apology and promised to reform.[77]

In February 1862, Secretary of War Stanton sent the following order to officers in various cities: "All newspaper editors and publishers have been forbidden to publish any intelligence received by telegraph or otherwise respecting military operations by the United States forces. Please see . . . that this order is observed. If violated . . . seize the whole edition and give notice to this department, that arrests may be ordered." Several months after this order, the Knights of the Golden Circle expressed their outrage for the unnecessary yet numerous cases of arbitrary arrests. On October 31, 1862, in Southern Illinois, this circular was distributed by the secret organization:

RESISTANCE TO TYRANTS IS OBEDIENCE TO GOD

To all Patriotic Men in the United States:

> Whereas, the repeated violations of the Constitution of the United States by the present party in power, do most seriously threaten the liberties of the people and tend to the destruction of constitutional liberty, the great anchor of a democratic republic, we, who are hereby united in order to check these outrages upon the rights of loyal citizens, and to prevent this Government from degenerating to a military despotism, to be controlled by unscrupulous fanatics, "do pledge our lives, our property, and our sacred honor," to maintain constitutional liberty, to the extent guaranteed by our fundamental laws, and determine that no more citizens shall be illegally arrested and detained, and that we will resent such usurpation in every legal and peaceable mode, and in the event of defeat we will fall back upon that God-given right—physical resistance to despotic power.[78]

The lifting of phrases from the Declaration of Independence reveals a rhetorical sophistication among the Knights, who operated on many fronts to advance their cause.

Two Cases of Importance

The circumstances surrounding the Chicago *Times* and the New York *World* provide two cases of press censorship based on fears of internal subversion. The suppression of the Chicago *Times* was triggered by an incident closely tied to the Vallandigham case. After hearing the *Times'* comments severely attacking the administration and expressing sympathy for Vallandigham, General Burnside, on June 1, 1863, issued General Order N. 84, which contained the following passage: "On account of the repeated expression of disloyal and incendiary sentiments, the publication of the newspaper known as the Chicago *Times* is hereby suppressed." Brigadier General Ammen, commanding the district of Illinois, was ordered to execute this order, and under his authority Captain Putnam, in command at Camp Douglas, Chicago, warned the management that the paper must not be published on the morning of the 3rd, under penalty of military seizure.

According to Secretary Welles, the president and every member of the Cabinet regretted Burnside's orders; Stanton directed a letter to Burnside expressing the president's disapproval. He advised Burnside that the dissatisfaction within his jurisdiction would only be increased "by the presence of an indiscreet military officer who will . . . produce irritation by assuming military powers not essential to the preservation of the public peace." After learning that the orders were given to suppress the *Times*, Lincoln wrote to Stanton that he had "received additional despatches, which, with former ones, induce me to believe we should revoke or suspend the order suspending the Chicago 'Times'; and if you concur in opinion, please have it done."[79] The publication of the paper was resumed as soon as the order was revoked.

A year later, Lincoln revealed his uncertainty about intervening in the *Times* case in a letter to I. N. Arnold: "In regard to the order of General Burnside suspending the Chicago 'Times,' now nearly a year ago, I can only say I was embarrassed with the question between what was due to the military service on the one hand, and the liberty of the press on the other, . . . I am far from certain today that the revocation was not right.' "[80] Lincoln's ambivalence is also evident in a conversation he had in the winter of 1864. In his reply to another request that he suppress the Chicago *Times*, the president wrote, "I fear you do not fully comprehend the danger of abridging the liberties of the people. Nothing but the very sternest necessity can ever justify it. A government had better go the very extreme of toleration, than to do aught that could be construed into a interference with, or to jeopardize in any degree, the common rights of its citizens."[81] One result of the Chicago *Times* crisis was the adoption of resolutions by a meeting of 15 New York journalists. The resolutions denied the right of the press to uphold treason or rebellion but insisted upon the right to criticize both civil and military acts of the government.

The case of the New York *World* presents some differences from that of the Chicago *Times*. Unlike Burnside, General Dix in New York acted reluctantly. Moreover, in the New York case, the legal methods of resistance attempted in the city and state differed widely from those taken in Chicago. On May 18, 1864, the *World* published a false presidential proclamation listing the recent battles and setting aside a day for public humiliation and prayer. It concluded by calling for the conscription of 400,000 men. On the day of publication, Lincoln sent General Dix the following order:

> Whereas, there has been wickedly and traitorously printed and
> published this morning, in the New York *World* . . . a false and

spurious proclamation purported to be signed by the President . . . which publication is of a treasonable nature, designed to
give aid and comfort to the enemies of the United States and to
the rebels now at war against the Government and their aiders
and abettors, you are therefore hereby commanded forthwith to
arrest and imprison . . . the editors, proprietors and publishers of
the aforesaid newspapers, and all such persons as, after public
notice has been given of the falsehood of said publication, print
and publish the same with intent to give aid and comfort to the
enemy; and you will hold the persons so arrested in close custody
until they can be brought to trial before a military commission
for their offense. You will also take possession by military force,
of the printing establishment of the New York *World*, and hold
the same until further orders, and prohibit any further publication therefrom.[82]

General Dix executed the order and took newspaper managers into custody,
holding them under military guard for three days.

Conclusion

Following in the ideological footsteps of Daniel Webster, one of his Whig
mentors, Lincoln was forced by the circumstances he inherited to place survival of the Union above some civil liberties guaranteed by the Constitution.
Though Lincoln had often been a defender of the Constitution during his
career, he was also a critic of some of its consequences, as in his opposition
to the *Dred Scott* decision. In fact, by the time of the Gettysburg Address,
Lincoln had concluded that the principles of the Declaration of Independence
were more important than a strict construction of the Constitution. He ended
that address echoing a phrase from Webster's Reply to Hayne when Lincoln
pledged a new birth of liberty from a government of, by, and for the people.
He sought to return the country to its "unalienable" rights.

His defense of the Union, however, had serious implications for freedom of expression during the Civil War. Lincoln and his supporters not
only tried to suppress dissent with persuasive appeals; they also used legal
and extra-legal action to accomplish their ends. This policy led to the suspension of habeas corpus, the use of extra-constitutional measures to quiet
both his external and internal opposition, and the censoring and closing of
newspapers which opposed his war policies. Lincoln's transgressions were
forgiven because of the dire situation and because Lincoln used his powers
judiciously and politically to keep his opponents at bay. Perhaps the boldest
stroke being the signing of the Emancipation Proclamation after the war

turned in the North's favor. That event placated Lincoln's Radical rivals in
the Republican Party and, combined with the victory at Gettysburg, assured
his re-election in 1864.

He was then able to move to a more conciliatory approach to the South.
However, in fairness to Lincoln, we need to remember that the scene was
far different when he first became president. Even before Lincoln took his
oath in March, 1861, seven Southern states had seceded from the Union.
He deemed the secessions a full-scale rebellion and suspended habeas corpus
in military jurisdictions and where martial law had been imposed. Nonetheless, Lincoln anguished over these cases, particularly those of Congressman
Vallandigham and the Chicago *Times*. Once Salmon Chase replaced Roger
Taney as Chief Justice, the Supreme Court supported Lincoln's actions, as
did the Republican Congress after the victory at Antietam.

After the war, Lincoln's leniency with regard to the South would have
extended to Copperheads in the North. However, Lincoln's assassination
opened the door on an era of vengeful reconstruction where further violation of rights occurred and the Constitution was significantly amended to
guarantee that the people would take primacy over the states when it came
to civil liberties. It is too that reconstruction of the South and the Constitution that we now turn our attention.

Notes

1. For a view of what went on in the Confederacy at the same time see
Steven A. Smith, "Freedom of Expression in the Confederate States of America," in
Perspectives on Freedom of Speech, eds. Thomas L. Tedford, John J. Makay, and David
L. Jamison (Carbondale: Southern Illinois University Press, 1987), 24–45.

2. Literally "body of law." It includes such rights as a speedy trial by a jury
of peers.

3. As quoted in Joseph Wheelan's *Mr. Adams Last Crusade* (New York: Public
Affairs, 2008), 109.

4. Richardson, *A Compilation of the Messages and Papers of the Presidents,
1789–1902*. Vol. 3, (Washington DC: Bureau of National Literature and Art, 1907,
1987), 175–176.

5. Senate Document [118], 24th Congress 1st Session. The report went to
condemn the tactics and the rhetoric of the abolitionists and to discuss the states'
right to resist it.

6. Richardson, *Messages and Papers*, 296–298.

7. Don E. Fehrenbacher, ed. *Abraham Lincoln: Speeches and Writings, 1859–1865*
(New York, 1989), 456–457.

8. For a historic approach to this question see, Harold Nelson, *Freedom
of the Press From Hamilton to the Warren Court* (New York: Bobbs-Merrill, 1967),
221–247; Dean Sprague, *Freedom Under Lincoln* (Boston: Houghton Mifflin, 1965):

James Randell, *Constitutional Problems Under Lincoln* (Urbana: University of Illinois Press, 1951).

9. U.S. Constitution, Article I, section 9, part 2.

10. See Sydney G. Fisher, "Suppression of the Writ of Habeas Corpus During the War of the Rebellion," *Political Science Quarterly*, 3 (1888): 454–488.

11. Opinion of David Dudley Field, *Ex parte Milligan*; S.C. 4, Wall. 2–142. For more on this case and other military tribunals, see Marouf Hasian, Jr., *Military Tribunals and the Loss of American Civil Liberties* (Tuscaloosa: University of Alabama Press, 2005).

12. For a closer look at questions regarding Congressional power versus Presidential power, see James G. Randall, *Constitutional Problems Under Lincoln* (Urbana: University of Illinois Press, 1951), 119.

13. James McPherson, *Battle Cry of Freedom* (New York: Oxford University Press, 1988), 696.

14. Eventually, Maryland would contribute 20,000 troops to the Southern effort and 30,000, including 9,000 Blacks to the Union effort. The state was badly divided and highly explosive.

15. Fehrenbacher, *Abraham Lincoln*, 237.

16. Fehrenbacher, *Abraham Lincoln*, 237.

17. McPherson, *Battle Cry*, 286.

18. Lincoln had already signed several extra-constitutional proclamations, which called for troops to repress the rebellion, expanded the size of the army, and blockaded the South. Richard N. Current, T. Harry Williams, and Frank Freidel, *American History: A Survey* (New York: Knopf, 1963), 390.

19. As reprinted in Current, *American History*, 392.

20. McPherson, *Battle Cry*, 287.

21. Dred Scott was a slave who argued that because he had held prolonged residence in a free state (the Illinois Territory) he (and his wife) should be set free. After an 11-year battle, the court ruled against Scott claiming that no person of African ancestry could declare citizenship in the United States, and consequently, could not bring a case to federal court.

22. Randall, *Constitutional Problems*, 124. *Ex parte Merryman*, 17 Fed. Cas. 144.

23. President Nixon used the same argument during the Watergate crisis.

24. The military authorities, however, refused. See *Ex parte Merryman*, 17 Fed. Cas. 144.

25. James D. Richardson, ed., *Messages and Papers of the President*, vol. 6, (Bureau of National Literature and Art, 1897), 24–25.

26. James McPherson, *This Mighty Scourge: Perspectives on the Civil War* (New York: Oxford University Press, 2007), 212.

27. This was not the first nor the last time that Lincoln would argue that there was a law higher than the Constitution. His best rendition of this position occurred in the Gettysburg's Address in November 1863. It is a position now represented on the Supreme Court by Justices Clarence Thomas and Anthony Kennedy.

28. This position was used by Democrats to justify the charge that Lincoln was a tyrant. This charge seems unjust given Lincoln's reluctance to suspend the writ.

29. See Horace Binney, *The Privilege of the Writ of Habeas Corpus Under the Constitution* (Philadelphia: C. Sherman, 1862).

30. Randall, *Constitutional Problems*, 123.

31. Randall, *Constitutional Problems*, 123.

32. Randall, *Constitutional Problems*, 123.

33. Fehrenbacher, *Abraham Lincoln*, 456–457.

34. See, for example, Samuel Eliot Morison & Henry Steele Commager, *The Growth of the American Republic*, vol. 1, (New York: Oxford University Press, 1962), 739.

35. For a more complete discussion of the Constitutionality of military commission issues during the Civil War see Randall, *Constitutional Problems*, 169–185. *Ex parte Milligan*, 71 U.S. 2 (1866). *Ex parte Vallandigham*, 68 U.S. 243 (1864).

36. Randall, *Constitutional Problems*, 174.

37. Randall, *Constitutional Problems*, 174–175.

38. Randall, *Constitutional Problems*, 175.

39. Randall, *Constitutional Problems*, 175.

40. For a more detailed account of the military commissions, see Randall, *Constitutional Problems*, 170–185.

41. Randall, *Constitutional Problems*, 175.

42. Randall, *Constitutional Problems*, 176.

43. Morrison and Commager, *Growth of American Republic*, 740.

44. Joel H. Silbey, *A Respectable Minority: The Democratic Party in the Civil War Era, 1860-1868* (New York: Norton, 1977), 101.

45. McPherson, *Battle Cry*, 592.

46. John G. Nicolay and John Hay, *Abraham Lincoln: A History*, vol. 7 (New York: Century, 1890), 338.

47. Michael Kent Curtis, *Free Speech, "The People's Darling Privilege," Struggles for Freedom of Expression in American History* (Durham, NC: Duke University Press, 2000), 302–304.

48. James G. Blaine, *Twenty Years of Congress*, vol.1 (Norwich, CT: Henry Bill), 489–493.

49. It should be noted that the Proclamation, which was made official on January 1, 1863, applied only to states in revolt against the Union, not border states that remained loyal. Thus, slavery was not abolished in Maryland, Missouri, or Tennessee. Universal abolition would only come with the passage of the Thirteenth Amendment.

50. Blaine, *Twenty Years*, 489–493.

51. Nicolay and Hay, *Abraham Lincoln*, 338.

52. *Ex parte Vallandigham* at 591.

53. William B. Hesseltine, *Lincoln and the War Governors* (New York: Knopf, 1948), 331.

54. Fehrenbacher, *Abraham Lincoln*, 45.

55. M. Birchard and others to the President, July 1, 1863, in Richardson.

56. By 1864, the Democrats vilified Lincoln at their convention for "being guilty of interfering with freedom of speech . . ." See Blaine, *Twenty Years*, 489–493.

57. "To Erastus Corning and Others" in Fehrenbacher, *Abraham Lincoln*, 459–463.

58. See Blaine, *Twenty Years*, 489–493.

59. See Blaine, *Twenty Years*, 489–493.

60. *Ex parte Milligan*.

61. *Ex parte Milligan*.

62. *Ex parte Milligan*.

63. *Ex parte Milligan*.

64. See Blaine, *Twenty Years*, 455.

65. This same privilege was given to President Grant in 1869 to deal with Southern states that refused to implement the Thirteenth, Fourteenth, and Fifteenth Amendments.

66. See Blaine, *Twenty Years*, 455.

67. Although the president permitted all of the arrests, there were instances in which the president directed arrests himself. See Randall, *Constitutional Problems*, 186–214.

68. In cases of delay or refusal to obey the order, the officer was to be subject to indictment for misdemeanor, punished by a fine of at least $500, and imprisonment in the common jail for at least six months. Randall, *Constitutional Problems*, 165.

69. The enforcement of the Habeas Corpus Act is a difficult historical problem. Some contend the act was not carried out in sufficient degree to make any noticeable difference in the matter of the arrest, confinement, and release of political prisoners. Randall, *Constitutional Problems*, 166.

70. Particular newspapers subjected to military "suppression" included: the Chicago *Times*, the New York *World*, the New York *Journal of Commerce*, the Dayton (Ohio) *Empire*, the Louisville (Kentucky) *Courier*, the New Orleans *Crescent*, the *South* of Baltimore, the *Maryland News Sheet* of Baltimore, the Baltimore *Gazette*, the *Daily Baltimore Republican*, the Baltimore *Bulletin*, the Philadelphia *Evening Journal*, New Orleans *Advocate*, the New Orleans *Courier*, the Baltimore *Transcript*, the Thibodaux (Louisiana) *Sentinel*, the Cambridge (Maryland) *Democrat*, the Wheeling *Register*, the Memphis *News*, the Baltimore *Loyalist*, and the Louisville *True Presbyterian*. See Randall, *Constitutional Problems*, 492–493.

71. The military branch of the Knights of the Golden Circle was the American Legion. Early in their formation, the Knights proposed to invade Mexico as the first step in adding a tropical slave plantation state, surrounding the Gulf of Mexico, to the United States. This is how "Golden Circle" became part of the group's name. See Wood Gray, *The Hidden Civil War* (New York: Viking Press, 1942), 70–71.

72. James E. Pollard, *The Presidents and the Press* (New York: Macmillan, 1947), 380.

73. Pollard, *The Presidents*, 380.

74. Gray, *Hidden*, 142.

75. The Ohio *Republican* sustained damages estimated at $800.

76. Gray, *Hidden*, 164.

77. Gray, *Hidden*, 70–88; Pollard, *The Presidents*, 380.

78. The circular appeared in the Belleville *Weekly Advocate*.

79. Pollard, *The Presidents*, 378.

80. Pollard, *The Presidents*, 378.

81. Pollard, *The Presidents*, 378.

82. Richardson, *Messages and Papers*, vol. 6, 237.

Chapter 3

The Radical Republicans
and Reconstruction

Craig R. Smith

When he should have been scouting the Union army for General Lee, J.E.B. Stuart decided to raid an iron works just south of Harrisburg. His mission was successful in the immediate sense: the foundry was destroyed and several workers were killed. Unfortunately, the iron works belonged to Republican Congressman Thaddeus Stevens and one of those killed was his nephew. When the war ended, Stevens, perhaps more than any other Republican, wanted his revenge.

That desire for revenge would not only result in the muzzling of the South, it would lead to a civil war within the Republican Party when its leaders, including Stevens, turned on their own presidents, first Lincoln for being too conciliatory and then Andrew Johnson for allegedly conspiring with the South. This case of silencing the opposition has significant similarities and differences with the Alien and Sedition crisis. It revolves around a war, around an external threat prompted by Southern arrogance, around a perceived threat of internal subversion by the president, and around a threat to the power of a major political party. In this case, however, the crisis arises just as the war ends and it leads to a division in the ruling party between the Congressional and executive branches. Furthermore, it contains an example of those being suppressed by one group trying to silence a third group. The circularity of these forces is impressive as Republicans free Blacks and disenfranchise the ex-Confederate leadership, while the ex-Confederates attempt to disempower newly freed Blacks.

As with the Federalists, the Radical Republicans ran a strong rhetorical operation that helped them pass significant and constitutionally suspect legislation; but the Radicals faced an intransigent president absolutely opposed to their program, a debacle the Federalists avoided with the acquiescence of

President John Adams. Since the Radicals succeeded in the face of perhaps tougher resistance at the outset, their success at emasculating the South and rendering President Johnson ineffective deserves special attention.

I should also note that this period of history is important for several other reasons. First, the passage of the Thirteenth, Fourteenth, and Fifteenth Amendments to the Constitution complete a movement toward a stronger federal government first started with the ratification of the Constitution in 1789. As we have seen, the Federalists led by Hamilton used it to expand the army and federal taxing power. The Whigs led by Clay and Webster would use it to protect private property, individual rights, and to advance a national agenda at the expense of states' rights. Clay's American System used a national tariff to fund internal improvements. In many cases before the Supreme Court, Webster was able to protect private contracts and the federal government's right of preemption. He crowned his thinking on this issue in his famous reply to Senator Hayne in 1830 proclaiming "Liberty and Union, one and inseparable." Just as the Federalist Party had evolved into the Whig Party, the "Conscience Whigs" evolved into the Republican Party, while the "Cotton Whigs" atrophied. And Lincoln carried on the work of Webster, particularly in his Gettysburg address and his saving of the Union. After his death, the Radical Republicans seized control and completed the job of turning the United States into a singular noun.

Second, the context of the passage of these three amendments creates a tension that runs from the way the amendments were passed to the way they should be read. As we shall see, Southern states were coerced into ratifying the amendments as the price of reentry into the Union even as some Northern states were rescinding their ratification. Once the amendments were adopted, however, the interpretation of them, if based even partially on their legislative history, implies a Unionist reading. For example, the "due process" and "equal protection" clauses of the Fourteenth Amendment clearly were meant to apply the Bill of Rights to the states. That change greatly enhanced First Amendment rights once it was accomplished in 1925. Thus, this crucial juncture in history is important to an understanding of these new amendments and to how civil liberties have evolved since their passage.

The Inception of the Crisis

The constituents of the civil war crisis quickly morphed into the constituents of the reconstruction crisis. The external threat of a militant South changed into the threat of a reborn politically powerful South, unbowed and unbroken. The internal threat of Copperheads changed into the threat of northern Democrats allying with returning Southern Democrats to steal power back from the Republicans. Soon added to the mix was a Democratic vice president, Andrew Jackson Johnson, who became president on the assassination of Lincoln. Instead of the president initiating restrictions on freedom of expression, it was the congressional leadership of the Republican Party. The Supreme Court was kept at bay through most of the legislative activity since the most radical legislation was in the form of amendments to the Constitution and the Court was dominated by Republicans. The conflict would be brought to a head with an impeachment trail, but would go fully unresolved until the settlement of the election of 1876.

The story of this crisis begins during the Civil War. In February 1862, Senator Charles Sumner of Massachusetts had set out a plan for post–Civil War reconstruction of the Union. As he saw it, any state that had voted to secede forfeited all rights under the Constitution and was reduced to the status of a territory. That was an important legal point because if Sumner was right, as he argued in *Atlantic Monthly*, then "rebel" states could only be readmitted to the Union with congressional approval, which would place control of reentry in the hands of Radical Republicans in Congress.

President Abraham Lincoln did not reveal his "restoration" plan until his proclamation of December 8, 1863, which made clear he did not share Sumner's view.[1] Under Lincoln's plan, any Southern state would receive executive recognition as soon as one-tenth of the voters in the state took an oath to support the United States Constitution. The House condemned the president's plan by passing the Wade-Davis Bill on May 4, 1864, by a vote of 73 to 59. It was a draconian measure requiring far greater obeisance from the Southern states if they were to receive recognition. Still smoldering over his burned iron works and loss of a nephew, Representative Thaddeus Stevens opposed the plan because it did not go far enough!

The bill reinforced Sumner's position that reconstruction was the prerogative of Congress not the president. When the bill passed the Senate easily, Lincoln killed it with a pocket veto. In response, at the Republican Convention of 1864, Thaddeus Stevens of Pennsylvania, Roscoe Conkling of New York, and George Boutwell of Massachusetts wrote radical planks into the party platform calling for what would eventually become the Fourteenth and Fifteenth Amendments. They also published a "Manifesto" in leading newspapers that was extremely critical of Lincoln. When it reconvened, Congress said it would refuse to admit any representatives from restored states. On April 11, 1865, Lincoln delivered what would become his last major public address; he pledged to reexamine his policy of restoration and make a "new announcement" soon.[2]

Any hope of reconciliation between the executive and congressional branches was destroyed by the bullet that felled the president on Good Friday; he died the next morning. Andrew Johnson, a Democrat, had been

the only Southern Senator to oppose secession. Before that, he had served
in the House for 10 years, so he knew how the Congress worked. He had
then served as governor of Tennessee for two terms before being elected to
the Senate and then military governor of Tennessee by appointment from
Lincoln in 1862. In 1864 he was elected vice president on Lincoln's ticket and
succeeded him upon his death. Johnson, however, lacked Lincoln's political
acumen and intellectual credibility; he had not attended one day of school.
This would render him particularly open to William Seward's influence
once the Secretary of State recovered from the wounds he suffered in the
conspiracy against the Lincoln administration.

When the phlegmatic Johnson assumed the presidency, he wanted to
"hang all traitors"; he had a visceral hatred for aristocrats and plantation
owners. As his middle named indicated, he was a Jackson Democrat and,
therefore, something of a populist. His actions concerning the apprehension
of Southern Confederate leaders and the conspirators pleased the Radicals
in Congress as did his good relations with Generals Grant and Sherman.[3]
However, when Seward resumed his full duties in May 1865, he was able
to talk Johnson into embracing Lincoln's more magnanimous plan of reconstruction.[4] Johnson also heard the siren song of praise from moderates and
pro-Union Southerners in his old party. Thus, despite his original call for
a clenched fist in dealing with "traitors," he opposed congressional attempts
to modify Lincoln's lenient policy toward the South.[5] He decided he would
recognize Southern states on his own and "restore" them to the Union.

Radicals were shocked and asked for a special session of Congress. Johnson not only refused to call one but began to appoint governors of Southern
states, some of whom had been loyal to the Confederacy. For example, he
issued a proclamation naming William Holden provisional governor of North
Carolina.[6] His war with the Radical Republicans was underway by June 1865.
Its implications for presidential rhetoric were clear by August when Johnson
sent the following telegram to the Mississippi State Convention:

> If you could extend the elective franchise to all persons of color
> who can read the Constitution of the United States in English
> and write their names, and to all persons of color who own real
> estate valued at not less than two hundred and fifty dollars, and
> pay taxes thereon, you would completely disarm the adversary
> and set an example the other States will follow. This you can
> do with perfect safety, and you thus place the Southern States,
> in reference to free persons of color, upon the same basis with
> the free States. I hope and trust your convention will do this,
> and, as a consequence, the radicals, who are wild upon negro
> franchise, will be completely foiled in their attempt to keep the

Southern States from renewing their relations to the Union by not accepting their senators and representatives.[7]

This was hardly the blanket enfranchisement of freedmen that Radicals wanted. Worse yet, the president overruled Sherman and the head of the Freedmen's Bureau, General Howard, and restored freedmen-tended properties to their previous owners.

The Radical Republicans officially broke with the president by forming the "Universal and Equal Suffrage Association," which fronted myriad speeches, editorials, and pamphlets supporting the Radicals' goals and condemning the president's plan. Johnson faced another setback when no state seeking reentry into the Union offered to enfranchise its newly freed Black citizens. The fact is that Black suffrage was opposed in the North, too. Referendums on the issue regularly went down to defeat.[8]

No precedent existed in America for the conduct of conquerors who had won a civil war that was fought to preserve national unity. Policy had to be invented in the face of postwar bitterness. Seward believed that the Executive Branch, not the Congress was in charge of rehabilitation. He immediately laid out a policy that granted amnesty to all Southerners except:

> "diplomatic officers and foreign agents" of the Confederacy; all who left "judicial stations" or "seats in the Congress" to join the rebellion; "all military and naval officers of the Confederacy above the rank of colonel in the army or lieutenant in the navy;" all who resigned from the armed forces to "evade duty" in the war; all who were absent from the United States to aid the rebellion.

The order continued through 14 more categories of exceptions and concluded that all others would be pardoned if they took an oath to serve the Union and endorse emancipation. These were similar to the terms that Lincoln had set out on December 8, 1863. Johnson approved the plan but made one amendment. Because he believed the revolt was the work of slaveholders, Johnson excluded them from the amnesty. He then set about a liberal policy of granting pardons and paroles, further upsetting the Radicals.

The External Threat of Southern Resurgence

Johnson's unwillingness to compromise, and disputes concerning executive powers gave additional ammunition to the Radicals. Worse yet, Southern Reconstruction Conventions had moved too quickly for the taste of most Northerners. Though the Thirteenth Amendment had emancipated all slaves, the new "reconstructed" governments began to act as the puppets of Confederate Generals and slaveholders. They passed "Black Codes" authorizing Southern law-enforcement officials to apprehend unemployed Blacks, fine them for vagrancy, and hire them out to satisfy the fine.[9] Blacks were forced to obey curfews that did not apply to whites and were often arrested for simply looking at a white woman. This was clearly a case of suppression within suppression as conservative Southerners attempted to disempower Blacks. Under the banner of "home rule," Southerners had acted because they believed the president would support them.

By differentiating "Negro" labor from other labor, the Codes offended some Northerners and increased public support for Radical Reconstruction. For example, the Black Code of Louisiana stated:

> Sec.1. Be it enacted by the Senate and House of Representatives of the State of Louisiana in General Assembly convened, That all persons employed as laborers in agricultural pursuits shall be required, during the first ten days of the month of January of each year, to make contracts for labor for the ensuing year, or for the next year ensuing the termination of their present contracts. All contracts for labor for agricultural purposes shall be in writing, signed by the employer, and shall be made in the presence of a Justice of the Peace and two disinterested witnesses, in whose presence the contract shall be read to the laborer, and when assented to and signed by the latter, shall be considered as binding for the time prescribed.
>
> Sec.2. Every laborer shall have full and perfect liberty to choose his employer, but, when once chosen, he shall not be allowed to leave his place of employment until the fulfillment of his contract . . . and if they do so leave, without cause or permission, they shall forfeit all wages earned to the time of abandonment.

These same governments flaunted the Freedmen's Bill signed by Lincoln just before his death. It was to protect newly freed "negroes" and "white refugees" who had been forced from their homes because they were loyal to the Union; it also provided educational opportunities for Blacks. However, reports filtered into Washington, D.C. that Alabama and Florida had passed vagrancy laws that required the poor to work for the state. Their income was given to widows and orphans of Confederate soldiers thereby returning many Blacks to the status of state-owned slaves. Other states passed laws denying the right of "negroes" to bear arms, denying business licenses to "negroes," and garnishing wages from "negroes" under various pretexts.

On top of that, Alexander Stephens, an ardent defender of slavery, in what must be seen as one the most arrogant acts in history, asked to be seated in the convening U.S. Senate. Stephens had been the vice president of the Confederacy and had spent four years trying to destroy the very Senate in which he asked to be seated. Northerners were further infuriated by Southern editors who defended the reconstruction conventions and egged Stephens on. Clearly, the South invited some of the vengeful measures that would soon pass the new United States Congress.[10]

Seizing the Initiative

The president and the South had provided Radical Republicans with incredible rhetorical resources. By being confrontational and moving quickly to "restore" the Southern states to the Union, the president exacerbated his weak position, lost credibility, and increased suspicions that he was in league with the South. Southern leaders made a similar mistake. Demonstrating *hubris* and a lack of remorse, they had themselves elected to congressional and statewide posts in appalling numbers. Radicals had reason to believe the South was ready to rise again because Johnson had frittered away much of the advantage the North had gained after the assassination of Lincoln and the surrender at Appomattox.

Thaddeus Stevens wasted no time in taking the initiative on the issue of how reconstructed states were to be readmitted into the Union. On December 18, 1865, he opened the debate on reconstruction by citing the Fourth Article of the Constitution, which states that "new States may be admitted by the Congress." Stevens argued that "none of the rebel States shall be counted in any of the Amendments to the Constitution, until they are admitted into the family of States by the law-making power of their conqueror." Like Sumner in 1862, Stevens concluded on December 18, 1865, that the Southern states should be reduced to territories as a means of cleansing their guilt and filtering their motives: "There they can learn the principles of freedom and the fruit of foul rebellion. . . . I know of no better place nor better occasion for the conquered rebels. . . . If we fail in this great duty now when we have the power, we shall deserve and receive the execration of history and of all future ages."[11] The actions of the president and Southern leaders allowed Stevens and other Radicals to seize the moral and rhetorical high ground, which they badly needed since they were only a portion of the Republican Party.[12] They strengthened their position by arguing that they were fighting for the war aims for which Union soldiers had died. The weight of the past four years and half a million deaths came down on Stevens' side, as did the action of the South and the president over the summer of 1865. Moderate Republicans like Grimes, Sherman, and Fessenden were outflanked as the debate carried over into the new year. For example, Congressman Henry Raymond, a moderate—they were known as "conservatives" at the time—Republican from New York, asserted that Stevens' vengeance was incompatible with Lincoln's plan and that Lincoln had repeatedly claimed that the Southern states had never left the Union. This remark stirred Republican Congressman Shellabarger to deliver one of the most stinging attacks on the South, the kind of rhetoric that would mark the next two election cycles. One can see in these remarks the two types of suppression we have examined in these chapters. The first, as exemplified in the following paragraph, describes activity that is extra-constitutional. The second, as exemplified in the next paragraph, is a rhetorical attack that is legal but ethically dubious because it attributes to the whole South, extreme actions of a few including the assassination of Lincoln:

> What is before the Congress? I at once define and affirm it in a single sentence. It is, under our Constitution, possible to, and the late Rebellion did in fact, so overthrow and usurp, in the insurrectionary States, the loyal State governments, as that during such usurpation such States and their people ceased to have any of the rights or powers of Government as States of this Union, and this loss of the rights and powers of Government was such that the United States may, and ought to, assume and exercise local powers of the lost State Governments, and may control re-admission of such States to their powers of Government in this Union, subject to, and in accordance with, the obligation to guarantee to each State a republican form of Government.[13]

The Congressman then let fly with a litany of sins on the part of Southern states to drive home his point:

> They discarded all their official oaths, and took, in their places, oaths to support your enemies' government. They seized, in their States, all the Nation's property. Their senators and representatives in your Congress insulted, bantered, defied and then left you. They expelled from their land or assassinated every inhabitant of known loyalty. They betrayed and surrendered your arms. They passed sequestration and other Acts in flagitious violation of the laws of nations, making every citizen of the United States an alien enemy, and placing in the treasury of their rebellion all money and property due such citizens. They framed iniquity and universal murder into law. For years they besieged your

Capital and sent your bleeding armies . . . back here upon the very sanctuaries of your national power. Their pirates burned your unarmed commerce upon every sea. They carved the bones of your unburied heroes into ornaments and drank from goblets made out their skulls. They poisoned your fountains, put mines under your sailors' prisons, organized bands whose leaders were concealed in your homes, and whose commissions ordered the torch to be carried to your cities, and the yellow-fever to your wives and children. . . . They destroyed, in the four years of horrid war, another army so large that it would reach almost around the globe in marching-columns. And then to give the infernal drama a fitting close, and to concentrate into one crime all that is criminal in crime and all that is detestable in barbarism, they murdered the President of the United States.

The Radicals in the Senate supported the legislation emanating in the House. Senator Sumner introduced a resolution from the House that stated:

All laws, statutes, acts, ordinances, rules and regulations in any of the States lately in rebellion, whereby inequality of civil rights and immunities among the inhabitants of said States is established or maintained by reason of differences of color, race, or descent, are hereby declared null and void.

In his speech for the resolution, Sumner developed his own rhetorical screed by detailing the sins of the South and called on his colleagues to make the Emancipation Proclamation a reality. Mocking President Johnson's claim that he would be a Moses to the Negro, Sumner warned: "An avenging God cannot sleep while such things find countenance. If you are not ready to be the Moses of an oppressed people, do not become their Pharaoh."

Despite the ardor of the Radicals, there was, according to Blaine, no "disposition among Republicans to confer upon the negro the right to vote."[14] On top of that, the president let it be known that he opposed any further amendments to the Constitution and opposed Black suffrage in the District of Columbia. He then refused to meet with Frederick Douglass on these issues,[15] and the Radicals stepped up their attack on what was to them a threat internal to the government and their Party, the president himself.

In February, the first major battle in the war between President Johnson and the Congress erupted over extensions to the Freedmen's Bureau Bill. Twice Johnson vetoed them and twice he was overridden as moderate Republicans were persuaded as much by the Radicals as annoyed by the president's mean spiritedness. For example, on Washington's birthday in 1866 in the midst of this battle and while the president was being feted at the White House by his friends, a crowd gathered outside and began to serenade him. Carried away by their adulation and his drinking,[16] Johnson gave a long rambling speech that was interrupted by cries from the audience begging the president to name the "traitors" to whom he had alluded. "I have fought traitors and treason," said the president, "in the South. I opposed Davis, Toombs, Slidell, and a long list of others whose names I need not repeat. And now, when I turn around at the other end of the line, I find men—I care not by what name you call them. . . ." Johnson was interrupted again with cries of "Call them traitors." He continued saying that it was those who opposed his plan of "restoration." The crowd demanded names and finally Johnson gave way:

> I say Thaddeus Stevens of Pennsylvania. I say Charles Sumner. I say Wendell Phillips and others of the same stripe among them. . . . They may traduce me, they may slander me, they may vituperate, but let me say to you that it has no effect upon me; and let me say in addition that I do not intend to be bullied by my enemies. . . . If it is blood they want, let them have the courage enough to strike like men.[17]

There could be little doubt that Johnson was a threat to the Radicals and they used his words to produce the majorities they needed in the Senate and the House.

The Senate responded by passing the Civil Rights Bill of 1866 "to protect all persons in the United States in their civil rights." The vote was 33 to 12; in March it passed the House 111 to 38. On March 27, again ignoring the pleas of moderates, the president vetoed the bill not on the grounds recommended by Seward, which was that it trampled states' rights, but on the grounds that he objected to making the Chinese, Indians, and Negroes citizens of the United States. He said that European immigrants had to qualify for citizenship and so should others. Furthermore, he claimed the bill was reverse discrimination in that it granted more rights to Blacks than Whites.

Senator Trumbull, the author of the bill, answered the president point by point. He quoted from a speech Johnson had given when he was a Senator wherein Johnson said the argument of rights for immigrants was a "mere quibble." Then Trumbull launched into a powerful peroration, again surfacing the rhetorical strategies of the Radicals. They would play to pathos; they would wave the bloody shirt; they would try to suppress the president.

Tell it not, sir, to the father whose son was starved at Anderson-
ville, or the widow whose husband was slain at Mission ridge, or
the little boy who leads his sightless father through the streets
of your city, or the thousand other mangled heroes to be seen
on every side of us today, that this Government, in defense of
which the son and the husband fell, the father lost his sight and
the others were maimed or crippled, had the right to call these
persons to its defense, but now has no power to protect the
survivors or their friends in any rights whatever in the States.
Such, sir, is not the meaning of our Constitution: such is not
the meaning of American citizenship.[18]

On April 6, the president's veto was overridden in the Senate by a vote
of 33 to 15; the House followed 122 to 41. A spontaneous demonstration
broke out on the floor of the House; the Civil Rights Bill became law and
is influential to this day. The Republicans had taken a huge risk because this
Bill went further than any state in the North had gone in protecting the
rights of Blacks. Obviously, the chance to control governments in the South
and to isolate the president outweighed other Republican concerns.

On April 30, 1866, a draft of the Fourteenth Amendment was introduced in the House and debate opened on May 8. While the president
granted more pardons,[19] the amendment was approved 128 to 37. A few
weeks later, the Senate passed its version of the amendment 33 to 11. On
June 13, the House accepted the Senate version 120 to 32. The ratification
process among the states began quickly when Connecticut ratified on June
30, followed by New Hampshire on July 7, and Tennessee on July 19, which
led to its readmission to the Union on July 24.

Johnson was delighted to have his home state back in the Union but in
a special message to Congress on July 25, he wrote, "My approval, however,
is not to be construed as an acknowledgment of the right of Congress to
pass laws preliminary to the admission of duly qualified representatives from
any of the states." Johnson noted opposition to the Fourteenth Amendment
was being suppressed in Confederate states; they were being blackmailed into
ratifying amendments to the Constitution. Alexander Stephens testified to
that effect before Congress to no avail.[20]

The way these and other "reforms" had been pushed through the Joint
Committee on Reconstruction reveals a measure of suppression of speech in
the committee itself. It was composed of 15 members of Congress with only
one Senator and two House members being Democrats.[21] The Committee
had called 144 witnesses, all in favor of the measures; this procedure became
a model for congressional hearings during this time.[22]

Johnson was appalled when he received the formal Report of the Joint Committee in June; it attributed base motives to the South as whole rehearsing again its threat to the nation:

> It must not be forgotten that the people of these states, without justification of excuse, rose in insurrection against the United States. . . . They continued this war for four years with the most determined and malignant spirit.

Here, as in the case of the Hamiltonian Federalists, the opponents' *positions* were not made the objects of criticism, but the opponents' *motives* for holding their views were assaulted and treated as permanently debarring them from civil considerations. The rhetorical uses of this "conspiracy" seemed limitless to the Radicals and applied the strategy to their internal threat, Johnson, by spreading stories that he was found hung over the morning he was sworn in, allowing the public to infer that he had celebrated Lincoln's assassination. They cited the fact that John Wilkes Booth had left his card at Johnson's boarding house, a charge that ignored the report that a co-conspirator happened to also be staying there at the time.[23]

The Radical Agenda

Underlying the Radical Republicans' political intolerance was the ideal of racial equality as embodied in the Thirteen Amendment, the proposed Fourteenth Amendment, and the soon-to-be-drafted Fifteenth Amendment. Racial equality had not been an official goal when the War began. President Lincoln had needed to keep the border states of Missouri, Kentucky, and Maryland in the Union, so he had overruled abolitionists in his cabinet. But after bitter battles and the North's quasi-victory at Antietam (Sharpsburg, Maryland) in 1863, Lincoln signed the Emancipation Proclamation. With freedom finally established as a war goal, Radicals resolved to reconstitute the Southern state governments so that Southern representatives in Congress would be loyal unionists. As we have seen, suggestions of leniency to the South were deemed an internal threat to Union; Johnson's opposition was in fact characterized as treason.

The Radicals took these issues to the public soon after Congress adjourned on July 28, 1866. They continued to use their three part rhetorical strategy with great success: first, an unrepentant South needed to be punished; second, the president was conspiring with the South to undo the victory of the North; third, the war goals of freedom for all must be preserved and propagated. Events played into the Radicals hands. In Memphis a riot occurred when a Black soldier shot at a White policeman. A vigilante group entered the Black district of the town and killed 46 Blacks. The perceived external threat of the rise of the South was strengthened.

Two days after Congress adjourned, the country was stunned to learn that Blacks in New Orleans had been slaughtered in order to stop a riot. The Chicago *Tribune*, the New York *Independent*, and *Harper's Weekly* blamed the president because those governing Louisiana had been put in place under his "restoration" plan.

As the midterm election campaign began in earnest, the president played into the hands of the Radicals when he called a convention of Democrats, conservatives, and Administration Republicans to meet in Philadelphia. When every state and territory sent representatives, the Radicals used the event to magnify the internal threat the nation face.[24] At the convention, Congressman Henry Raymond of New York argued for the "restoration" policy in his keynote address. The convention passed resolutions of support for Johnson's policy on August 15. When the proceedings were delivered to the president, he greeted the delegation with General Grant standing by his side. Then much to the embarrassment of Grant, Johnson gave an inflammatory speech in which he defended his policies:

> So far as the Executive Department is concerned, the effort has been made to restore the Union, to heal the breach, to pour oil into the wounds which were consequent upon the struggle.... We have seen hanging upon the verge of the government, as it were, a body called, or which assumes to be, the Congress of the United States, while it is in fact a Congress of only a part of the states.[25]

Since many Copperheads, including Clement Vallandigham (see chapter 2) participated in the convention, even moderate Republicans were appalled. The New York *Tribune* extrapolated that the convention was "ninety per cent Rebels and Copperheads."[26] Evidence useful to the Radicals mounted when former Senator Wade Hampton of South Carolina supported the president. When Johnson failed to bring Jefferson Davis to trial in a timely manner, Radical claims of conspiracy were strengthened. When Johnson extended the amnesty proclamation to Texas, which had been excluded from it in April, the paranoia among Radicals knew no bounds.

To provide yet another venue for their rhetoric of conspiracy, Radicals held conventions of their own. They started in Philadelphia on September 3; on September 25 and 26 in Cleveland, the Radicals organized a huge convention of "soldiers and sailors of the Union." They condemned the president, while delegates waved their blood-stained shirts from the Civil

War.[27] Throughout the ensuing election campaign, Johnson was frequently heckled and threatened, and his "swing around the circle" during the campaign had disastrous results because of his intemperate rhetoric. His replies often contained profane and blasphemous language that incited his enemies.[28] At huge gatherings in Cleveland and St. Louis, he yelled "Hang Thad Stevens."[29] When someone in a crowd would call Johnson a traitor, he would respond by calling his heckler a coward and often challenge who ever it was to step forward. By the time he got to Chicago, he was met with placards that read "No Welcome to Traitors." The protests were so vociferous in Indianapolis and Pittsburgh that Johnson could not speak.

In the elections of November, Republicans, especially Radicals, won overwhelming victories. Republicans would rule the new House by a margin of 143 to 49. They carried the Northern states with an aggregate majority of 400,000 votes. The 39th Congress convened on December 3, 1866, and received a conciliatory message from the president calling for the readmission of the 10 states left in the Confederacy. However, these states had overwhelmingly rejected the Fourteenth Amendment; Radicals seethed when Johnson included that sentiment in his annual message to Congress. Republicans were quick to respond. They admitted Nebraska to the Union over the president's objections to their reworking of the state's constitution to mandate universal male suffrage. They then removed the president's power to grant pardons, previously given in the Confiscatory Act of 1862.[30]

Doubling Their Efforts

In January 1867, the Supreme Court sided with congressional moderates. In the *Milligan* and *Test Oath* cases, the Court overturned the "internal security policies" Lincoln had imposed on Copperhead counties in Indiana (see chapter 2). With the war over, the Court came down in favor of restoring civil liberties but not in the South. The Radicals planned new legislation and used these unpopular decisions to stir up public fervor for the elections of 1868.

By now, however, the Radicals knew they could achieve their most radical goals. Perhaps the most severe measure was the one introduced in the Joint Committee by the ailing Thaddeus Stevens on February 6, 1867.[31] It called for dividing the 10 states still outside the Union into five military districts and proposed that habeas corpus be suspended in the districts so that military tribunals could take control and Southern freedom of expression be curtailed. Speeches critical of the Radicals' plans were dubbed incitements to riot. Proponents of the bill claimed that whites loyal to the Union were being driven from the homes and killed, that new Black citizens needed to be protected, that the South had arrogantly rejected the Fourteenth Amendment, and that they had established illegal governments. Opponents of the bill said it was unconstitutional, unduly harsh, and imperialistic. In the Capitol, the *National Intelligencer*, a newspaper that supported Johnson, said it was "treason enveloped in the forms of law."

With their newfound, lop-sided majority, Republicans were able to pass the bill 109 to 55 in the House. On February 14, the Senate took up the bill and rehearsed the arguments of the House with one exception. Several Senators wanted to know how the bill would ever be repealed if a new president wanted to keep the military districts in place. A substitute bill was passed 20 to 10 and back in the House, Stevens complained that the Senate had weakened his bill by giving the president too much power over the activities of the military governors in the districts. Congressman James Garfield of Ohio responded that if president acted improperly, he could be impeached, which was what Stevens wanted anyway. This retort was the first public evidence that impeachment was on the minds of the Radicals. If the plan succeeded, it would certainly remove the president from the rhetorical stage.

Despite Garfield's argument, the House rejected the Senate version and a conference committee developed a new version that emphasized suffrage for all male citizens and stated that all Southern governments would be considered provisional until the states were admitted to the Union. The military district bill was passed by the House and Senate, and when it was passed again over a presidential veto, the South officially became occupied territory allowing for further confiscation of property and suppression of dissent, particularly in the Southern press. While he was being vilified, Johnson suffered the further humility of having to carry out the legislation he had vetoed. In consultation with General Grant, he created the military districts mandated by the Radicals. General Schofield was assigned to the military district that contained Virginia; General Sickles controlled the Carolinas; General Pope was given Georgia, Alabama, and Florida; General Ord was given Mississippi and Arkansas; General Sheridan was given Louisiana and Texas.

If the election results of November 1866 were a calamity for President Johnson, the Reconstruction Acts of 1867–1868 verified his worst fears. Soon after the 39th Congress adjourned and the 40th opened under the leadership of Senator Benjamin Wade and House Speaker Schuyler Colfax, the Second Reconstruction Act was passed. It gave specific orders to the Army on how to implement reconstruction. Yet another piece of legislation known as the Supplementary Act, giving even more power to the military was passed on July 19, despite even Sumner's feeling that military force should not be used to achieve reconstruction aims. However, it was the feeling of the vast majority in Congress that the Attorney General had watered down the previous

Reconstruction Acts and that even more specific language was required. The Supplementary Act was passed and Johnson's veto was overridden. The reinstatement process now required: 1) registration of voters, including all adult Black males, 2) each voter had to swear a loyalty oath, 3) voters must elect a convention to prepare a new state constitution providing for Black suffrage, 4) the new state constitution must be ratified, 5) the state must hold elections for public office holders, 6) the state must ratify the Fourteenth Amendment, and 7) once the Fourteenth Amendment was adopted by the mandated number of states, a state having fulfilled the other requirements would be readmitted to the Union.

Clearly, the Radicals were at the height of the power and were unafraid to use it. The Radicals imposed an unprecedented straightjacket on the South, muzzling all criticism as sedition, particularly in newspapers (see below). The Act stripped former rebels of running for public office, perhaps the worst infringement of their rights. For example, General John Pope, who was in charge of the Third Military district, issued orders from his Atlanta office that kept those favorable to the Union in office after their terms were up by postponing elections. He forced judges to put Blacks on juries. President Johnson replaced him with General Meade because of these excesses.

Clearly exceeding the letter if not the intent of the Act, General Sheridan, in charge of the Louisiana-Texas district, removed ex-Confederates from office. Taking the Act as a mandate, General Grant told his commanders to continue to enforce the law as they saw fit.[32] With ex-Confederates off the ballots, it was not difficult for the Union League to carry election after election in the South. Republicans, including postwar opportunists from the North known as "Carpetbaggers," rallied the newly enfranchised Blacks to support this pro-Union effort. By the end of 1867, Blacks held majorities in terms of voters in Louisiana, South Carolina, Mississippi, Florida, and Alabama. White Republican voters were mainly from the poor upland counties and northern parts of their states. They hated the plantation owners and the aristocrats. Many had been Unionists and now were dubbed "Scalawags" by their Democratic foes. Together with Black Republicans, the Scalawags simply overwhelmed the Democratic Party. In the November elections of 1867 in the South, 80percent of registered Blacks voted; less than half of the White voters came to the polls. Republicans took complete control of the reconstruction conventions. Sullen Democrats labeled these the "black and tan" conventions and some migrated to Mexico to start new lives.

Conventions assembled, constitutions were written and ratified, governments organized, and the Fourteenth Amendment endorsed. These conventions included large percentages of Blacks and Northern Carpetbaggers. For example, they alone constituted 45 percent of the Alabama convention, 47 percent in Arkansas, 73 percent in Florida, 25 percent in Georgia, 71 percent in Mississippi, 25 percent in North Carolina, 78 percent in South Carolina, and 68 percent in Virginia.[33] Where they did not have a majority between them, Blacks and Carpetbaggers could usually find enough votes among Scalawags and disaffected Southern White delegates to form a majority. The constitutions written by these conventions were noxious to most Southerners. They resulted in the dominance of Reconstruction Republicans in the South through at least one election cycle. In no state was a conservative Democrat elected governor. Thus, the old liners were deprived a venue from which to plead their case. Eventually during the Reconstruction era, 226 Black citizens would serve as officials in Mississippi, including as United States Senator Blanche K. Bruce; the other Southern states followed suit to a lesser degree.[34] In fact, Blacks were only elected to 6 percent of the available House seats during Reconstruction and in their states Blacks never held more than 20 percent of the nonlegislative offices available.[35] They did better in the state legislatures, where they won 61 percent of representative seats and 42 percent of the state senate seats. However, White Carpetbagger Republicans constituted half of the governors, U.S. Representatives, and U.S. Senators though they only represented a tiny percentage of the vote.[36] To add insult to injury, many of these Carpetbaggers were former Union officers.

As late as 1875, Ruben Davis, a former member of the U.S. Congress complained, "You took $16,000 in cotton and left me a beggar. I call that an act of oppression. You denied my right to vote; I call that an act of oppression. You denied me the right hold office; I call that an act of oppression." Earlier, Davis had seen that without permission of the president, the Treasury Department loosed a posse of agents into the South to confiscate property and crops to compensate for the losses the Union had sustained during the war.[37]

Silencing Southern Newspapers

As one might expect, once the generals who ran the five military districts were in place, newspapers became a target of their censorship. While Republican papers were allowed to flourish, some old line Whig and most Democratic newspaper came under close scrutiny. Disparaging comments about the behavior of Union soldiers often resulted in suspensions of publication of newspapers by General Hancock and the other generals. The practice came easy to them since they had regularly shut down newspapers in the South in occupied territory.[38] As early as 1867, General John Pope, in charge of Alabama, Georgia, and Florida, cut off advertising in Democratic papers such as the

Mobile *Advertiser and Register*. Several Georgia papers, such as the Americus *Summer Republican* and the Albany *News*, had their publications suspended because they were not supportive of the Reconstruction program.

Being jailed for sedition was not uncommon, even when the criticism was sound. For example, the editor of the Petersburg *Daily News* went to jail for three months for ridiculing charges that Jefferson Davis was involved in the conspiracy to assassinate Lincoln. In Louisiana, the St. Martinsville *Courier de Tech* saw its editor arrested for commenting on a local political feud.[39] Forcing dissent underground was one of the causes of the formation of secret societies such as the Ku Klux Klan.[40] In fact, in his dissent in the *Slaughter House Cases*, which upheld the Fourteenth Amendment in 1872, Justice Bradley wrote, "intolerance of free speech and free discussion . . . often rendered life and property insecure, and led to much unequal legislation."[41]

With the South humbled and hence the external threat to the North finally quashed, Radicals focused their attention on Johnson. As usual, persuasion, allowed in a free North, preceded action. Using the rhetorical ploy of *guilt by association*, the Radicals strengthened their case for conspiracy by reasoning that since Johnson was a Southerner, his sympathies lay with the Confederacy. They published and distributed the words of a few Southerners in an attempt to prove that the whole South might rebel under the new "Southern" President, claiming:

> It is the old troop of slavery, with a few recruits, ready as of old for violence—cunning in device. . . . With the President at their head, they are now entrenched. . . . The safety of the Republic requires action at once.[42]

During this period of legislative fecundity, Radicals also reinforced the Freedmen's Bureau, a federal agency established to counteract the impact of the so-called Black Codes that were adopted by Southern legislatures during the sessions of 1865–1866 (see above). Radical leaders saw the Black Codes as a return to slavery. Wendell Phillips claimed, "The rebellion has not ceased, it has only changed weapons."[43] He called for extreme remedies to prevent the South from retrieving prejudice from the ashes of defeat.

Crippling the Presidency

Congress heard his call. On March 2, 1867, it passed the Command of the Army Act, which heavily restricted the president's military power; Congress overrode the veto of the new Reconstruction Act and then passed the Tenure of Office Act designed to prevent President Johnson from removing officers from his cabinet and other government posts. The specific motivation for this piece of legislation was to protect Secretary of War Stanton, a supporter of Radical Reconstruction and a critic of Lincoln's softness.

Overturning 80 years of precedent, the Tenure of Office Act required the advice and consent of the Senate to remove someone from office during the term of the president under which they were appointed.[44] If the Congress was not in session, then the undesirable appointee could only be suspended until it reconvened. The Act was introduced on January 10, 1867, three days after the first impeachment measures had been defeated in the House because a majority believed them to be too extreme. Thus, from the first, the Act was seen as a vehicle to foment impeachment. As debate raged in the House, the bill was amended to include the cabinet and then passed 111 to 38. The Senate followed suit.

Seward wrote the president's veto message of March 2, 1867, which raised grave constitutional concerns.[45] It had no effect on the Congress, which promptly overrode the president again. All through this period, the Radicals continued to gather evidence for impeachment. By November 1867, 95 witnesses had been deposed. The most interesting was General Grant, who refuted charges of conspiracy against Johnson. Grant had traveled with Johnson on the political tour of 1866 and often shared a bottle with him.

Less friendly witnesses accused the president of selling offices, improperly corresponding with Jefferson Davis, and acting illegally under provisions of the newly passed Reconstruction Act. Nonetheless, a vote on impeachment was defeated on December 7, 1867; only 57 Republicans supported the bill, while 108 members of both parties opposed it.

While the Radicals were plotting, President Johnson did little to allay their fears or to protect his flanks. For example, when General Sheridan, who was close to Secretary Stanton, dismissed the governors of Texas and Louisiana against the president's wishes, Johnson decided Stanton had to go, too. He notified Stanton on August 5, 1867, after learning that Stanton had interfered in the case of the Southern spy Mary Surratt.[46] That was the last straw. Stanton refused to resign, so the president suspended him on August 12 under the provisions of the Tenure of Office Act.[47] He appointed General Grant as the interim Secretary of War and asked Stanton to vacate his office. Stanton complied and Grant moved in. Next, Johnson asked for the head of General Sheridan, but Grant protested. Finally, after several exchanges and private meetings, Grant agreed to the removal of Sheridan. Encouraged, Johnson issued new pardons in South Carolina and then removed General Sickles as district commander. The Radicals claimed that Johnson was dismantling reconstruction.

However, they were beginning to lose momentum. In the off-year elections of 1867, Northerners let it be known that the Radicals had gone too far. The South had been forced to allow Blacks to vote; no Northern state had approved enfranchisement of Blacks. Negro suffrage went down to defeat in Ohio by 38,000 votes and the citizens returned a Democratic legislature.[48] New Jersey kept the word "white" in its suffrage requirement. In 18 states Republican strength declined. House Speaker Schuyler Colfax illustrated the panic among Radicals when he wrote to Garfield: "Before July, the majority of our party was against [impeachment] as a matter of policy. Now they are solidly for it. It must come. And the election returns & his wicked advisers have so excited [him] that he is decidedly on the war path."[49] They didn't have to wait long. Johnson removed heavyhanded General Pope and replaced him with the more moderate General Meade. Radicals claimed that Southerners were rejoicing over Johnson's decision. In December 1867, the Congress reconvened only to receive a hostile message from the president in which he opposed the effort to "Africanize half of our country."

On January 13, 1868, the Senate invoked the Tenure of Office Act and told Johnson it did not "concur" in the suspension of Stanton. Grant deserted the president by vacating his office and Stanton promptly moved back in. The president then ordered Grant to appeal the Senate action to the Supreme Court, but Grant refused. Their angry exchange of letters hit the press in early February when they were leaked by Congressmen who had asked to see them. It is now clear that Grant had his eye on the presidential nomination for 1868 and could stay with Johnson no longer if he did not want to offend the Radical wing of the Republican Party.

On February 21, the president notified the Senate he was again removing Stanton and replacing him with Lorenzo Thomas whom Johnson had appointed adjutant general over Stanton's objections. Stanton was immediately supported by many in the Senate, including Sumner who wired Stanton to "Stick" in place.

The next day Stanton ordered the arrest of Thomas, while Thaddeus Stevens introduced a resolution of impeachment with no particulars. Thomas posted bail and the Attorney General began to prepare his defense. When Stanton realized that the Thomas case could decide the constitutionality of the Tenure of Office Act before the president was tried, he promptly dropped the charges against Thomas and the impeachment case moved forward.

It lasted three days and filled 200 columns in the *Congressional Globe*. The lead speaker for impeachment was Ben Butler who cited the president's rhetoric on his swing around the campaign circle as demonstrating that he was "unmindful of the high duties of his office and the dignity and propriety thereof, and of the harmony and courtesies which out to exist and be maintained between the Executive and Legislative branches of the government." Butler claimed that the president attempted to bring into "disgrace, ridicule, hatred and reproach the Congress."[50] By such a standard, many a president might have been impeached. But the Constitution normally protects what Butler condemned as "loud threats and bitter menaces" of the president.

In this case, however, the vote was 128 in favor (all Republicans), 47 against (all Democrats), 17 not voting. A special committee then drew up specific articles of impeachment. Those selected to prosecute the case before the Senate included Congressmen Stevens, John Bingham, George Boutwell, James Wilson, Ben Butler, and John Logan. The Senate proceedings, over which Chief Justice Salmon P. Chase presided, began on March 5, 1868, when the House presented its charges. Chase had been a senator from and governor of Ohio; he had served as Secretary of Treasury before Lincoln appointed him Chief Justice to replace Lincoln's nemesis Roger Taney.

The defense team told the president not to appear and, most importantly, to keep his mouth shut during the trial. The political nature of the tribunal was evident from the outset; the Senate consistently voted to overrule the Chief Justice on questions of evidence and procedure. The president told his defense team to make the point that the Tenure of Office law should have been ruled on by the Supreme Court, not by the Senate that passed it, and certainly not in an impeachment trial.[51]

Having finished with procedural issues, the forum was adjourned on March 13. It reconvened on March 30 for an official opening of the trial phase. During his presentation of the case against the president, Representative Butler actually waved the bloody shirt of a Union soldier continuing an oratorical fad. He told the Senate, "You are bound by no law. You are a law unto yourselves." In his conclusion he pulled out all the stops: "By murder most foul did he succeed to the Presidency and is the elect of an assassin to that office, not the people."

On April 9 the president's defense team began its case. Henry Stanbery had resigned as Attorney General to defend Johnson; he was joined by William Evarts, the impressive New York lawyer who would eventually become Secretary of State, Benjamin Curtis, a former Associate Justice who had dissented in the *Dred Scott* case, Democrat William Groesbeck, and lawyer Thomas Nelson. Opening the defense, Curtis argued that since Stanton was a Lincoln appointment, Johnson had every right to remove him, and the Tenure of Office Act did not apply. He claimed that the last two articles of impeachment were a clear violation of the president's *freedom of speech*. He should not be held a criminal for simply stating the opinions in which he believed, no matter how troublesome they were to the Radicals. Over the next few days the defense was successful in portraying the president as intending to act lawfully. Furthermore, the cabinet, including Stanton, had unanimously advised the president that the Tenure of Office Act was unconstitutional.

After each side made summations, 29 Senators rose to speak on the issues. There were several long orations and even a challenge to a duel.

Charles Sumner's vitriol proved typical. He had been caned by a Southern member of the House during the debate over the Kansas territory in 1856. Now he proclaimed: "This is one of the last great battles with slavery. Driven from these legislative chambers, driven from the field of war, this monstrous power has found a refuge in the Executive Mansion."[52]

Behind the scenes Radicals worked feverishly to gather the necessary votes. Extra-constitutional activity was again pondered when Wade revived a plot to admit Colorado to the Union so that two more senators could be added to the pro-impeachment side. However, he was undone by the fact that if Johnson were convicted, Wade would fill out the president's term. On May 16, the Senate was ready to vote. The first vote was on the last article of impeachment, number 11. Each Senator was called and asked to respond "guilty" or "not guilty." The tension was palpable because the Radicals could not succeed without the votes of moderates like Grimes of Iowa and Fessenden of Maine.

What few in the room knew was that Grimes was an opponent of Wade's, and had had a private dinner with the president to gain assurances that Johnson would stop meddling with the reconstruction effort.[53] Johnson convinced Grimes of his sincerity by letting him know he intended to appoint General John Schofield as the new Secretary of War. Johnson also gave assurances to Senator Ross of Kansas that he would impose reconstruction constitutions in South Carolina and Arkansas. The formerly intransigent and hapless president compromised with some moderate Republicans to save his neck.

It worked. Fessenden voted for acquittal. Grimes, who had had a stroke and was thought to be too sick to attend the final vote, arrived on a stretcher and voted "not guilty." Then Senator Ross, an abolitionist from Kansas, shocked his fellow Republicans and also voted "not guilty." The president was saved by that one vote on a 35 guilty, 19 not guilty count. Radicals immediately moved for an adjournment to May 26 in order to lobby for more support on the other articles of impeachment. But the vote held at 35–19 on each one. The seven Republicans who voted against the removal of President Andrew Johnson were protecting the social fabric of the country. The institution of the presidency was for them larger than the particular charges leveled against Johnson. Senator Grimes put it this way: "I can not agree to destroy the harmonious working of the Constitution for the sake of getting rid of an unacceptable President."

Some of the press also played a responsible role when they went after the excesses of Radical Republicans. The New York *Times* led rational sentiment when it said on March 3, 1868:

> [W]hat else are the heated appeals of party organs, the fervid
> exhortations of party orators, the instructions of party majorities

in State Legislatures, and the resolutions of party meetings, but attempts to use the forms of the most solemn judicial proceeding known to our Constitution, for the purpose of accomplishing party ends and anticipating the results of next Fall's election? If President Johnson may thus be ejected from office—not because he is guilty of the "crimes and misdemeanors" for which he has been impeached, but because he is deemed "unfit" for the place, and because the "country will be safer," in the Senate's judgement—so may his successor: so may any President who shall come after him. And, under such a precedent, whenever the President shall belong to one party and the Congress to another, the former may be removed, and the Senate may appoint one of their number to take his place.

A month later, the *Times* issued another appeal for rational action:

[I]f the President is removed merely for a mistake, or because he is in the way of party triumphs, or from partisan hatreds, having committed no crime or misdemeanor in the opinion of the nation, when it read the testimony and arguments, *even then* the people will be calm, because they will fall back on justice, and know that wickedness and passion will be avenged. Then the perpetrators of injustice will lose all their *prestige*, and no other harm will come than a wound to a party which cannot rule but by passion. We take it for granted that, whatever the verdict, there is patriotism and intelligence enough left to the nation to see the right ultimately vindicated. What is *any party*, to the eye of the patriot, compared with the dominion of truth, and the integrity of institutions?

No doubt these sentiments helped to moderate opinions in the population of which the Radicals were only a part.

When the trial was over, Stanton resigned. Johnson served the remaining nine months of his term but had been broken. The failure to remove Johnson hardly slowed the Radical Republicans during 1868. They succeeded in admitting state after state on their terms under the Reconstruction Acts. By the end of June, seven states—Arkansas, North Carolina, South Carolina, Louisiana, Georgia, Alabama, and Florida—were readmitted to the Union. All of the new Southern Senators were Republicans, and only half of them were from the South. White Carpetbaggers had reached their zenith of power.

On July 28, 1868, the day after the purchase of Alaska was complete, Secretary of State Seward certified that the Fourteenth Amendment had been ratified. In the entire Union, no Democratic legislator had voted for it. No Democratic member of Congress supported it; no Republican opposed it.

That summer the Republicans nominated General Grant for president, and he handily defeated Horatio Seymour of New York in the national election. However, Democrats cut into the Radicals' strength around the country and in the Congress. The Democratic platform called for an end to the Freedman's Bureau. The Democratic nominee for vice president, Frank Blair of Missouri, had traveled the country attacking the Reconstruction Acts and the havoc they wreaked on the South. He referred to the reconstructed governments in the South as "bastard and spurious."[54] The Republicans responded by waving the "bloody shirt" of Northern soldiers and touting their hero Grant over the pacifier Seymour. Grant carried California by only 514 votes. In the North, Oregon went Democratic along with New Jersey, Delaware, and New York, and Seymour carried Maryland and Kentucky and half of the reconstructed South as Democrats returned to the polls and used intimidation tactics to scare Blacks from them.

Once the election was over, the Radicals realized that they might not have another chance at passing the last amendment they sought for the Constitution. The movement for the Fifteenth Amendment was motivated by the argument that it was unfair to impose Black suffrage on the South through the Reconstructions Laws without imposing the same requirement on the rest of the nation.

Senator Henderson of Missouri, who had introduced the Thirteenth Amendment, brought forward the draft amendment, which said, "No State shall deny or abridge the right of its citizens to vote or hold office, on account of race, color or previous condition." He had written a section for the Fourteenth Amendment, which called for "impartial suffrage among men," but it had been rejected.

The Fifteenth Amendment received strong support in the House. For example, due to the Fourteenth, "citizens in Kentucky and Maryland," claimed Representative Boutwell, "[were] eligible to the office of President ... yet cannot vote for representation in Congress." On January 30, 1869, the House passed the new amendment 150 to 42 with 31 abstentions.

The Senate amended the House version by adding a provision that prohibited the testing of voters' knowledge. Then the Senate approved the amendment 39 to 16 and sent it back to the House. The House refused to accept it and the bluff worked. The Senate adopted the original House version. However, the House then changed the language again to include the Senate's call for no discrimination based on nativity, property, or creed. In a snit, the Senate continued the comic opera by rejecting all versions and demanded a conference. On February 26, 1869, the Senate and House adopted the version that now resides in the Constitution. It allowed educational testing and poll taxes, two loopholes through which the South would disenfranchise millions of poor Blacks and Whites over the next decades. These Jim Crow laws helped reestablish a monolithic Democratic Party for almost a hundred years.

President Grant took office on March 4, 1869, soon after which the Tenure of Office Act was repealed. Georgia's Senators and Representatives were refused entry to Congress until the state legislature ratified the Fifteenth Amendment, which it had recently rejected. This act of blackmail by the Radicals led to Georgia's capitulation, but demonstrates that the amendment was ratified under duress and despite opposition from New Jersey, Delaware, Maryland, Kentucky, Tennessee, California, and Oregon. The Carpetbagger legislators had done their job for the Radicals.

Led by Charles Sumner in the Senate and Thaddeus Stevens in the House, Radicals passed a number of laws to enforce the Fifteenth Amendment. The votes on this legislation split down party lines. One piece of legislation gave the president the right to suspend habeas corpus, a right Lincoln had claimed on his own during the Civil War.

For admission, the three "unreconstructed" states, Mississippi, Virginia, and Texas, faced the additional requirement of ratifying the new Fifteenth Amendment. It was not until 1870 that they were admitted back into the Union.[55] The Republican Carpetbaggers provided enough of a supplement in Congress for the Republicans to pass the Civil Rights Act and the Force Act of 1871, which sought to protect Southern Blacks from attacks by the Ku Klux Klan and others.

Grant won the election of 1872 by defeating a coalition ticket led by Liberal Republican Horace Greely. This election reveals one of the early cracks in the Grand Old Party, between the conservatives who favored business and the progressives who favored political reform. Grant's euphoria over winning reelection was dampened by a financial panic. While he fretted, the Radicals in Congress were instrumental in keeping Union troops in the South through Grant's second term despite severe setbacks in the congressional elections of 1874. The presidential election of 1876 brought more bad news for the Radicals. Rutherford B. Hayes of Ohio, who had been nominated on the seventh ballot at the Republican Convention, lost the popular vote to Samuel Tildon of New York. Representative James Garfield worked mightily behind the scenes to cut a deal with the South in which enough electors were challenged to force a reexamination of the vote by a special commission. Garfield promised that Hayes would only serve one term and that he would end the military supervision of the Southern states. The commission saw to it that Hayes was elected by one electoral vote. In the next election, free of military rule, the South voted solidly for the Democratic nominee and threw out the Carpetbaggers. The Republicans won with Garfield in 1880; however, in 1884 and 1892, Democrat Grover Cleveland broke the Republican hold on the presidency. Ironically, one of the legacies of the Radical Republicans was a solidly Democratic South from 1876 until 1964.

Conclusion

The Radicals were successful at silencing their opponents for many reasons. The South handed the Radicals a rhetorical sword when Southern leaders seemed unrepentant for the damage it had caused the Union during the Civil War. They embarked on a strategy of denigrating newly freed Blacks and restoring members of the Confederacy to power. The arrogance of some of the Southern leaders presented Radicals with evidence by which they could rile up Northern sentiment and preserve their status as the dominant political force in the Congress. Clearly, in a democracy the public is open to the most radical persuasion once it has endured a civil war. War must be vindicated; the fruits of victory must not be allowed to rot. The Radical Republicans understood this in the nature of their audience, while President Johnson, Secretary of State Seward, and members of the Confederacy did not.

The president also played into the Radicals' hands. By approving Seward's plan for "restoration," by pardoning Southerners, and by conferring with moderates and Democrats, he allowed himself to be portrayed as an internal threat not only to his party, but also to the nation. His boorish behavior inflamed his enemies and undercut the support he enjoyed from moderates. His flaws were seen in relief against the tall shadow of his martyred predecessor.

The Radicals promptly capitalized on these rhetorical opportunities in the election of 1866. Achieving huge majorities in the Congress, they were able to override the president's opposition to Radical Reconstruction and put in place a system that guaranteed them control over newly forming Southern governments. They were able to disenfranchise Southern citizens, censor Southern newspapers and confiscate Southern property. They were able to amend the Constitution, sometimes by dubious means, particularly in the case of the Fourteenth and Fifteenth Amendments. And they nearly impeached the president using the clearly unconstitutional Tenure of Office Act.

Their zeal was fired by threats real and imagined. They were able to translate that zeal into rhetorical appeals to voters who empowered them to carry out the most significant changes in the Union since the adoption of the Bill of Rights. It is a lesson that should not be lost on a democratic republic such as our own. Rhetoric, as the Sophist Gorgias said, is a powerful lord with narcotic powers over an audience, particularly a democratic one.

Notes

1. James D. Richardson, *A Compilation of the Messages and Papers of the Presidents, 1789–897*, vol. 6, (Washington DC: Government Printing Office, 1911).

2. One is reminded of John Kennedy's speech on Vietnam at American University in 1963 shortly before his assassination.

3. Hans L. Trefousse, *Andrew Johnson: A Biography* (New York: Norton, 1989), 210–213.

4. Seward himself had been converted to Lincoln's plan because of Seward's growing admiration for Lincoln from 1860. Initially, Seward was a fire brand on the issue of abolition and had opposed the 1850 Compromise. See Craig R. Smith, "Daniel Webster's July 17th Address as a Mediating Influence in Conflict Situations," *Quarterly Journal of Speech*, 71 (1985): 349–361.

5. James G. Blaine, *Twenty Years of Congress*, vol. 2, (Norwich, CT: Henry Bill, 1888), 68.

6. Howard Nash, *Andrew Johnson: Congress and Reconstruction* (Rutherford, NJ: Fairleigh Dickinson University Press, 1972), 31.

7. Trefousse, *Andrew Johnson*, 224.

8. On October 2, 1865, a referendum for Black suffrage was defeated by a vote 55 percent to 45 percent in Connecticut; in Minnesota and Wisconsin on November 7, referenda were defeated by the same margin.

9. In 1866, Congress voted to extend the appropriations of the Bureau and to strengthen it. Johnson vetoed the bill, but Congress overturned the veto. Richard N. Current, *The Essentials of American History* (New York: Knopf, 1976), 170.

10. See Philip Dray, *Capitol Men: The Epic Story of Reconstruction Through the Lives of the First Black Congressmen* (New York: Houghton Mifflin, 2008).

11. www.let.rug.nl/~usa/D/1851-1875/reconstruction/steven.htm

12. Trefousse, *Andrew Johnson*, 234.

13. Blaine, *Twenty Years*, vol. 2, 134–137.

14. Blaine, *Twenty Years*, vol. 2, 168.

15. Trefousse, *Andrew Johnson*, 241.

16. Hugh McCulloch is one of the few historians who disputes the fact that Johnson was unable to hold his liquor. He argues that Johnson was simply a vituperative personality incapable of civil speech. See *Men and Measures of Half a Century* (New York: Charles Scribner's Sons, 1889), 393.

17. This speech of February, 1866, can be found at www.teachingamericanhistory. org/library/index.asp?document=1932

18. Blaine, *Twenty Years*, vol. 2, 177.

19. In this case, both Blaine and Garfield argued that Johnson was merely carrying out the policy of Lincoln. See Blaine, *Twenty Years*, vol. 2, 205–206.

20. The controversy continues to this day, some believing the Fourteenth Amendment was never properly ratified For example, on June 13, 1967, Congressman Rarick of Louisiana rose to speak on the floor of the House of Representatives and to make a case against the ratification process for the Fourteenth Amendment. He claimed that, "The Joint Resolution proposing said Amendment was not submitted to

or adopted by a Constitutional Congress. . . . The Joint Resolution was not submitted to the President for his approval. . . . The proposed 14th Amendment was rejected by more than one-fourth of all States then in the Union, and it was never ratified by three-fourths of all the States in the Union." *Congressional Record—House*, (1 Session, 90th Congress, 1967), 15641.

21. The five Republican Senators were Fessenden of Maine, Grimes of Iowa, Harris of New York, Howard of Michigan, and Williams of Oregon. Grimes, as we shall see, played a key role in saving the president from being removed from office. The lone Democrat was Johnson of Maryland. The seven Republicans from the House were Stevens of Pennsylvania, Washburne of Illinois, Morrill of Vermont, Conkling of New York, Bingham of Ohio, Boutwell of Massachusetts, and Bow of Missouri. The two Democrats were Grider of Kentucky and Rogers of New Jersey.

22. Franklin, *Reconstruction*, 57.

23. Trefousse, *Andrew Johnson*, 195–196.

24. Nash, *Andrew Johnson*, 94.

25. As printed in Edward McPherson, *Political History of the United States during the Period of Reconstruction* (Washington, DC: Philip and Solomons, 1871), 127.

26. Nash, *Andrew Johnson*, 94.

27. The audience continued a fad. The first orator to use this tactic was Ben Butler during the Johnson impeachment trail discussed below.

28. Trefousse, *Andrew Johnson*, 264–265. See also Nash, *Andrew Johnson*, 107–110.

29. Franklin, *Reconstruction*, 69.

30. Trefousse, *Andrew Johnson*, 276.

31. The Committee had been formed in January 1866.

32. James M. McPherson, *Ordeal by Fire: The Civil War and Reconstruction* (New York: Knopf, 1982), 528.

33. Based on numbers of John Hope Franklin, *Reconstruction After the Civil War* (Chicago: University of Chicago Press, 1964), 102.

34. McPherson, *Ordeal by Fire*, 535.

35. McPherson, *Ordeal by Fire*, 556.

36. McPherson, *Ordeal by Fire*, 557.

37. Franklin, *Reconstruction After the Civil War*, 40.

38. Michael Ken Curtis, *Free Speech, "The People's Darling Privilege"* (Durham, NC: Duke University Press, 2000), 338–339.

39. Donna Lee Dickerson, *The Reconstruction Era: Primary Documents on Events from 1865 to 1877* (Westport, CT: Greenwood Press, 2003), xii, xiv.

40. Curtis, *Free Speech*, 373.

41. *Slaughter-House*, 83 U.S. 36, 123 (1872).

42. Richard Hofstadter, *Great Issue in American History*, vol. II, (New York: Random House, 1958), 26.

43. Franklin, *Reconstruction*, 55.

44. The founders, especially Madison and Justice Marshall, had opposed requiring the Senate to advice and consent to firings.

45. Blaine, *Twenty Years*, vol. 2, 273.

46. Trefousse, *Andrew Johnson*, 295. Johnson had signed her death warrant in ignorance of certain pleas on her behalf. He believed Stanton had blocked the pleas.

47. It is ironic that Stanton had all along opposed the Tenure of Office Act as unconstitutional.

48. Franklin, *Reconstruction*, 74.

49. *James A. Garfield Papers*, Library of Congress, (September 11, 1867); Gideon Welles, *Diary of Gideon Welles*, Ed. Howard K. Beale, vol. 3, (New York, 1960), 239.

50. *Congressional Globe*, 40th Congress, 2nd session, pt. 2, 1615.

51. Trefousse, *Andrew Johnson*, 321.

52. Hofstadter, *Great Issues*, 36.

53. Trefousse, *Andrew Johnson*, 323.

54. McPherson, *Ordeal by Fire*, 543.

55. Current, *The Essentials*, 171.

Chapter 4

Suppression of Native American Culture

Craig R. Smith, Karen Rasmussen, and Stephanie J. Hurst

> There was a time when our people covered the whole land, as the waves of
> a wind-ruffled sea cover its shell-paved floor. But that time has long since
> passed away with the greatness of tribes now almost forgotten.[1]

This chapter differs from those surrounding it in two ways. First, it spans
a much greater time period than the other cases. We have placed our
discussion right after the epoch of Radical Republicanism because the years
from 1870 to 1895 are those during which Native- and Euro-Americans
visited their worst terrors on one another. The period includes the massacres
at Sand Creek and Wounded Knee and the slaughter of General George
Custer and his men at the Little Big Horn.

However, the epoch of Native American persecution stretches back
and forward from this crisis point. The tension between established White
governments and Native Americans dates to the first attempted settlement
off the coast of North Carolina, where the only clues to what occurred were
the word "Crohattan" carved on a tree and a report of the birth of child
named Virginia Dare marked on a log. When Captain John Smith founded
Jamestown in 1607, the conflict with the Powhatans nearly cost Smith his
head. The landing of the Pilgrims in 1620 triggered a terrible plague among
the indigenous natives of New England. And despite efforts of most tribes
to help the new Englanders, no Native American was allowed to become a
member of the Puritan Church until 1660.

At the same time, the history of interaction between Euro and Native
American cultures reveals a serious tension that continues to this day. The
latest form of suppression began in 1978 when the Bureau of Indian Affairs

established a review procedure to "acknowledge Indian groups" so that they could qualify for federal assistance. In that year, 114 petitions were received; by January of 1993, only 19 had been acted upon, and 12 of those were rejected. The government is silencing Native Americans' abilities to express their cultural heritage. Twenty-one of the tribes that petitioned from California had lost their tribal status when in the 1950s and 1960s Congress passed several "termination acts" eliminating protected status.

The current silencing of Native Americans through poverty and alcoholism is well documented. Census data regularly indicate that the nation's poorest county encompasses the Pine Ridge Reservation of the Oglala in South Dakota, where a majority of the people live below the poverty line despite the sale of mineral rights to multinational companies in the mid-1980s.[2] Because of alcoholism among Native Americans, New Mexico has the worst record of per capita alcohol related deaths in America. And though the courts have provided some relief, they have also severely restricted the religious freedom of Native Americans by further stifling freedom of expression and religion, clear infringements on First Amendment rights.[3]

A second difference between this chapter and the others is the fact that this one looks at an attempt to silence entire cultures rather than a politically active group or individual, and thus it considers the relationship of cultural difference to suppression in general and denial of First Amendment freedoms in particular. Our analysis of strategies of suppression reveals the manner in which a Eurocentric culture responded to an alien one. When convenient, Native Americans were treated as members of a separate nation, a strategy that often co-opted the need to provide First Amendment rights. Nontraditional, specifically non-Anglo-Saxon, forms of expression seemed pagan and barbaric to the early settlers. This symbolic speech included sand painting, war paint, hieroglyphics, ghost and rain dancing,[4] belts, necklaces, and other artifacts that functioned as mnemonic devices. It was the expression of cultures "dominated by religion,"[5] an appeal to spirits that demanded respect.[6] Hence, Indian nations were treated as if they were foreign nations to be subjugated and undeserving of rights guaranteed to British subjects under common law or American citizens under the Bill of Rights.

Third, this chapter is a longitudinal study of the means of silencing a co-culture, perhaps the most stifling example of restrictions on freedom of expression, inclusive of cultural traditions. We examine four suppressive strategies, *isolation, annihilation, transformation*, and *marginalization*. In most, the means of suppression are more physically active than rhetorical. We treat these strategies separately and chronologically, realizing that the various tactics often overlapped. Our discussion frames each strategy within the context of cultural difference, focusing on the impact of suppressive actions on the lives and First Amendment freedoms of Native Americans. To conclude, we examine the implications of our analysis, arguing first that silenced groups make gains to the extent that they adopt the tools and principles of the dominant culture and second that denial of First Amendment rights of indigenous peoples is especially severe because the dominant culture elevates the political over the religious.

The Means of Suppression

The various of means of suppression discussed in the chapter vary in the subtlety and level of violence. We begin with the strategic use of isolation and move on to annihilation, transformation, and marginalization.

Isolation

When European settlers first came to North American, they faced the question of how to deal with its natives, particularly regarding ownership of territory. Historically western "laws of discovery" dictated that "[t]hose who discovered . . . other lands were entitled to them" and all their resources.[7] European expansion invariably followed the pattern of "conquest, assimilation, or extinction, and yet more conquest." The historical roots of settlers' dealings with Native Americans date to 1532 when Spain's Catholic emperor sought the counsel of theologian Francisco de Vitoria. Vitoria concluded that Indians owned the land and that, therefore, Spain could acquire territory legitimately either through just wars or by purchase from the natives.[8] Because early pioneers needed the protection of larger tribes, they tended to exercise the second option. Hence, the policy of treaty-making was born, a policy that would yield more than 600 pacts and remained in tact until well into the nineteenth century.

This policy had several important consequences. First, it affirmed the sovereignty of indigenous peoples, thereby defining both political and legal relationships between natives and settlers. Article 1, Section 8 of the U.S. Constitution, for example, affirms the sovereign nature of Native nations by stating that "the Congress shall have power . . . to regulate commerce with foreign nations, among the several states, and with Indian tribes." Second, the policy provided a means for purchasing lands, hence facilitating an orderly transfer of property to Europeans. And, third, it served to distance the two groups from each other, thus ultimately subverting Native Americans' right to freedom of speech, assembly, and religion through the suppressive strategy of isolation. This strategy allegedly protected aboriginal peoples from conflict with and contamination by more powerful Europeans. The "protection" actually denied Native Americans a voice through withholding access to power and, perhaps more importantly, by undermining the *validity of Indian concepts of language* and the land.

Europeans tended to rely on the written document though they often unilaterally altered treaties. Written language was the instrument of an historical record that prioritized recent events. Because native languages were oral, not written, because they attributed meaning to the word as spoken,[9] not to a concept represented by a symbol, because they subscribed to renewal[10] rather than progress, verbal contracts were as binding as written ones. As Dorris explains, "some . . . leaders . . . committed the agreements in their entirety to memory. [Hence, they considered t]his oral record as immutable and stable as its written counterpart in Washington."[11] Therefore, for indigenous tribes, the breaking of verbal agreements was equally as serious as transgressing a written commitment. Because Congress did not always ratify treaties made by its agents—particularly oral agreements—the trust native peoples had for the word of Whites eroded rapidly.

Furthermore, immigrants considered land a commodity, a resource, an avenue to profit. It yielded lumber and crops, furs and game, and, above all, precious metals and other minerals. Because Europeans viewed themselves as the pinnacle of creation, the land and the life it supported was theirs to use, to control, to mold for their own gain.[12] By signing treaties with indigenous peoples, they secured rights to territory. Some lands might be better than others for certain purposes, but because land was an "inanimate" thing, it was subject to the laws of exchange. For Native Americans, however, the land was part of an organic whole and a basis for the expression of their culture.

Because they viewed humans as inextricably related to *all* creation, because they saw ongoing creation as wedding them to specific areas, because they perceived land as the ground for a "spiritual substance" that was the "source, sustenance, and end of all cosmic life and forms," aboriginal peoples' notions of ownership differed radically from those of Europeans. Bands or tribes, not specific individuals, had the right to occupy land. Furthermore, the source of sovereignty was not human but spiritual, the creative source that gave and continues to give life to all creation and hence, cultural expression. "No human, not even a tribal chief" could "own the land." In addition, a people retained their right to stewardship only if they fulfilled a compact to live in harmony with the rest of nature.[13] Thus, to the Native American, the concept of land *use* was an anathema and the idea that human beings could exchange that which ultimately they could not possess was nonsensical. As a consequence, the removal of nations to other lands, even if desirable or comparable to their ancestral homes, separated them from sacred, spiritual space and thereby alienated them from the core of their culture.

Complicated by cultural misunderstanding rooted in different views of language and the land, the history of treaty-making between Europeans and

Native Americans is an account of broken promises and of progressive cultural subversion. By 1980, for example, the American government had cancelled or violated more than 370 separate treaties. The Delawares signed the first pact with the new United States government in 1778; that document promised them leadership of the Indian nations after independence, provided they joined the colonists in fighting the British during the Revolutionary War. Over the next 100 years, Americans, by signing and subsequently breaking no fewer than 18 treaties, forced the Delawares to move into and out of Indiana, Missouri, and Kansas; that is, they were repeatedly removed from the basis of their cultural expression. Of the 18, the one most egregiously violated was the Northwest Ordinance of 1787, which allegedly set the ground rules for western expansion. It pledged that "[t]he utmost good faith shall always be observed toward the Indians; their land and property shall never be taken from them without their consent." Not surprisingly, Pachgantschilias of the Delaware protested: "There is no faith to be placed in their words. . . . They will say to an Indian, 'My friend; my brother.' They will take him by the hand, and, at the same moment, destroy him."[14] Those Delawares who survived European diseases and forced migration finally received 160 acres each in Oklahoma, only to face further conflict after the discovery of oil on their land.

In 1825 President Monroe echoed the position of his mentor, Thomas Jefferson, when he argued that the only means of saving Native Americans was to escalate the policy of removal. He recommended eastern tribes submit to voluntary relocation on new western land equal in extent and quality to that surrendered in the East. Many nations agreed and moved to territory that later became Kansas; but a significant majority of southeastern tribes—the Cherokees, Chickasaws, Choctaws, Creeks, and Seminoles—refused to leave their sacred land, the foundation of their cultural expression.

After his Inaugural in 1829, Andrew Jackson, who had fought the Seminoles in Florida, advocated forced colonization of these tribes[15] and on May 28, 1830, a new Indian Removal Bill became law. Jackson celebrated the policy in his Annual Message to Congress:

> [T]he benevolent policy of the Government . . . in relation to the removal of the Indians beyond the white settlements is approaching to a happy consummation. . . . It puts an end to all possible danger of collision between the authorities of the General and State Governments on account of the Indians. . . . The tribes which occupied the countries now constituting the Eastern States were annihilated or have melted away to make room for the whites. The waves of population and civilization are rolling to the westward, and we now propose to acquire the countries occupied by the red men of the South and West by a fair exchange.[16]

Within two years, three of the five southern nations had forfeited their home-lands: the Choctaws in 1830, the Chickasaws and the Creeks in 1832. More than 90 similar agreements effected the migration west of more than 60,000 Native Americans from 1829 to 1837. For example, a pact signed in Chicago on September 26, 1833, gave the Chippewa, Ottawa, and Potawatomi tribes a tract in western Iowa in exchange for territory east of the Mississippi.

One incident demonstrates the depth to which this policy affected our national leadership. In 1831 Abraham Lincoln captained one company of the Illinois militia in its pursuit of Chief Black Hawk's Sauk (Sac) tribe into the Wisconsin wilderness where the militia engaged in a wholesale slaughter of men, women, and children.[17] While Lincoln saw no action himself, he must have been well aware of the militia's atrocities.

Having trusted Whites since the treaty of 1791, the Cherokees sought redress in the federal courts after gold was found in their territory and it was invaded by outsiders. In *Cherokee Nation v. the State of Georgia* (1831), Chief Justice Marshall, no friend of President Jackson, argued that Indians were not subject to state law, thus "prevent[ing] the state of Georgia from extending its power over the Cherokee Nation's lands."[18] In a second test case, *Worcester v. Georgia* (1832), Chief Justice Marshall found for the Cherokee, to which President Jackson is supposed to have said, "John Marshall has made his decision. Now let him enforce it." Jackson chose to circumvent the Court's ruling and pursue the policy of removal. He sent troops to South Carolina and Georgia to remove the Cherokees. In his annual message of December, 1835, he continued to advocate the "removing . . . [of] aboriginal people . . . to the country west of the Mississippi River . . . [because a]ll preceding experiments for the improvement of the Indians have failed."[19] His message of December 1836 indicates the extent of his commitment to this policy: "The military movements rendered necessary by the aggressions of the hostile portions of the Seminole and Creek tribes . . . have required the active employment of nearly our whole regular force, including the Marine Corps, and of large bodies of militia and volunteers."[20] The Seminoles and Creeks soon were "pacified." In essence, then, "Jackson's refusal to enforce Marshall's decision" showed that even if America's "highest court" "affirmed" their "legal rights," Native Americans' lack of political power allowed the "void[ing] of such rights"[21] by a sitting president.

Thus, the Cherokee ultimately lost their battle with the administration and were ordered to evacuate their homeland and relocate. As General Winfield Scott escorted 18,000 members of that nation west of the Mississippi River, more than 4,000 perished along the "Trail of Tears." The survivors built a new society in Oklahoma complete with a government consisting of executive, legislative, and judicial branches. But even in the modern era, Cherokees have faced abridgment of the First Amendment rights they were finally granted in 1924. Soon after they began publishing a newspaper called the *Phoenix*; in 1928, the government confiscated the printing press.

In the Oregon Territory, Native Americans in the Willamette Valley—the Calapooya, Moolalla, Clakamas, and Chinook—celebrated the resources of a rich land, "migrating with the seasons, gathering wild plants, berries, seeds, and roots, hunting deer, rabbits, birds, and rodents with bow and arrow, sling, and trap, collecting grasshoppers and other insects, and taking fish, eels, and shell fish from streams and lakes."[22] Their comparatively peaceful coexistence ended abruptly with White settlement. Between 1830 and 1834, their numbers plummeted from 15,000 to 2,000 because of an epidemic—probably malaria—likely brought on by contact with whites.

In 1851 a federal commission sought to establish a reservation for the Willamette Valley Indians on the eastern side of the Cascades, thereby effectively separating them from settlers and freeing land for development. Colonel Beverly Allen told the natives that "it would be better for you to be entirely separated from the whites. . . . Then your people would be furnished with teachers to teach your children and teach you how to farm. . . . There our Government would protect you both from encroachment by whites and neighboring tribes."[23] Through a series of compromises, the parties negotiated a treaty, which ceded approximately six million acres of land to the United States while maintaining small reservations on traditional tribal lands. Congress, however, deeming the agreement too "generous," refused to ratify the treaty.[24]

Thus, a new round of talks began, which resulted in the removal of the Indians to Grand Rounde on the Pacific coast in 1856. The development of that agreement is instructive. The "representatives of the bands had negotiated in good faith with little awareness of the political realities, the selfish interests and the fierce lobbying . . . which doomed the treaties."[25] Hence, as whites continued to invade what Indians assumed were inviolate lands, confusion, conflict, and distrust grew. Furthermore, after the agreement that the tribes would move to the coast was reached, their compensation came, not in direct payments, but at the discretion of the president. The clear intent of the government, therefore, was to "expend . . . funds in establishing and maintaining reservations," thereby not only confining the Native Americans to a specific area but also retaining strict control over their development, in effect perpetuating their status as dependents further stifling their voices.[26]

The experiences of the Delaware, Cherokee, and Willamette Valley peoples are but a small sample of events typical of the policy of removal. The coerced ceding of territory by Native Americans uprooted them from their ancestral homelands, altered their lifestyle and subjected them to a control that promoted dependence and impotence. By isolating them from white settlers while treating them as pseudo-sovereign, the policy denied them access to decision-making systems that determined their fates. Thus silenced in the name of protection, they found themselves with no legitimate voice until at least 1924, the year of Native American suffrage. More significantly, however, their being uprooted from their lands severely restricted their religious freedom because of the centrality of land to their notion of spirituality. Hence, a policy with at least some benevolent motivation effectively stifled many peoples and significantly altered the basis for their spiritual existence.

Annihilation

In 1607 Jamestown became home for settlers sent by an English trading company expecting to make profit in the colonies. Although saved from starvation by the Powhatan, the colonists seized lands the Indians had cleared, killing many in the process. The tribe watched as the colony grew. In desperation, they attacked a White settlement in 1622, killing 346 Europeans. Edward Waterhouse of the Virginia Company describes settler's response to the attack:

> We many now by right of Warre, and law of Nations, ... destroy them who sought to destroy us. ... [C]onquering them is much more easie then of civilizing them, ... for they are a ... barbarous ... people. ... [V]ictorie ... may be gained ... by force, by surprise, by famine in burning their corn, by destroying and burning their Boats, Canoes, and Houses, by breaking their fishing Weares. ... [These] naked, tanned, deformed Savages ... are so fierce, ... may their ruine or subjection be soone effected.[27]

The settlers' rationale for subduing the Powhatan and appropriating their lands was not simply self-defense; it was the *telos* demanded by a hierarchical culture's commitment to the progress of "civilization," which in turn warranted action steeped in self-interest.

The assumption of cultural superiority and the privilege it brings was natural to Europeans. Hierarchy implies an ideal, which in turn determines who has the privilege of choice, expression, and control. Because Europeans perceived humans as the pinnacle of God's creation, because they saw their religion as right, because they viewed their civilization as better than all that had come before, because they believed in the moral authority of progress, they could paint harmful actions as the fulfillment of a destiny ordained by God. Not surprisingly, in the nineteenth century, they adopted concepts such as the "white man's burden" and "manifest destiny," euphemistic notions vindicating cultural intolerance of the expression of others.

That intolerance manifested itself in a cultural monism that stood in stark contrast to the pluralism of the indigenous population. Although certainly not one people, Europeans did share key similarities: most of their languages were Indo-European derivatives; their religions—whether Protestant, Jewish or Catholic—shared common roots as well as the heritage of control by the Roman Church in the middle ages; the bases for their legal system included the Ten Commandments, Solon's precepts, and Blackstone's commentary on common law; and they subscribed to a hierarchical and authoritarian model of leadership. Hence, they regarded those whose culture diverged from theirs as inferior, barbarous, and savage.

Indigenous peoples lived in a world in which others looked, spoke, dressed, believed, and prayed in ways singularly *appropriate to themselves*. Although each nation likely saw itself as "more enlightened" than its neigh-bors, Native Americans routinely faced the "inescapable observation that other groups whose ways and beliefs seemed bizarre and inexplicable similarly felt themselves to be the center of the universe." They therefore were far less ethnocentric than Europeans whose convictions all too often justified anni-hilation of those considered alien in the name of destiny and progress.[28]

Some of the annihilation was *passive*, though certainly not rhetorical, the simple product of Native American's being exposed to diseases for which they had no immunity. Death by pestilence began with the first contact between Native and European: between 1492 and 1514 in Haiti, the initial center for explorers from Spain, the numbers of Native Americans plum-meted from 200,000 to 29,000; in North America, the years spanning 1789 and 1890 saw death from disease alone decimate 30 percent to 40 percent of the population. Some tribes faced virtual extinction: for example only 31 out of 1,600 Mandan survived an outbreak of small pox in 1837 and between 1849–1850 a wave of cholera spread by migrating whites wiped out thousands more on the Great Plains. In addition, the introduction of alcohol created an ongoing physiological and psychological plague.

A more active form of annihilation involved forms of environmental destruction having disastrous impact on the lifestyles of peoples all across the continent. The most notorious example was the slaughter of the buffalo of the Great Plains. By the end of the Civil War, the building of railroads made movement west more feasible. The Northern Pacific, chartered in 1864, received 40 million acres of land as an incentive to construct what is a clear example of the western idea of linear progress—the seemingly endless railroad tracks that would carry harbingers of civilization westward.

The impact on Native American cultures was stunning. Hoards of hunters exterminated the seemingly inexhaustible herds of buffalo to clear the way for expanding railroads, as well as for the animals' skins. Prior to this slaughter, a traveler on the Santa Fe Trail noted, "Every acre was covered [with buffalo], until in the dim distance the prairie became one black mass from which there was no opening."[29] The killing of as many as 150 animals a day[30] virtually destroyed the herds. This depletion of the buffalo population created havoc for the horse Indians of the plains who used them for food, clothing, shelter, and cultural expression. Native Americans made hides into robes, moccasins, saddles, tepees, bedding, and boats. Hooves yielded glue, horns became cups and spoons, and muscle tendons furnished bowstrings. Dried manure provided fuel, and stomachs were made into water bottles. As Lakota Chief White Cloud observed, "Wherever the whites are established, the buffalo is gone, and the red hunters must die of hunger."[31]

The "civilizing" of the Willamette Valley provides an example of cultural impact. The inhabitants of the area roamed according to the seasons, harvesting plants, animals of the forests, and fish. White possession of the land restricted the movement essential to their way of life. Cultivation and the insertion of pigs into the eco-culture disrupted the area's natural balance, destroying plants and animals integral to Native American existence and cultural expression.[32]

This pattern of conflict between one culture dedicated to *control* of the land and another dependent on existing in *harmony* with it[33] recurred countless times, always to the detriment of the aboriginal population. Santana, chief of the Kiowa, expressed the plight of a people asked to abandon their way of life:

> I have heard that you intend to settle us on a reservation near the mountains. When we settle down, we grow pale and die. A long time ago this land belonged to our fathers; but when I go up to the river I see camps of soldiers on its banks. These soldiers cut down my timber; they kill my buffalo; and when I see that, my heart feels like bursting; I feel sorry. I have spoken.[34]

Although the words of Santana and others garnered sympathy, which eventually ameliorated some of the more exploitative actions of Euro-Americans, such sympathy came far too late to stem massive environmental and cultural annihilation.

Colonists and, later, American citizens also participated in a second form of active annihilation: *military* destruction through the Indian Wars. Those encounters reached a peak during and after the 1840s as the country witnessed a dramatic increase in westward movement by pioneers. At mid-decade, the Democratic party took up the call John O'Sullivan printed in the July–August issue of the New York *Democratic Review*: "Our manifest destiny," he declared, "is to overspread the continent allotted by Providence for the free development of our yearly multiplying millions." He called for "annexation" of the west. Much to the consternation of Senator Daniel Webster and a freshman Representative named Lincoln, Senator John C. Calhoun claimed, "Our great mission is to occupy this vast domain."[35]

Hence, although warned periodically of the dangers of venturing into "Indian Country" and advised to treat Natives with respect, immigration west as well as blatant encroachment on Indian lands continued and then accelerated after the United States expanded its territory by winning the war with Mexico in 1848. That victory augmented the size of the country by about a fifth. The discovery of gold in California in 1849 followed by that state's being admitted to the Union the next year spurred more migration westward. Steamboats expedited the building of new forts along the Mississippi. Inevitably, the stream of covered wagons destroyed the Madison–Jackson policy of separation of Native from Euro-Americans.

By 1851 the flow of settlers had created such problems that the Bureau of Indian Affairs sent representatives to Fort Laramie in Wyoming to reach an agreement that would ensure the safety of travelers and define "Indian territories."[36] Ten thousand Native Americans from nine nations attended; many, such as the Sioux and Crow, signed subtreaties of understanding. A more general agreement provided the tribes with $50,000 a year for 10 years but greatly reduced the land area the Sioux could claim as their own.

The treaty did not last long. In the summer of 1854, when the tribes gathered in Laramie to collect that year's annuity, a young brave killed a farmer's cow. Fort Laramie's Commander Gratten demanded the surrender of the brave, a request the terms of the treaty rendered patently illegal. The chief in charge refused and Gratten's men opened fire. The Indian leader and his braves along with 30 U.S. troops died; both sides followed the skirmish with retaliatory raids.[37] Between 1853 and 1857, the first year of the stagecoach, the federal government shifted 174,000 acres of land from Native Americans to Whites, while denying southwestern tribes like the Hopi, Navaho, and Apache the right to renegotiate after the Mexican American War. In 1861 the Arapaho became the first to accept the BIA's reservation policy when they gave up land rights in Nebraska, Kansas, and Wyoming in exchange for a reservation in Colorado. Other tribes resisted, seeing the Civil War as an opportunity to take advantage of the then-preoccupied federal government. Eventually, led by Red Cloud, the Sioux chose war, attacking white settlers in Minnesota and killing 450 of them.[38] A quickly-organized militia destroyed the offending war party. Elsewhere results were no different.

In 1863 Kit Carson laid waste to Navajo farms in New Mexico territory in retaliation for raids on White farmers. Forced to surrender and march to new reservation lands, many starved along the route.[39] Those who survived had lost their sacred land and much of the basis for their cultural celebrations. One of the worst incidents was the slaughter at Sand Creek in 1864 of a band of Cheyenne who were led by the pacifist Black Kettle. The ensuing insurrection forced the government to call 8,000 troops from services in the Civil War to protect settlers across the Missouri.[40]

With the end of the Civil War, the government could spend military resources on the "Indian problem." In 1868 a second treaty signed at Fort Laramie further reduced Sioux lands to give Whites access to gold in Montana.[41] Additional discoveries of gold and silver, however, destroyed the peace. Black Kettle, who had escaped Sand Creek, met his nemesis in November of 1868 when General George Armstrong Custer attacked a band of Cheyenne camped on the Washita River. Custer and his troops slaughtered Black Kettle, his wife, and 40 women and children.

War chiefs Red Cloud and Crazy Horse, however, achieved military success. At Fort Laramie in 1866, Red Cloud had rejected the policies of the Peace Council: "You have heard the sound of the white soldier's ax upon the Little Piney. His presence here is . . . an insult to the spirits of our ancestors. Are we then to give up their sacred graves to be plowed for corn? Dakotas, I am for war."[42] Using guerilla tactics, he forced federal troops to abandon Fort Reno. In November 1868, Red Cloud agreed to peace with the government for, as he said, "Our nation is melting away like the snow on the sides of the hills where the sun is warm, while your people are like the blades of grass in the spring when summer is coming."[43] In 1870 the Chief met with President Grant and spoke at Cooper Union Institute in New York City to a group sympathetic to the plight of Native Americans; subsequently, he made seven more journeys to the nation's capital on peace missions. Until his death in 1909, he consistently called for universal kinship of all people united under the Great Spirit, and hence became one of the few Indian voices not easily marginalized.

However, his views fell on deaf ears when it came to Oregon. On August 12, 1868, Chief Joseph of the Nez Perces agreed to surrender prime farmland in exchange for the security of a protected reservation. That security evaporated the next year with the discovery of gold nearby. Though President Grant ordered settlers to stay out of "Indian territories," Congress passed laws in 1871 clearing the way for the abrogation of the treaty. In 1873 the American Baptist Home Missionary Association justified the opening of Oregon territory to Whites by alleging that Native Americans had more land than they needed. Subsequent attempts to confine the Nez Perces to small reservations motivated their run for Canada in 1877.

In 11 weeks, they traveled 1,600 miles, fighting 13 battles with Federal troops. Finally, in the Bear Paw Mountains of Montana on October 5, they surrendered to General Nelson A. Miles. Chief Joseph's speech on this occasion is one of the most moving in Native American history:

> Tell General Howard I know his heart. . . . I am tired of fighting. Our chiefs are killed. The old men are all dead. . . . It is cold and we have no blankets. The little children are freezing to death. . . . I want to have time to look for my children and see how many I can find. Maybe I shall find them among the dead. . . . I am tired; my heart is sick and sad. From where the sun now stands *I will fight no more forever.*[44]

Newspaper accounts of the speech and the events surrounding it finally generated sympathy for the plight of an embattled people. Until his death in 1904, Chief Joseph, like Red Cloud, tried to build on this sympathy by giving speeches and writing letters in support of Indian rights.

Gold continued to prove the undoing of many nations, particularly of the Sioux, but not before they achieved what likely is the most famous victory of the Indian Wars. 1874 saw the discovery of gold in the Black Hills of South Dakota, holy land of the Oglala,[45] prompting the government to make several attempts to purchase the land. Sitting Bull and Crazy Horse, however, overruled Red Cloud's counsel to cooperate. Reports claiming that the Sioux leaders were directing warriors to terrorize Whites drew a quick response from the Department of the Interior to Red Cloud in December of 1875: "Sir, I am instructed . . . to direct you to notify Sitting Bull's band and other wild and lawless bands . . . that unless they shall remove within the bounds of the reservation . . . they shall be deemed hostile and treated . . . by military force.[46]

On February 1, 1876, the War Department proclaimed that all Sioux, Northern Cheyenne, and Arapaho not residing on the Great Sioux Reservation to be at war with the United States. Fresh from his tour of duty as a reconstruction district commander, General Sheridan ordered Custer and the Seventh Cavalry to capture Sitting Bull and Crazy Horse. The Sioux, however, quietly mobilized into two forces. Early on June 25, 1876, a warrior named Gall prevented Colonel Reno from joining Custer. After Crazy Horse engaged the General and his forces, Sioux warriors caught federal troops in a pincer movement as Gall attacked from the rear at the Little Big Horn killing Custer and 261 soldiers only days before the centennial of the Declaration of Independence. The nation was shocked; Grant was appalled.

During the 1880s, Geronimo of the Apache replaced Crazy Horse and Sitting Bull as the Native American's most famous warrior.[47] Born at the head waters of the Gila, Arizona Territory, in 1829, this leader of the Nedni Apache lived in relative peace until 1858. In the summer of that year, his band traveled south to Jarnos in Chihuahua, Mexico to trade for goods. While the men were in town, Mexican regulars raided their camp, killing and scalping women, children, and a small band of warriors who had been left behind as guards.[48] Geronimo's wife, mother, and his three children were among the dead.

Enraged, Geronimo created a war council drawn from various Apache tribes and promised them victory over their enemies.[49] Moved by Geronimo's appeal, Cochise, the powerful leader of the Chiricahua, pledged support.[50] The summer of 1859 saw Geronimo's warriors inflict heavy losses during a two-hour battle at Arizpe, Mexico.[51] For the next 15 years, he continued his raids against the people who had killed his family, always retreating to safety across the American border. However, the Gadsden Treaty eliminated the possibility of using the border into Mexico as a refuge because the treaty allowed both Mexican and U.S. troops to pursue raiding warriors into each other's territory.

Discovery of gold and silver in the area around Prescott, Arizona further increased the Apache's plight as hostile actions on the part of Whites became common. For example, Mangas Colorada, a chief who had been harassing settlers, came to the camp of General West under a flag of truce. His reward was being taken prisoner, tortured, shot, scalped, and beheaded.[52]

Geronimo went on a rampage of reprisal, prompting American and Mexican troops to stalk him in an attempt to restore calm to the area. The press supported this effort by reporting and probably exaggerating stories of atrocities. One dispatch from Silver City, New Mexico read:

> Some particulars of the killing done by Geronimo's band near Silver City are learned. . . . The family consisted of Phillips, his wife and two children, aged 3 and 5 years. This morning Geronimo's band attacked him and his family, killing the entire family excepting the oldest child, a girl, whom they hanged on a meat hook.[53]

Geronimo later denied the accusations.

Captured and taken to the San Carlos reservation in 1877, the Apache leader faced charges of murder and robbery. Escaping to Mexico in 1881 with a large party of followers, he eluded authorities until January of 1884, when he surrendered to General George Cook rather than submit to Mexican authorities. A few months after his second incarceration at San Carlos the government transferred his band to Turkey Creek, demanding that they discard their traditional lifestyle and become farmers. Not surprisingly, the proud Apache engineered one more dramatic escape. This defiance greatly annoyed President Cleveland, who pressured General Sheridan to take action because news from Arizona likely would affect the impending midterm elections.[54] Sheridan promptly instructed Cook to demand an unconditional surrender.[55] Surrounded and outnumbered, Geronimo, 17 warriors, and 19 women and children surrendered near Sonora. Federal soldiers moved him and other Apaches to Florida and then to Fort Sull, Oklahoma where he was forced to farm and become a curiosity piece for tourists. He died in poverty on February 17, 1909; his skull was eventually taken into the possession by Yale University.

The "official" end to the Indian wars came on December 29, 1890, with the massacre of a band of Oglala Sioux by the Seventh Calvary at Wounded Knee in South Dakota. During the 1880s, an apocalyptic religion inspired by the prophecy of a Native millennium had spread among the western nations. Alarmed by the predictions that Native Americans would again control their land, the government banned practice of the new faith's centerpiece, the Ghost Dance. A few hundred Sioux led by Big Foot tried to flee to the Dakota Badlands only to be taken as prisoners to the small settlement of Wounded Knee.

On the morning following their capture, while the Sioux were being disarmed, a shaman urged the braves to resist. One pulled a rifle from under his blanket and fired into the massed soldiers. In the ensuing firefight, the cavalry massacred nearly 300 Sioux men, women, and children. Black Elk, an Oglala Holy Man, recalls the event:

> Dead and wounded women and children and little babies were scattered . . . where they had been trying to run away. . . . Sometimes they were in heaps because they had huddled together; . . . sometimes bunches of them had been killed and torn to pieces where the wagon guns hit them. I saw a little baby trying to suck its mother, but she was bloody and dead.[56]

After the massacre, Whites charged the Sioux two dollars a body for the burials of those left behind in the snow.

Thus, disease, environmental destruction, and war depleted the indigenous population of the North American continent. Although annihilation was not an official policy of colonizing powers or of the American government, it was the product of a Euro-American value structure that helped to rationalize events that contributed to the greatest holocausts in American history. Though part of this strategy was accidental and passive, far too much of it was active. However, even this strategy failed to eradicate the Native American. And so in the end, white America turned to a policy of transformation to achieve the goal of an integrated society dominated by Judeo-Christian values that in turn suppressed the expression of Native American values.

Transformation

In 1877, newly elected President Rutherford B. Hayes told the Congress that "Many, if not most, of our Indian wars have had their origin in broken promises and acts of injustice on our part." Hayes' message signaled the increasing uneasiness of political leaders concerning the tactics used to deal with Native Americans:[57] the burgeoning White population had made isolation unworkable; the destruction of native peoples was morally repugnant. Hence, national policy shifted to attempts to transform and thus assimilate the indigenous population into mainstream American culture, to make them "white" by educating and Christianizing them as well as by training them to farm and appreciate the value of private property. Those efforts at transformation put into stark relief the subversion that results when a linear, instrumental culture dominates one grounded in harmony and cyclical renewal.

The *linearity* of Euro-American culture was pervasive:[58] knowledge was cumulative, advancing principally through the scientific testing of ideas, so that newer concepts replaced old ones; in law recent statutes and rulings superseded those of the past; civilization progressed so that the life of today and tomorrow was better than an existence left behind; religion prepared people for an after-life to be found in a heaven of the future. Indigenous peoples, however, embraced circular metaphors, notably the sacred hoop that stood for the earth, the sun, the moon, the planets, as well as for the endless cycles of the seasons and other natural patterns. Even the history of some Native Americans was recorded in a spiral path on a buffalo skin. One such work composed by Sioux begins in 1800 and runs to 1871 using 24 symbols depicting intertribal warfare.[59]

John Lame Deer explains the significance of the hoop for the Sioux:

> [T]he hoop . . . stands for the togetherness of people who sit with one another around the campfire, . . . united in peace. . . . The camp . . . was also a ring . . . and all the families in the village were in turn circles within a larger circle, part of the larger hoop which was the seven campfires of the Sioux. . . . The nation was only a part of the universe, in itself circular and made of the earth, . . . the sun, . . . the stars. . . . The moon, the horizon, the rainbow—circles within circles within circles, with no beginning and no end. [60]

The hoop, then, embodied the cyclical principle of living in and renewing harmony with the natural world. Hence, to impose linearity on native peoples was to inflict on them a "psychic nightmare" of straight lines and boxes that suppressed their cultural expression.[61]

In 1881, President Arthur told Congress that the solution to dealing with Native peoples was to "introduce among the Indians the customs and pursuits of civilized life and gradually absorb them into the mass of our citizens."[62] A major tool for effecting this assimilation was the Dawes Act of 1887. It promised 160 acres and eventual citizenship to persons who would work the land, thus abandoning tribal ways in favor of farming and private business. The act pledged increased aid to Native Americans but also allowed the president to abrogate treaty agreements with the tribes. This latter provision along with other facets of the act allowed whites to usurp vast expanses of Native American holdings.[63] The result was a reduction in Indian control of land from "138 million acres in 1887 to 48 million in 1934. Of this 48 million acres, nearly 20 million were desert or semi-arid and virtually useless for any kind of . . . farming."[64] The loss of sacred lands demoralized Native Americans while it also denuded some of their religious expression.

According to the Meriam Report, a government study commissioned 50 years after the adoption of the Dawes Act, the land allotment was a dismal failure, principally because it attempted to force indigenous peoples to live in ways antithetical to their own cultures.[65] Although some nations were agrarian, many, such as the Sioux, Apache, and various Oregon Tribes, were not, and thus saw tilling specific pieces of land as anathema because it destroyed their ability to live in harmony with nature. For example, Apaches confined on the San Carlos Reservation in the 1880s found farming an inadequate substitute for a way of living that involved raiding for horses and cattle. To relieve their boredom, many drank *tiswin*, an alcoholic beverage, the consumption of which often resulted in behavior labeled criminal by White society.[66]

Living in "boxes" on reservations or individual farms curtailed the adaptability of traditional lifestyles, which depended on movement based on changes brought by the seasons, on adjusting to the conditions of the land rather than on using it. In his recounting of the destruction of Big Foot and his people at Wounded Knee, Black Elk explains the Native American aversion to the white mode of allotting and using land: "The Wasichus [whites] have put us in these square boxes [reservations]. . . . They slaughtered all the bison and shut us up in pens. Our power is gone and we are dying. . . . [T]he nation's hoop is broken and scattered. There is no center any longer, and the sacred tree is dead."[67]

The native way was to "unite . . . with the sacred," to close the circle; they therefore "perceive[d] land use as an intimate relationship with the cosmic mother," not as the utilization of finite resources.[68] At the Lake Mohawk Conference Proceedings in 1900, Merrill Gates, a reformer, noted that the Dawes Act was "a mighty pulverizing engine for breaking up the tribal mass. It has nothing [useful] to say to the tribe, nothing to do with the tribe. [Rather i]t breaks up that vast 'bulk of things' which the tribal life sought to keep unchanged."[69] Hence, the linearity of land development and private ownership mandated by allotment were forms of cultural suppression, not vehicles for Indian emancipation.

The Eurocentric approach to education also ran counter to native norms. Western education prioritized the objective, divided the knower from the known, divorced the personal from the professional. "English education [made] an effort to effect a complete transformation of beliefs . . . [through its insistence on] implanting a particular body of knowledge and a specific view of the world."[70] As early as 1839, T. Harvey Crawford, Commissioner of Indian Affairs, linked education with the objective of making "the Indian better than he is."[71] Its purpose was to dispel the "dark clouds of ignorance and superstition" so that the "light of Christianity and general knowledge" could remediate the "moral and intellectual darkness" of Native peoples. Not surprisingly, the Secretary of the Indian Rights Association proclaimed that the goal of reform was to guide the Indian "from the night of barbarism into the fair dawn of Christian civilization."[72] In essence, the importing of objective knowledge would improve Indians so that the lines between Native and white society would disappear.

The principles guiding Indian education, however, were unity and renewal, concepts integral to completion of a circle or the closing of the sacred hoop. Deloria explains that the "old ways . . . affirmed the . . . principle" of the "responsibility to be a contributing member of a society" so that "society as a whole would function."[73] Such a perspective granted knowledge status to a wide range of data. "Individuals consider[ed] their own . . . experiences, the accumulated wisdom of the community . . . gathered by previous generations, their dreams, visions and prophecies, and any information received from . . . animals and plants as data."[74] Thus, native education stemmed from unity with the entirety of existence and that unity led to a continuous closing of the sacred hoop.

The impact of a Euro-American educational system failed to admit the viability of traditional expression. In other words, reeducation meant acculturation. Eddie Benton-Banai, of the Ojibwa, describes his first American educational experience at a BIA boarding school:[75]

> We'd been riding on a school bus the better part of that day from Wisconsin to southern Minnesota, and we arrived at Pipestone around midnight. . . . [E]verybody got their hair lopped off. I remember how I cried. . . . [T]hey cut it right down to the skin. . . . [T]here on the floor lay my pretty eagle plume and the braids that my mother had so carefully fixed and tied. . . . Then all of our clothes were taken away from us and we were all dressed

in blue coveralls. If we were wearing moccasins, those were taken away and we were all put into government-issue black shoes.[76]

Such a stripping of vestiges of cultural identity undoubtedly suppressed and stigmatized tribal custom. Morris and Wander describe Native American children as being "taken away to 'Indian' schools far from their friends, families, traditions, rituals, systems of belief, languages, principles, ancestors—nearly everything that made them who they were." Since a people live on in their stories, literature, ceremonial speeches, music, dance, poetry, dreams, this process of reeducation was particularly suppressive.[77]

The most striking efforts to transform Native Americans involved their Christianization and the concomitant suppression of traditional religious practices. Both Protestants and Catholics adhered to a creed based on the linear metaphor of descent/ascent. The fall (descent) in the Garden of Eden and resulting original sin required the redemption (ascent) through God's grace in the person of Christ. His sacrifice created the possibility of deliverance, but individuals needed to live the Christian life to attain personal, future redemption. Such a creed differed markedly from religions founded on a cyclical unity and harmony with creation. As a result, rituals affirming that unity through various modes of closing the sacred hoop were especially foreign. Government attempts to eradicate native dances are illustrative for they highlight the conflict between linear transformation endorsed by Christian Euro-Americans and the cyclical principle of renewal integral to the concept of the sacred hoop.

Opposition to Native American religious practices entailed a depicting of such acts as superstitious, cruel, and licentious.[78] One such attempt to steer indigenous peoples away from the "barbarism" of their own religions involved legislation in 1883 that outlawed the Sun Dance practiced by the Oglala. One of seven vital tribal rites, this dance serves the purpose of offering one's body and soul to Wakan-Tanka, the Creator. It attempts to validate the unity implicit in the concept of the sacred hoop by affirming a oneness binding humans with ongoing creation. Whites considered the ritual particularly savage and primitive because often it included the piercing of the skin. On March 30, 1883, the Secretary of the Interior informed Commissioner of Indian Affairs, Hiram Price, that the Sun Dance was an uncivilized rite that stimulated warriors' warlike passions.[79] Price declared the ceremonial dances, practices of medicine men, and the giving and destroying of property during funeral rituals illegal. A Court of Indian Offenses would mete out punishment.[80]

Similarly, a 1920 report by the Rev. E. M. Sweet, an Indian Bureau investigator, alleged that the Snake Dance of the Hopi, a supplication for rain and bountiful harvest and hence an affirmation of kinship between people and nature, involved torture and immoral sexual practices. Commissioner of Indian Affairs Charles H. Burke issued a directive recommending sanctions be imposed on participants in the Snake Dance.[81] Hence, both the Hopi and the Sioux ran afoul of a bureaucracy dedicated to "improvement" of Native Americans by abolishing traditional religious practices.

The most famous of Native rituals suppressed by the government were various forms of the Ghost Dance, a ceremony grounded in the message of Wovoka, a Paiute born in Nevada in 1858. His promise of "renewal, rebirth, and revitalization" was one of the few things that encouraged Indians to envision a brighter future. Demoralized Native Americans saw in Wovoka's teachings a promise of "deliverance from their depression and sorrow."[82] Hence, more than half of the Indians west of the Missouri River embraced a shared cultural and spiritual response, which constituted the largest Indian movement of the nineteenth century.

Variously called Wovoka, Kwotisauq, Jack Wilson, Jesus—or Juses, Wovoka claimed to have experienced a rebirth in which he returned from God's heaven graced with divine messages directing life and worship. James Mooney describes the prophet's revelation of New Year's Day, 1889:

> [H]e saw God, with all the people who had died long ago, . . . all happy and forever young. . . . God told him he must go back and tell his people they must be good and *love one another*, . . . and *live in peace* with the whites; that they must work, and not lie or steal; that they must *put away all the old practices that savored of war*; that if they faithfully obeyed his instructions they would at last be reunited with their friends in this other world, where there would be no more death or sickness or old age. He was then given the dance which he was commanded· to bring back to his people [emphasis added].[83]

Wovoka's dream thus promised an Indian millennium, provided Native Americans performed the dance and adopted peaceful ways. The dance itself was an exhausting experience producing a "delirium" that supposedly enabled "participants" to communicate with "the dead."[84]

Word of the Paiute prophet's teachings spread through the Western nations. Because of the differences among the cultures influenced by his ideas, the Ghost Dance movement was diverse. Each tribal culture "built a structure from its own mythology,"[85] one that embodied the hope that their way of life could be restored. Many traveled to hear Wovoka, returning to their homes with a "Messiah Letter." Those instructions counseled adherents to partake in the dance, to live in peace, to work with White people and to take heart that the dead—their ancestors—would return.[86] Such a philosophy, grounded as it was in an endless circle uniting the living with their ancestors as well as with future generations, was foreign to Whites who labeled the movement "Ghost Dance" because of the promise to awaken the dead.

Sensational newspaper accounts about the movement emphasized predictions that Indian redemption would bring about the destruction of White invaders and linked the practice of what was essentially an apocalyptic religion grounded in fraternity and peace with images of rebellious Sioux driven mad by a savage dance. Hence, the government banned the dance. The banning led to the last tragedy of the Indian Wars, the massacre in South Dakota, a massacre in which a "dream" based on a "religion of Hope died with the Sioux on the snow-swept plains . . . [of] Wounded Knee."[87]

In 1909 the Secretary of the Interior delineated the discriminatory impact of the attempt to transform Native Americans:

> That Christianity and federal interests were often identical became an article of faith, . . . and this pervasive attitude initiated the . . . religious persecution of the Indian religions. It was . . . an oblique attack on the Indian way of life that had as its by-product the [supposed] transformation of Indians into American citizens. Had a Christian denomination . . . or the Jewish community been . . . [treated similarly], the outcry would have been tremendous. But Indians, from an exotic community which few understood, were thought to be the proper subject of this concern.[88]

Thus, as Cadwalader and Deloria argue, "[a] century ago, the assimilationists . . . confidently envisioned a future in which tribes had disappeared . . . to be remembered only as symbols of a by-gone and primitive era."[89] This attempt to remake indigenous peoples into images of Whites failed to work because it required Indians to abandon their cultures, to forsake their identities by adopting the creeds and behaviors or a highly linear culture which ran counter to their beliefs and behaviors.[90] Hence, although the motivation behind the strategy may have been humane, transformation was repressive. It denied the legitimacy of the voice of Native Americans by curtailing their ability to live in harmony with the land, discounting the methods and aims of traditional native education, and outlawing important religious rites. It was, therefore, a unilateral suppression of both speech and religion.

Marginalization

The Indian Citizenship Act of 1924 and the Wheeler-Howard Act 10 years later marked the beginning of the modern era for Native Americans. The former granted the continent's native inhabitants constitutional rights while the latter encouraged Native self-government, expanded reservations and extended educational programs related to cultural heritage. Those two pieces of legislation embodied a curious tension that is the product of dual sovereignty of Native Americans: members of Indian tribes are, on the one hand, like all other citizens and, on the other, are set apart by virtue of their membership in pseudo-sovereign nations that have special privileges such exclusive rights to the control of fishing, gambling and harvesting on various reservations. This set-apart people were marginalized by patronizing them, condemning their cultural practices and/or minimizing or ignoring of their actions and problems.

Strategies for circumventing the Indian Citizenship Act emerged early. The handling of suffrage in Arizona is illustrative. Passage of the 1924 legislation seemed to extend voting privileges to residents of reservations.[91] However, in 1928, Arizona's Supreme Court denied their right to the franchise because, it argued, they were "under guardianship" and therefore "not capable of handling [their] own affairs in competition with whites."[92] It took 20 years to undo this patronizing ruling.[93]

Arizona also withheld the right to vote from anyone not able to read English,[94] in effect declaring Native and other languages to be inferior and/or illegitimate. Given the centrality of language to Indian culture, such a prohibition significantly diminished native freedom of expression. In no case is this tendency more apparent than in the sensitive area of religious freedom.

"Religious intolerance and suppression," Echo-Hawk argues, "have been primary features . . . [of] the relationship between native people . . . and the newcomers from the Old World."[95] Europeans came to North America laden with a legacy of religious suppression: Spain and Italy had their inquisitions; England its Cromwell, Bishop Laud, and Bloody Mary; France its clashes between Catholic and Huguenot. In like manner, German princes quelled the Ana-Baptist revolt; the entirety of Europe in its witch burnings of the 1500s and 1600s. Not surprisingly, then, Euro-Americans used similar means to safeguard their own beliefs by attempting to cleanse the New World of religions they regarded as pagan, corrupt, or heretical. This zealousness invaded the legal arena through laws that prohibited behaviors integral to Native rites and entered the political realm through decisions made by Christian bureaucrats in the Office of Indian Affairs.[96] Especially perplexing to Native Americans were the Indian Offenses Acts of the 1880s.

Although the government reversed that policy in 1934 and passed the American Indian Religious Freedom Resolution in 1978, myriad forms of harassment related to Native religious practices continue. Chief Walking Buffalo described the feelings of peoples denigrated by a more powerful cultural group:

When we sang our praises to the sun or moon or wind, you said we were worshiping idols. . . . [Y]ou condemned us as lost souls just because our form of worship was different than yours. We saw the Great Spirit's work in almost everything: sun, moon, trees, wind, and mountains. [W]e have a true belief in the supreme being, a stronger faith than that of most of the whites who have called us pagans.... Indians living close to nature and nature's ruler are not living in darkness.[97]

Walking Buffalo's lament reflects a factor key to the suppression of Native religions, the contrast between Native and Euro-Americans views of nature. That difference is central to controversies over sacred sites, use of hallucinogenic plants, and ritualistic use of animal parts.

For centuries most Euro-Americans viewed themselves as separate from and above the rest of creation; Native Americans accept the principle of universal kinship, a unity with all of existence.[98] Hence, the dominant culture had difficulty accepting religions that view nature as sacred, particularly given the heritage of the rationalism of the Enlightenment and exceptionalism of early settlers. Kirkpatrick Sale explains:

The task of rationalism ... was to ... prove that there was no sanctity about ... nature, that ... [it was] not animate or purposeful or sensate, but rather nothing more than measurable combinations of ... properties subject to scientific analysis, prediction, and manipulation. Being de-godded, ... [nature] could thereby be capable of human use and control according to human whim and desire.[99]

This de-godding was especially important to a religion that fought for survival against a variety of pre-Christian faiths that venerated nature. Consequently, sacred objects in Christianity are ones created by people such as crosses and statues, not products of nature such as animal feathers and hides. Similarly, Judeo-Christians respect the sanctity of the Wailing Wall, the Mount of Olives, Calvary, the Vatican, not the sacredness of the holy places of the Oglala in the Black Hills of South Dakota.

In a string of rulings starting in 1977 with *Rosebud Sioux Tribe v. Kneip,*[100] the Supreme Court has denied First Amendment protection to religious practices established long before the colonization of the United States.[101] Similar rulings have allowed infringement on sacred sites. For example, in *Sequoyah v. Tennessee Valley Authority* (1980)[102] the Supreme Court refused to grant *certiorari* when a federal circuit court ruled the flooding of holy places, ancestral burial grounds, and gathering sites did not violate religious freedom of Cherokees because they had no property rights in the area.

More recently, the Supreme Court refused to extend sacred status to natural terrain in *Lyng v. Northwest Indian Cemetery Assn.* (1988). In the early

1980s, Indian groups opposed road construction and timber harvesting in the Six Rivers National Forest, a site where various tribes held vision quests and gathered medicines. After the District Court of Northern California and the Ninth Circuit Court used the Free Exercise Clause to *uphold* an injunction to protect the forest, the Supreme Court reversed their decisions. It ruled that First Amendment rights do not include "protecting tribal religious areas on federal lands for worship purposes. [It held further] that Free Exercise Protection arises *only* in those rare instances when government *punishes* a person for practicing religion or *coerces* one into violating his religion."[103] The decision in *Lyng* stripped Native Americans of legal safeguards protecting worship at sacred sites.[104]

Ironically, during the first Gulf War allied forces took care to avoid damaging areas having religious significance in Iraq. Euro-American culture thus has respected places venerated by Muslims but has refused, as Morris Udall remarked, to "understand" that "[f]or many tribes the land is filled with physical sites of religious and sacred significance."[105] Nonetheless, the Supreme Court undercut the 1978 American Indian Religious Freedom Resolution, which sought to protect the "inherent right of freedom to exercise the traditional religions."[106]

The continuing controversy over the use of peyote further underscores contemporary inequities in the guarantees of religious freedom by exemplifying the dominant culture's tendency to denigrate Indian rites and to sanction behaviors it regards as dangerous or sinful. Use of peyote was one of the "Indian Offenses" of the 1880s. At various times numerous states scattered throughout the intermountain, mid-, and southwest have banned use of the substance. Thus, in 1909 Indians founded what was to become the Native American Church of North America hoping they could practice peyotism under the protection of the First Amendment. Various governments, however, continued penalizing use of peyote. In 1914, for example, when a U.S. District Court failed to prohibit its use under anti-alcohol statutes, the Office of Indian Affairs labeled it a narcotic. Even when it was legal, Indians have faced harassment, arrest, conviction, and incarceration.[107]

The most significant case relevant to peyotism was *Employment Div., Dept. of Human Resources of Oregon v. Smith* (1990). Because they had used peyote in religious rites, several members of the Native American Church lost their jobs and subsequently were denied unemployment benefits.[108] The Supreme Court refused them protection under the First Amendment, thereby limiting the application of the Free Exercise clause. This ruling overturned the previous test that was established in *Sherbert v. Vernor* (1963),[109] "a three-step process for determining when the state could . . . impinge on religious activities, the most important step being a demonstration that . . . [it] had a compelling interest in controlling specific kinds of behavior." The Smith decision abandoned the compelling interest test, substituting in its place the "proposition that the right of free exercise of religion had to be linked to some other freedom guaranteed in the Bill of Rights."[110] The 1993 Native American Free Exercise of Religion Act attempted to overcome state objections to Native religious practices.[111] It proposed protection of "sacred sites, . . . use of peyote, . . . religions rights of North American prisoners, . . . use of eagle feathers and other surplus animal parts in ceremonies" and extension of "the compelling state interest test to religious practices."[112] However, in 1997, the Supreme Court struck the law down and protected states' rights to enforce laws against narcotics in a 6–3 decision in *City of Beorne v. Florida*.

These decisions exemplify techniques of suppression grounded in marginalizing a co-culture: the Euro-American prioritizing of the rational over the mythical, the humanly created over the natural, the civil over the religious, and Christian "morality" over any competing ethic in effect marks indigenous cultures as subordinate, as inferior, as unimportant. Such a prioritizing denigrates and renders impotent groups perceived as alien others.

Marginalization is also evident in the way protests by Native Americans have been handled in the modern era. The activist movement started in the late 1960s professed to be a mending of the sacred hoop. Eddie Benton-Banai, an Ojibwa, explains, "A renaissance is taking place among Native American peoples. This renaissance is not of a material nature. It is a spiritual renaissance, a retrieving and reviving of our original covenant with the Creator. We are reaffirming our relationship and stewardship with our Mother the Earth."[113] That renaissance was not always civil, particularly when land was involved. During the 1960s several Indian activist groups emerged. The most prominent was the militant American Indian Movement (AIM), founded by Vernon and Clyde Bellecourt of Minneapolis.[114] On November 20, 1969, AIM members became part of the coalition "Indians of All Tribes"; they staged a 19-month takeover of Alcatraz Island, demanding attention to Indian health, educational, and cultural needs.[115] The *Akwesasne Notes*, a publication of the Mohawk nation, describes the event: "We came to Alcatraz with . . . little hate or anger in our hearts for the thought of a lasting unity kept us whole and in harmony with life. From this island would grow a movement which must surely encompass the world, . . . not as a fire of anger but as a warming glow."[116] The tactics used at Alcatraz carried into the 1970s.

On September 13, 1972, 40 Indians seized the Bureau of Indian Affairs office in Pawnee, Oklahoma after learning that Federal funds intended to benefit Indian children had been mishandled. Once a settlement was negotiated, Vernon Bellecourt of AIM organized seven automobile caravans to drive to Washington, D.C. to dramatize common mistreatment and neglect of American Indians. This soon came to be known as the "The Trail of Broken

Treaties" reminiscent of the "Trail of Tears" of 1838. On November 2, about 500 Native Americans seized control of the Bureau of Indian Affairs building after scuffles with Capitol police, barricading themselves inside the building. A force of about 150 law enforcement officers surrounded the building for six days just at the time of the presidential election.

The Nixon administration ignored their demands and challenged the movements' legitimacy. On November 6, a Washington judge ordered the Indians be held in contempt and directed their arrests. After reaching accord with White House negotiators to hear Indian grievances, the occupying group agreed to leave the building on November 8, taking what they called "incriminating" documents from federal files. Officials estimated more than $1 million in damage to the building.

Militant tactics escalated further on February 27, 1973, when more than 200 Native Americans seized the village of Wounded Knee as a means of protesting and publicizing deplorable physical, economic, and political conditions. Their goal was to gain "the freedom to determine their own lives and destinies as a sovereign people" by establishing "their own government, where they [could] run their affairs according to their own traditions."[117] Eddie Benton, executive director of St. Paul's chapter of AIM, situates the protest within his peoples' cultural heritage:

> "Why Wounded Knee 1973?" . . . We are the poorest of the poor. We have no control over the destiny of our communities, no economy of our own, the poorest health facilities. We are rapidly losing our natural resources and our land base. Organized religion and big Government have conspired . . . to annihilate, assimilate, inundate, legislate, excavate, segregate, separate, and at all time to HATE us. . . . We ask you, America, . . . [W]hy have you broken every treaty? . . . [W]hy do you kill? . . . Why do you try to change the universal order? . . . Wounded Knee 1973 is . . . the result of the divisionary tactics . . . [that] pit Indian against Indian, tribe against tribe, brother against brother. It is our voice petitioning government. . . . It is our blow for freedom.[118]

A skirmish between federal troops and the militants led to the wounding of one soldier and the death of two Native Americans, before the violence dissipated, ending the armed occupation of Wounded Knee ended on May 8, 1973.

The next and perhaps most serious confrontation began nearby in early 1975 when AIM leader Leonard Peltier traveled to the Sioux reservation at Pine Ridge, South Dakota to help organize Ghost Dance dissenters who opposed the Tribal Council's decision to lease reservation lands to multinational mining companies. Soon after they set up a Spiritual Camp on the reservation's Jumping Bull Ranch, the FBI began training a BIA SWAT team nearby. On June 26, 1975, FBI agents Coler and Williams arrived at the ranch claiming they were looking for a man accused of stealing boots. A shoot out ensued that ended in the deaths of the agents and one of the dissenters. Peltier and three other men were charged with murder. After extradition from Canada, Peltier was convicted of two counts of first degree murder in April 1977. Currently he is serving double life sentences.[119]

Like other contemporary protest groups, AIM achieved considerable success by involving the press. Media reports of the seizure of the BIA building in Washington, D.C., for example, set off sympathetic actions elsewhere. On November 6, 1972, 50 Native Americans invaded the Bureau of Indian Affairs office in Seattle and began a sympathetic sit-in. During the siege at Wounded Knee in 1973, the press provided global coverage, thus embarrassing the United States by reminding the international community of domestic injustice on the part of a nation fighting an unpopular war in Vietnam. By publicizing protest, the media not only served as a buffer against a possible government attack, but also forged bonds between Native Americans and an array of other groups.

For example, in response to news reports, the Iroquois sent a delegation to Wounded Knee to demonstrate their support. Two hundred Lumbee and Tuscarora Indians along with blacks and whites advanced on the town of Lumberton in North Carolina. In Denver, 2,000 Chicanos marched in support of the Independent Oglala Nation. Letters and telegrams came to Wounded Knee from Australia, Finland, Germany, Italy, Japan, England, and all over the U.S. and Canada. Leonard Peltier has won the support of Amnesty International, Jesse Jackson, Bishop Tutu, and eight Episcopal Bishops, among others, in his ongoing legal struggle. Thus, Native American protest made inroads against marginalization by becoming part of a civil rights and antiwar movement adamantly opposed to racial discrimination and military solutions to national and international problems.

The protests did much to create Red pride and raise national consciousness. "Holding the Rock" at Alcatraz was a proactive move embodying the "collective expression of modern Native Americans seeking control over their lives in a society that had long before robbed them of such control."[120] Wounded Knee, with its tie to the massacres of the 1800s, caught the imagination of the larger public. In July 1970 Richard Nixon decried the "suffocating paternalism" of contemporary Indian policy. "The time has come," he said, "to . . . create the conditions for a new era in which the Indian future is determined by Indian acts and Indian decisions."[121]

The bureaucracy's response was to deflect, thereby marginalizing a culturally different people. It ignored the position paper advanced by

Indians participating in the caravan to Washington, acknowledging it only after violence broke out.[122] Officials at Wounded Knee minimized the significance of that takeover by defining the conflict as a problem unique to Pine Ridge. In like vein, the government accused dissenters of engaging in a public relations ploy. It also condemned Native American actions as those of unreasonable radicals, describing the protesters as "criminals," "savages," "militants,"and "agitators."[123] Similarly, it denied a request to hold religious services at Arlington Cemetery because that request conflicted with regulations prohibiting any services "closely related" to "partisan activities." In Hardin, Montana Native Americans on the "Trail of Broken Treaties" were refused permission to erect a cast-iron plaque at Custer National Battlefield as a memorial to their ancestors who died in the Battle of the Little Big Horn.[124] In essence, then, the dominant society engaged in a self-protective marginalization of distressingly different dissidents.

Conclusion

The preceding analysis points to the centrality of cultural tensions to suppressive strategies that have denied voice to Native Americans since Euro-Americans first came to this continent. The policy of *isolation* stripped Native peoples of two sources of cultural power. Prioritizing written English subverted native voice for, as Luther Standing Bear argues, written language has promoted "a blind worship of . . . history, of books, of the written word, that has denuded the spoken word of its power and sacredness."[125] Similarly, because land for Native Americans was not simply a commodity, removal to territory away from whites was a denial of spiritual sovereignty that tore them from the sacred spaces so essential to their religion and cultural identity. The cultural superiority inherent to *annihilation* through disease, environmental destruction, and war points to a worldview steeped in hierarchy and wedded to progress rather than the parity and continuity inherent in concepts of continuous creation[126] and universal kinship. Hence, phrases such as "manifest destiny" and the "advancement of civilization" were emblematic of a discourse which has silenced indigenous peoples by painting "native cultures as outdated and regressive."[127]

Eurocentric attempts at *transformation* of Indian peoples, to "improve" them so that they allegedly can occupy an "equal" place in the larger society, required that members of those co-cultures forsake their religion, language, and lifestyle. Similarly, *marginalization*, as manifest in quashing of religious practices and the deflecting of protest constitutes an acute denial of native voices for it denigrates and thus trivializes the languages and spiritual bases for entire cultures.

However, by adopting Euro-American strategies, Native Americans have achieved some mark of success, especially in the legal realm. For example, in 1961 the Ak-Chin Indian reservation won freedom from the Bureau of Indian Affairs by gaining the right to farm its own lands rather than lease them to non-Indians for negligible revenues. In 1971 Congress awarded the 60,000 natives of Alaska $962 million and 40 million acres to settle land claims. Since the passage of the 1975 Indian Self-Determination Act, various tribes have taken over the administration of education and other social programs; as a result, Indian governments now control most of the Bureau of Indian Affairs' budget. In addition, some treaty rights have been restored. The Klamath of Oregon, in 1986, won the right to acquire new timber and funding to restore their tribal government and in the future dams will be removed along the Klamath River to allow the return of the salmon and the stealhead. In 1988 the Puyallup Indians of Acoma, Washington received $66 million and 300 acres of prime land in the port of Tacoma based on an 1854 treaty. In 1990 the Shoshoni-Bannock people of the Fort Hall reservation in Idaho secured their right to use 581,000 acre-feet of water flowing through the Snake River in recognition of an 1868 treaty. In December 2009 the federal government agreed to pay $3.4 billion in recognition of the fact that it had mismanaged Indian trust funds for more than a century. While these gains are substantial, all involve rights consistent with a Eurocentric perspective: legal control of land and natural resources.

Similarly, the rhetoric of Red power raised consciousness of native cultures and problems by capturing the imagination of the press. However, that success points to a dilemma facing Native Americans: to speak to the dominant culture, they must adopt behaviors contrary to their own. Indian activists had to violate Native norms: they communicated competitively through militant activity that attracted attention of the dominant culture through the mainstream press; they abandoned an oral tradition by issuing printed proclamations; they went outside Indian institutions for effecting justice by entering political and legal arenas. In essence, then, Native Americans have made gains by subscribing to Euro-American principles and behaviors, not by adhering to their own.

Not surprisingly, then, efforts in the area of religious freedom have encountered significant roadblocks because of a Eurocentric reading of the First Amendment. The first provision in the Bill of Rights contains two kinds of prohibitions: one exclusive, the other inclusive. The latter forbids the making of laws that abridge free speech, press, petition, and assembly. The former bans the government from establishing a religion or interfering in its free exercise. In essence, it guarantees political liberties but not religious ones, thereby prioritizing the former over the latter. The Supreme Court consistently has ruled that individuals are free to *believe* what they want but are not free to *practice* that belief in ways that violate the law.[128]

To make religious freedom secondary to other government interests is a denial of the core of many cultures to which religion is all-encompassing. Blaeser describes the difference between Native and Western faiths as she distinguishes religion from the spiritual: "[R]eligion . . . involves the imposition of the already-established, the fixed order or structure. . . . [S]pirituality . . . involves the interactive formation of relationships, . . . [for] [i]n an alive world, forces . . . change, shift, and develop, requiring, therefore, equal life, equal vitality, in the forms of ritual or the means of connection with [them]."[129] Significantly, since most Indian nations do not delineate religion from other aspects of existence, many Native languages have no separate word for it.

The lesson implicit in the experience of Native Americans is simple: a subordinate culture must adopt the means and ends of the more powerful to protect itself. That the area of greatest weakness for Native Americans should be religious freedom is truly ironic given the genesis of this nation. In the evolution of the First Amendment, religious and expressive freedoms were bound to each other inextricably. Catholics, Jews, Quakers, and Puritans all sought haven in America to escape religious persecution in Europe. Preachers were leaders in articulating revolutionary sentiments. And since underground presses and public orators had helped foment revolt, freedom of expression and freedom of religion became aims for which the American Revolution was fought. After ratification of the Constitution, those aims were united with each other in the first provision of the Bill of Rights. And yet, historically the government has guaranteed these freedoms to its citizens while denying them to Native Americans. Redress for the situation within the strict confines of a Eurocentric perspective will inevitably be only partial. Therefore, the dominant culture needs to expand its horizons to admit the legitimacy of divergent perspectives on the regulation of religion if it is to effect equal justice for all of its citizens.

Notes

1. These words were spoken by Chief Seattle when Governor Stevens was appointed the Commissioner of Indian Affairs and given a reception in Seattle, Washington, on October 29, 1854.

2. For Native Americans on reservations, death from heart disease occurs at double the national rate; from alcoholism, at 10 times the U.S. average.

3. See also *Montana v. U.S.*, 450 U.S. 544 (1981); *Sioux Nation v. U.S.*, 448 U.S. 371 (1980); *Lyng v. Northwest Indian Cemetery Assn.*, 485 U.S. 439 (1988); and *Employment Div., Dept. of Human Resources v. Smith*, 494 U.S. 872 (1990). The *Smith* ruling requires those seeking free exercise of religion to link the exercise to some other right guaranteed in the Constitution. In *Smith* (494 U.S. 872, 876), the Court makes clear that ingesting peyote is not protected by the First Amendment even though ingestion is integral to religious practice. (See below for more on this case.)

4. For an excellent study of the importance of symbolic speech to Native Americans, see Richard Morris and Philip Wander, "Native American Rhetoric: Dancing in the Shadows of the Ghost Dance," *Quarterly Journal of Speech*, 76 (1990): 164–191.

5. Benjamin Capps, *The Indians* (New York: Time Life Books, 1973), 123.

6. Capps, *The Indians*, 118.

7. Vine Deloria Jr. and Clifford M. Lytle, *American Indians, American Justice* (Austin: University of Texas Press, 1983), 3.

8. Felix Cohen, *Handbook of Federal Indian Law* (Albuquerque: University of New Mexico Press, 1942), 46–47.

9. Joseph Epes Brown, quoted in Richard Morris and Phillip Wander, "Native American Rhetoric," 167; see also Gayle High Pine, quoted in Randall A. Lake, "The Rhetor as Dialectician in 'Last Chance for Survival,'" *Communication Monographs* 53 (1986): 271.

10. Russell Lawrence Barsh, "The Nature and Spirit of North American Political Systems," *American Indian Quarterly* 10 (1986): 181.

11. Michael A. Dorris, "The Grass Still Grows, the Rivers Still Flow: Contemporary Native Americans," *Daedalus* 110 (1981): 50.

12. In *Steps to Ecology of Mind* (New York: Ballantine, 1972), Gregory Bateson describes the Euro-American posture in relationship to her or his environment: "If you . . . have the idea that you are created in . . . [God's] image, you will . . . see yourself as . . . against the things around you. . . . [Y]ou will see the world around you as mindless and therefore not entitled to moral . . . consideration. This environment will seem to be yours to exploit. Your survival unit will be you and your folks . . . against . . . other social units, other races and the brutes and vegetables" (462).

13. John D. Loftin, "Anglo-American Jurisprudence and the Native American Tribal Quest for Religious Freedom," *American Indian Culture and Research Journal* 13 (1989): 3–4.

14. Pachgantschilias, quoted in Frederick W. Turner III, ed. *The Portable North American Indian Reader* (New York: Viking Press, 1974), 245.

15. While fighting the Seminoles, Jackson had destroyed whole villages. Then the Seminoles under the leadership of Himollemico ambushed an army detachment traveling with women and children. Jackson's reprisal was vicious. Himollemico was chased to St. Marks in the Caribbean where he was captured and imprisoned. Samuel Elliot Morison and Henry Steele Commager, *The Growth of the American Republic*, vol. 1 (New York: Oxford University Press, 1962), 449.

16. James D. Richardson, ed., *A Compilation of the Messages and Papers of the Presidents, 1789–1902*, vol. 2, (Washington, DC: Bureau of National Literature and Art, 1907), 519–521.

17. Samuel Elliot Morison and Henry Steele Commager, *The Growth of the American Republic*, vol. 1, (New York: Oxford University Press, 1962), 488.

18. Deloria and Lytle, *American Indians*, 4.

19. James D. Richardson, ed., *A Compilation of Messages and Papers of the Presidents, 1789–1897*, vol. 3, (Washington, DC: Government Printing Office, 1911), 171.

20. Richardson, *Messages and Papers of the Presidents*, vol. 3, 253.

21. Deloria and Lytle, *American Indians*, 4.

22. Ronald Spokes, "Too Small a Place: The Removal of the Wilamette Valley Indians, 1850–1856," *American Indian Quarterly* 17 (1993): 173.

23. Beverly Allen, quoted in Spokes, "Too Small a Place," 176–177.

24. Spokes, "Too Small a Place," 171–178.

25. Spokes, "Too Small a Place," 179.

26. Spokes, "Too Small a Place," 182.

27. This excerpt also illustrates the European pursuit of land and prosperity at the expense of the Native American. See *Chronicles of American Indian Protest* (New York: Council on Interracial Books for Children, 1979).

28. Dorris, "The Grass Still Grows," 44, 45.

29. Peter Nabokov, *Native American Testimony* (New York: Penguin, 1992), 173.

30. Nabokov, *Native American*, 174.

31. Capps, *The Indians*, 167.

32. Joel B. Palmer, quoted in Spokes, "Too Small a Place," 173.

33. Barsh, "The Nature and Spirit," (187) details the key dimensions of Native American views of unity or harmony: "Continuity in time connects ancestors with the unborn.... [E]ach family extends both backwards and forwards through time, bridging the physical and spiritual worlds.... Continuity in space connects family with family.... [R]elationships among families [are political bonds that] transcend time.... Continuity across species connects human beings with all life.... [Such ecological unity implies] there is no 'ownership' of land, ... only the right to live in a place with one's relatives, both human and nonhuman."

34. Capps, *The Indians*, 154.

35. Capps, *The Indians*, 156.

36. In 1806, the Office of Superintendent of Indian Trade was established in the War Department. In 1824, the Secretary of War created the Bureau of Indian Affairs which was transferred to the Department of Interior in 1849.

37. Capps, *The Indians*, 165.

38. Capps, *The Indians*, 168.

39. Capps, *The Indians*, 165–168.

40. Capps, *The Indians*, 183–192.

41. A final "agreement" in 1889 would deprive the Sioux of another 11 million acres and contribute to the crisis at Wounded Knee.

42. John Bartlett, *Familiar Quotations*, 15th edition. (Boston: Little, Brown, 1980), 591.

43. Capps, *The Indians*, 200.

44. Bartlett, *Familiar Quotations*, 642.

45. According to Matthew King, spokesperson for the Lakota, the Black Hills are the birthplace of the Lakota people, where their ancestors are buried, and where they go for sacred ceremonies. See Steve Wall and Harvey Arden, *Wisdomkeepers: Meetings With Native American Spiritual Elders* (Hillsboro, OR: Beyond Words, 1990), 34.

46. Capps, *The Indians*, 210.

47. S. M. Barrett, *Geronimo: His Own Story* (New York: Dutton, 1970), 19.

48. Dan L. Thrapp, *The Conquest of Appacheria* (Oklahoma City: University of Oklahoma Press, 1967), 9–10.

49. Barrett, *Geronimo*, 89.

50. Alexander Adams, *Geronimo: A Biography* (New York: Putnam, 1971), 88.

51. During this battle the Mexicans gave him the name Geronimo because of his ferocity as a fighter and because the battle was fought on St. Geronimo's Day.

52. Barrett, *Geronimo*, 126. Thrapp, *The Conquest*, (16–18) discusses other incidents.

53. Thrapp, *The Conquest*, 320.

54. Odie B. Faulk, *The Geronimo Campaign* (New York: Oxford University Press, 1969), 77.

55. Faulk, *The Geronimo Campaign*, 94. Some evidence suggests that Cook had come to respect Geronimo and had even looked the other way during his escape.

56. John G. Neihardt, *Black Elk Speaks* (Lincoln: University of Nebraska Press, 1932/New York: Washington Square Press, 1959), 259.

57. In 1980 the Supreme Court awarded eight Sioux tribes $105 million in compensation for the land grabs of 1874 and 1877.

58. For a discussion of the contrast between linear (Euro-American) and cyclical (Native American) concepts of time, see Randall A. Lake, "Between Myth and History: Enacting Time in Native American Protest Rhetoric," *Quarterly Journal of Speech* 77 (1991): 123–151.

59. Capps, *The Indians*, 20. Navaho medicine men placed their sand paintings inside circles. See Capps, *The Indians*, 140–141.

60. John Fire/Lame Deer and Richard Erdoes, *Lame Deer Seeker of Visions* (New York: Simon and Schuster, 1972), 112.

61. Robert Fleck, "*Black Elk Speaks*: A Native American View of Nineteenth-Century American History," *Journal of American Culture* 17 (1994): 68.

62. Chester A. Arthur, quoted in Dorris, "The Grass Still Grows," 8.

63. Dorris, "The Grass Still Grows," 51.

64. Deloria and Lytle, *American Indians*, 10.

65. Deloria and Lytle, *American Indians*, 12–13; Dorris, "The Grass Still Grows," 52.

66. Clare V. McKanna Jr., "Murderers All: The Treatment of Indian Defendants in Arizona Territory, 1880–1912," *American Indian Quarterly* 17 (1993): 360.

67. Neihardt, *Black Elk Speaks*, 166, 195, 230.

68. Loftin, "Anglo-American Jurisprudence," 4, 5.

69. See Francis Paul Prucha, *Indian Policy in the United States* (Lincoln: University of Nebraska Press, 1981), 28.

70. Vine Deloria Jr., "Knowledge and Understanding: Traditional Education in the Modern World," *Winds of Change* 5 (1986): 15.

71. Prucha, *Indian Policy*, 16–17.

72. Prucha, *Indian Policy*, 27.

73. Deloria, "Knowledge," 16, 17.

74. Vine Deloria Jr., "Ethnoscience and Indian Realities," *Winds of Change* 7 (1992): 15.

75. Although Indian schools had functioned for decades, beginning in 1879, off-reservation vocational boarding schools became a dimension in federal Indian education.

76. Wall and Arden, *Wisdom Keepers*, 54–55.

77. Morris and Wander, "Native American Rhetoric," 170.

78. Wilcomb E. Washburn, "Indian Policy Since the 1880s," *The Aggression of Civilization: Federal Indian Policy Since the 1880s*, ed. Sandra L. Cadwalader and Vine Deloria Jr. (Philadelphia: Temple University Press, 1984), 52.

79. The Sun Dance is one of the seven rites of the Oglala Sioux. It is held each year during the Moon of Fattening (June) or the Moon of Cherries Blackening (July). The dance is an offering of one's body and soul to Wakan-Tanka (the Creator). See Joseph Epes Brown, *The Sacred Pipe* (Norman: University of Oklahoma Press, 1953), 67–68.

80. See Paul B. Steinmetz, *Pipe, Bible and Peyote Among the Oglala Lakota* (Knoxville: University of Tennessee Press, 1990), 17.

81. David M. Strausfield, "Reformers in Conflict: The Pueblo Dance Controversy," *The Aggressions of Civilization: Federal Indian Policy Since the 1880s*, ed. Sandra L. Cadwalader and Vine Deloria Jr. (Philadelphia: Temple University Press, 1984), 25–26.

82. L. G. Moses, "'The Father Tells Me So!' Wovoka: The Ghost Dance Prophet," *American Indian Quarterly* 9 (1985): 336, 335.

83. James Mooney, "The Ghost Dance Religion and the Sioux Outbreak of 1890," *Fourteenth Annual Report of the Bureau of Ethnology* (Washington, DC: Government Printing Office, 1896), 770–771.

84. Moses, "The Father Tells Me So!" 339.

85. Mooney, "The Ghost Dance Religion," 23.

86. Mooney, "The Ghost Dance Religion," 780–781.

87. Moses, "The Father Tells Me So!" 342.

88. Quoted in Walter R. Echo-Hawk, "Native American Religious Liberty: Five Hundred Years After Columbus," *American Indian Culture and Research Journal*, 17 (1993): 36.

89. Sandra L. Cadwalader and Vine Deloria Jr., *The Aggressions of Civilization: Federal Indian Policy Since the 1880s* (Philadelphia: Temple University Press, 1984), x.

90. In some areas, the effort continues. *Rider v. Board of Education of Independent School District*, 414 U.S. 109, has so far upheld the right of an Oklahoma school district to require Pawnee Indian children to cut their braids before being admitted to school. The Pawnees argue that the braids religious and cultural are a symbol.

91. Glenn A. Phelps, "Representation Without Taxation: Citizenship and Suffrage in Indian Country," *American Indian Quarterly* 9 (1985): 136.

92. *Porter v. Hall*, 34 Ariz. 308, 411(1928). This ruling by the Arizona Supreme Court ignored the Indian Citizenship Act and prevent Native Americans from registering in the state for 20 years.

93. *Harrison v. Laveen*, 67 Ariz. 337 (1948).

94. Phelps, "Resurrection," 136.

95. Echo-Hawk, "Native American Religious Liberty," 34.

96. Paul E. Lawson and Jennifer Scholes, "Jurisprudence, Peyote and the Native American Church," *American Indian Culture and Research Journal* 10 (1986): 14.

97. Chief Walking Buffalo quoted in Rennard Strickland, "Implementing the National Policy of Understanding, Preserving, and Safeguarding the Heritage of Indian Peoples and Native Hawaiians: Human Rights, Sacred Objects, and Cultural Patrimony," *Arizona State Law Journal* 24 (1992): 175.

98. Exceptions include the Romantic Movement, holistic healing, and some ecological advocates.

99. Kirkpatrick Sale, *The Conquest of Paradise* (New York: Knopf, 1990), 40.

100. 430 U.S. 584.

101. See also *Montana v. U.S.*, 450 U.S. 544 (1981); *Sioux Nation v. U.S.*, 448 U.S. 371 (1980); *Lyng v. Northwest Indian Cemetery Assn.*, 485 U.S. 439 (1988), and *Employment Div., Dept. of Human Resources v. Smith*, 108 L. Ed. 2d 876 (1990). In these cases, the Court draws a sharp line between religious *beliefs* and religious *conduct*. The Smith case is particularly disturbing because it overturned the three part test established in *Sherbert v. Verner*, 374 U.S. 398 (1963), which placed a heavy burden on states seeking to restrict religious practices. (See also John Rhodes, "An American Tradition: The Religious Persecution of Native Americans," *Montana Law Review* 52 [1991]: 42–44, 58; Lawson and Scholes, "Jurisprudence, Peyote," 13–27). In *Church of the Lukumi Babulu Aye, Inc. v. City of Hialeah*, 113 S. Ct. 2217, 2233 (1993), a plaintiff won for the first time in twenty years when the Court ruled that "A law burdening religious practice that is not neutral or not of general application must undergo the most rigorous scrutiny." The decision somewhat mitigates *Smith* but has created confusion. See Rod Fliegel, "Free Exercise and the Religious Freedom Restoration Act of 1993: Where We Are, Where We Have Been, and Where We Are Going," *Constitutional Law Journal* 5 (1994): 81, 83–88.

102. 620 F. 2d 1159, 1164-65 [6th Cir.] *cert. denied*, 449 U.S. 953 (1980).

103. Echo-Hawk, "Native American Religious Liberty," 42–43.

104. For a careful analysis of this issue, see Luralene D. Tapahe, "After the Religious Freedom Restoration Act: Still No Equal Protection for First Amendment Worshipers," *New Mexico Law Review*, 24 (1994): 331–363. Tapahe contends that "native claims challenging the development of sacred land sites have not been given the same doctrinal treatment as those claims brought by mainstream Judeo-Christian plaintiffs" (332).

105. Morris Udall, quoted in Echo-Hawk, "Native American Religious Liberty," 40.

106. Loftin, "Anglo-American Jurisprudence," 30.

107. Lawson and Scholes, "Jurisprudence, Peyote," 15–16, 25.

108. Echo-Hawk, "Native American Religious Liberty," 47.

109. Adell Sherbert had been fired for refusing to work on her Sabbath day, Saturday. The Court ruled that such an infringement on the practice of religion required justification through a "compelling state interest" (374 U.S. 398. 403).

110. Vine Deloria Jr., "Secularism, Civil Religion, and the Religious Freedom of American Indians," *American Indian Culture and Research Journal* 16 (1992): 13.

111. On November 19, 1990, the Native American Graves Protection and Repatriation Act became law.

112. Echo-Hawk, "Native American Religious Liberty," 49–50.

113. Wall and Arden, *Wisdom Keepers*, 50.

114. See R. S. Cathcart, "Movements: Confrontation as Rhetorical Form," *Southern Speech Communication Journal*, 43 (1978): 233–247.

115. For a description of the Alcatraz affair by Adam Fortunate Eagle, a Red Lake Chippewa, see Peter Nabokov, *Native American Testimony*, 367–370.

116. *Akwesasne Notes*, (Early Winter 1973): 7.

117. Kenneth Tilsen, quoted in *Akwesasne Notes*, (June 1973): 5.

118. These thoughts were first published in the "The Seventh Fire," a chapter newsletter sent out in St. Paul, Minnesota in March 1973.

119. Before Peltier's trial, two of the defendants were acquitted and the government dropped charges against the remaining defendant. This led Peltier's lawyers to suspect something was amiss. In the meantime, Peltier was transferred from Marion prison to Lompoc, California, from which he escaped for six days. On January 22, 1980, he was given an additional seven-year sentence for the escape. In 1984 the Eighth U.S. Circuit Court of Appeals ordered a hearing on the issue of whether the FBI had withheld evidence that might clear Peltier. His attorney, William Kunstler, obtained information through the Freedom of Information Act that indicated that the rifle that killed the agents was not the rifle that Peltier used during the confrontation. During the hearing, the FBI admitted that an affidavit used to convict Peltier was a fabrication. Several witnesses against Peltier in the original trial claimed they were coerced by the FBI. While the hearing progressed, Peltier was not allowed to meet with reporters. When the court reaffirmed the conviction, Peltier was transferred to Leavenworth, Kansas. From there he continues to file appeals to this day.

120. Jeff Sklansky, "Rock, Reservation and Prison: The Native American Occupation of Alcatraz Island," *American Indian Culture and Research Journal* 13:2 (1989): 60.

121. Richard M. Nixon, quoted in Sklansky, "Rock, Reservation," 62.

122. D'Arcy McNickle, *Native American Tribalism: Indian Survivals and Renewals* (New York: Oxford University Press, 1973), 9, ix.

123. Morris and Wander, "Native American Rhetoric," 182.

124. *Akwesasne Notes* (Early Winter 1973): 4, 5.

125. Luther Standing Bear, "Land of the Spotted Eagle," *Chronicles of American Indian Protest*, ed. The Council on Interracial Books for Children (Greenwich, CT: Fawcett, 1971), 271.

126. Barsh, "The Nature and Spirit," (181–184) argues that many Native nations saw original creation as an act of love, which through time has been embellished through an ongoing recreation that results in ever-increasing complexity.

127. Lake, "Time," 125.

128. See *Lemon v. Kurtzman*, 403 U.S. 602 (1971). In *Everson v. Board of Education*, 330 U.S. 1 (1947) Justice Rutledge persuaded his brethren that the establishment clause meant no government aid to any religions. In the majority opinion, Justice Black writes, "Neither [the Federal Government nor the states] can force nor influence a person to go to or to remain away from church against his will or for him to profess belief or disbelief in any religion. . . . No tax in any amount, large or small, can be levied to support any religious activities or institutions, whatever they may be called, or whatever form they may adopt to teach or practice religion" (330 U.S. 1,

15). See also *Engel v. Vitale*, 370 U.S. 421 (1962), which outlawed prayer in public schools. See Mark Fischer, "The Sacred and the Secular: An Examination of the 'Wall of Separation' and Its Implications on the Religious World View," *University of Pittsburgh Law Review*, 54 (1990), which concludes, "Underlying many of the theories used in Establishment Clause jurisprudence is an implicit disdain for the religious world view" (340); for further analysis, see Robert S. Alley, "Public Education and the Public Good," *William & Mary Bill of Rights Journal*, 4 (1995): 277–350.

129. Kimberly M. Blaeser, "Pagans Rewriting the Bible: Heterodoxy and the Representation of Spirituality in Native American Literature," *Ariel* 25 (1994): 23.

Chapter 5

Silencing the Union Movement

Andrew Sachs

Between 1871 and 1910, worker organizations in the United States experienced prodigious growth and activity. A dialectical tension was created when the forces of capital induced the government to suppress these organizations' First Amendment rights of speech, press, and assembly to such an extent that the labor movement was seriously impeded. The tactics of suppression pervaded government at state and national levels because governments usually supported business against labor. Because of the destruction wrought by the Civil War, the need to repair America was especially acute. Railroads crossed the nation carrying materials out to the plains and bringing back raw materials and foods. A postwar industrial boom set in. Under these circumstances, those advancing "Social Darwinism," that is, competition to determine the fittest, held the "social gospel," the obligation to care for the needy, in check.[1] The government most often chose to protect business by guaranteeing it freedoms granted under various clauses of the United States Constitution rather than to grant labor unions speech, press, and assembly freedoms guaranteed under the First Amendment.[2] Looking at government responses to labor movement activities is valuable because it reveals how the inherent tension between capitalism and communal needs of workers is managed in a First Amendment environment. It is particularly valuable to look at this tension in the post–Civil War era because the need for and success of industrial expansion was so great. At no time in our history would the hand of business be so powerful and unrestrained. Its threat to workers would never be so great.

The purpose of this chapter is to describe the extent and effects of suppression as it was manifest over time by local, state, and federal governments through legislative, military, and judicial branches.[3] Government suppression of unions' First Amendment rights can be divided into two major strategies.

The first comprised immediate and direct acts of intimidation; organizers and workers who engaged in union activity were arrested, beaten, even killed by government enforcement authorities sent to quell such activity.

State and federal legislatures passed legislative acts aimed at suppressing labor. Specific legislative acts were passed against labor by state and federal legislatures. These acts are clearly beyond persuasive speech and they were enforced by the courts often through wholesale application of the labor injunction, which itself further prohibited labor from carrying out activity. The effects of suppression were cumulative, ultimately leading to a considerable weakening of the labor movement as a whole.

I begin with a historical review of circumstances after the Civil War that led to government suppression of labor unions' First Amendment rights. Then, I discuss the techniques of government suppression. This discussion has two main sections. First, I review police and military suppression (hereafter referred to as martial suppression) during various labor movement events from 1877 to 1910. In this section I focus specifically on a key event in that sparked the most severe martial suppression, the Chicago Haymarket Square bombing. But I hope to make clear that the elements that provoked the massive martial suppression against anarchists were in place long before the bombing on May 4, 1886; they came together at Haymarket, had a protracted effect on the labor movement, and led to massive administrative suppression. That is the second technique of government suppression of First Amendment rights of labor unions, and it includes principal federal and state laws and court actions that attempted to silence labor's First Amendment activities. I close the chapter with a discussion of the overall significance of First Amendment suppression for the labor movement.

The Exigency

The nineteenth-century rise of capitalism is a principle factor that led to union suppression. As early as 1863 in England, Henry Fawcett wrote, "It would appear that social terrorism is the source of [union] power."[4] With the second phase of the industrial revolution in full swing during reconstruction after the Civil War, great business enterprises emerged, notably those of J. Pierpont Morgan, Andrew Carnegie, Jay Gould, H. L. Frick, E. C. Knight, Edward H. Harriman, and John D. Rockefeller. These individuals exercised what they believed to be rights of acquiring, possessing, and protecting property in the name of Social Darwinism.[5] Further, the government was invested with the role of protecting these rights especially insofar as business established commerce among the states. Article 1, Section 8 of the United States Constitution, for example, invests the federal government with the power to regulate commerce among the states. These individuals exercised these guaranteed rights to the fullest. Railroads proliferated throughout the United States; the natural resources of the South were devoured. Wealthy Carpetbaggers moved in to oversee the operation and founded cities like Birmingham (1872) along the way. Steel, oil, coal, timber, transportation, and textile businesses developed into large industries; monopolies and trusts soon formed out of the capitalistic boom. This was the Gilded Age, an era of increased mechanization of industry, business expansion, rampant individualism, and laissez-faire dominance.

Nonetheless, this was also a time of great economic instability and consequent unemployment for working people. Periods of national financial panic, such as those occurring in 1873, 1886, from 1892 to 1894 and from 1907 to 1911, occasioned runs on banks, drops in the stock exchange, and dramatic business failures.[6] With these events, wrought in part by the unscrupulous business practices of the chieftains of industry, massive unemployment, hunger, homelessness, and despair rent the working class. In October 1884, for example, *Bradstreet's Journal* conducted a field survey of "the Industrial Situation" in the northeastern states; it arrived at a figure of some 350,000 unemployed persons, or about 13 percent of total population. Analysts estimated that wage reductions were occurring at rates from 20 to 30 percent, and they saw little hope for improvement in the new year.[7] In 1885, Terence Powderly, master workman of the Knights of Labor, a national union then in its ascendancy, calculated unemployment to be much higher, at 2 million persons.[8]

Extreme economic conditions provoked worker discontent. As working-class people found it difficult to partake of the fruits of capitalism, the episodic and gradually increasing impact of depression upon production, wages, and employment became a subject for complaint. In 1879, for example, a currier (one who works on leather or tans hides) testified to the Massachusetts Bureau of Labor Statistics about deteriorating labor conditions:

> During working hours the men are not allowed to speak to each other, though working in close together. Less than five years ago wages were from 12$ to 18$ a week currency; now they are from 6$ to 12$, and work not as steady.... What do the mechanics of Massachusetts say to each other? I will tell you. We must have a change. Anything is better than this. We cannot be worse off, no matter what the change is.[9]

Six years later the discontent remained. With foreboding, Powderly noted in 1885 that "A deep rooted feeling of discontent pervades the masses; ... the army of the discontented is gathering fresh recruits day by day."[10]

As a result of such dissatisfaction, citizens demanded and defined a more active role for the government in regulating business. Reform penetrated thinking in many circles. For example, the platform of the American Economic Association in 1886 advanced its objectives in language whose formality underscored the statement's earnestness:

> We regard the state as an educational and ethical agency whose positive aid is an indispensable condition of human progress. While we recognize the necessity of individual initiative in industrial life, we hold that the doctrine of laissez-faire is unsafe in politics and unsound in morals. . . . We hold that the conflict of labor and capital has brought to the front a vast number of social problems whose solution is impossible without the united efforts of church, state, and science.[11]

Statements such as this demanded that the government along with other institutions correct the effects of uncontrolled free enterprise. In the preamble of their Omaha platform of 1892, the Populists promised to remedy "falling prices, the formation of combines and rings, the impoverishment of the producing class . . . by wide and reasonable legislation, in accordance with the terms of our platform." But, if this proved insufficient, they went on to declare:

> We believe that the powers of government . . . should be expanded (as in the case of the postal service) as rapidly and as far as the good sense of an intelligent people and the teachings of experience shall justify, to the end that oppression, injustice, and poverty shall eventually cease in the land.[12]

This call for reform culminated in the Progressive Era in the first and second decades of the twentieth century.

The Emergence of Unionism

In the late nineteenth century, however, this pronounced anti-big business drift away from laissez-faire individualism and toward social and political responsibility was limited to third parties, such as the Populists, and the labor movement. The economic conditions provoked the rise of unions, especially during severe depressions. Several organizations formed and/or met to advocate workers' causes against the ravages of the industrial system as it evolved during the decades after the Civil War. These organizations courted working people of all trades and levels of skill. Through such unions, workers were offered a panoply of rhetorical media and strategies in various degrees of radicalism by which they might better their lives. While their structure, politics, and strategies varied from 1877 to 1910, these organizations and the people they attracted represented the American labor movement.

One type of organization was the craft union, which already had a long history in the United States. The crafts had been organized since colonial times. However, by the end of the Civil War craft unions appeared in numbers unprecedented in American history. In most major cities, cigar-makers, dressmakers, bookmakers, machine makers, artisans and craft-persons of all trades might have a union, and common to most crafts was a restriction of membership to specific trades. Members had cooperative stores, free libraries and reading rooms, legislative lobbies, apprentices, and a labor press. In addition, approximately 30 powerful national unions of specific trades arose, and several of these unions published their own journals.

The political tendencies of the craft and trade unions varied. Some of them embraced the radical socialist, anarchist, and communist ideas current in Europe, particularly in Paris at the time, and brought them to the United States. Among his confreres at least, Samuel Gompers, a member of a cigar-makers' trade union in New York City, for instance, endorsed the ideas of Karl Marx. However, rather than attempting to overthrow the capitalist system by revolution, as Marx advocated, Gompers sought to work within that system to improve the everyday lives of workers, by stressing bread and butter issues.[13] Some individuals entered political life. For example, in 1877, H. J. Walls, secretary of the molders' national union, became the first commissioner of the Ohio Bureau of Labor and Statistics. This position allowed Walls to work for improvement through conventional channels. Generally, the tenor of trade unions' actions followed this track: whether moderate or radical, the trades sought to improve the well-being of laborers by working within the capitalistic system rather than seeking to replace it. In terms of free expression, this included the establishment of such conventional media as newspapers and speaking societies to advance craft causes. Further, for the most part, the rhetorical discourse associated with these media sought not to foment rebellion, but to cement fraternal relationships among trade members and fellow unions.

Perhaps the most significant development in labor history from 1877 to 1910 was the rise of mass national unionism, that is, the call for one union for all workers. From 1866 to 1872 the National Labor Union held a yearly congress. But as the panic of 1873 swept over the country and opened a six-year period of industrial distress, employers took steps against workers and stalled the national movement. Though wage reductions were followed by prolonged and desperate strikes, black lists and prosecutions intimidated labor leaders into submission. Under the onslaught of capital, this first attempt at nationalism failed. The failure induced the leaders of the four big national craft unions—the iron molders, machinists, coopers, and typographers—to attempt to nationalize along new lines.

Consequently, in 1879, the Knights of Labor succeeded in secretly organizing working people to combat the forces of capital in the industrial arena. The Knights, originally founded in 1869, had a national emphasis. The union admitted both skilled and unskilled workers, excluding only lawyers, managers, and owners. It was dedicated to reform of the capitalistic system through collective ownership of industry and an egalitarian improvement of the status of all laboring people, regardless of race, gender, education or level of skill. During their three-decade existence, the Knights modified their objectives and their membership. However, the union's advocacy of labor solidarity and its idealistic agenda remained permanent characteristics. In contrast to the exclusiveness of the existing craft unions, the Knights' appeal was far-reaching, embodied in its motto, "An injury to one is the concern of all."[14]

The primary rhetorical vehicles of the Knights of Labor were newspapers, marches, strikes, boycotts, speech making, and journals. The Knights held frequent conventions during which leaders would make speeches and issue statements of purpose. In 1884, the Knights began lobbying in state capitals and in Washington, D.C. to advance their demands.[15] At that time, they were a growing organization of more than 70,000 members. They frequently engaged in strikes, which, although contrary to the principles of his Order and the wishes of its general officers, were nevertheless acknowledged by Powderly as aiding the movement's growth.

During the early 1880s, when the Knights were in their ascendancy, a small number of independent national trade unions composed of skilled workers continued to operate independently. In 1881, these formed into a loosely knit organization called the Federation of Organized Trades and Labor Unions of the United States and Canada, a forerunner of the American Federation of Labor (AF of L), which Samuel Gompers organized in 1886. The AF of L quickly became a competitor with the Knights for worker association. The AF of L evolved into a decentralized federation of craft unions with almost 300,000 members by 1898, and more than a million by 1914 despite the fact that it only enlisted skilled workers. The AF of L looked to the immediate betterment of skilled unionists' conditions under the wage system, rather than to the far-reaching reforms of the capitalist system envisaged by the Knights. One measure of its success is the fact that the AF of L has existed continuously since 1886, and today still exercises, after merger with the Congress of Industrial Organizations (CIO), a steady influence on the ideology and practice of organized labor in the United States.[16]

The most radical union organizations that emerged in the last quarter of the nineteenth century were the anarchists and socialists.[17] Their vanguard was composed of artisans and craft-persons, the majority of them newly emigrated from Europe. They tended to concentrate in large cities like Chicago and New York, where the great industrial plants were located. The two principal political organs were the Socialist Labor Party and the anarchistic International Working People's Party. Because of their radical methods and ideas, the anarchists represented the strongest post–Civil War rejection of a developing, large-scale industry, which embodied the mechanization of labor. Along with the socialists, they generally favored direct, confrontational action rather than political machination as a means of expression. They engaged in elaborate public ceremonies, demonstrations, and protest marches.

However, like their antagonists, they also advocated extra-rhetorical means to accomplish their ends. Most incendiary was the anarchists' martial element, which organized paramilitary groups and openly advocated the use of guns and dynamite for its causes.[18] On the eve of the Haymarket Riot of May 4, 1886, the anarchists became dedicated to the "propaganda of the Deed": the overthrow of the capitalistic system by sabotage if necessary. They would pay dearly for this position. When anarchist's bomb killed seven Chicago policemen at Haymarket Square, it brought on the first major Red Scare in American history, and with it, massive labor suppression.

While the anarchist movement after Haymarket was, for the most part, quelled, it resulted in the assassination of President McKinley in 1901, and reemerged during World War I (see chapter 7). In the meantime, a new organization cutting across craft and trade lines came to the fore; it was called the Industrial Workers of the World (IWW), a revolutionary industrial union organized in Chicago in 1905 by delegates from the Western Federation of Miners. These delegates and representatives of 42 other labor organizations formed the nucleus of the IWW. Leaders of the IWW were forceful, often violent characters. They employed Marxist rhetoric and endorsed civil disobedience and sabotage.[19] They made free speech a major issue of their various platforms until 1913 when they shifted their focus to union building.

The leaders included the "gentleman from Terre Haute," Eugene V. Debs, who would eventually run for president on the Socialist ticket (see chapter 7), William "Big Bill" Haywood, an imposing man who did not hesitate to beat in the head of anyone who opposed him, and Daniel DeLeon, a Venezuelan with a flamboyant reputation who claimed to be a direct descendant of the explorer, Ponce De Leon. Its members were called, among other appellations, the "Wobblies." The organization was especially strong in the lumber

camps of the Northwest, in the docks of port cities, in the wheat fields of
the central states, and in textile and mining areas. The aim of the IWW
was to unite all skilled and unskilled workers into one body for the purpose
of overthrowing capitalism and rebuilding society on a socialistic basis. Its
revolutionary credo was "Complete surrender of industry to the organized
workers."[20] The IWW became the chief United States' representative of the
doctrine of syndicalism, a political and economic doctrine that sought control
of the means of production by organized bodies of workers. Its methods were
direct action and propaganda, very much like those of the anarchists, with
whom they were associated. However, the IWW stopped short of sabotage.
Its stand against political action led to controversy among its members, with
DeLeon emphasizing direct intervention. He and his followers were expelled
in 1908, a proceeding that weakened the IWW but confirmed its position
against violence. Nonetheless, the IWW was involved in a series of protests
illustrating that the clash between business and labor was essentially a clash
between free expression and assembly for unions and freedom of contract and
business for industry. It culminated in the protests lodged by the IWW in
the first decade of the twentieth century. At that juncture, the "free speech
fight" became the special trademark of the Wobblies. While they won little
in terms of actual concessions from business and government during their
15-year existence, they made the "free speech fight" a dominant factor in
the labor movement. In order to challenge all forms of institutional First
Amendment suppression, members were willingly arrested, beaten, jailed,
and harassed.[21]

The common denominator among all of these worker organizations was
a preoccupation with asserting certain remedies and reforms through various
speech and assembly activities allowed under the First Amendment. The
persistent variable among them was the issue of whether that assertion should
take the form of a quest for moderate solutions effected through compromise
within the political process, or take the form of alien and socialistic programs
challenging the very existence of the post–Civil War industrial order.

The Voices of Unionism

Workers struck, picketed, published newsletters, pamphlets and notices of
boycotts, marched, printed placards, lectured, debated, elaborately celebrated
labor victories, and sang. Through these rhetorical activities, worker status
was advanced, as powerful labor agencies and reform laws were passed.
The Interstate Commerce Act of 1887 ushered in the federal regulation of
railroads, the provision for an Interstate Commerce Commission, and the

establishment of the Bureau of Labor in the Department of the Interior. The effective functioning of such agencies called for the zealous and dedicated services of a new, charismatic type of public servant devoted to labor reform. These public figures were able to focus wide public attention on labor causes, and included such persons as Carroll D. Wright, the first Commissioner of Labor, appointed in 1885, Edward Moseley, the first secretary of the Interstate Commerce Commission, and Henry C. Adams, academic economist and chief statistician of that commission.[22] In addition, many measures that would eventually come to fruition during the Progressive Era—the income tax, restrictions of immigration, the initiative and referendum, compulsory school attendance of children up to the age of 15, free school textbooks, and child labor laws—had their origin in the agitation by union organizations during the last quarter of the nineteenth century.

However, these gains emerged from a long arduous struggle that can be interpreted as essentially a free speech, militant, and legal battle between labor on one side, and business and government on the other. This contentious relationship came about largely through government's conflicted attitude toward labor and business. When labor found it necessary to agitate for certain policies, laws, and changes, government was enrolled to act as an arbiter. The government was, therefore, the entity charged with balancing business's claim to be protected in its inherent rights to pursue wealth with labor's First Amendment demands that certain policies, laws, and changes be enacted.

The Response of Big Capital

Feeling the onslaught of labor protest, business sought to protect what it believed to be its right to operate without interference, and appealed to the government for protection and assistance to quell labor uprisings. Generally, the government chose the side of business. In many cases, this was to be expected, since many government leaders had strong business connections, backing, and experience. President Cleveland's Attorney General Richard Olney had been a railway executive, and used the labor injunction to end a strike by the American Railway Union in 1894. In scores of labor disputes, local police and sheriffs deputized company employees, who thus became officers of the law. In many such cases, the deputized company employees continued to be paid by the companies. As John Roche observes, "this practice merely institutionalized the convergence of business and government interests during the 1873–1937 period."[23] Thus, government was biased toward business. Particularly when labor seemed to threaten the capitalist system with rhetoric and action that was incendiary or anarchic, government responded forcefully to maintain or restore a capitalist status quo. In quieting labor, the government used various techniques to suppress the First Amendment rights of worker organizations.

The specific dynamics of suppression were these. First, government would respond with martial suppression to particular labor uprisings. The response would be relatively indiscriminate: martial force was often imposed whether the uprisings were violent or not, based simply upon the perception by the government that any stand by labor was bound to be radical and dangerous. When these uprisings were violent and incendiary, a characteristic usually sparked by anarchist rhetoric, then martial suppression would occur with particular force. A prime example of such an uprising is the Haymarket Riot of 1886. Violent uprisings such as Haymarket, indeed any uprisings for which martial force was called, were seen as an internal threat and served as precedents to legitimate more suppression. Thus, the impact of martial suppression was cumulative and self-justified.

The second form of government suppression of labor's First Amendment rights was administrative: that is, the legal system, including local, state, and federal legislative, executive, and judicial bodies would avail themselves of laws that further prohibited First Amendment activity. Usually, administrative suppression occurred subsequent to violent clashes between labor and government. For example, legislative bodies would invoke, pass, or strengthen laws that could prevent future violent clashes and the courts would issue orders enforcing these laws. The extreme nature of the Haymarket Riot justified further legislative suppression. After this affair, conspiracy laws were strengthened. Administrative suppression was used especially against radically inspired union uprisings and protest. But no violent tendency need necessarily have been present for administrative suppression to occur; it was used indiscriminately against unions regardless of their temperament.

As I show in the following sections, the principle federal acts and laws used against labor were the statute against conspiracy, the Interstate Commerce Law, the Sherman Anti-Trust Act, and criminal syndicalist laws. State legislatures followed the federal government's lead, passing their own measures using federal laws as examples. Or, as sometimes happened, the federal government would follow a state's example when it proved effective.

The courts, too, had their own arsenal of suppressive measures. These measures included issuing arrest warrants, contempt of court citations, and holding hearings in front of a judge where a union advocate did not have to be present. The major judicial technique of suppression, however, was the court injunction, which came into widespread use after the Pullman Strike of 1894.

Martial Suppression

From 1877 to 1910, martial suppression followed a consistent pattern. It would begin at a strike location where the challenge posed to capital was perceived as threatening. This suppressive action was itself often aggressive and violent even when the strikers were not. This tactic unfairly reinforced the perception of the labor movement as violent, leading to more suppression. Typically, the local police or sheriff's department would respond first using martial force. For example, in 1897 sheriff's deputies fired on unarmed striking miners near Hazelton, Pennsylvania; they killed 21 and wounded 40 others.[24]

If local enforcement authorities proved insufficient in quelling violence, officials of the state and federal government would be called on, and the situation would escalate. Strikers, their wives and children were frequently fired on. While exact figures of workers arrested, beaten, or killed by authorities do not exist, hundreds of accounts describe the violence. John A. Fitch, a historian and associate editor of the *Survey*, reported retrospectively in an open letter of 1914 to Labor Commissioner John Williams, "I found large numbers of special policemen and deputy sheriffs patrolling the streets in the neighborhood where the working people live. . . . They walk about in groups, carrying clubs in their hands, and their attitude toward strikers and strangers upon the streets is constantly menacing and evidently designed to discriminate."[25] Further reports by actual participants in the violent clashes between workers and authorities are far less understated and record outright attacks on workers and their families. "The law," Albert Parsons, a leading anarchist would exclaim in the context of the Haymarket affair, "protected only the rich, leaving the poor defenseless. The police clubbed and beat unarmed strikers, shot them down in the streets, even shot at their women and children with impunity. How long was this to be tolerated?"[26] As in other movements, labor used these incidents to justify reform and more militant responses to the government.

In fact, acts of intimidation marked the whole period from 1877 to 1910. The Railway Strike of 1877 was the first violent clash between capital and labor, and the first major suppression of labor by federal troops since Andrew Jackson's administration. The roots of violence began on July 16 when the Baltimore and Ohio Railroad instituted a 10 percent wage cut. State troops were sent to Buffalo and Rochester in advance of a threatened strike on the Erie Railroad. Nonetheless, a nonviolent strike spread throughout the country. Its nationwide scope was unprecedented, and posed a serious threat to the interests of capital. In New York, police and militia suppressed the strike by killing 12 workers. In response, President Rutherford B. Hayes became the first president after the Civil War to call up federal troops to quell an insurrection.[27] Thus, one of the earliest attempts to unionize the railroads on a national scale failed.

Throughout the years, authorities practiced intimidation in much the same manner as in New York in 1877. For example, in 1891, state militia in Pennsylvania fired on coke strikers who, far from instigating violent action, were fleeing from the militia. Ten workers were killed, and 50 were wounded. Andrew Carnegie used Pinkerton detectives to help quash the great Homestead Strike against his steel company in 1892.[28] When that failed, he demanded government intervention; he got his wish and the AF of L backed down. When the American Railway Union led by Eugene Debs struck against the Pullman Company in 1894, the government was there in the form of troops: ultimately, the Railway Union lost the battle. During extremely serious strikes that occurred when the nation was at war with Spain or when state troops were already committed, federal troops intervened to quell labor disturbances. This happened during the 1899 Coeur d'Alene, Idaho coal strike and in 1902 when the United Mine Workers led the Anthracite coal strike.[29]

Other techniques that authorities used clearly violated the First Amendment right to assembly. The least noxious of these tactics was to disperse strikers or bar them from meeting. More ominous and effective was the use of massive and indiscriminate arrest of striking and strike sympathizers. For example, when the anarchist-influenced United Mine Workers struck at Coeur d'Alene in 1892 and again in 1899, federal troops made mass arrests. This intervention may well have been justified in that serious violence by workers had occurred. However, instead of merely reestablishing peace in the area, the troops imposed martial law to stymie the strikers' cause. They jailed hundreds of men in make-shift bull pens, and literally barred union men from reemployment in the mines, drawing on the unemployed in the area. Frequently, arrests of workers were made for much less aggressive and constitutionally guaranteed activity. Goldstein observes that this was particularly true in the immediate wake of Haymarket; workers were arrested for simply picketing, or on charges such as "intimidation," "inciting to riot," "obstructing the streets" and "trespass."[30] Anarchist-inspired unions were liable to suppression even if their activities were not "radical." With government employing such broad and ambiguous standards, however, members of less radical unions were arrested as well.

As we have seen, in most cases disturbances of some nature occurred before the introduction of state and federal troops; however, in several instances force was sent to strike locations that had experienced no disturbances or had suffered only disorders of a trivial nature. Almost invariably, the result of such action was to intimidate the workers into calling off a strike. For example, when one of the earliest miners' unions attempted to organize in Leadville, Colorado, in 1880, the most serious disorder occurred when a deputy sheriff opened fire on a group of strikers and injured three of them. When strikers were not intimidated by a vigilante citizens' organization that was supplied with guns and ammunition by the state governor, state troops were sent in and martial law was declared. The strike ended within two days. As Paul Bechtol observes, "the fledgling union could not survive the appearance of the state militia."[31]

Also in 1880, state militia was sent and federal troops were alerted during a strike at the nation's largest smelting works in Omaha, Nebraska. Though there had been no work disruption during the strike, troops were sent at the request of the plant managers without consultation with workers, and with local officials' approval. The strike quickly collapsed. Although little serious violence appears to have occurred, Louisiana state militia broke a strike of sugar workers in 1880 by arresting strike leaders. In 1882, both federal and state troops were sent again to Omaha after a second smelting strike by railroad workers resulted in minor violence. Although the only casualty in the strike occurred when a soldier bayoneted and killed a man who tried to cross military lines, a number of strike leaders were arrested for "assault with intent to kill" because of fights that broke out among picketers. This strike also collapsed.[32]

Cumulatively, this violence directed against labor by martial forces functioned to impede First Amendment activity that would lead to organizing workers. In responding to violent behavior on the part of workers, or more often to the threat against capital by even nonviolent strike activity, martial forces undercut workers' First Amendment rights by dispersing, arresting, beating, even killing strikers and their supporters.

Secondary effects of these tactics included breeding the perception that labor was violent, provoking fear among the public in general, and thereby, providing a rationale for further martial acts. One sees this fear in a letter of July 24, 1877, by John Hay, soon to become assistant secretary of state. During the high point of the Great Railway Strike, he wrote in alarm to his wealthy father-in-law: "Any hour the mob chooses it can destroy any city in the country— that is the simple truth."[33] No wonder the government sat ready to act with force against labor.

The Haymarket Riot

Among instances of martial suppression between 1877 and 1910, the Chicago Haymarket Affair of May 1886 stands out with particular vividness. Like many conflicts, it took place within the context of increasing worker dissatisfaction and agitation in a major industrial city during a national depression. Like other such conflicts, it was composed of endemic clashes between police

and workers that led up to one cataclysmic clash. Since it was typical of
the conflict between government and worker organizations and justified later
armed action, I want to examine it in more detail at this juncture.

At Haymarket Square, the AF of L, the Knights of Labor and the
crafts were allied in fraternal spirit with anarchists. This meant that the
government, ever sensitive to extreme, anarchistic rhetoric, was inclined
to respond with especially repressive martial force. And the effects of this
incident, both in the short and long term, were extreme for the labor movement in general and for the anarchist movement in particular. This surge of
national anti-anarchist feeling spilled over to more mainstream labor unions
with less violent tendencies. The result was that bread and butter labor issues
suffered. Overall, an upsurge in popular condemnation of labor as a whole
took place, legitimating and furthering widespread legislative forms of suppression of labor First Amendment rights.

Several significant events led up to the Chicago riots in Haymarket
Square, which culminated in the bombing of May 4. The principle conces-
sion for which the workers were agitating was the eight-hour workday. The
AF of L and the Knights of Labor supported this cause although it was the
anarchists who led the strike. From February 1886, conflicts between workers
and police centered on a lockout and strike at the McCormick Harvester
factory, one of the nation's largest manufacturers of farm equipment. During
the months of the strike, the police on horseback had regularly attacked with
clubs gatherings of workers and strikers. They had done so at the behest
of McCormick executives; one witness recounted that "the Chicago police
force responded by operating as though it were a private police force in the
services of the employer."[34]

By early May the situation in Chicago was extremely tense, and it was
not just police and the forces of capital that were acting provocatively. In print
and speech, anarchists, whose violent rhetoric had inflamed worker passions in
Chicago for 10 years prior to 1886, were calling for a decisive confrontation
with capitalists. Referring to the coming revolution, the anarchist newspaper
Alarm incited its readers to realize that "Gunpowder brought the world some
liberty, and dynamite will bring the world much more. . . ."[35] Anarchists in
other cities joined in the agitation. As the *Nemesis* of Baltimore put it, "The
discovery of gunpowder overthrew feudalism. Chemistry will liberate the
laborer from modern wage-serfdom. . . . Dynamite is the emancipator! In the
hands of the enslaved it cries aloud: 'Justice or—annihilation!' "[36]

On May 3 Chicago police fired on a crowd of McCormick strikers who
had attacked strikebreakers leaving the plant. On the evening of May 4, the
International Working People's Association, the chief anarchist organization
representing workers, sponsored a meeting to protest police brutality. This
meeting, to be held at the Haymarket Square, was to be peaceful, despite an

English anarchist who had begun inciting a mob of about 1,000 strikers to violence. Just as the meeting was adjourning, 180 police, led by the notoriously violent Captain Bonfield, appeared and demanded that the few hundred people still in attendance immediately disperse. Suddenly a person whose identity has never been conclusively determined threw a bomb into police ranks. The police began to shoot indiscriminately into the crowd. Mayhem ensued, and the casualties from the bomb and the shooting amounted to seven police killed and about 70 wounded, and an undetermined number of civilian dead and wounded.[37]

A wave of anti-anarchist hysteria convulsed the country. In Chicago particularly, as both the mainstream and radical presses drew constant attention to the violence, the police began a reign of terror consisting of raids and mass arrests. On May 7, without a warrant, Chicago police arrested about 150 persons; they were held for hours without charges being issued. Police shut down the *Alarm* for three days allowing it to publish again only on the understanding that it would be closed if it carried articles deemed inflammatory by government authorities.

The protests spread to other cities. As Goldstein notes, "[I]n New York, police attacked a peaceful crowd of about ten thousand with clubs during a June, 1886, street car strike; in September, 1886 they assaulted a reception held in honor of arriving German socialists; and, within a two-month period arrested one hundred strikers and boycotters for 'conspiracy.' "[38] Judges and juries who were "swept along by the panic and outrage following the Haymarket Square riot" sentenced more than 20 workers in New York City to jail terms for boycott activity.[39]

Subsequent to the bombing at Haymarket, eight anarchists were found guilty of murder and sentenced to hang. The verdict against the men was rendered in the absence of credible evidence linking these persons to the act of bombing the policemen. Four men were actually hung, one committed suicide in prison, and the remaining three were pardoned by Governor John Altgeld, who was then widely denounced as an abettor of anarchy.[40]

The Haymarket Riot provoked long-term consequences not only for anarchists but for the labor movement as a whole. For months and years, the press was filled with imprecations damning labor unions, particularly anarchistic unions, with the stain of violence. Anarchists were stereotyped as "ragged, unwashed, long-haired, wild-eyed fiend[s], armed with smoking revolver[s] and bomb[s]."[41] Soon anti-labor legislation began to make its way through state legislatures. Many states strengthened the application of common law doctrines of conspiracy to labor disputes, and many participants in strikes and boycotts were convicted of conspiracy, especially during 1886 and 1887.[42] In uprisings subsequent to Haymarket, the authorities frequently took steps particularly prohibitive against labor organizers, agitators, and their meetings. Speech against the government, particularly of a more violent brand, was less tolerated after Haymarket.

In 1902 and 1903, federal and state anti-anarchist laws were strengthened in reaction to the assassination of President McKinley in September 1901. Using these laws, the government extinguished the reputedly anarchist-influenced Western Federation of Miners in the period from 1903 to 1907. New Jersey had a peace-time sedition law in 1908 and enforced it several times against labor organizers before World War I.[43] Like the Alien and Sedition Acts of 1798, these laws went beyond outlawing specific actions to criminalizing opinions, speech, and associations. The recession of 1907–1911 combined with a huge influx of immigrants deepened the anarchist scare, producing a federal campaign to deport alien anarchists (though almost none could be found). In addition the post office refused, without any legal authority, to handle two anarchist newspapers. This refusal amounted to press suppression since no other means of wide distribution was available. So devastating and complete were these First Amendment suppressions that during the period from 1907 to 1911, no major strike was won by a union. The drought was broken when the International Workers of the World won the Lawrence, Massachusetts strike in 1912.[44] But even this was a short-lived victory for no other major strike was won by a union in America until the eve of World War I.

As a result of the suppression flowing from the Haymarket incident, labor was forced to relinquish many of its established tactics and lost ground. In the last years of the 1880s, strike activity was reduced drastically. In addition, the Illinois Bureau of Labor statistics reported that the bomb "abruptly ended" the eight-hour workday movement; the Bureau explained that "Men who would have ventured far on behalf of the principle . . . shrank from any assertion of that principle because to do so could hardly fail to involve misinterpretation."[45] In other words, for a union—any union—to advocate the eight-hour day, and to strike, especially during periods of less severe economic distress, was to present a clear and present danger to the nation.

Haymarket had a long-term impact on labor politics. Mass national unions were persuaded to avoid radical policies. The American labor movement moved to the political mainstream. According to Goldstein, the major lesson for the national unions such as the AF of L, which were just beginning in 1886 to organize workers on a national scale, was probably that the affiliation with a radical union might well lead to jailing or even hanging, regardless of whether union members had connection with violent disorders. Revolted by the violence that issued from both the workers and the authorities, Powderly's Knights of Labor also "worked to keep radicals and workers separated in the public mind, by issuing strong denunciations of anarchism."[46] The Knights and the AF of L concluded that if the American community's hostility to social movements was so keen that a belief in anarchism could be punishable by death, it was safest for members to eschew any extremist organization.

In terms of the practical sense of politics, government suppression may have kept Gompers from forwarding the AF of L's positions on an independent political basis. To be an independent political force was acceptable only if one were a capitalist. Gould, Carnegie, and Rockefeller all testify to the possibilities of independent action in the post Civil War era. If one were not a capitalist, and happened also to be a voice of labor, one risked being perceived as radical to be separated from the party system. Thus, Gompers kept the AF of L inside the Democratic party. He had already studied the Populist Party and believed that its confrontational style violated acceptable political and rhetorical boundaries. He was not inclined to alienate the AF of L from the Democratic party, the political body that held the best chance of forwarding the AF of L's political and social goals. Gompers' political decisions were driven, in part, by his fear of the radical stain of Haymarket.

As far as the labor movement as a whole is concerned, "the net impact of public reaction to Haymarket . . . was to . . . set back the labor movement in general for about ten to fifteen years."[47] Haymarket interrupted the eight-hour workday movement; it led to legislative prohibition of speech and assembly, and turned labor away from radical doctrines and toward more cautious politics. In the early portion of the twentieth century, the state and federal government added new weapons to their arsenal of suppressive laws: new ways of controlling and stigmatizing dissent offered by the unions, and new laws to control the radicalism with which labor unions associated themselves.

Administrative Suppression

While the Haymarket bombing gave government an excuse to pass new anti-labor legislation, such legislation generally transcended Haymarket. Among the federal laws often used against labor in the period from 1877 to 1910 were sedition and conspiracy laws, and the Interstate Commerce Law, passed in 1881. The most potent federal law used to suppress labor speech and assembly was the Sherman Anti-Trust Act of July 2, 1890. The judicial procedure that most powerfully enforced these laws was the labor injunction, which was used with greater frequency after the Pullman Strike of 1894. Ultimately, the 1907 fight between Samuel Gompers (representing the AF of L) and the Buck Stove and Range Company culminated in a momentous decision in 1908 by Judge Gould in federal court; his judgment against Gompers solidified a pro-business and anti-free expression bias against unions.

Even before the Civil War the legal system suppressed union activity on the grounds that unions constituted criminal conspiracies to destroy businesses. The government believed conspiracies could lead to the destruction of lawful free enterprise, particularly of small businesses. It accepted some strikes as legal in principle but also treated the activities connected with them, such as boycotts, meetings, and publications, as criminal conspiracies. After the Civil War, criminal prosecutions against unions for conspiracies surged.[48] In short, the government reverted to its antebellum policy.

The use of decisions made subsequent to the Great Railway Strike of 1877 provides a case in point. The courts revived the doctrine of conspiracy as applied to labor combinations; subsequently, new conspiracy laws were enacted by many state legislatures.[49] These laws were applied in 1894, when a New Jersey court ruled in *Barr v. Essex Trades Council* that a strike, picketing, or boycott by employees constituted an unlawful conspiracy.[50] In the early twentieth century, many courts agreed on labor's "general right" to strike but declared many strikes illegal because of "the increase of power which a combination of citizens had over the individual citizen," as the Massachusetts Supreme Court held in 1906.[51]

While union activity was always liable to suppression by the use of criminal conspiracy laws, by far the biggest administrative blow to union activity came in 1890, when Congress enacted the Sherman Antitrust Act. No House member and only one Senator voted against the Act.[52] Section I of the Sherman Act states that "Every contract, combination in the form of trust, or otherwise, or conspiracy in restraint of trade or commerce among the several States, or with foreign nations, is hereby declared to be illegal."[53] Although this act originally was passed to reduce the power of large business combinations that were found to be restraining interstate commerce, it quickly became a tool to hinder the labor unions from organizing and carrying out First Amendment activities of all kinds that were directed against businesses.

Federal acts, however, had no teeth without court orders. And, of all the anti-labor legal weapons, perhaps none so vividly illustrated the direct hostility of the government to union First Amendment activities than did the labor injunction. Simply defined, the labor injunction is a judicial order that could command an individual or a union to refrain from a strike, boycott, march, picket, the publication of a flyer, or any other speech and assembly activity which the court considers injurious to the property rights of the employer. Temporary injunctions were customarily issued by judges on the request of company attorneys without notice or hearing for the union and threatening violators with immediate arrest. Generally, these orders were sufficient to break strikes. If the strike continued, permanent injunctions could be issued. Between 1880 and 1930, federal and state courts issued a total of 1,845 strike injunctions against labor unions.[54]

Injunctions were often designed specifically to prohibit speech, print, and assembly activities in order to discourage union agitation. According to Goldstein, "Usually an injunction prohibited such activities as the use of coercion and intimidation by workers, prevented or regulated picketing, and barred boycotts, trespassing, the use of the word 'scab' and the payment of strike benefits."[55] Occasionally they incorporated such absurdities as barring striking clothing workers in New York City from "standing in the street within ten blocks . . . of the plaintiff's business," although this area was the center of the New York City clothing industry and included the strikers' headquarters.[56]

Though employed regularly during the uprisings of the Great Railway Strike of 1877, the labor injunction developed as the government's most effective tool of administrative suppression of First Amendment activity during the Pullman Strike of 1894. In that strike Eugene Debs, the leader of the American Railway Union, attempted to establish industrial union-ism on the nation's railroads by leading a boycott and strike against the Chicago-based Pullman Company, America's leading producer of railway cars. For his efforts, Debs was enjoined from continuing the boycott with an injunction obtained by the United States government. The government alleged that the boycott of the Pullman Company would hinder the nation's rail service, a clear violation of Interstate Commerce Act and an unlawful interruption of mail service.[57]

From the beginning of the strike, the railroad's General Managers' Association sought to involve the federal government in breaking the strike. Support for the policy came from President Grover Cleveland's Attorney General Richard Olney, as we have seen, a former corporation attorney with close ties to the railroads. The strategy adopted by Olney was to blanket the country with injunctions. Although technically not outlawing the strike, the injunctions barred the American Railway Union from taking any action to further the strike, including peaceful persuasion of workers to cease work. Almont Lindsay, the leading historian of the Pullman strike, claims the injunctions "were so sweeping and all inclusive that the union leaders could not move without running afoul of it. The purpose of the [injunction] was designed not so much to protect property as to crush the strike."[58] Debs aborted the strike after three months proving that the government's injunc-tion was an effective tool that squelched First Amendment activities. The technique effectively crushed the first effort by a union to establish mass unionism on the nation's railroads.

After tasting success in Pullman, the government used the injunction tool frequently in the following years. All types of unions suffered. But, because the injunction was most often directed against boycott activity, the AF of L, which favored the boycott, suffered most severely. The courts gener-ally ruled that boycotts, including the secondary or the combined sort, were illegal as was publishing them. Boycotters often countered by contending that to prevent them from boycotting and publishing notices of boycotts, or otherwise announcing them in print, was an infringement of freedom of the press and speech; for the most part, however, the courts held the free speech argument was without merit. They did so by contending that no right was absolute, and that the law could and should interfere when unbridled exercise of the right infringed on the equal rights of others, and deprived others of such rights as acquiring, possessing, and protecting property.

Judge Robb of the Appellate Court of the District of Columbia articulated this principle amid Gompers' attempt to boycott the Buck Stove and Range Company in 1907:

> "While the right of free speech is guaranteed to all citizens of the Constitution," holds a California judge (*Jordahl v. Hayda, Cal., 1905*), there is also guaranteed to them by the same Constitution the rights "of acquiring, possessing and protecting property and obtaining safety and happiness" (see Art. 1, Sec. 1) . . . and it is a maxim of jurisprudence prescribed by the statute law of this state that one must use his rights so as not to infringe upon the rights of another.[59]

Robb delineated specifically what free speech and assembly activities would be prohibited. He enjoined "each of their [union's] agents, servants, attorneys, confederates, and any and all persons active in aid or conjunction with any of them," and enjoined them as officials, or as individuals from "conspiring, agreeing, or combining in any manner to restrain or destroy the business of the company or its agents." This meant that the union was restrained from carrying on a host of constitutionally guaranteed First Amendment freedoms. It was prohibited, for example, from publishing in its newspaper the company's name in the "We Don't Patronize" or "unfair" list, or from calling attention to the existence of a boycott.[60] The legal outcome was an unquestioned victory for industry.

When the court had so clearly supported the side of business, Gompers recognized the decision's broad impact in terms of free speech and press, and countered by angrily defending the union's First Amendment rights. He pointed to dangers inherent in the decision: "This injunction is the most sweeping ever issued," he wrote in the *Federationist*, which was now enjoined from furthering the boycott, "It is an invasion of the liberty of the Press and the Right of free speech" for all. This was not an issue that concerned labor alone, he said, for "Tomorrow it may be another publication or some other class of equally law-abiding citizens, and the present injunction may then be quoted as a sacred precedent for future encroachments upon the liberties of the people."[61]

Labor leaders backed Gompers in his defiance of the injunction. They were threatened by what they called "a new form of judicial tyranny," through which all union activity against property might be broken via injunction. When Gompers violated the injunction, he and two others were sentenced to a year in prison by Judge Gould. Gompers was punished for contempt of court, an action that did not call for trial by jury but merely the hearing of a judge. Gompers never served his term, but Gould's decision convinced him that the courts were interested not only in quelling particular union activity against industry, but were against the very existence of unions. This understanding led him to challenge the use of injunctions by conducting more boycotts. In the twentieth-century's first decade, AF of L affiliates conducted several hundred boycotts and faced almost as many court injunctions. Preoccupation with obtaining injunction relief from Congress became the AF of L's main political objective.

Injunctions issued by the courts, sanctioned by the Conspiracy Act, Interstate Commerce Act, and/or Sherman Anti-Trust Act, were a major deterrent to union First Amendment activity, particularly after the 1880s. With this potent writ, a judge could almost entirely impede unions from exercising First Amendment activities of press, speech and assembly; by doing so, courts could stop activities crucial to carrying on the labor movement.[62] In short, while claiming to "balance" employers' right to hold property and the union advocates' right to speak, print, and assemble against holders of property, the courts usually acted against labor. While the AF of L was dramatically affected by the use of injunction, other forms of national unionism were also attacked. For example, in 1908 when the Wobblies began fomenting their "Free Speech fights," they immediately faced all forms of institutional suppression of free expression. Although the Wobblies engaged in an effective demonstration of the unions' ideology and its opposition to suppression of First Amendment rights, as far as the injunction order was concerned, it was not until 1931 when Congress passed the Norris-La Guardia Act, that the government established a provision to protect some "legitimate" activities of labor from injunctions. Regarded as a "new Magna Carta" for labor, the Norris-La Guardia Act (also known as the Federal Anti-Injunction Act) provided provisions broad enough to start labor on the road toward injunction emancipation, and introduced a new era of government/labor relations.[63]

Conclusion

This era of development of the unions ends in 1910, a particularly difficult year for them because they became tainted by a bomb blast that killed 21 people. It happened on October 1 at the Los Angeles Times building and was eventually traced to J. J. McNamara, of the Ironworkers Union. He and two co-conspirators were represented in court by Clarence Darrow and in the public arena by Gompers, who claimed the charges were trumped up. Darrow's behavior during the trial came under serious newspaper and prosecutorial scrutiny because he fed the press fabricated evidence, induced false testimony, and may have arranged to bribe a juror or two. When Darrow was caught in one of these payoffs, McNamara and his allies pleaded guilty to the charges against them, and Darrow then had to face his own trial for jury tampering. Darrow's emotional and tearful summation saved him from condemnation but not the unions.

During the period from 1877 to 1910, the government, whether city, state, or federal, interfered often, and rarely proved itself impartial toward worker organizations. Furthermore, a violent public image of labor unions, provoked ironically in large part by aggressive government suppression, turned popular sympathies against labor, legitimated anti-labor legislation, and turned the tide of the labor movement's major mass unions from socialism toward political moderation. The violence itself undermined and even eliminated union leadership and membership, and retarded labor momentum. Administrative suppression was able to restrict First Amendment rights of speech, press, and assembly, and thus to curtail crucial union activities. Overall, the labor movement's agenda was diluted and, though many of its causes were adopted and furthered by other political organizations, labor itself was undermined as a coherent force in American society for many years.

In protecting the principles of private property and freedom of contract, the government, almost without exception, sent its police, sheriffs, militia, and federal troops to crush union speech, print, and assembly activity. The courts sustained this dispatch of the government's forces by allowing the arrest of workers on charges such as vagrancy, conspiracy, contempt of court, riot, and rebellion. Legislation frequently operated against labor; even the Sherman Anti-Trust Act, ostensibly enacted to curb the monopolistic tendencies of industry and commerce, was used to justify the labor injunction at the time of the Pullman Strike.

First Amendment suppressions by the government are a distinct feature of labor history from 1871 to 1910. The government perceived labor as a threat to capital. As a result, government techniques of suppression were immediate, direct, and cumulative. Given the evidence, the post–Civil War alliance between government and business leaders constituted no less than an attack on union speech, press, and assembly. Worker organizations learned that the use of rhetorical discourse to dissent, deliberate, or act against the state's interest in protecting business would lead to suppression. Yet, despite all the killings, beatings, arrests, laws, and court orders, the labor movement never stopped its speeches, marches, boycotts, banners, books, pamphlets, lectures, debates, or rallies. The tenacity of labor is best represented by the last words of August Spies, a radical anarchist sentenced to hang for the bombing at Haymarket. "The time will come," he predicted on the scaffold, "when our silence will be more powerful than the voices you strangle today!"[64] Communication may have been suppressed, but the ideas of the movement lived on. Sometimes ideas were taken over by other political arms of the labor movement. Sometimes the nature of the movement itself changed, as when the AF of L became more moderate in the aftermath of anarchist suppression.

Consistently, however, unions established and then increased the tension between communal needs of workers and the production interests of business. They tried to correct business practices that they believed were exploiting workers by seeking First Amendment protections, which were violated by the government and denied by the courts. Their battle was a long one which was not completely won until after World War II.

Notes

1. For a closer look at the rhetorical tactics of the Social Darwinists, see Craig R. Smith, *Freedom of Expression and Partisan Politics* (Columbia: University of South Carolina Press, 1989), 24–40.

2. Zechariah Chafee has discussed how various rights guaranteed under the Constitution have historically come into conflict with other rights. For example, the Fourteenth Amendment, which had been passed ostensibly to protect the rights of former slaves, became an instrument used by the courts to protect business against state regulation. Likewise the First Amendment has been modified in specific cases where such rights come in conflict with other rights. According to Chafee, the courts have been especially burdened with balancing First Amendment rights with "other purposes of government, such as order, the training of the young, protection against external aggression." Unlimited discussion, as stipulated under the First Amendment "sometimes interferes with these purposes." Zechariah Chafee Jr., *Free Speech in the United States* (Cambridge: Harvard University Press, 1946), 31–35.

3. See Richard J. Goldstein, *Political Repression in Modern America from 1870 to the Present* (Cambridge: Schenkman, 1918), ix–xxi; 1–93; Patricia C. Sexton, *The War on Labor and the Left, Understanding America's Unique Conservatism* (Boulder: Westview Press, 1991).

4. Henry Facett, *Manual of Political Economy* (New York: Macmillan, 1888), 242.

5. J. C. Furnas, *The Americans, A Social History of the United States, 1587–1914* (New York: Putnam's Sons, 1969), 655.

6. National depressions may have been more than episodic problems. David A. Wells interprets the depression of the 1880s as only one stage in a sequence of

"Economic Disturbances since 1873," constituting a relapse from the brief recovery of 1879–1881. It was fitted into the pattern of a "Great Depression" extending from the 1870s into the 1890s. D. A. Wells, "Economic Disturbances since 1873," *Popular Science Monthly*, vols. 31, 32 (1887), passim, and his *Recent Economic Changes* (New York, 1890), 1ff.

7. *Bradstreet's*, 10 (Dec 20, 1884): 386 ff.

8. *North American Review*, 140 (April, 1885): 369.

9. Massachusetts Bureau of Statistics of Labor, *Tenth Annual Report* (Boston, 1879), 133.

10. *North American Review*, 140 (April, 1885): 369; Henry David, *History of the Haymarket Affair* (New York: Collier, 1963), 17ff.

11. *Publications of the American Economic Association*, vol. 1 (Baltimore, 1887), 6–7.

12. Chester McArthur Destler, *American Radicalism 1865–1901, Essays and Documents* (New London: Connecticut College, 1946), 191.

13. Stuart B. Kaufman, *Samuel Gompers and the Origins of the American Federation of Labor, 1848–1896* (Westport: Greenwood Press, 1973).

14. For a brief history of unions in the United States, see Marc Karson, *American Labor Unions and Politics, 1900–1918* (Carbondale: Southern Illinois University Press, 1958), 13; see also Mary Beard, *A Short History of the American Labor Movement* (New York: George H. Doran, 1924), 116–126.

15. Karson, *American Labor Unions*, 151.

16. Karson, *American Labor Unions*, 18–19.

17. For a definitive treatment of the anarchists and socialists, see Paul Avrich, *The Haymarket Tragedy* (Princeton, NJ: Princeton University Press, 1984).

18. After the railway strike of 1877 paramilitary groups emerged out of the ranks of the anarchists. The Illinois legislature responded by passing a law banning all paramilitary groups, unless they were affiliated with state militia, and making it a punishable offense for any body of men to assemble with arms and drill or parade within the state without authorization. Robert V. Bruce, *1877: Year of Violence* (Chicago: Quadrangle, 1970), 53–55.

19. David M. Rabban, "The IWW Free Speech Fights and Popular Conceptions of Free Expression Before World War I," *Virginia Law Review*, 80 (1994): 1055–1063.

20. Karson, *American Labor Unions*, 175.

21. See Leon Litwack, *The American Labor Movement* (Englewood Cliffs, NJ: Prentice Hall, 1962), 27; Terry W. Cole, "The Right to Speak: The Free Speech Fights of the Industrial Workers of the World," in *Perspectives on Freedom of Speech: Selected Essays from the Journals of the Speech Communication Association*, Thomas L. Tedford, John J. Makay, and David L. Jamison, eds. (Carbondale: Southern Illinois University Press, 1987), 46N52.

22. William Z. Ripley, *Railroads, Rates and Regulation* (New York, 1924), 441ff.; Thomas C. Cochran, *Railroad Leaders* (Cambridge, MA, 1953), 197; James Morgan, *The Life Work of Edward A. Moseley in the Service of Humanity* (New York, 1913).

23. *Quest for a Dream* (New York: Macmillan, 1963), 19.

24. Jerry M. Cooper, "The Wisconsin National Guard in the Milwaukee Riots of 1886," *WMH*, 55 (1971): 31–48; John Higman, *Strangers in the Land* (New York: Atheneum, 1970), 88–90.

25. Quoted in Harry W. Laidler, *Boycotts and the Labor Struggle Legal and Economic Aspects* (New York: John Lane, 1914), 318–319.

26. *The Alarm*, December 13, 1884.

27. Goldstein, *Political Repression*, 31.

28. Robert L. Heilbroner, "Andrew Carnegie, Captain of Industry," in *Historical Viewpoints: Volume Two, Since 1865*, ed. John A. Garraty (New York: American Heritage, 1970), 96.

29. See Cooper, "The Wisconsin National Guard," 31–48; Higman, *Strangers in the Land*, 88–90.

30. Goldstein, *Political Repression*, 41.

31. "The 1880 Labor Dispute in Leadville," *Colorado Magazine*, 47 (Fall, 1970): 325.

32. William Ivy Hair, *Bourbonism and Agrarian Protest* (Baton Rouge: Louisiana State University Press, 1969), 172–174.

33. Tyler Dennett, *John Hay* (New York: Dodd, Mead, 1933), 122.

34. Henry David, *The History of the Haymarket Affair*, 161.

35. *The Alarm*, October 25, 1884.

36. *Nemesis*, May 17, 1884.

37. Estimates, however, of civilians killed range from 10 to 60. Michael J. Schaack, *Anarchy and Anarchists* (Chicago: F. J. Schulte, 1889), 155. Exact figures are not known because the workers feared reprisal and therefore spirited the dead quickly away from the scene and buried them privately.

38. Goldstein, *Political Repression*, 41; see also Chester Destler, *American Radicalism, 1865–1901* (Chicago: Quadrangle, 1966), 101.

39. Michael A. Gordon, "The Labor Boycott in New York City, 1880–1886," *Labor History*, 16 (1975): 225.

40. Ray Ginger, *Altgeld's America, 1890–1905* (Chicago: Quadrangle, 1965), 176–178.

41. David, *History of Haymarket*, 436.

42. Philip S. Foner, *History of the Labor Movement in the United States*, vol., 2 (New York: International, 1947–1965), 25; David, *History of Haymarket*, 443–444.

43. N.J. Laws, 1908, c. 278 now N.J.S.A. 2:173–10, 11.

44. Sidney Lens, *Radicalism in America* (New York: Thomas Y. Crowell, 1966), 235–243.

45. John A. Garraty, *The New Commonwealth* (New York: Harper & Row, 1968), 168.

46. Goldstein, *Political Repression*, 42; Daniel Bell, *Marxian Socialism in the United States* (Princeton, NJ: Princeton University Press, 1967), 39–40.

47. Goldstein, *Political Repression*, 41.

48. For a brief account of conspiracy law and labor union history see Sexton, *The War on Labor*, 68–69.

49. J. R. Commons et al., *History of Labour in the United States*, vol. 2 (New York: Macmillan, 1921), 191.

50. Sexton, *The War on Labor*, 68–69.

51. Slason Thompson, "Violence in Labor Disputes," *World's Work* (December, 1904).

52. Thurman Arnold, "Economic Reform and the Sherman Antitrust Act," in Garraty, *New Commonwealth*, 154. The Act's directive against trust was delay by the Supreme Court in *United States v. E. C. Knight & Co.* It would not be resurrected until the administration of Theodore Roosevelt. The Northern Securities case reversed E. C. Knight and businesses were henceforth under the scrutiny of the government.

53. Everett J. Burtt, *Labor Markets, Unions, and Government Policies* (New York: St. Martin's Press, 1963), 246.

54. Irving Bernstein, *The Lean Years* (Baltimore: Penguin, 1966), 200.

55. Goldstein, *Political Repression*, 19.

56. Bernstein, *The Lean Years*, 194–196.

57. *In re* Debs, 158 U.S. 654, 15 S. Ct. 900 (1895).

58. Almont Lindsay, *The Pullman Strike* (Chicago: University of Chicago Press, 1964), 275.

59. *A. F. of L. v. Buck Stove and Range Co.*, Ct. of A, D. of C., 1909.

60. J. C. Kennedy, "Important Labor Injunction in the Bucks' Stove and Range Company Suit," *Journal of Political Economy*, vol. 16 (1908): 98.

61. *American Federationist* (January, 1908): 98.

62. Lovestone, *Government Strikebreaker*, 217–218.

63. Burtt, *Labor Markets*, 253.

64. Avrich, *Haymarket Tragedy*, 393.

Chapter 6

Suppression of the Suffrage Movement

Katie L. Gibson and Amy L. Heyse

Mr. President, What Will You Do For Woman Suffrage?

—Message on a National Woman's Party Banner, 1917

When the woman suffragists of the National Woman's Party (NWP) picketed the White House from 1917 to 1919, they carried banners that asked President Woodrow Wilson what he would do to support women's democratic rights and if he would endorse their push for suffrage.[1] Wilson and the federal government responded by suppressing the suffragists' First Amendment rights to petition the government, to free speech, and to assemble peaceably. This treatment was not new and not surprising: suppressing women's freedom of expression was the norm and enjoyed a long history in the United States. It is the governmental and societal efforts to quiet women's voices and limit their citizenship rights that are the subjects of this chapter as we focus on rhetorical and legal resistance to the woman suffrage movement from the early 1800s to 1920. We argue that the government employed a variety of inventive strategies to rob women of their First Amendment rights as well as their right to vote.

We begin the chapter by contextualizing American women's suppression in public life. This first section is devoted to discussing how the law of coverture, dominant gender ideologies, and religious appeals functioned as rhetorical strategies to limit women's freedom of expression and citizenship rights. We argue that this context of cultural and religious restraint provided powerful warrants that the government would later use to formalize the suppression of women's freedom of expression in laws and other legal actions. The early rhetorical strategies will be illustrated in the responses to two early women orators—Sarah and Angelina Grimké—and their efforts to put women's issues on the national agenda. In the second section of this chapter, we analyze the early efforts of women to make their voices heard, the beginnings of the woman suffrage movement, and the legal and extra-legal strategies the government employed to keep women silent. Specifically, we identify strategies of legislative and judicial suppression. The third and fourth sections of the chapter examine the middle and latter parts of the woman suffrage movement as well as the continued governmental efforts to suppress women's First Amendment rights. Here we find that in addition to legislative suppression, the women faced martial suppression and government suppression-by-proxy. Government suppression-by-proxy, we argue, is the government's failure to protect women's freedom of expression from intimidation, harassment, and circumvention.

Rhetorical Context: Denying Women a Civic Voice

Before written into law, women's citizenship rights had long been suppressed in the United States under the common law of coverture whose roots may be traced back to Sir William Blackstone's 1765–1769 treatise, *Commentaries on the Laws of England.*[2] Blackstone was an English jurist and professor who explained *femme couvert*, or "a woman under cover," as the unconditional unity of a man and woman in marriage. Suffragist Elizabeth Cady Stanton paraphrased Blackstone's position this way: "The husband and wife are one, and that one is the husband."[3] Thus, coverture denied women legal status once they were married; and as such, they were unable to own property, enter into legal contracts without permission from their husbands, inherit from their husbands, sue or be sued, obtain a divorce, or have custody rights to their children. JoEllen Lind adds, "In addition to the notion that a woman should have no independent existence apart from her husband, it was the dominant view that her activities should be confined to the private domestic sphere. As a result, women were not to seek paid employment outside of the family nor to enter the public forum of politics to speak and agitate for reform."[4] The public sphere, after all, was exclusively masculine. The law of coverture ruled common law gender relations in the United States from our founding well into the nineteenth century.

Alongside the law of coverture, gendered social expectations allowed for the further suppression of American women's voices and citizenship rights. Before and especially after the Revolutionary War, the ideology of republican motherhood rigidly defined White women's roles as mothers and teachers of their children. Women were expected to serve the nation by staying at home and raising their sons to be virtuous citizens.[5] On the one hand, republican motherhood was empowering because it carved out a political-by-proxy role for women, but on the other hand, it limited their opportunities by defining women's position as solely domestic. The cult of domesticity, or the cult of true womanhood, was another gendered ideology that narrowly defined women's role as domestic. Normally assumed of middle- and upper-class White women, "true women" were expected to embody the four "cardinal virtues" of piety, purity, submissiveness, and domesticity.[6] Most dominant between 1820 and the start of the Civil War in 1861, the cult of domesticity represented yet another set of ideas that defined women out of the public sphere and undermined the legitimacy of their civic voice.

Religious organizations reinforced the cultural silencing of women by suppressing their positions in the church and by explicitly calling for their subservience to men. Although Quakers allowed women a voice in church and church affairs, most dominant religions did not. Known as the Pauline injunction, Christian churches often evoked St. Paul's dicta to inform women that they were to remain silent in church and beholden to their men. Citing St. Paul's letter to the Corinthians, for example, it was declared, "Let your women keep silent in the churches: for it is not permitted unto them to speak; but they are commanded to be under obedience, as also saith the law. And if they will learn any thing, let them ask their husbands at home."[7] Not only did the rhetoric of the Pauline passages help to justify women's suppression in the church, but the passages also reinforced the domesticity and submissiveness of women and endowed the silencing of women with a divine and unalterable authority.[8]

Although several successful attempts had been made by American women such as Anne Hutchinson, Frances Wright, and Maria Stewart to challenge and sometimes overcome these rhetorical constraints, the work of two abolitionist sisters in the mid-1830s stands out as groundbreaking.[9] According to Flexner and Fitzpatrick, the Grimké sisters "paved the way for the long roster of famous women orators in the anti-slavery cause."[10] Angelina and Sarah Grimké were the daughters of a slaveholding family in South Carolina and by all accounts, "loathed slavery and all its works" from earliest childhood.[11] Shortly after moving to Philadelphia and meeting members of the American Anti-Slavery Society, the sisters were invited to speak against slavery to "promiscuous audiences" of men and women. Not long thereafter, the women began to face resistance and were repeatedly met with harassment and intimidation: "Officials often denied them meeting places. Critics called them names. The venom spewed at the Grimkés and the women who followed them was part of a larger public antipathy toward the abolitionist movement that sparked an assault upon fundamental American values such as free speech, a free press, and the right to assemble peaceably."[12]

In response to the public appearances of the Grimké sisters, Reverend Dr. Nehemiah Adams of the General Association of Congregational Ministers of Massachusetts issued a Pastoral Letter in July 1837 inviting "attention to the dangers which at present seem to threaten the female character with widespread and permanent injury."[13] Making appeals to his readers with the rhetoric of the Pauline passages and the assumed domesticity of women, Adams explained:

> The appropriate duties and influence of women, are clearly stated in the New Testament. Those duties and that influence are unobtrusive and private, but the sources of mighty power. When the mild, dependent, softening influence of woman upon the sternness of man's opinions is fully exercised, society feels the effects of it in a thousand forms. The power of woman is in her dependence, flowing from the consciousness of that weakness which God has given her for her protection and which keeps her in those departments of life that form the character of individuals and of the nation.[14]

The letter admitted, though, that there were areas in which women's influence was deemed necessary and appreciated:

> There are social influences which females use in promoting piety and the great objects of christian [sic] benevolence, which we cannot too highly commend. We appreciate the unostentatious prayers and efforts of woman, in advancing the cause of religion at home and abroad:—in Sabbath schools, in leading religious inquirers to their pastor for instruction, and in all such associated effort as becomes the modesty of her sex; and earnestly hope that she may abound more and more in these labours of piety and love.[15]

The appeal made here to women's domestic responsibility was consistent with the tenets of republican motherhood and the cult of true womanhood because women were expected to raise good Christian children at home and remain pious beings themselves. The letter was clear, however, in denouncing a public voice for women:

> But when she assumes the place and tone of a man as a public reformer, our care and protection of her seem unnecessary, we put ourselves in self defence against her, she yields the power which God has given her for protection, and her character becomes unnatural. . . . We cannot, therefore, but regret the mistaken conduct of those who encourage females to bear an obtrusive and ostentatious part in measures of reform, and countenance

any of that sex who so far forget themselves as to itinerant in the character of public lecturers and teachers.[16]

Although such critical responses reportedly took a heavy toll on Angelina and Sarah,[17] the most heated controversy over their new role as "public lecturers and teachers" emerged when the sisters began linking abolition to the condition of American women. The sisters even faced resistance from members of their own camp: abolitionists such as John Greenleaf Whittier and Theodore Weld asked Sarah and Angelina to stop speaking on women's rights for fear it might injure the abolition cause.[18] Most importantly, the success of women such as the Grimké sisters on the public stage made the government more creative in its efforts to suppress women's freedom of expression, specifically, the First Amendment right to petition government.

Before women officially organized to fight for suffrage, they exercised their civic voice and opposition to slavery through the right to petition.[19] Lumsden found that, "More than half of the signatures on the annual flood of anti-slavery petitions to Congress throughout the [1830s] belonged to women."[20] The government quickly exerted its legislative resistance to this display of women's expression. In 1836, the House of Representatives passed the Pinckney Gag Rule in response to the American Anti-Slavery Society's petition campaign (see chapter 2 of this book). The Gag Rule was designed to table the presentation of anti-slavery petitions to Congress, particularly those gathered by women.[21] According to Marilley, "As fierce debate erupted about the right to petition—especially for women—and the appropriate action to take, the woman's rights issue was raised for the first time in Congress."[22] Weighing in on the topic of women's right to petition, Senator Benjamin Tappan of Ohio addressed Congress in 1840 to assert, "The field of politics is not her appropriate arena. The powers of government are not within her cognizance, as they could not be within her knowledge unless she neglected her higher and holier duties to acquire it."[23] The appeals to coverture and the domestic norms for women are clearly evident in Tappan's remark and closely reflected the sentiments of those many who opposed women's right to speak in public.

Although the Gag Rule and its subsequent congressional iterations were not discontinued until 1844, it is significant that the issue of women's rights was brought to the attention of government. Furthermore, the women learned important lessons, one of which is that they had a friend in former president and then congressman John Quincy Adams, who, despite being censored, argued tirelessly for eight years in favor of the women's right to petition.[24] The women also found that by their association with the abolition movement, they had support from those who saw anti-slavery as a freedom of expression issue. As Lerner explains, "the fight against the 'gag rules' made the connection between slavery and the denial of free speech persuasively clear to large numbers of citizens who had been previously indifferent to anti-slavery."[25] In response to the Grimkés' success and their bringing the woman's rights issue to public attention, the government began codifying into law the common laws of coverture, the gendered ideologies of women, and religious arguments of women's place. The government also escalated its legislative and judicial suppression of the suffrage movement.

Women Assemble for Suffrage and Face Legislative and Judicial Suppression

Women's participation in the public work of abolitionism quickly highlighted their own circumscribed status and lack of individual liberties. In 1840, after women delegates were barred from the World's Anti-Slavery Convention in London, England, Elizabeth Cady Stanton and Lucretia Mott pledged to assemble a conference to address the oppression of women in the United States. The origin of the suffrage movement in the United States traces back to this first women's rights conference held in 1848 in Seneca Falls, New York. The main concerns to emerge from this first meeting at Seneca Falls were married women's disabilities, religious discrimination, and the denial of opportunities for education and employment. The conference attendees signed a Declaration of Sentiments, authored by Elizabeth Cady Stanton, which outlined a list of grievances and advanced a series of resolutions. Notably, the resolution that provoked the most controversy and debate read: "Resolved, that it is the duty of the women of this country to secure to themselves their sacred right to the elective franchise."[26] Considering the context of restraint that had undermined women's voices so completely, the idea of woman suffrage was simply unthinkable to many. Although the attendees eventually voted to support the resolution for suffrage, it would take years before advocates for women's rights realized that their efforts to improve their legal, religious, and social positions would ultimately be futile without a civic voice. Throughout the 1850s, women continued to assert their right to assembly and national women's rights conventions were held regularly until the Civil War. Charles Conrad points to the convention of 1860 as a watershed event, "when feminism started to become suffragism."[27] It was shortly after this conference in 1860 that the government answered the call for woman suffrage with legislative suppression.

Advocates for women's rights willingly set aside their agenda during the Civil War to support the Union cause. While most advocates for women's rights were fierce supporters of abolition, they also believed that their loyalty to country would be rewarded once the war came to an end and that women would be extended the vote alongside African Americans. The Reconstruction amendments, however, did not enfranchise women (see chapter 3 of this book).[28] In fact, a series of legislative suppressive acts would mark Reconstruction as a dramatically low point for women's rights. The first debate on woman suffrage in the Senate took place during Reconstruction, in 1866, after an amendment was proposed to strike the word "male" from a bill extending the vote to African Americans in the District of Columbia.[29] The arguments against woman suffrage emerged from the topoi of cultural and religious suppression that had silenced women since the founding. Listen to the arguments from the floor of Congress in favor of the government's continued suppression of women's vote. Senator George Williams of Oregon argued that, "The woman who undertakes to put her sex in an adversary position to man, who undertakes by the use of some independent political power to contend and fight against man, displays a spirit which would, if able, convert all the now harmonious elements of society into a state of war, and make every home a hell on earth."[30] Similarly, the cult of domesticity rang from Senator Frelinghuysen's exclamation, "It seems to me as if the God of our race has stamped upon [the women of America] a milder, gentler nature, which not only makes them shrink from, but disqualifies them for the turmoil and battle of public life. They have a higher and a holier mission . . . Their mission is at home, by their blandishments and their love to assuage the passions of men as they come in from the battle of life, and not themselves by joining in the contest to add fuel to the very flames. . . . It will be a sorry day for this country when those vestal fires of love and piety are put out."[31]

Post–Civil War, the topoi of cultural and religious silencing remained effective as warrants for the government's suppression of women's vote. Women were dismissed by many who echoed the senators. Others, more sympathetic to the idea of woman suffrage, claimed that it was not the right time and that "this [was] the Negroes' hour."[32] The post–Civil War amendments included the Thirteenth Amendment, which abolished slavery and the Fourteenth Amendment, which described the rights of full citizenship and inserted the word "male" into the Constitution. The word was used three times in the second article of the Fourteenth Amendment in a passage that addressed voting rights and proportional representation in the South.[33] For the first time in the history of the United States, the government's suppression of women's vote was explicitly inscribed into the Constitution.

Women's rights advocates such as Lucy Stone and Frederick Douglass supported the Fourteenth Amendment as a step forward for the civil rights of all men, but others, like Elizabeth Cady Stanton and Susan B. Anthony, actively campaigned to defeat the Fourteenth Amendment for its failure to include women.[34] After losing the fight to remove the references to "male" in the second article, Stanton and Anthony turned to the first article of the Fourteenth Amendment to argue for full citizenship.[35] The Fourteenth Amendment was ratified in July 1868. Six months later, the Radical Republicans introduced a Fifteenth Amendment to Congress, seeking to guarantee the right to vote to African Americans. The Fifteenth Amendment resulted in another act of legislative suppression. It read: "The right of citizens of the United States to vote shall not be declined or abridged by the United States or any State on account or race, color, or previous condition of servitude." Incensed by the exclusion of "sex" from the Amendment's list of intolerable discriminations, Stanton and Anthony led the more radical faction of the suffrage movement in a campaign against the Fifteenth Amendment that angered many of their former abolition compatriots and deepened the divide among advocates for women's rights. The conflict over the Reconstruction amendments created a rift in the woman suffrage movement that would split the energies and efforts of the advocates for more than 20 years.

Women's rights litigation began appearing in the courts of the United States shortly after the Reconstruction amendments were ratified in 1868. Despite hopes that the arguments for women's rights would receive a fairer hearing in the courtroom than in the halls of the legislature, the government responded with judicial suppression that was equally as sharp and unwavering. A review of Justice Bradley's concurring opinion in the 1873 case of *Bradwell v. Illinois* demonstrates the extent to which judicial rhetoric mirrored public argument. In this case, the topoi of cultural and religious silencing are codified into law and affirmed by the nation's highest bench as appropriate warrants for restricting women's public personhood.[36] Justice Bradley wrote:

> Man is, or should be, woman's protector and defender. The natural and proper timidity and delicacy which belongs to the female sex evidently unfits it for many of the occupations of civil life. The constitution of the family organization, which is founded in the divine ordinance, as well as in the nature of things, indicates the domestic sphere as that which properly belongs to the domain and functions of womanhood. . . . The paramount destiny and mission of woman are to fulfill the noble and benign offices of wife and mother. This is the law of the Creator.[37]

The doctrine of separate spheres advanced by the Court represented the philosophical core of republican motherhood and the cult of domesticity. *Bradwell* affirmed these cultural arguments for women's silence as appropriate judicial warrants for government suppression. For decades, Justice Bradley's judicial rhetoric stood as a touchstone for judges and legislators seeking to restrict women's public activity and expression.

Drawing on the rights of full citizenship spelled out in the first article of the Fourteenth Amendment, Susan B. Anthony and Virginia Minor challenged the government's suppression of their right to vote and attempted to cast ballots in the presidential election of 1872. At the time, there was a growing number of lawyers and members of Congress who believed that the Fourteenth Amendment could be extended to protect women's votes.[38] Anthony's and Minor's challenges served as a test case. The suffragists initiated two historic court cases in which the government would reaffirm its commitment to silencing women's civic voice: *United States v. Susan B. Anthony* (1873)[39] and *Minor v. Happersett* (1874).[40] The government declared that the Fourteenth Amendment to the Constitution does not expand or protect women's rights.

Susan B. Anthony registered to vote and cast a ballot in New York in the general election of 1872. Two weeks later, Anthony was arrested by a U.S. Deputy Marshal and later convicted of unlawful voting in a presidential election. Anthony's trial underscored the extent to which her freedom of expression was denied; the judge refused to allow her to testify on her own behalf, citing her incompetence as a woman. When her attorney finished arguing her case, Judge Ward Hunt read a statement prepared before the trial, before he heard the evidence or listened to the arguments, stating that the Fourteenth Amendment "gives no right to a woman to vote, and the voting of Miss Anthony was in violation of the law." Judge Hunt directed the jury to find Anthony guilty. When asked if she had anything to say before her sentencing, Anthony unleashed a scathing criticism of the government, which had silenced her voice in the voting booth and the court of law. She exclaimed:

> Yes, your honor, I have many things to say; for in your ordered verdict of guilty, you have trampled underfoot every vital principle of our government. My natural rights, my civil rights, my political rights, my judicial rights, are all alike ignored. Robbed from the fundamental privilege of citizenship, I am degraded from the status of a citizen to that of a subject; and not only myself individually, but all of my sex, are, by your honor's verdict, doomed to political subjection under this, so called, form of government.[41]

The U.S. Supreme Court echoed Judge Ward Hunt and the Circuit Court's decision in *United States v. Anthony* when it decided *Minor v. Happersett* a year later. Virginia Minor, a suffrage leader in Missouri, argued that the Missouri state registrar, Reese Happersett, violated her civil rights under the Fourteenth Amendment by refusing to allow her to register to vote. The registrar argued that he was upholding the Missouri state constitution that read, "Every male citizen of the United States shall be entitled to vote." After losing the case in the state Supreme Court, Minor's husband brought her case to the United States Supreme Court.[42] In a unanimous decision the Court reaffirmed the exclusion of women from voting rights and announced that suffrage was not a right of citizenship. It would take more than 100 years after the passage of the Fourteenth Amendment before the courts would rule that the Equal Protection Clause of the Fourteenth Amendment protected women's rights.[43] Recognizing that judicial suppression would persist in the federal courts, advocates for woman suffrage would shift their strategy after *Minor* toward securing a federal amendment to the United States Constitution and working state-by-state to secure residentially-based suffrage.

Suffrage Moves into the Streets: Turn-of-the-Century Tactics and Continued Suppression

The shift toward securing a federal amendment and the strategy of the state-by-state campaign demanded that suffragists take their arguments public. To their advantage, the changing roles of women combined with the spirit of Progressivism created a more supportive public context and drew a new generation of activists to the growing movement for woman suffrage.[44] By the turn of the century, increased opportunities for women outside of the home blurred the public/private divide that fueled anti-suffrage arguments throughout the nineteenth century. The increasing reality of women in the workforce introduced new warrants for woman suffrage and encouraged more public strategies of advocacy. Woman suffragists working in separate camps came together under the National American Woman Suffrage Association (NAWSA) and organized outreach efforts to include working-class women among the ranks of their membership. Sarah Hunter Graham appropriately described this period as the "suffrage renaissance."[45] In this environment of new members and new arguments, Harriot Stanton Blatch orchestrated new "open-air" rhetorical strategies that took the arguments for woman suffrage out of the parlor rooms and speaking halls and into the city streets. The government suppression that followed Blatch's new public strategies proved inconsistent and illustrated the arbitrary nature of the government's protection of freedom of expression at the turn of the twentieth century. Government suppression-by-proxy was perhaps the staunchest enemy of the suffragists' freedoms of expression during this period. For it was not the legislature or the judiciary, but the *public* harassment, threats, and intimidation *allowed* by the government that silenced the advocacy for suffrage most effectively.

Beginning in 1908, soapbox speakers were appearing on street corners across the nation. Soapbox speaking deeply embodied the spirit of freedom of expression. "The suffragists' open-air campaign exemplified classic arguments on the paramount importance of the right of assembly," Lumsden explained. "Street meetings were cheap, easily arranged, attracted publicity, and forced the issue upon indifferent audiences."[46] Reflecting on her own experience atop a soapbox, Maude Malone wrote, "It was in the broadest spirit of democracy that we went out into the streets inviting all passersby to listen to our arguments and offer their objections or ask questions."[47]

Requiring meeting permits was a common tactic of legislative suppression used to regulate the assembly of soapbox speakers and their audiences on public property. The Supreme Court ruled in *Davis v. Massachusetts* (1897) that a municipality could prohibit the use of its parks by public speakers unless a permit was secured by the speaker.[48] City and police officials regularly cited "police power" to deny permits for dissidents seeking a public audience. "Police power," an especially broad term at this time, represented the authority of the state to regulate personal liberty in defense of public health, safety, morals, and welfare. "Under the police power," Blanchard explains, "governments were permitted to engage in a wide range of repressive functions."[49] The Supreme Court did not guarantee the right to assemble peaceably until the 1930s.[50] Throughout the early 1900s, a broad right of the public to enjoy public property routinely overrode a dissident's right to speak.[51] Suffragists were routinely denied meeting permits, barred from assembling on public grounds, and forced to retreat to private halls or homes.

Obtaining a meeting permit was not the only obstacle to soapbox speaking. The failure of police to protect the speakers from angry crowds also silenced suffrage soapboxers and represented a powerful form of government suppression-by-proxy. Women were routinely brought down from their platforms by harassment and violence. They were pelted with rocks and apple cores; they were tripped and kicked; and the police often ignored their requests for protection.[52] Despite suppressive efforts to censor their speech, though, the suffragists persisted with their new public strategies.

The "open-air" strategies that defined the suffrage movement after 1909 also included the suffrage parade. Advocates for women's votes turned to the parade as a powerful form of assembly with the hope that such a forum would allow them to reach a broader audience and increase public sympathies for their cause.[53] From the early days of the republic, parades were understood as an expression of collective identity and civic participation. Parading was also expressly protected by the Supreme Court in 1886.[54] Harriot Stanton Blatch and the Equality League of Self-Supporting Women organized the first large scale parade in New York City in 1910.[55] Six more Fifth Avenue suffrage parades followed over the next seven years, one attracting 50,000 marchers in 1915, and another drawing 20,000 marchers to New York City in 1917. Borda writes about the rhetorical power of the suffrage parade:

The parades functioned as an instrument of resistance enacted to challenge traditional views of woman and her limited roles. When thousands of woman suffragists took to the streets, the rhetorical force of their orderly processions threw the sexual hierarchy into disorder. The parades articulated women's desire to enter the world of politics in the same capacity as man, and demonstrated her ability to do so.[56]

Considering the challenge that the suffrage parade waged on cultural norms, the public sphere, and the sexual hierarchy, it is no surprise that efforts were made to prevent women from marching. A form of government suppression-by-proxy emerged as employers threatened women who participated in the parades and the government offered no protection. A large business firm, for example, issued a warning to its female employees that they would lose their jobs if they marched in the 1911 parade.[57] A year later, a parading Catholic schoolteacher was fired for setting a bad example for her students.[58] The government, complicit in such suppression, offered little protection to women who marched.

The most memorable parade was the first national woman suffrage parade organized by Alice Paul in Washington, D.C. The parade was scheduled to march up Pennsylvania Avenue on March 3, 1913, the day before President Wilson's inauguration. Paul believed that a parade at that time in the nation's capitol would announce women's political presence and call the attention of the nation to the demand for woman suffrage. The first sign that the 1913 parade exceeded the "tolerable" limits of suffragists' speech came the afternoon before the march. In an act of administrative suppression, police superintendent Major Richard Sylvester refused to grant a permit for the proposed march down Pennsylvania Avenue, arguing that it was "totally unsuitable for women."[59] The superintendent proposed that the women move their parade away from the White House and march down Sixteenth Street instead. Recognizing that Sixteenth Street was small compared to the thoroughfare that was Pennsylvania Avenue, Paul asked the suffragist wife of a Connecticut congressman to help secure a permit for the parade to pass the White House. Lumsden explains, "The women's success in obtaining a permit indicated the arbitrary nature of protections for exercising the right to assemble peaceably."[60]

On March 3, 1913, 8,000 suffragists marched down Pennsylvania Avenue. In a second move of government suppression, the police failed to protect the marchers. The police stood by passively as onlookers took their turn at silencing the arguments for suffrage. The crowd of a half million included many who were hostile not only to the arguments for woman suffrage but to the very presence of women marching in the streets. The parading suffragists were harassed, spat on, burned with cigars, and threatened as they approached the White House. Soon, the crowd rioted; the marchers were beaten and their banners and clothing were torn. The violent attack on the D.C. marchers disrupted the parade and suppressed the arguments of the suffragists. Although some reports recount the passivity of the police, others recall the blatant amusement of the police as they stood by and watched the riot. In any case, the lack of response and police protection enabled the government's suppression-by-proxy of the national suffrage parade. However, the suppression of the national suffrage parade backfired. Press coverage of the riots increased public sympathies for the suffragists and a national outcry forced a Senate committee to investigate the reported mishandling of the situation by the police.

While women struggled against government suppression-by-proxy on the streets, an insidious force was at work behind the scenes to ensure the continued government suppression of women's vote. Historian Eleanor Flexner writes that the influence of the liquor interest, "reached openly into the halls of legislation."[61] The liquor interest feared women's enfranchisement because women were chief supporters of the temperance movement dating back to the early nineteenth century. The emergence of the Women's Christian Temperance Union in 1874, and its rapid growth to become the largest organization formed by women in the United States, prompted the United States Brewer's Association to adopt an anti-suffrage resolution in 1881. Thereafter, the influence the liquor interest exerted on elected officials and democratic processes became a second powerful form of government suppression-by-proxy.

The liquor interest was responsible for stalling the federal amendment for decades and for interfering with multiple state referenda by bribing voters and stealing entire elections. After the state-by-state strategy resulted in victories for state suffrage in the West, the liquor lobby mounted a sweeping opposition effort to halt further victories. To the surprise of the liquor lobby, the suffragists' public strategies of persuasion had convinced the male electorates in Washington (1910), California (1911), Arizona (1912), Kansas (1912), and Oregon (1912) that the time for woman suffrage had come. These early victories prompted the liquor interest to begin aggressively circumventing democratic processes.[62] Referring to their successes at shutting down state referenda, suffragist Carrie Chapman Catt describes the 50 years spanning the end of Reconstruction to the adoption of the Nineteenth Amendment as the "saloon's hour."[63] Catt and Shuler write:

> Those invisible influences that were controlling elections; that invisible and invincible power that for forty years kept suffragists waiting for the woman's hour; for forty years circumvented the

coming of suffrage; that power that made Republican leaders hesitate to fulfill their promises to early suffragists; restrained both dominant parties from endorsing women's suffrage; kept Legislatures from submitting suffrage amendments. And organized droves of ignorant men to vote against suffrage amendments at the polls when its agents had failed to prevent the submission of the question, was, manifestly, the power that inhered in the combined liquor interest.[64]

The influence of the liquor lobby thwarted democratic processes and prolonged the suffragists' battle for full citizenship. The consequence of failing to protect against such circumvention implicated the government in the liquor lobby's surreptitious effort to suppress woman suffrage and restrain their civic voice.

After repeated disappointment in the states, many advocates for the woman's vote returned their focus to the federal amendment and took their fight directly to the White House. Their persuasive efforts in the streets had endowed their voices with new confidence and their "open-air" strategies had won them a growing public audience. Both would be necessary for the new phase of their fight. As the advocates for suffrage gained the confidence to ratchet up their demand for a civic voice, World War I shifted the political climate and government strategies of suppression became much more aggressive.

Silencing the Sentinels:
The NWP Pickets in a Time of War

Frustrated by limited victories in the states and exhausted by seemingly futile efforts to lobby Congress, the National Woman's Party (NWP) formed a more militant wing of the women's movement in 1916.[65] After severing all ties with NAWSA, the NWP's more radical tactics—such as staging demonstrations, lighting watch fires of freedom at the White House gates, sending delegations of women to the White House, and unfurling banners in sessions of Congress that displayed support for woman suffrage—"signified a new daring and seriousness in the movement."[66] Suffragist Alice Paul led the NWP in the fight for a constitutional amendment for woman's vote. Historians and critics have consistently pointed out that the NWP "established a legacy defending the exercise of free speech, free assembly, and the right to dissent—especially during wartime."[67] Of course, it may be argued that women and the NWP were able to forge such a legacy because they never had to defend their First Amendment rights more. That is, the government under

President Wilson had significantly ramped up its suppression of women's freedom of expression, more than any other time in history and before it began its censorship of antiwar propagandists.[68]

President Wilson was initially somewhat receptive to the NWP's early delegations, but he remained unmoved by the women's appeals for suffrage. Wilson insisted that he would not stand against the will of his Democratic Party and that the issue of woman suffrage should be decided by the states.[69] Tired of Wilson's dismissals, and after he rebuffed a series of suffrage resolutions presented to him in early January 1917, the women of the NWP did something no one had ever done: they began picketing the White House. On January 10, 1917, a dozen women marched to the White House carrying flags and banners that read, "Mr. President, What Will You Do For Woman Suffrage?" and "How Long Must Woman Wait for Liberty?"[70] For the next few months, regardless of the weather, the women stood as "silent sentinels" at the front gates of the White House holding their flags and banners, every day and night except Sunday. The women took turns at the sentinel stations and reported having nearly 2,000 suffragists from 30 states travel to Washington, D.C. to take turns on the picket line.[71] At first, public responses to the sentinels were restrained as the women expressed their First Amendment rights to petition the government, peaceably assemble, and speak freely.

In April 1917, after the United States entered World War I, responses to the NWP's pickets changed. At that point, some women resigned from the NWP because they believed that protests were unpatriotic during a time of war; others resigned after the sentinels were harassed and intimidated by mobs and violence on the picket line. The most violent resistance against the women came in response to the banners that compared President Wilson with the Russian czar and the German Kaiser—the NWP justified the comparison by explaining that each leader denied citizenship rights to their people. Paired with words from his own speeches, the sentinels hoped to point out Wilson's hypocrisy in fighting for democracy in Europe but denying it to women here at home.

The mobs that gathered around the sentinels physically attacked the women. They pulled the "traitorous" banners from their hands and tore them to shreds. Day-to-day intimidation included "slow growth of the crowds; the circle of little boys who gathered about . . . first, spitting at them, calling them names, making personal comments; then the gathering of gangs of young hoodlums who encourage the boys with further insults; then more and more crowds; more and more insults."[72] In her account of the violence visited upon the sentinels, suffragist Inez Haynes Irwin went on to explain, "Sometimes the crowd would edge nearer and nearer, until there was but a foot of smothering, terror-fraught space between them and the pickets."[73]

The woman suffrage pickets endured government suppression-by-proxy. The police often stood by and watched, just like they did at the suffrage parade in 1913. Perhaps more importantly, the government made no moves to protect the women from the angry mobs or from the negligent police who failed to safeguard them and their First Amendment rights.

On June 22, 1917, the first of the sentinels—Lucy Burns and Katherine Morey—were arrested for "obstructing the traffic on Pennsylvania Avenue."[74] According to suffragist Doris Stevens' account of the arrest, the police chief and his staff did not know how to answer Burns' and Morey's question about why they had been arrested: "The Administration had looked ahead only as far as threatening arrest. They doubtless thought this was all they would have to do. People could not be arrested for picketing. Picketing is a guaranteed right under the Clayton Act of Congress. Disorderly conduct? There had been no disorderly conduct. Inciting to riot? Impossible! The women had stood as silent sentinels holding the President's own eloquent words."[75] The arrest of Burns and Morey started a wave of martial suppression of the women's freedom of expression that Wilson did nothing to stop, if not willingly endorse.

The women could not understand how their freedom of expression was punishable under law, but reportedly Wilson and his administration believed the women had finally gone too far and needed to be stopped. As Abbott explains, "The man responsible for the arrests awkwardly enough for him, was President Woodrow Wilson. It was awkward because, though he had not shown himself a great friend of suffrage, he did not wish to be known as an enemy. Moreover, he was trying to wage a war in Europe and tended to regard any distraction as subversive. He had tried to ignore the pickets at the White House gates. But when they began to carry banners reading DEMOCRACY SHOULD BEGIN AT HOME, it was more than he could endure."[76] Therefore, Wilson and his administration endorsed the martial suppression of the NWP's freedom of expression by allowing the police to arrest the women under trumped up charges and letting the mobs attack them while they legally protested.

From then on, the sentinels were subjected to martial suppression and arrested on a regular basis. At first, the women were released on their own recognizance or forced to pay a fine, but as the years wore on and the U.S.'s involvement in war intensified, the penalties for the women's "obstructing traffic" became more severe. From the summer of 1917 until June of 1919, (when the NWP ceased picketing), the arrested women faced longer prison sentences and endured unconscionable treatment. Most of the women were sentenced to weeks and months in jail, usually in the D.C. jail or the Occoquan Workshop in Virginia. Alice Paul and Lucy Burns both served sentences in Occoquan where they demanded to be treated as political prisoners. Instead,

Paul, Burns, and the other women were forced to eat food infested with worms and insects, to use and reuse dirty sheets from previous prisoners, and to work long hours in the sweatshop doing hard manual labor and sewing. The women were also attacked by the prison guards on occasion and beaten, pushed, dragged, thrown into cells, and like Lucy Burns, had their arms handcuffed above their heads in their cells. When the women protested against such harassment, torture, and intimidation by staging a hunger strike, they were force-fed liquids by the jailers. Alice Paul was even subjected to psychiatric evaluation and threatened with a transfer to an insane asylum after being solitarily confined and violently force-fed.

Meanwhile, moves in Congress were being made to legislatively suppress free speech and peaceable assembly in wartime. On August 18, 1917, Senator Henry L. Myers of Montana introduced a bill in direct response to the suffragists' picketing designed to restrict the freedom of expression of all U.S. citizens:

> That when the United States shall be engaged in war it shall be unlawful for any person or persons to carry, hold, wave, exhibit, display, or have in his or her possession in any public road, highway, alley, street, thoroughfare, park, or other public place in the District of Columbia, any banner, flag, streamer, sash, or other device having thereon any words or language with reference to the President or the Vice President of the United States, or any words or language with reference to the Constitution of the United States, or the right of suffrage, or right of citizenship, or any words or language with reference to the duties of any executive official or department of the United States, or with reference to any proposed amendment to the Constitution of the United States, or with reference to any law or proposed law of the United States, calculated to bring the President of the United States or the Government of the United States into contempt, or which may tend to cause confusion, or excitement, or obstruction of the streets or sidewalks thereof, or any passage in any public.[77]

Cloaked in the language of legislative initiative and framed as a wartime measure, Myers made his case against the suffragists. Myers' bill was not passed and women's rights were defended by some congressmen sympathetic to their cause, but the anti-suffrage sentiment was still heard loud and clear: silence women's voices, suppress their rights, and keep them disfranchised.

Even though their freedom of expression was suppressed in multiple and creative ways, and even though the treatment they received at the hands of the public and government was inexcusable, it could be argued that the sentinels in particular and suffragists in general were not treated as harshly as they could have been. As Bosmajian argues, the application of laws and First Amendment rights was a double-edged sword: "The practice of selectively enforcing the law . . . worked against the suffragists when they were arrested and jailed for 'obstructing traffic,' 'climbing a statue,' and 'unlawful assembly,' but this practice of selective enforcement worked in their favor when it came to enforcement of the federal and state espionage statutes."[78] In fact, no suffragist was ever arrested under the Espionage Act (see chapter 7 in this book) for treason even though they compared Wilson to tyrants and displayed his words as examples of his hypocrisy.[79] Lumsden argues that it may have been the women's strategy of using Wilson's words on their banners that actually saved the suffragists from charges of treason.[80]

Once reports of the women's treatment leaked out of the prisons and into the newspapers, public opinion became more sympathetic for the women and their cause. After 500 women had been arrested and at least 168 were jailed,[81] President Wilson finally agreed to support suffrage for women on January 9, 1918, the day before the Anthony amendment was scheduled in the House. On the morning of September 30, 1918, Wilson appeared before the Senate and urged them to pass the woman suffrage bill as a war measure. Wilson proclaimed, "I tell you plainly that this measure which I urge upon you is vital to the winning of the war and to the energies alike of preparation and of battle."[82] The point to be made here is that Wilson did not support woman suffrage for its constitutionality but rather for the service it could bring to the war effort. Thus, Wilson framed suffrage as a war measure that privileged the war and subordinated women's vote. As the war drew to a close, state after state ratified the Nineteenth Amendment.

Regardless of the way Wilson framed the issue, or perhaps because of it, the suffrage amendment was finally certified by the Secretary of State on August 26, 1920, after being ratified by the last state, Tennessee. The 1920 presidential election became the first in which women were allowed to vote; Republican Warren G. Harding of Ohio won an overwhelming endorsement. Since then, and after decades of governmental and societal suppression of their freedom of expression, women have enjoyed the right to vote as guaranteed by the Nineteenth Amendment.

Conclusion

The study of the government's suppression of women's freedom of expression reveals several important lessons. First, this study demonstrates how the government formalized cultural and religious warrants to suppress women's freedom of expression. Legislative suppression mirrored public argument and judicial suppression—far from emerging from an idealized and a rhetorical field of argument—drew directly from the topoi of cultural and religious restraint. The relationship between public argument and legislative and judicial discourse demonstrates that advocates of all stripes may shape legal discourses through their contributions to public argument. "In a representative form of government," Hasian, Condit, and Lucaites note, "the law can only function effectively within the rhetorical boundaries set up by a public vocabulary. The law flows from public discourse. It is therefore at least partially dependent upon the political action of the community in which it operates."[83] Indeed, understanding the symbiotic relationship between the law and the public vocabulary imbues the individual citizen's freedom of expression with added significance.

This study also argues that the government's failure to protect women's freedom of expression from intimidation, harassment, and circumvention resulted in a powerful form of government suppression-by-proxy. Woman suffrage advocates were harassed and attacked on the streets, they were threatened by employers, and they were denied a fair hearing by a powerful liquor lobby that circumvented democratic processes. We argue that it is important to recognize each of these suppressive efforts as a part of the government's suppression of women's freedom of expression. While public mobs or private interests might have enacted the restraint, the government's complicity made such restraint possible. The study of the suffrage movement underscores the argument that government protection is a necessary prerequisite to the realization of the First Amendment's promise of free expression.

Finally, the martial suppression of the suffragists provides yet another example of aggressive governmental restraint in a time of war. The shift in response to the NWP pickets demonstrates how appeals to patriotism and to fear allow the government to reign in the tolerable limits of free expression in a time of war. While this theme persists throughout the history of free expression in the United States, understanding the case of the suffragists and others may prepare citizens to guard against the suppression of free expression in a time of war.

Notes

1. We choose to honor women's struggle for the elective franchise by employing their terminology, "woman suffrage," rather than the contemporary phrase "women's suffrage."

2. Originally published by Clarendon Press of Oxford, the *Commentaries* are now available at avalon.law.yale.edu/subject_menus/blackstone.as

3. Elizabeth C. Stanton, Susan B. Anthony, Matilda J. Gage, and Ida H. Harper, Eds. *History of Woman Suffrage* (New York: Arno Press, 1969), 738.

4. JoEllen Lind, "Women Trailblazers: The Changing Role of Women in American Legal History," *The Amicus* (Valparaiso, IN: Valparaiso University School of Law) 7 (1994): 12.

5. Linda K. Kerber, *Women of the Republic: Intellect and Ideology in Revolutionary America* (Chapel Hill: University of North Carolina Press, 1980), 145.

6. Barbara Welter, "The Cult of True Womanhood: 1820–1860," *American Quarterly* 18 (1966): 151–174.

7. I Corinthians 14:34–35.

8. Glenna Matthews, *The Rise of Public Woman: Woman's Power and Woman's Place in the United States, 1630–1970* (New York: Oxford University Press, 1992), 4–5.

9. Lind, "Women Trailblazers," 12–14.

10. Eleanor Flexner and Ellen Fitzpatrick, *Century of Struggle: The Woman's Rights Movement in the United States* (Cambridge: Harvard University Press, 1975), 40.

11. Flexner and Fitzpatrick, *Century of Struggle*, 42.

12. Linda J. Lumsden, *Rampant Women: Suffragists and the Right of Assembly* (Knoxville: University of Tennessee Press, 1997), xxiv.

13. "Pastoral Letter," www.assumption.edu/users/mcclymer/His130/P-H/Grimke/PastoralLetter.html

14. Pastoral Letter.

15. Pastoral Letter.

16. Pastoral Letter.

17. Flexner and Fitzpatrick, *Century of Struggle*, 43.

18. Flexner and Fitzpatrick, *Century of Struggle*, 44.

19. Alisse Theodore, " 'A Right to Speak on the Subject': The U.S. Women's Antiremoval Petition Campaign, 1829–1831," *Rhetoric and Public Affairs* 5 (2002): 601–624. Theodore argues that although women did petition local, city, and state governments before 1830, the first national petition campaign by women was in 1829–1831 to protest the removal of Southern Indian tribes (602).

20. Lumsden, *Rampant Women*, 55.

21. Suzanne M. Marilley, *Woman Suffrage and the Origins of Liberal Feminism in the United States, 1820–1920* (Cambridge: Harvard University Press, 1996), 28.

22. Marilley, *Woman Suffrage*, 28.

23. As quoted in Lumsden, *Rampant Women*, 56.

24. Adams argued mercilessly against the Gag Rule citing its clear violations of the First Amendment. Anti-slavery petitioners recognized Adams' support and began mailing their petitions directly to him. Adams was eventually threatened with censure from his fellow congressmen in 1837 when he presented the petitions of 22 slaves to Congress. For more on Adams' opposition to the Gag Rule and his eventual victory, see chapter 3 of John T. Morse Jr., *John Quincy Adams* (Boston: Houghton Mifflin, 1883).

25. Gerda Lerner, *The Grimké Sisters from South Carolina: Pioneers for Women's Rights and Abolition* (New York: Oxford University Press, 1998), 206.

26. Stanton et al., *History of Woman Suffrage*, 72.

27. Charles Conrad, "The Transformation of the 'Old Feminist' Movement," *Quarterly Journal of Speech* 67 (1981): 290.

28. The Reconstruction amendments include the Thirteenth, Fourteenth, and Fifteenth Amendments.

29. Flexner and Fitzpatrick, *Century of Struggle*, 151.

30. *Congressional Globe*, 39th Congress, 2nd Session, pt. 1, 56.

31. *Congressional Globe*, 66.

32. Carrie Chapman Catt and Nettie Rogers Shuler, *Woman Suffrage and Politics: The Inner Story of the Suffrage Movement*, (Seattle: University of Washington Press, 1969), 47.

33. Section two of the Fourteenth Amendment reads:

Representatives shall be apportioned among the several States according to their respective numbers, counting the whole number of persons in each State, excluding Indians not taxed. But when the right to vote at any election for the choice of electors for President and Vice President of the United States, Representatives in Congress, the executive and judicial officers of a State, or the members of the Legislature thereof, is denied to any of the male inhabitants of such State, being twenty-one years of age, and citizens of the United States, or in any way abridged, except for participation in rebellion, or other crime, the basis of representation therein shall be reduced in the proportion which the number of such male citizens shall bear to the whole number of male citizens twenty-one years of age in such State.

34. Angela Ray notes that the framing of this debate resulted in an acute difficulty for African American women: "White supremacist and ethnocentric rhetoric suffused the movement during this period. Because the debates were often framed as race versus sex, activist African American women faced painful, impossible choices." See "The Rhetorical Ritual of Citizenship: Women's Voting as Public Performance, 1868–1865," *Quarterly Journal of Speech* 93 (2007): 1–26.

35. The first article sets out the privileges of citizenship and reads, "No state shall make or enforce any law which shall abridge the privileges or immunities of citizens of the United States; nor shall any state deprive any person of life, liberty, or property without due process of law; nor deny to any person within its jurisdiction the equal protection of the laws."

36. Myra Bradwell studied law under her husband and passed the Illinois bar examination, but the Illinois Supreme Court refused to admit her on account of her sex. Bradwell's attorney argued that she was denied the protection granted to her by the privileges and immunities clause of the Fourteenth Amendment.

37. *Bradwell v. Illinois*, 83 U.S. 422 (1873).

38. Catt and Shuler, *Woman Suffrage and Politics*, 92.

39. 24 Fed. Cases, 829–833 (1873); or 11 Blatchford, 200–12 (1873).

40. 88 U.S. 162 (1874).

41. John D. Lawson, ed. *American State Trials* (St. Louis Thomas Law, 1915), 50–51.

42. Virginia Minor did not have legal standing to appeal the case herself on account of gender.

43. *Reed v. Reed*, 404 U.S. 71 (1971).

44. Doris Stevens argues that the influence of the Progressive Era (1890–1925) provided an impetus to all reform. See *Jailed for Freedom* (New York: New Sage Press, 1995), 15.

45. Sarah Hunter Graham, "The Suffrage Renaissance: A New Image for a New Century, 1896–1910." *One Woman, One Vote: Rediscovering the Woman Suffrage Movement.* Ed. Marjorie Spruill Wheeler. (Troutdale, OR: New Sage Press, 1995), 159.

46. Lumsden, *Rampant Women*, 23.

47. "Miss Malone Quits the Suffragettes," New York *Times*, (March 27, 1908): 4.

48. *Davis v. Massachusetts*, 167 U.S. 43 (1897).

49. Margaret A. Blanchard, *Revolutionary Sparks: Freedom of Expression in Modern America* (New York: Oxford University Press, 1992), 63.

50. In the 1937 case *De Jonge v. Oregon*, the Supreme Court ruled that the Fourteenth Amendment's due process clause protected the freedom of assembly. The Court ruled that Dirk de Jonge had the right to organize and speak at Communist Party meetings. In the 1939 case *Hague v. Committee for Industrial Organization*, the Supreme Court held that it was a violation of the First Amendment right to freedom of assembly to prohibit labor meetings on public property. See *De Jonge v. Oregon*, 299 U.S. 353 (1937) and *Hague v. Committee for Industrial Organization*, 307 U.S. 496 (1939).

51. Lumsden, *Rampant Women*, 34.

52. Lumsden, *Rampant Women*, 35.

53. Jennifer Borda, "The Woman Suffrage Parades of 1910–1913: Possibilities and Limitations of an Early Feminist Rhetorical Strategy," *Western Journal of Communication* 66 (2002): 25–52.

54. Simon Newman, *Parades and the Politics of the Street: Festive Culture in the Early American Republic* (Philadelphia: University of Pennsylvania Press, 1997), 64.

55. Blatch organized the Equality League of Self Supporting Women (later to become the Women's Political Union) to bring working and professional women together. The group was affiliated with NAWSA but was organized to support the referendum for woman suffrage in New York State.

56. Borda, "The Woman Suffrage Parades," 47.

57. "Suffragists March in Procession To-Day," New York *Times* (May 6, 1911): 13.

58. "Suffrage Parader Loses Teaching Job," New York *Times* (May 22, 1912): 1.

59. Lumsden, *Rampant Women*, 78.

60. Lumsden, *Rampant Women*, 78.

61. Flexner and Fitzpatrick, *Century of Struggle*, 308.

62. Flexner and Fitzpatrick, *Century of Struggle*, 265, 307–309.

63. Catt and Shuler, *Woman Suffrage and Politics*, 113.

64. Catt and Shuler, *Woman Suffrage and Politics*, 132.

65. The NWP was originally organized under the NAWSA banner in 1913 as the Congressional Union for Woman Suffrage (CU). The NWP broke away from the more conservative NASWA when the organization objected to the militant strategies advocated by Alice Paul and the CU.

66. Lumsden, *Rampant Women*, 7.

67. Library of Congress, "Tactics and Techniques of the National Woman's Party Suffrage Campaign," http://lcweb2.loc.gov/ammem/collections/suffrage/nwp/tactics.html 1

68. See chapter 7 of this book for more instances of Wilson's suppression of free speech during the Red Scare of 1917–1920.

69. Library of Congress, "Tactics and Techniques," 2.

70. Library of Congress, "Tactics and Techniques," 7.

71. Library of Congress, "Tactics and Techniques," 7.

72. Inez Haynes Irwin, *The Story of Alice Paul and the National Woman's Party* (Fairfax, VA: Denlinger's Publishers, 1920; reprint 1977), 473.

73. Irwin, *The Story of Alice Paul*, 473.

74. Haig Bosmajian, "The Abrogation of the Suffragists' First Amendment Rights," *Western Speech* (1974): 221.

75. Doris Stevens, *Jailed for Freedom* (New York: Boni and Liveright, 1920), 94–95.

76. Shirley Abbott, *The National Museum of American History* (New York: Harry N. Abrams, 1981), 427.

77. Stevens, *Jailed for Freedom*, 133.

78. Bosmajian, "The Abrogation," 231–233.

79. According to Bosmajian, "The 1918 amendment to the 1917 Espionage Act made it a federal offense punishable by up to $10,000 fine or twenty years' imprisonment (or both) to utter, print, write, or publish in wartime '. . . any disloyal, profane, scurrilous, or abusive language about the form of government of the United States, or the Constitution of the United States . . . , or any language intended to bring the form of government of the United States, or the Constitution, or the military or naval forces of the United States, or the flag of the United States, or the uniform of the Army or Navy of the United States into contempt, scorn, contumely, or disrepute' " (230).

80. Lumsden, *Rampant Women*, 129.

81. Lumsden, *Rampant Women*, 114.

82. Flexner and Fitzpatrick, *Century of Struggle*, 303.

83. Marouf Hasian, Celeste Condit, and John Lucaites, "The Rhetorical Boundaries of 'The Law': A Consideration of the Rhetorical Culture of Legal Practice and the Case of the 'Separate but Equal' Doctrine," *Quarterly Journal of Speech 82* (1996): 335.

Chapter 7

The Red Scares

Craig R. Smith

In other studies I have advanced the thesis that new technologies prove so threatening that they are almost always regulated by those in power.[1] This was certainly true of Gutenberg's printing press with moveable type and it was equally true of the film industry's "silent pictures." The new medium was barely commercially viable when in 1915 the Supreme Court ruled that films were subject to the prior restraint of state censorship boards.[2] The Court argued that it was matter of "common sense" that the First Amendment was not designed for movies. Not overturned for 37 years,[3] this ruling opened the door for federal censorship during World War I, which halted the momentum of freedom arising from the Progressive movement.[4]

President Wilson's Suppression of Free Speech

The length of that war was undoubtedly extended in 1917 when Russia withdrew from the allied effort due to a revolution in part fomented by Communists. The success of the Communist Revolution in Russia led to a fear of worldwide Marxist activity, not unlike the fear that gripped the civilized world after the French revolution (see chapter 1). The United States was not spared the anxiety. Woodrow Wilson's administration sent a force of U.S. troops to Archangel, Russia to join with other allies in support of the White Russian armies opposing Lenin's Communist Bolsheviks.

Throughout the time of America's direct intervention into World War I and its attempt to prop up the White Russians, Wilson and his administration conducted an unremitting campaign of suppression of free speech at home.[5] Once war was declared, Wilson was aware of ethnic opposition to his policies, particularly among Irish, German, and other central European immigrants. However, he knew that the majority of Americans would close ranks behind their president with the advent of war. Evidence of the bipartisan nature of support for suppression can be seen in former Republican President Theodore Roosevelt's call for sanctions on those opposing U.S. entry into the war.[6]

Despite Wilson's claim to respect civil liberties, the administration was quick to call for legislation that paralleled the Alien and Sedition Acts of 1798. In fact, Wilson had sought to repress his critics as early as 1915, when Roosevelt had launched a withering attack on Wilson's measured response to the sinking of the passenger liner *Lusitania*. Wilson soon claimed that German agents were subverting national will.

Once war was declared, the Congress passed the Espionage Act of 1917 and strengthened it in 1918. It passed the Trading with the Enemy Act in 1918 along with the Sedition Act. Section 3 of the Espionage Act was an outright assault on the First Amendment. One could be arrested for "willfully" making "false reports or false statements with intent to interfere with the operation or success of the [U.S.] military." One could be arrested for "willfully" causing "or attempting to cause, or incite, or attempt to incite, insubordination, disloyalty, mutiny, or refusal of duty, in the military or naval forces of the United States, or . . . willfully obstruct . . . the recruiting or enlistment service of the United States." One could be arrested for uttering, printing, writing, or publishing "any disloyal, profane, scurrilous, or abusive language about the form of government of the United States, or the Constitution of the United States, or the uniform of the Army or Navy . . . in contempt, scorn, contumely or disrepute." One could be arrested for displaying the "flag of any foreign enemy." Fines of up to $10,000 could be imposed along with prison sentences of up to 20 years.[7]

Eugene Debs, the union leader (see chapter 5) and Socialist candidate for president, would be incarcerated under these acts, and Justice Oliver Wendell Holmes would speak for the majority of the Supreme Court in condemning Debs antiwar rhetoric. After the war, Wilson refused to pardon him.[8]

In the meantime, the Espionage Act's censorship provisions allowed Postmaster General Albert Burleson to suppress journals, letters, or whatever he believed to be a threat to national security.[9] Wilson often defended Burleson's judgment.[10] The Trading with the Enemy Act allowed the president to create the Committee on Public Information, better known as the "Creel Committee" after its head George Creel, a former Muckraker who had supported Wilson in 1912 and again in 1916. The committee was charged with coalescing a divided public behind the war effort by putting out "information" and "correcting" disinformation.[11] Faced with the surprising growth of the motion picture industry, Creel initiated a policy of "benign censorship" that often crossed swords with Burleson's activism.[12] With Wilson's support,

Burleson overruled or circumvented Creel and also assumed more powers when the Sedition Act was passed in 1918. Though Burleson came under continued attack from the nation's press and such strong liberal voices as Norman Thomas and Upton Sinclair, Wilson continued to back the man who helped him win the presidential nomination in 1912. In fact, at one juncture, Wilson sought the indictment of a newspaper editor for seditious treason.[13] Even after the war, from his deathbed Wilson continued to support Burleson's suppressive tactics.[14]

Throughout this period, Burleson found a soul mate in Wilson's new Attorney General, A. Mitchell Palmer,[15] who used the previously mentioned legislation to round up suspected Communists and "Reds." He often encouraged state governments to follow his lead. Like many state legislatures, New York's had established, on March 26, 1919, a joint committee to investigate seditious activities. This group instigated the case against Socialist agitator Benjamin Gitlow that reached the Supreme Court (see below). Before that ruling, the same Court would condemn the secretary of the Socialist Party of Philadelphia in *Schenck v. United States* (249 U.S. 47 (1919)) upholding the Espionage Act. Writing for the majority, Justice Holmes argued that Charles Schenck presented "a clear and present danger" to the United States during the war. Holmes refused to accept the argument that Schenck's circular opposing the draft was "speech" or "press," instead Holmes said it was an action.[16] In *Abrams v. United States*, also in 1919, the Supreme Court upheld the conviction of Jacob Abrams and his four cohorts who circulated a leaflet condemning U.S. policy in Russia and calling for a general strike.[17] Crucially, however, in *Abrams*, Holmes and Brandeis dissented. Holmes seemed to realize that these publications were in fact expression, not action. He argued that the "silly leaflets" did not present a danger. Holmes, with Louis D. Brandeis concurring, wrote:

> [T]hese pronunciamentos in no way attack the form of government of the United States.... I do not see how anyone can find the intent required by the statute in any of the defendants' words.... In this case sentences of twenty years imprisonment have been imposed for the publishing of two leaflets that I believe the defendants had as much right to publish as the Government has to publish the Constitution.... [T]he best test of truth is the power of the thought to get itself accepted in the competition of the market.... [T]he United States through many years had shown its repentance for the Sedition Act of 1798, by repaying fines that it imposed.[18]

It was in this case that Holmes developed his famous "marketplace" of ideas conceptualization that would eventually become the majority position of the court in *Gitlow v. New York* (1925),[19] which was the first to apply the First Amendment through the Fourteenth against the states.

In January 1920, however, following the Supreme Court's lead in *Abrams* and *Schenck*, the New York State Legislature did not allow five legally elected Socialists to take their seats in the assembly for fear they would spread Communist propaganda. The speaker of the assembly claimed that the Socialists did not belong to a legitimate party, "You are seeking seats in this body, you who have been elected on a platform that is absolutely inimical to the interests of the State of New York and of the United States." After a hearing, the members were expelled.

The Red Scare of 1919–1920 died away because of a number of short- and long-term factors.[20] First, some heroic politicians, such as Governor Al Smith of New York, refused to sign suppressive legislation. Second, Wilson's Democrats lost the presidential election of 1920 when the Republicans returned to full control of the government on the promise of a return to "normalcy." Third, under the leadership of Leon Trotsky, the Communist Bolsheviks won astounding military victories over their enemies, firmly establishing them as the authoritarian leaders of the new Soviet Union. Fourth, during the depression and into the 1940s, many Americans, particularly the young and academic, were attracted to the messages of Socialists and Communists. Idealists not only hoped to find new solutions to economic calamity, they were in the forefront of the war against fascism in Italy, Spain, and Germany. Little did they know that such activity would open them to harassment during the McCarthy era in the 1950s. Fifth, President Franklin Roosevelt finally recognized the Soviet government in the 1930s; it eventually became an ally against Hitler in 1942. Thus, during World War II, the Supreme Court protected membership in the Communist Party saying it was a movement no different from many others.[21] But all that soon changed.

President Franklin Roosevelt's Attempts at Suppression

FDR had his own problems with sedition during the war. Having endured years of vilification by Republican-owned newspapers over such issues as trying to pack the Supreme Court, failing to end the depression, and angling to get America into the war, Roosevelt was ready, as he wrote J. Edgar Hoover, to "clean up a number of . . . vile publications."[22] The president proceeded to criticize—which was his right—and call for investigations of—which was at least an unethical use of his powers—the New York *Daily News*, Henry Luce the publisher of *Time* and *Life*, and editorialists Drew Pearson and Robert S. Allen, among others. He also tried to keep newspapers from acquiring ownership of radio stations, the first instantiation of the cross-ownership rules of the Federal Communication Commission (FCC).

Blocking Roosevelt's way was his liberal Attorney General Francis Biddle, a man very much committed to civil liberties. J. Edgar Hoover already suspected Biddle of disloyalty because he had opposed the internment of Japanese-Americans. Hoover began a campaign to undercut Biddle. Hoover was not alone. Congressman Hale Boggs of Louisiana, for example, claimed that Biddle was running a "benign policy . . . toward treasonable publications."[23] In March 1942, Roosevelt demanded that Biddle investigate the Chicago *Tribune*, the Washington *Times-Herald*, and the New York *Daily News* for disclosing classified information.

Biddle finessed the situation by going to Hoover to get information on flagrant, right-wing seditionists. He then prosecuted those involved in "a nation-wide conspiracy to destroy the morale of our armed forces through systematic dissemination of sedition."[24] Leading publications, including *Newsweek* and the *New Republic*, supported the Justice Department's decision invoke the Smith Act (The Alien Registration Act) and the Espionage Act against right-wing agitators.[25] The Smith Act imitates the language of the Espionage Act of 1918. The 1940 version makes it "unlawful for any person to knowingly or willfully advocate, abet, advise, or teach the duty, necessity, desirability, or propriety of overthrowing or destroying any government of the United States by force or violence, or by the assassination of any officer of any such government." Section 3 made it illegal to "organize or help to organize any society, group, or assembly of persons who teach, advocate, or encourage the overthrow or destruction of any government of the United States by force or violence; or to be or become a member of, or affiliate with, any such society, group, or assembly of persons, knowing the proposes thereof."[26] This time the fines were up to $10,000 and the sentence was up to 10 years in prison. (This law is mainly still in force. See 18 *U.S. Code Annotated*, section 2385).

Near the end of March 1942, George Christians, the chief officer of the Fascist Crusader White Shirts, and Rudolph Fahl of Denver were arrested for disseminating material that could demoralize the army. In early April, five more seditionists were arrested. The president took pride in the operation during his radio "Fireside Chat" later in the month: "this great war effort . . . must not be impeded by a few bogus patriots who use the sacred freedom of the press to echo the sentiments of the propagandists in Tokyo and Berlin."[27] All of those from the March–April group were convicted by the end of the summer 1942 except Fahl. By the end of the year, 150 persons had been arrested for sedition statements or publications.[28] Biddle's policy of going after only the most radical fascists helped protect the mainline press, but certainly compromised his commitment to the First Amendment. Once the war ended, many believed civil liberties would be restored. But Biddle's activity would pale in the face of what followed.

Cold War Suppression

After 1946, deteriorating U.S.–Soviet relations evolved into a "Cold War" as fear of nuclear retaliation prevented a "hot war." Efforts to stem the spread of Communism became a dominant part of United States foreign policy. The Truman Doctrine, the Marshall Plan, the Berlin Airlift of 1948, the North Atlantic Treaty of 1949, and the Mutual Security Act of 1951 were all parts of this policy to contain the spread of communism. The fear of the Red menace was bipartisan. In one of the most interesting quotations of the time, John Foster Dulles made an analogy that haunts contemporary times. In 1948 he said, "For the first time since the threat of Islam a thousand years ago, Western civilization is on the defensive."[29] Five years later, Dulles was Secretary of State under Eisenhower and calling for the liberation of Eastern Europe.

Truman's Curtailment of Freedom of Expression

Containment suffered several severe blows during the second term of the Truman Administration. The Soviet Union's aggressive policy of nation grabbing inspired Winston Churchill's famous line of 1946 about an "iron curtain" descending across Eastern Europe. In 1949, the Communist threat intensified. The Soviet Union exploded an atom bomb. China fell to the Communists led by Mao Tse-tung, who then joined the "Communist Bloc." Due in part to the China lobby, which partly consisted of former missionaries, the United States had supported the Nationalists led by Chiang Kai-shek.[30] When evidence surfaced that American advisors had hindered Chiang's ability to retrieve Japanese weapons at the end of World War II, the lobby attacked Truman despite the prediction by many State Department advisors that Mao would succeed if reforms weren't made in Chiang's Kuomintang government. Ironically, those responsible for these warnings would come under attack from Senator Joseph McCarthy in the early 1950s. He would not attribute the fall of China to Communist forces to the incompetence of Chiang Kai-shek but to American policy makers in the State Department.

In 1950, the United States led a United Nations' "Peace Keeping Force" to protect South Korea from invading Communists from North Korea. During the first phase of that undeclared war, General Douglas MacArthur, a World War II hero, pushed the North Koreans out of the South and eventually over the Yalu River, the northern border with Red China. There was bitter division in the Truman Administration about what action to take next. General MacArthur advocated bombing the bridges that crossed the Yalu, and he suggested that if Red China entered the war, tactical nuclear weapons should be used to stop the incursion. As heated discussion of MacArthur's disagreement with the administration over the conduct of the war ensued, Communist Chinese forces poured across the Yalu into North Korea, driving the Americans back below the 38th Parallel and inflicting severe losses on MacArthur's forces. When MacArthur expressed further dissent from Truman's policy, he was removed, and the war fell into a bloody stalemate. MacArthur's farewell speech to a joint session of Congress stirred strong emotions: "There are some who for varying reasons would appease Red China. They are blind to history's clear lesson, for history teaches with unmistakable emphasis that appeasement but begets new and bloodier war."[31] Truman's popularity, already low, plummeted.

Many in America saw the conflict in Korea as an indication of a real threat to all governments bordered by Communist powers. This view was intensified by a new domestic crisis. FBI Director Hoover and presidential advisor Clark Clifford claimed that the Soviet Union was fostering spying operations in the United States. Hoover had regularly fed information about potential spies to congressional committees searching for subversives. The rhetorical advantage of this means of leaking information was that members of the House and Senate were immune from libel and slander when operating in an official capacity. Thus, witnesses or those accused of various activities had no legal recourse if they were defamed.

The House Un-American Activities Committee (HUAC) evolved from a series of Hoover-fed committees that began with the Fish Committee (1930–1934) whose charge was carried forward by the McCormick-Dickstein Committee (1934–1935). In 1938 Congressman Martin Dies converted it into the House Un-American Activities Committee, which he used as an anti-Communist pulpit until the U.S. alliance with Stalin during World War II.

When the war ended, HUAC became a permanent standing committee that looked into "subversive and un-American propaganda activities." In 1947, Eugene Dennis, secretary of the Communist Party, was held in contempt of HUAC when he would not testify. In the same year, Truman initiated the Loyalty Oath for federal employees and most states followed by instituting loyalty oaths for their employees, including teachers and professors at public schools and colleges. Thirty-one professors in the University of California system were fired when they refused to sign the loyalty oath passed by the state of California in 1949. None of these professors were found unfit to teach, and many had tenure. Representative Karl Mundt and Senator

Alexander Smith were key players in the passage of legislation (Public Law 402), which established America's overseas propaganda operations, including the "Voice of America" radio program.

In 1948, during hearings held by the House Un-American Activities Committee, Congressman Richard Nixon compromised Alger Hiss, a top State Department official. During the hearings, Hiss was accused by Whittaker Chambers, a former editor for *Time* magazine, of having been a member of a Communist cell. Hiss was eventually convicted of perjury. Senator Karl Mundt of South Dakota joined Congressman Nixon in proposing a bill that made it a crime to attempt the establishment of a Communist dictatorship in America. It passed the House 319 to 58.

During the 1948 election year, fears were further heightened in July when the FBI arrested six members of the Communist Party in their New York City offices. Eventually, 11 leaders of the Party were brought to trial for teaching and advocating "the overthrow and destruction of the government of the United States by force and violence," directly violating the Smith Act. At this juncture most of the press sided with the federal government, and so did the courts. The 11, including Eugene Dennis, were convicted under the Smith Act despite protests from Socialist presidential candidate and former Vice President Henry Wallace and the ACLU. The Dennis 11 were fined $10,000 each and sentenced to five years in jail. In 1951, the Supreme Court upheld the Dennis decision; only Hugo Black and William O. Douglas dissented. Such "liberal" papers as the New York *Times* and the Washington *Post* published editorials in praise of the majority on the Court.[32]

The fear gripping the nation was heightened in 1950 when Julius and Ethel Rosenberg were apprehended for spying. Their sensational trial in 1951 included testimony against them by David and Ruth Greenglass, the brother and sister-in-law of Ethel Rosenberg; Ruth Greenglass confessed to providing information to the Soviets about the Manhattan Project to create nuclear weapons. David Greenglass had been a wartime machinist in Los Alamos, New Mexico, where nuclear research was done, and some speculated that he may have turned on his sister Ethel in order to save the life of his wife. In any case, the sentencing judge claimed that the Rosenbergs were responsible for the Soviets obtaining the Atom Bomb, which encouraged their entry into the Korea War, which led to the deaths of many American soldiers. Therefore, he argued, the death penalty was warranted.[33] The Rosenberg's were executed in June 1953; later examination of cables in the Soviet Union indicate that Julius Rosenberg and David and Ruth Greenglass did provide information. But Ethel Rosenberg is not mentioned. In 2008, co-defendant Martin Sobell, 91, after years of denial, finally admitted that he and Julius were spies for Soviets.

Also in 1950, nearly 2,000 Communist demonstrators fought with police in New York City to protest the Korean War. Congress responded with the Internal Security Act, which required registration of "Communist action, Communist front, and Communist infiltrated" organizations. At the same time, the Soviet Union launched a major propaganda effort to which President Truman responded with his "Campaign of Truth." Many in Congress argued that the Soviet Union was consolidating its hold on Eastern Europe and that the administration's response was ineffective.

Out of these crises, there arose an obsession with preventing persons having unorthodox, left-wing political views, or who might once have entertained such ideas, from assuming positions of prominence, authority, and political leadership. The Taft-Hartley Act, which sought to reform labor unions' excesses, required union officials to pledge that they were not Communists.

Thus, it is clear that the Truman Administration was as anxious as any other political entity to be seen on the right side of this problem.[34] In 1947, three years before Senator Joseph McCarthy came to the fore, Truman was supporting congressional investigations of unions, including the Screen Actors Guild, then headed by Ronald Reagan. However, Truman's record on these issues was fogged by his partisan attacks on McCarthy and his veto of the McCarran-Walter Immigration Act. His record in the late 1940s matches that of many liberal groups clamoring to avoid the soft-on-communism label.[35] Even Americans for Democratic Action, a liberal lobby formed in 1946, purged its ranks of Communists and former Communists in 1947.

The Rise of Senator Joseph McCarthy

Robert L. Ivie's analysis of George Kennan's political rhetoric shows that Kennan was partially at fault for encouraging the environment that spawned McCarthy.[36] Specifically, Kennan "was largely responsible for creating in the earliest phase of the cold war . . . an overly frightful image of the Soviet threat."[37] Kennan's descriptions of Soviet leaders, particularly of Stalin, were grist for the propaganda mills of the far right. Perhaps more than any other foreign service diplomat, it was Kennan who attributed conspiratorial motives to the Soviets.

We should also note that the threat of internal subversion was real. Communists under instruction from the Soviet Union were trying to take over various unions.[38] Thus, there were real external and internal threats to United States' security during this era.

These threats would serve as proof for Senator McCarthy's less well-documented claims. He had been elected to the United States Senate from

Wisconsin in 1948. McCarthy's rise to political power is explained in part by his appeal to Irish and German Catholics, who generations earlier opposed World War I and Woodrow Wilson. As they witnessed the fall of Eastern Europe and heard the anti-Communist litany from the Catholic hierarchy, they were receptive to McCarthy's call to arms. In the context of the times, he perceived that the threat of Communist infiltration into the federal government could be portrayed in realistic terms that would produce political capital. He saw that the political instability that prevailed on a global scale and the domestic crisis of confidence in the Truman Administration created political turmoil and fueled fears of subversion. He sensed that American citizens were especially sensitive to, and fearful of, a Communist threat to their government, the very government that was supposed to be leading the battle to contain Communism. The United States was deeply embroiled in a United Nations "police action" against Communists in Korea, and the reality of at least some infiltration into branches of the federal government was coming to light. McCarthy stepped forward to *save* the American government from Communist infiltration.

McCarthy employed a rhetoric of purification that was featured at the 1952 Republican Convention in Chicago. After a rousing introduction by Walter Hallahan, McCarthy stirred the crowd with a pledge to purge the United States of all Communists:

> I say, one Communist in a defense plant is one Communist too many. One Communist on the faculty of one university is one Communist too many. One Communist among American advisors at Yalta was one Communist too many. And even if there were only one Communist in the State Department, that would be one Communist too many.[39]

As McCarthy studied his subject, he also brought a set of tactics into play that would eventually undermine his credibility two years later. One of his favorites was to establish his assertions using an inartistic and unethical proof such as a cropped photo or claiming that he had the evidence for his claims secreted away somewhere else. For example, McCarthy presented what he claimed was a list of 205 Communists that had infiltrated the State Department. The speech announcing this news was delivered in February 1950 at an obscure GOP women's meeting in Wheeling, West Virginia. The proof for this assertion was a list he waved at the audience, a list that turned out to be his laundry slip from his hotel, though the audience and national media did not know that at the time.[40]

Another tactic, McCarthy's general use of exaggeration, is clearly documented by a review of his speeches. At various times he claimed he

could name more than 200 Communists in the State Department, then in
Reno and Salt Lake City he said they numbered 57, then 81, respectively.
Later the numbers changed again, first to 121, then to 106. In an attempt
to refute McCarthy's accusations, Democratic Senate Majority Leader Scott
Lucas of Illinois secured passage of a motion to have the Foreign Relations
Committee conduct a full investigation into McCarthy's charges of Com-
munist infiltration. The investigating committee, headed by Senator Millard
Tydings of Maryland, called the charges a "fraud and a hoax perpetrated on
the Senate of the United States and the American people."[41]

McCarthy's Rhetorical Tactics

Nonetheless, McCarthy won this rhetorical skirmish and emerged from the
early hearings as something of a hero for many Americans. In the 1950 congressional elections, McCarthy gained revenge by helping Republican candidate
John Marshall Butler defeat Tydings in a vile, low, unscrupulous campaign. As
the 1952 election approached, McCarthy traveled the country drawing large
crowds. He was joined by Republican Senators Jenner, Mundt, and Wherry
as he pressed his attack. And in the process, he built a strong coalition that
included the dispossessed of the military, such as those in the Pentagon who
vehemently disagreed with Truman's Korean policy and who supported General
MacArthur's desire to take the war into Red China.[42] The coalition included
Joseph P. Kennedy and other isolationists who had opposed entry into World
War II.[43] It included the China lobby, a group dedicated to Chiang Kai-shek's
dream of overthrowing Mao Tse-tung; Chiang had taken refuge on the island
of Formosa (Taiwan) and imposed his government-in-exile on the island. And
it included such religious groups as the missionaries who had returned from
China and lay Catholics who opposed atheistic Communism and the Soviet
Union for its takeover of Catholic countries in Europe.

McCarthy was appealing to these groups for several reasons. First,
each wanted something purified. Isolationists tended to be xenophobic; they
wanted immigration restricted and immigrant stock reduced. The military
dispossessed wanted to clean the military of civilian control and manipulation.
The religious groups wanted to rid the world of Godless Communism.

Second, these groups were also open to McCarthy's paranoid style.[44]
Only four years after World War II, when America seemed at the height of
its power, the world had lost its bearings. Nations were falling under Communist control at an appalling rate. The Soviets were developing nuclear
weapons. America was at war again and not winning it. The State Department housed Communists and spies who were being discovered on a regular
basis. These events defied logic and invited a conspiratorial explanation to
which the group adhered.

Another contributing factor to the strength of this coalition was McCarthy's ability to manipulate the press. The Hearst and McCormick papers, columnists such as Walter Winchell, Westbrook Pegler, and H. V. Kaltenborn converted McCarthy's allegations into headlines, thereby lending them credibility. Many others were intimidated by his tactics and feared that he could affect their readership and advertising revenue. Several reporters who opposed the Senator soon found their pasts being investigated.[45] Others were vilified from the floor of the U.S. Senate where McCarthy was immune from prosecution for slander. Reporters Joseph and Stewart Alsop, for example, were described as fellow travelers with the Communists.[46] McCarthy compared newspapers that opposed him with the Communists' *Daily Worker*.[47] During his feud with the Milwaukee *Journal*, he said, "[W]hen you send checks over to the *Journal* . . . you are contributing to bringing the Communist Party line into the homes of Wisconsin."[48] The *Journal* made it a habit of inserting corrections into McCarthy's statements and warning readers about the veracity of the senator's comments.

Furthermore, McCarthy's mastery of press deadlines served him well. Knowing that most reporters needed a lead story by 11 A.M., McCarthy would hold press conferences at 10 A.M. issuing serious charges and backing them up with "documentation." Newspeople rarely had enough time to check the documentation on the day of the story, so they printed it and then checked it later. Although this might lead to a correction or editorial slap at McCarthy later, the responses were never featured on the front page as were McCarthy's initial charges.

The press and others were also taken in by McCarthy's strategic use of research. For example, his 96-page pamphlet, modestly called *McCarthyism*, contained 313 footnoted references, thereby giving it a scholarly patina. Few had the time to check these references. And since they had been gathered with some care by McCarthy's aide, lawyer Roy Cohn, they had a legal burnish that was intimidating.[49] McCarthy reinforced this image by referring to his "bulging briefcase" of corroborating evidence, which he said held photostats of documents that could prove what seemed to be outlandish claims.

Like others we have examined, McCarthy and his supporters were not above exaggeration and claims of guilt by association. They argued that one former Communist employed by the State Department meant that a large section of the department had been infiltrated and subverted to Communism. McCarthy also used these tactics to great effect when questioning witnesses. Here is a typical exchange between McCarthy and one of his victims. In this case, Reed Harris, a civil servant from the information services division of the State Department had been called to testify:

McCarthy: You [worked at] Columbia University in the early thirties, is that right?

Harris: I did, Mr. Chairman.

McCarthy: You resigned from the University. Did the Civil Liberties Union provide you with an attorney at that time?

Harris: I had many offers of attorneys and one of those was from the American Civil Liberties Union, yes.

McCarthy: You know the Civil Liberties Union has been listed as a front for, and doing the work of, the Communist Party?

Harris: Mr. Chairman, this was 1932.

McCarthy: I know it was 1932. Do you know they since have been listed as a front for, and doing the work of the Communist Party?

Harris: I do not know that they have been listed so, sir.

McCarthy: You don't know they have been listed?

Harris: I have heard that mentioned or read that mentioned.

McCarthy: You wrote a book in 1932. I'm going to ask you again at the time you wrote this book did you feel that professors should be given the right to teach sophomores that marriage "should be cast off of our civilization as antiquated and stupid religious phenomena"? Was that your feeling at that time?

Harris: My feeling was that professors should have the right to express their considered opinions on any subject whatever they were, sir.

McCarthy: I'm going to make you answer this.

Harris: I'll answer, yes, but you put an implication on it and you feature this particular point out of the book which of course is quite out of context. . . . The American public doesn't get an honest impression of even that book, bad as it is, from what you are quoting from it.

McCarthy: Then let's continue to read your own writings.

Harris: From 21 years ago?

In this exchange, Harris was associated with a "Communist front organization" because he had considered using a lawyer from the ACLU in 1932. He was also badgered and his work was quoted out of context, another rhetorical practice commonplace in arousing fear in the public. The former passage, and there are many more like it, indicates an assumption of guilt where the evidence is made to fit the crime. The passage also reveals that several tactics are at work at the same time, making it difficult for the defendant to recover, let alone respond in an extemporaneous setting. When written down, such fallacies are not difficult to discern, but when uttered in a highly confrontational, pressurized oral situation, they often prove effective.

McCarthy used the Senate's subcommittee system to create spaces for his rhetoric. As we have already seen, it was a rhetoric of interrogation. On

March 26, 1953, for example, McCarthy convened his Permanent Subcommittee Investigation of the Senate Committee on Government Operations, with his trusted aide, Roy Cohn sitting as Chief Counsel to the committee. On this day, the committee called Dashiell Hammett, the famous author of detective stories, before the committee. Cohn and McCarthy peppered Hammett regarding his membership in the Community Party, his financial contributions to the Party, and his opinion of the viability of the Party in the United States. Hammett answered the ideological questions but took the Fifth Amendment privilege on pragmatic matters.

Then McCarthy asked one last question: "Mr. Hammett, if you were spending, as we are, over a hundred million dollars a year on an information program to fight communism, would you purchase the works of some 75 Communist authors and distribute their works throughout the world, placing our official approval upon those works?" Hammett replied, "If I were fighting communism, I don't think I would do it by giving people any books at all."[50] Those present broke into laughter, but Hammett's books were soon removed from the State Department libraries. President Eisenhower eventually intervened and the books were put back on the shelves.

McCarthy's most spectacular exaggeration occurred when he expanded the case of an Army mishap into a congressional hearing that lasted 36 days and produced 7,300 pages of transcripts.[51] Private Schine, who was a close friend of McCarthy's counsel Roy Cohn, claimed he had evidence of Communist infiltration into the Army. By mistake, the Army had prevented Schine from presenting his evidence to them. He then claimed there was a cover up. When the congressional committee at first refused to hear Schine, they gave McCarthy the opening he wanted. At a hearing on February 18, 1954, of McCarthy's Subcommittee, "McCarthy exploded into a personal attack on General Zwicker, roughing him up verbally and humiliating him. In this one act, McCarthy had taken on the full power of the elite officer corps of the Army. . . . The Schine incident was blown into a major crisis when McCarthy claimed that Schine . . . was being held 'hostage.' "[52]

Clearly, extrapolation from limited instances is one of the most potent methods of making an alleged danger salient for the public. This incident also caused the enmity of Secretary of Defense Stevens, who rose to defend Zwicker. Stevens eventually charged that McCarthy and his staff brought undo pressure on the Army to help out Cohn's friend Private Schine. Steven's claim led to the Army-McCarthy hearings where McCarthy turned attention from the Schine incident to Communist influence in the Army. It would be the zenith of McCarthy's power.

In the meantime, McCarthyists sought to remove Democrats in order to strengthen McCarthyists' power in particular and that of Republicans in general. As they charged Democrats with being "soft on communism," they generated added publicity and exacerbated public anxiety over the question of subversion. Here, as in the other cases in this book, ulterior political motives led to renewed and intensified claims about the nature of the alleged threat. To the McCarthyists, the danger of communism was expanded by the threat of the now partially documented infiltration of the State Department and the Armed Forces. In this exchange between Senators Stuart Symington and McCarthy during the famous Army-McCarthy hearings of 1954, McCarthy feeds the conspiracy claims he first outlined in 1950:

> Symington: Our people have been urged to entertain serious doubts as to the dedication and loyalty of our armed forces from top to bottom.
> McCarthy: One of the subjects of this inquiry is to find out who was responsible for succeeding in calling off the hearing of Communist infiltration in the government. At this point I find out there's no way of ever getting at the truth. The iron curtain is pulled down so we can't tell what happened.

McCarthy was also noted for his ruthless attacks on an individual's motives and trustworthiness. His targets included such prominent figures as General and Secretary of State George Marshall, Secretary of State Dean Acheson, and Owen Lattimore, a noted specialist on Asian affairs in the State Department. McCarthy was sweeping and vitriolic in his attacks: Professor Lattimore was "the top Soviet espionage agent" in the State Department, and President Truman was "a sonofabitch" who would let "red waters . . . lap at all our shores."[53] More than anything else, this sort of recklessness and character assassination probably contributed to his ultimate censure by the Senate, but in the early going, the attacks brought publicity that enlarged McCarthy's audience. His attack on one of attorney Joseph Welch's aides was his most widely noticed exploitation of senatorial immunity to destroy the character of those who opposed him. His charge and Welch's reply (cited below) occurred on national television during the 1954 "Army-McCarthy Hearings." Said McCarthy of a member of Welch's staff, "I think we should tell Mr. Welch that he has in his law firm a young man named Fisher whom he recommended incidentally to do work on this committee, who has been . . . a member of an organization which is named . . . as the legal bulwark for the Communist Party." In these instances, the identification of alleged new dangers served to fuel the radicals' resolve and to increase public anxiety.

Federal Legislation and Local Activities

Intimidating liberals such as Senator Hubert Humphrey, the McCarthyists were able to pass the Subversive Activities Control Act in 1950 and the McCarran-Walter Immigration Act in 1952. The former called for the use of various loyalty tests for government employees, and it promulgated several spurious investigations. The Act established a Subversive Activities Control Board to ensure registration with the U.S. Attorney General of Communist action and/or front groups. The Act also denied passports to members of the Communist Party and its "fronts," and required members of the Communist Party to register individually. The Control Board was given power to determine which organizations and individuals were Communist-action or Communist-front groups.

In 1952, the McCarran-Walter Immigration Act was passed over President Truman's veto by a vote of 278 to 133 in the House and 57 to 26 in the Senate.[54] It gave the State Department authority to prevent foreigners with alien political beliefs or affiliations from entering the country. This throwback to the Alien Act of 1798 remains in force today. Under the law, current and former Communists, as well as homosexuals, anarchists, and those whom the State Department deems "prejudicial to the public interest," may be excluded. The McCarran-Walter Act, a comprehensive codification of the immigration and naturalization system, was amended by Congress in 1987 to say that aliens may no longer be denied entry into the United States on the basis of "past, current, or expected beliefs, statements, or associations."[55]

McCarthy did not limit his activities to drafting and supporting legislation. McCarthy's supporters often initiated action on the local level. For example, his followers incited the citizens of Boston to take action against their own public library.[56] Once organized, his followers had books removed from the shelves and instituted other forms of censorship. In 1951, the Los Angeles City Council passed an ordinance condemning modern art as Communist propaganda and banned its display in public. On college campuses the picture was not much better. Those who admitted to being former Communists or left wing radicals or took the Fifth Amendment before congressional committees were often fired, censured, or placed on probation, even though Congress took no action against them. In fact, many of these professors had tenure and it did not protect them from losing their jobs. The University of California proved particularly egregious in this regard.[57] Harvard proved an exception. When Governor Christian Herter of Massachusetts asked Harvard President Nathan Pusey to fire physicist Wendell Furry because the professor had taken the Fifth Amendment before McCarthy's committee, Pusey refused, arguing that universities needed to preserve academic freedom.

What we learn in this case is that at the level of "community action," the end justifies the means. Radical elements are apt to become guilty of wide-ranging repression, and others, such as college administrators and librarians, often cower before them. McCarthyism inspired 26 states to enact laws barring Communists from running for public office. Twenty-eight states passed laws denying state or local civil service jobs to Communists, and 32 states required teachers to take a loyalty oath. In 11 states, Communists were denied the right to meet in school buildings. Furthermore, many private meeting halls, including Madison Square Garden, refused to rent to groups tagged as Communist Fronts by the Attorney General.[58] Suspected Communists were denied low-income housing, and could not obtain passports.[59]

Opposition

Voices had been heard in opposition to McCarthy. One of the first was Senator Margaret Chase Smith of Maine. As a Republican, she risked her career in a speech on the floor of the Senate on June 1, 1950, that called on her colleagues to search their "consciences" about what was going on. When President Eisenhower, who had appeared with McCarthy in Wisconsin during the 1952 presidential campaign, turned against him, Eisenhower was finally accepting responsibility to rid the party of its pariah.[60] Perhaps the first instance occurred while Eisenhower was delivering a commencement address at Dartmouth College on June 14, 1953, a year before the McCarthy hearings. McCarthy had used his Chairmanship of a subcommittee to attack the Voice of America and its stocking of overseas libraries with books McCarthy found questionable: "Frankly, I do not care what they do with the book after they remove it, whether they burn it or not. I can see no objection to destroying it."[61] Eisenhower attacked the Senator's excesses:

> Don't join the book burners. Don't think you are going to conceal faults by concealing evidence that they ever existed. Don't be afraid to go in your library. . . . How will we defeat communism unless we know what it is, and what it teaches; and why does it have such an appeal for men? . . . And even if they think ideas that are contrary to ours, their right to say them, their right to record them, and their right to have them at places where they are accessible to others is unquestioned[62]

Eisenhower's disavowal of McCarthyism did not satisfy Truman. In November 1953, the former president went on national television to issue a highly partisan attack: "It is now evident that the present administration has fully embraced, for political advantage, McCarthyism. I'm not referring to the Senator from Wisconsin—he's only important in that his name has taken on a dictionary meaning in the world. And that meaning is the corruption of truth, the abandonment of our historical devotion to fair play."[63] Perhaps stung by this criticism and fearing for the Army's credibility, Eisenhower was more direct in his criticism of McCarthy in his televised address to the nation in

1954: "[T]he greater is the need that we look at them, our anxieties, clearly face to face without fear like honest, straightforward Americans . . . so we do not fall prey to hysterical thinking. . . . First of all, this fear [of Communist subversion] has been greatly exaggerated as to numbers."[64]

Throughout this time period, senators rose to attack McCarthy and warn the nation of his dangerous tactics. On March 9, 1954, Senator Flanders of Vermont issued a statement that was made part of Edward R. Morrow's "See It Now" broadcast that evening (see below). Flanders, a Republican, concluded that "[McCarthy] is a one-man party, and that its name is 'McCarthyism,' a title which he has proudly accepted. . . . He goes forth to battle and proudly returns with the scalp of a pink Army dentist. We may assume that this presents the depth and seriousness of Communist penetration in this country at this time."[65] When Eisenhower read Flanders' speech, he asked him down to the White House to discuss the matter further.

The most dramatic assault on McCarthy was launched by Joseph Welch in response to McCarthy's smear of one of Welch's aides (see above). Welch, while on live television, provided the most dramatic moment of the Army-McCarthy Hearings:

> Until this moment, Senator, I think I never really gauged your cruelty or your recklessness. Fred Fisher is a young man who went to the Harvard law school and came to my firm and is starting what looks to be a brilliant career with us. . . . It is, I regret to say, equally true that I fear he shall always bear a scar needlessly inflicted by you. If it were in my power to forgive you for your reckless cruelty, I would do so. I like to think I'm a gentle man, but your forgiveness will have to come from someone other than me. . . . Let us not assassinate this lad further, Senator, you've done enough. Have you no sense of decency, sir, at long last?

Welch then stalked from the hearing room, tears streaming down his face. The scene was played and replayed on televisions across America. Attorney Welch's reply would win sympathy for his young aide and cut through McCarthy's rhetorical shield. It is important to note that it was not logic that revealed McCarthy for who he was; it was an emotional attack. Its impact was dramatic. In January 1954, the Gallup Poll showed a record high of 50 percent of the American people viewing McCarthy with some favor; 29 percent viewed him unfavorably, and 21 percent expressed no opinion. By the time the Army-McCarthy Hearings ended on June 17, 1954, McCarthy's standing in the Gallup Poll had dropped to 35 percent favorable and 49 percent unfavorable.[66] There seems little doubt that viewing McCarthy's televised attacks on the character of individuals established that he was too

unrestrained and insinuative to be credible on the general subject of the
threat of Communist influence in government and elsewhere.

The Media Counterattacks

Long before McCarthy's vile tactics were obvious to the nation, they were
clear to some opinion leaders in the media. Fortunately, a significant number
of the printed press assumed their historic role of guardian for the First
Amendment, while at the same time uncovering the truth about Senator
McCarthy. The truly encouraging fact from this period is that McCarthy
was attacked not only early and often by the print media, but that even
conservative Republican publications went after him.

For example, Republican Henry Luce's *Time* magazine printed this of
McCarthy on October 22, 1951:

> The Reds in Government, if any, were safe. After nearly two years
> of tramping the nation and shouting that he was "rooting out the
> skunks," just how many Communists has Joe rooted out? The
> answer: none. At best, he might claim an assist on three minor
> and borderline cases which Government investigators had already
> spotted. . . . The public quite correctly, thought that someone must
> be to blame. Joe McCarthy went into the business of providing
> scapegoats. It was easier to string along with Joe's wild charges
> than to settle down to a sober examination of the chuckle-headed
> "liberalism," the false assumptions and the fatuous complacency
> that had endangered the security of the U.S. That he got a lot
> of help from the Administration spokesmen who still insist that
> nothing was wrong with U.S. policy helps to explain McCarthy's
> success—although it in no way excuses McCarthy. Joe, like all
> effective demagogues, found an area of emotion and exploited it.
> No regard for fair play, no scruple for exact truth hampers Joe's
> political course. If his accusations destroy reputations, if they
> subvert the principle that a man is innocent until proven guilty,
> he is oblivious. Joe, immersed in the joy of battle, does not even
> seem to realize the gravity of his own charges.

McCarthy was infuriated by the attack and threatened to mount an advertiser
boycott of *Time*. Luce backed off for a short time, then in the September 8,
1952, issue of the popular *Life* magazine, his warning was reissued:

> If Mr. Truman & co. had not derided the issue of Communist
> infiltration of the U.S. government, it might never have gained

currency. But the President did call the Hiss case a "red herring" and Secretary of State Dean Acheson did "refuse" to turn
his back on Alger Hiss. So in 1950—a Congressional election
year—another smart politician with an elastic conscience aimed
low at an obvious target. The junior Senator from Wisconsin, Joe
McCarthy, charged there were 205 persons, known by Secretary
of State Dean Acheson to be Communists, who were still in
the State Department. Joe never proved his charge, numeri-
cally or otherwise; instead he went on making more sensational
accusations. . . . McCarthyism is a form of exaggerated campaign
oratory; it is also abuse of the freedom of speech we enjoy in this
country. Every single individual, including the editors of LIFE,
who lapses from his highest sense of responsibility to truth, is
guilty, in some degree, of McCarthyism. But we believe in free
speech—we believe that the best cure for exaggeration and distortion is the counter attack which will be and *is* made against the
exaggerations and distortions. Of this the history of McCarthyism
is a superb example. No one has more energetically counterattacked
than Senator Joe McCarthy. In fact, the very word McCarthyism
is the cannon fire of the anti-McCarthyist.

Luce's attack was only the tip of the iceberg. McCarthy was opposed by many
major newspapers including the New York *Times*, the Washington *Post*, the
Christian Science Monitor, the St. Louis *Post-Dispatch*, the Baltimore *Sun*, the
Chicago *Daily News*, the New York *Herald-Tribune*, the Kansas City *Star*,
and the Louisville *Courier-Journal*.

Individual journalists, many of them syndicated, proved to be modern
day Thomas Coopers. For example, Drew Pearson, who had used McCarthy
for a source when the senator first came to Washington, turned on him
after the Wheeling speech of 1950, and attacked him in 58 of his nationally syndicated columns.[67] On the floor of the Senate, McCarthy claimed
that Pearson was the "sugar-coated voice of Russia." Anthony Lewis wrote
a series of Pulitzer Prize winning articles in the Washington *Daily News* in
July 1954.[68] They resulted in the reinstatement of Abraham Chasanow in
the Navy after McCarthyists had had him removed.

The editorials and articles of the print media laid the groundwork for
what would be transmitted by television, a newly emerging force in American
society. The new medium attacked the monster that McCarthy had become
by doing what the print media could not: televise McCarthy and his tactics.
The public did not like what it saw through the camera's eye.

Edward R. Murrow opened his *See It Now* broadcast of April 6, 1954,
with: "Tonight's report consists *entirely* of certain remarks by Senator Joseph

R. McCarthy. . . ." Murrow's earlier program of March 9 had shown McCarthy
doing his worst. After McCarthy protested, Murrow gave McCarthy equal
time to reply. Both programs were carried at prime time in 36 major cities by
the CBS television network. For his March 9 program, Murrow had carved
a frightening picture of McCarthy from 15,000 feet of film.[69] To conclude
the program, Murrow put what the audience had seen in perspective:

> Often operating as a one-man committee, [McCarthy] has trav-
> eled far, interviewed many, terrorized some, accused civilian and
> military leaders of the past administration of a great conspiracy
> to turn the country over to Communism, investigated and
> substantially demoralized the present State Department, made
> varying charges of espionage at Fort Monmouth. (The Army says
> it has been unable to find anything relating to espionage there.)
> He has interrogated a varied assortment of what he calls "Fifth
> Amendment Communists." . . . Other critics have accused the
> Senator of using the bull whip and smear. . . . Two of the staples
> of his diet are the investigations (protected by immunity) and the
> half truth. . . . His primary achievement has been in confusing
> the public mind as between internal and the external threat of
> Communism. We must not confuse dissent with disloyalty. We
> must remember always that accusation is not proof and that
> conviction depends upon evidence and due process of law. We
> will not walk in fear. . . . We will not be driven by fear into an
> age of unreason if we dig deep in our history and our doctrine,
> and remember that we are not descended from fearful men,
> not from men who feared to write, to speak, to associate and
> to defend causes which were for the moment unpopular. This
> is no time for men who oppose Senator McCarthy's methods
> to keep silent. . . . [H]e didn't create this situation of fear, he
> merely exploited it and rather successfully. Cassius was right,
> "The fault, dear Brutus, is not in our stars, but in ourselves."
> Good night—and good luck.

CBS was inundated with calls, the vast majority favorable to Murrow's position. Responsible members of the media community rallied round Murrow,
praising his courage.

McCarthy chose to send a film of his remarks to CBS to rebut Murrow's
charges of March 9. CBS played it unedited for the April program. Here
are some excerpts, which show just how well television worked to reveal
McCarthy's nature. Although this kind of oratory might pass muster on the
stump, it clearly violated television's cool decorum:

[O]rdinarily, I would not take time out from the important work at hand to answer Murrow. However, in this case I feel justified in doing so because Murrow is a symbol, the leader and the cleverest of the jackal pack which is always found at the throat of anyone who dares to expose individual Communists and traitors. I am compelled by the facts to say to you that Mr. Edward R. Murrow, as far back as twenty years ago, was engaged in propaganda for Communist causes. For example, the Institute of International Education, of which he was the acting director, was chosen to act as a representative by a Soviet agency to do a job which would normally be done by the Russian Secret Police. Mr. Murrow sponsored a Communist school in Moscow. In the selection of American students and teachers who were to attend, Mr. Murrow's organization was known as Voks. V-O-K-S. Many of those selected were later exposed as Communists. Murrow's organization selected such notorious Communists as Isadore Bugin, David Zablodowsky. Incidentally, Zablodowsky was forced out of the United Nations, when my chief counsel presented his case to the grand jury and gave a picture of his Communist activities. Now, Mr. Murrow, by his own admission, was a member of the IWW—that's the Industrial Workers of the World—a terrorist organization cited as subversive by an attorney general of the United States, who stated that it was an organization which seeks (and I quote) "to alter the Government of the United States by unconstitutional means." Now, other government committees have had before them actors, screen writers, motion picture producers, and others who admitted Communist affiliations but pleaded youth or ignorance. Now, Murrow can hardly make the same plea. On March 9 of this year, Mr. Murrow, a trained reporter, who had traveled all over the world, who was the educational director of CBS, followed implicitly the Communist line as laid down in the last six months, laid down not only by the *Communist Daily Worker*, but by the Communist magazine. . . . Now, the question: why is it important to you, the people of America, to know why the Education Director and the Vice President of CBS so closely follows the Communist Party line? To answer that question we must turn back the pages of history. A little over a hundred years ago a little group of men in Europe conspired to deliver the world to a new system, to Communism. . . . What do the Communists think of me and what do the Communists think of Mr. Murrow? One of us is on the side of the Communists; the other is against the Communists. . . . Here is a *Communist*

Daily Worker of March 9, containing 7 articles and a principal editorial, all attacking McCarthy, and the same issue lists Mr. Murrow's program as—listen to this—"one of tonight's best bets on TV."

In this instance, as in later televised hearings, McCarthy's methods were more evident than on hustings. Sitting in living rooms, viewers could watch dispassionately and listen critically. McCarthy's shaky foundations of "fact" and his leaps in drawing inferences were more obvious on Murrow's "news program" than they were in heated political settings. Furthermore, he was attacking a highly respected reporter–commentator and one who had weighed his own words carefully in criticizing McCarthy. The public had the choice of rejecting their most credible leaders—Henry Luce, Dwight Eisenhower, Harry Truman, Edward R. Murrow—or rejecting McCarthy. Increasingly, McCarthy stood alone until, by the end of the televised Army Hearings, his strategies became obvious.[70]

The Collapse of McCarthyism

It appears that at the point where radicals' schemes of *implementation* are made clear through enactments or proposals, these groups become most fully open to attack or to partial co-optation by mainstream political groups. In the face of this counterattack, the McCarthyist collapse was dramatic. It demonstrates that because inflammatory rhetoric requires constant feeding, the lead rhetor overreaches himself or herself, and then descends into reck-lessness, character assassination, and myriad fallacies. To the end, McCarthy continued to claim that there were many Communists in the government, but his colleagues in the Senate grew impatient with his excesses. As in the case of the *See It Now* broadcasts, it was television that proved McCarthy's final undoing. His performance during the 36 days of the Army-McCarthy Hearings revealed the monster in the man to a majority of Americans. The thesis that permitting more speech better promotes civil liberties than less speech seems verified. What began as the Permanent Subcommittee on Investigations of the Senate Committee on Government Operations under McCarthy's chairmanship, now became the Army-McCarthy Hearings, the last gasp on a grand stage broadcast to America. From the cropping of the picture that made it appear that General Zwicker was physically, and hence personally, closer to Private Schine than he actually was, to the charge that the Army tried to get the hearing called off, McCarthy revealed his zest for the theatrical and sophistic.[71] He would learn the hard way that television is not a theatrical medium; it is personal and revealing. Furthermore, the public, unlike the courts of law, is unlikely to accept a defense built around a series of assertions that read like McCarthy's: "We didn't do it. Even if we did it, it wasn't improper. Even if it were improper, the other side did worse."[72] The manic snicker, the high-pitched whining, the constant overstatement, the verbal tricks and the five o'clock shadow didn't help. America tired of his points of order, Pentagon politicians, and Fifth Amendment Communists.

At the end of the hearings, Senator John McClellan (D-Arkansas) said, "Simply to say that this series of events is regrettable is a gross understatement. They are deplorable and unpardonable." On July 30, 1954, a resolution censuring McCarthy was introduced in the Senate. It passed by a vote of 67 to 22.[73] His powers were thus further diminished. His death in 1957 left his now enfeebled "crusade" without a leader. Ironically, it was not until that year that Supreme Court finally put limitations on the House Un-American Activities Committee requiring it to detail the purposes of its inquiries.[74]

That, of course, was not the end of McCarthyist tactics used to silence the opposition. In 1959, J. Edgar Hoover expressed his intolerance of "publications which are severely and unfairly discrediting our American way of life and praising directly or indirectly the Soviet system." He called for an investigation into "subversive factors in the backgrounds of some of the prominent columnists, editors, commentators, authors, et cetera, which could be influencing such slanted views."[75] Freedom of Information Act inquiries have revealed investigations of H. L. Mencken, Robert Frost, Thomas Wolfe, Dorothy Parker, Truman Capote, Lillian Hellman, Aldous Huxley, Carl Sandburg, Sinclair Lewis, Pearl Buck, William Faulkner, Ernest Hemmingway, and John Steinbeck, just to name the most prominent.

Clearly, we must be ever vigilant about what various branches of the government are up to. If this kind of thing could happen so recently in our history, it is not impossible to imagine it happening again in the near future. Rhetoric is a two-edged sword. It can be wielded in the defense of truth, but it can also advance causes that threaten our basic liberties. If all sides of a given dispute are equally versed in rhetorical theory, then perhaps they can keep one another from using unethical and fallacious tactics and hold those involved to the pursuit of the justice.

Notes

1. See Craig R. Smith, *To Form a More Perfect Union* (Lanham, MD: University Press, 1993), introduction.
2. See *Mutual Film Corporation v. Industrial Communication of Ohio*, 236 U.S. 230 (1915); *Mutual Film Corporation of Missouri v. Hodges*, 236 U.S. 248 (1915).

3. See *Joseph Burstyn, Inc. v. Wilson*, 343 U.S. 495 (1952).

4. See Donna Lee Dickerson, *The Course of Tolerance: Freedom of Press in Nineteenth Century America* (Westport, CT: Greenwood Press, 1990); Timothy L. Gleason, "19th Century Legal Practice and Freedom of Press: An Introduction to Unfamiliar Terrain," *Journalism History* 14 (1987): 27–33.

5. Many historians have examined this administration from different perspectives. Some of the more recent that highlight its suppressive nature include Robert H. Ferrell, *Woodrow Wilson and World War I, 1917–1921* (New York: Harper & Row, 1985), 208ff; Christopher C. Gibbs, *The Great Silent Majority: Missouri's Resistance to World War I* (Columbia: University of Missouri Press, 1988); August Heckscher, *Woodrow Wilson* (New York: Charles Scribner's Sons, 1991); Paul Murphy, *World War I and the Origins of Civil Liberties in the United States* (New York: Norton, 1979) particularly 26–32; David M. Rabin, "The Emergence of Modern First Amendment Doctrine," *University of Chicago Law Review*, 50 (1984): 1217–1219.

6. See Ferrell, *Woodrow Wilson*, 204; H. C. Peterson and Gilbert C. Fite, *Opponents of the War* (Madison: University of Wisconsin Press, 1957), 14.

7. 40 *U.S. Statutes at Large*, (1918), 553–554.

8. He was eventually pardoned by Republican President Warren G. Harding in 1921.

9. Donald Johnson, "Wilson, Burleson, and Censorship in the First World War," *Journal of Southern History*, 28 (1962): 46–58. For a thorough analysis of Burleson's role see also, Jon M. Suter and Jack A. Samosky, "Uneasy Reading: Censorship in Woodrow Wilson's Wartime Administration," paper presented at the annual convention of the Western States Communication Association, 1994.

10. See, for example, Woodrow Wilson, *The Papers of Woodrow Wilson*, ed. Arthur S. Link, vol. 43 (Princeton, NJ: Princeton University Press, 1979–1991), 246; vol. 44, 420. Johnson, "Wilson, Burleson," 54–55, points out that Wilson did defend some papers that Burleson had attacked in 1918.

11. See George Creel, *How We Advertised America: The First Telling of the Amazing Story of the Committee on Public Information that Carried the Gospel of Americanism to Every Corner of the Globe* (New York: Harper and Brothers, 1920). See also, Cedric Larson and James R. Mock, "The Lost Files of the Creel Committee of 1917–19," *Public Opinion Quarterly*, 3 (1939): 5–29; Thomas A. Hollihan, "Propagandizing in the Interest of War: A Rhetorical Study of the Committee on Public Information," *Southern Speech Communication Journal*, 49 (1984): particularly 240–246.

12. Donald Fishman and Joyce Lindmark, "George Creel and the Strategy of Benign Censorship during World War I," paper presented at the annual meeting of the Western States Communication Association, 1994; George Creel, *How We Advertised America* (1920; reprint New York: Arno Press, 1972). The Creel Committee's attempt to shut down a movie which contained a brutal scene involving the bayonetting of a baby by a British soldier resulted in *United States v. Motion Picture Film "The Spirit of '76"* (252 F. Su 946, S.D., California, 1917). As Fishman reports, the government argued that the producer of the film had violated Sections 1 and 3 of the Espionage Act by attempting to "cause insubordination in the army. [H]e was sentenced to ten years in jail and fined five thousand dollars. . . . [T]wo years later [it was] upheld by the Ninth Circuit Court." See *Goldstein v. United States*, 258 Fed. 908 (9th Circuit,

1919). Imagine the chilling effect these decisions must have had on the motion picture industry in its infancy.

13. Harry N. Scheiber, *The Wilson Administration and Civil Liberties, 1917–1921* (Ithaca, NY: Cornell University Press, 1960), 38–39.

14. Wilson, *Papers*, vol. 55, 327.

15. The erosion of rights during this period is laid out by Murphy in *World War I.*

16. In the same series of rulings, Holmes in *Frohwerk v. United States* (249 U.S. 204 (1919)) condemned the antiwar rhetoric of a German newspaper publisher.

17. *Abrams v. U.S.*, 250 U.S. 616 (1919).

18. 268 U.S. 652 (1925). In Montana alone 78 people were convicted of sedition during and immediately after World War I. They were not pardoned until 2008.

19. 268 U.S. 652 (1925). Benjamin Gitlow had written a "Left-Wing Manifesto" that allegedly violated the state's "Criminal Anarchy" law. The Court attempted to make a distinction between "academic discussion" or "abstract doctrine" and more threatening "language advocating, advising, or teaching the overthrow of organized government by unlawful means."

20. Julian F. Jaffe, *Crusade Against Radicalism: New York during the Red Scare, 1914–24* (Port Washington, NY: Kennikat, 1972), 200–225.

21. See *Schneiderman v. United States*, 320 U.S. 118 (1943).

22. Memorandum, Franklyn D. Roosevelt to J. Edgar Hoover. January 21, 1942, President's Secretary's File. Justice Department—J. Edgar Hoover folder, Roosevelt Library, Hyde Park, NY.

23. U. S. Congress, House. *Congressional Record, 77th Congress, 2d Session,* 1942, 88, pt. 2, 2566.

24. Lewis Wood, New York *Times*, (July 24, 1942): 1, 8.

25. Patrick S. Washburn, "FDR Versus His Own Attorney General: The Struggle over Sedition, 1941–42," *Journalism Quarterly*, 62 (1985): 717.

26. 54 *U.S. Statutes at Large*, 670–671 (1940).

27. Washburn, "FDR Versus," 720.

28. Washburn, "FDR Versus," 722.

29. Arch Puddington, *Broadcast Freedom: The Cold War Triumph of Radio Free Europe and Radio Liberty* (Lexington: University of Kentucky Press, 2000), 9

30. Robert Newman and Dale R. Newman, *Evidence* (Boston: Houghton Mifflin, 1969), 104–105.

31. www.americanrhetoric.com/douglasmacarthurfarewelladdress.htm

32. The *Dennis* (341 U.S. 494 (1951)) decision would be eviscerated in 1957 in *Yates v. United States* (354 U.S. 298 (1957)). Note that this restoration of First Amendment rights did not occur until the McCarthy crisis had dissipated.

33. The controversy surrounding the trial has shifted to the significance of what the Rosenbergs passed onto the Soviets. Many believe it was not significant enough to warrant the death penalty. However, at the height of the cold war, feelings were different.

34. See *Lead Time: A Journalist's Education* (Garden City, NY: Doubleday, 1983), 53–56.

35. See Martin J. Medhurst et al. *Cold War Rhetoric: Strategy, Metaphor, and Ideology* (New York: Greenwood, 1990).

36. "Realism Masking Fear: George Kennan's Political Rhetoric," paper presented at Annual Meeting of Speech Communication Association (Miami, Florida, 1993).

37. Ivie, "Realism Masking Fear," 2.

38. For a balanced account of this activity see Martin H. Redich, *The Logic of Persecution: Free Expression and the McCarthy Era* (Stanford, CA: Stanford University Press, 2005).

39. New York *Times*, (July 10, 1952): A1. The clip can be viewed on line at: www.wpafilmlibrary.com/detail/biography_joseph_mccarthy/3c93ee7e-f5f5-a481-cf6f-33dcc8eb2fe6.html. See also Herbert S. Parmet, *Eisenhower and the American Crusades* (New York: Macmillan, 1972), 95.

40. McCarthy startled his audience by charging that communists inside the State Department were responsible for American setbacks in the world, "I have here in my hand a list of 205." Robert A. Divine, *Since 1945: Politics and Diplomacy in Recent American History*, (New York: John Wiley & Sons, 1975), 33.

41. Divine, *Since 1945*, 34.

42. Conservatives were merely one segment of McCarthy's core group. Catholics, with strong ties to traditionally anti-communist areas of Europe or countries that had become Russian satellites, were strong supporters of McCarthy in Wisconsin; thus, McCarthy enjoyed strong support from Poles and Czechs. He was also strong among eastern Catholics including Irish and Italian Americans. Parmet, *Eisenhower*, 125.

43. This fact explains why the young Robert Kennedy became a committee staff member for Senator Joseph McCarthy.

44. For an extensive definition of the paranoid style, see Richard Hofstadter, *The Paranoid Style in American Politics and Other Essays* (New York: Random House [Vintage Books], 1967), particularly 36–37.

45. David Oshinsky, *A Conspiracy So Immense*, (New York: Macmillan, 1983), 183.

46. Stewart Alsop served with the British Army during World War II before transferring to an American unit. He had also worked for the OSS.

47. Oshinsky, *A Conspiracy*, 183.

48. Oshinsky, *A Conspiracy*, 184.

49. For more on McCarthy's use of evidence, see Barnet Baskerville, "The Illusion of Proof," *Western Speech*, 35 (1961): 236–242.

50. Richard Layman, *Shadow Man: The Life of Dashiell Hammett* (New York: Harcourt Brace Jovanovich, 1981), 231–232. Primary source: State Department Information Program, Proceedings of Permanent Subcommittee investigation of the Senate Committee on Government Operations, March 1953, 83–88.

51. It is estimated that 20,000,000 watched the hearings on the ABC and Dumont networks. NBC pulled out after the second day. CBS, to their undying shame, did not broadcast the hearings at all.

52. Emile de Antonia and Daniel Talbot, *Point of Order* (New York: screenplay, 1964), 9.

53. Devine, *Since 1945*, 34, 42

54. See Poyntz Tyler, ed., *Immigration and the United States* (New York: Wilson, 1956). For President Truman's veto message, see Henry S. Commanger, *Documents of American History*, 9th edition (Englewood Cliffs, NJ: Prentice-Hall, 1973), 578–582. See also Nat Hentoff, *The First Freedom* (New York: Delacorte Press, 1980), 137–138.

55. The Subversive Activities Control Act of 1950 was upheld by the Supreme Court in a 5–4 decision in 1961. See *Communist Party v. Subversive Activities Control Board*, 367 U.S. 1 (1961). In 1965 the Court reversed itself in *Albertson v. Subversive Activities Control Board*, 382 U.S. 70 (1965).

56. Ironically, the first public burning of a book in America took place in Boston in 1650. Hentoff, *First Freedom*, 61.

57. Ellen Schrecker, *No Ivory Tower: McCarthyism and the Universities* (New York: Oxford University Press, 1986).

58. See A. H. Rashin, "What Communists Can and Can't Do," New York *Times* (April 26, 1953): E12.

59. See Parmet, *Eisenhower*, 226–246.

60. Eisenhower was goaded in part by McCarthy's attempts to intimidate Eisenhower's beloved army and to obtain information from Eisenhower's State Department. See Raoul Berger, *Executive Privilege: A Constitutional Myth* (Cambridge: Harvard University Press, 1974), vii, 1–2.

61. Senate Subcommittee on Permanent Investigations, *State Department Information Program—Information Centers*, 83rd Congress, 1st Session, 1953, 461.

62. The full text is available at the Dartmouth College Library.

63. The speech was delivered on November 16, 1953. See "Truman Attacks McCarthyism," New York *Times* (November 17, 1953): 1, 26.

64. "Radio and Television Address to the American People on the State of the Nation, April 5, 1954," *Public Papers of the Presidents: Dwight D. Eisenhower, 1954*, (Washington, DC: Government Printing Office, 1960), 375–377.

65. *Congressional Record—Senate* (March 9, 1954): 2886.

66. Devine, *Since 1945*, 69–70.

67. Oshinsky, *A Conspiracy*, 180. McCarthy was so upset with Pearson he attacked him in the cloakroom after a Gridiron Club dinner. Richard Nixon pulled McCarthy away.

68. See "A Young Man Just Out of China," Washington *Daily News*, (July 28, 1954): 5; "After one Full Year Nave Still Sits on Chasanow Case," Washington *Daily News* (July 29, 1954): 9.

69. Oshinsky, *A Conspiracy*, 399. For a complete study of this incident see Thomas Rosteck, *"See It Now" Confronts McCarthyism* (Tuscaloosa: University of Alabama Press, 1995).

70. We should not neglect the role artists played in rallying to defend their own and to alert the country to danger. Though Arthur Miller has steadfastly refused to confirm it, his play in four acts, *The Crucible*, implied an analogy between the Salem witch trials and McCarthy's investigations. Miller's play was first performed on January 22, 1953, at the Martin Beck Theatre in New York City. Miller was subsequently denied a passport by the State Department to see the Brussels premiere of the play. Nonetheless, the play met with critical success and gave artists an articulate vehicle

by which to rally support. Miller was summoned before the House Un-American Activities Committee and eventually tried for contempt of Congress.

71. When asked for the originals of the photographs, McCarthy refused to turn them over to the committee.

72. Orville A. Hitchcok, "McCarthy's Answer: The Strategy of the Defense," *Quarterly Journal of Speech*, 41 (1955): 11.

73. See U.S. Sen. Select Committee to Study Censure Charges, 83rd Cong. Hearings . . . pursuant to Sen. Resolution 301. The resolution stated in part, "The Senator from Wisconsin, Mr. McCarthy . . . acted contrary to senatorial ethics and tended to bring the Senate into dishonor and disrepute, to obstruct the constitutional processes of the Senate, and to impair its dignity; and such conduct is thereby condemned." Commanger, *Documents of American History*, 601.

74. See Franklyn S. Haiman, *Speech and Law in a Free Society* (Chicago: University of Chicago Press, 1981), 349. Earl Warren wrote the majority decision in which he invoked the First Amendment. *Watkins v. U.S.*, 354 U.S. 178 (1957).

75. H. Mitgang, *Dangerous Dossiers* (New York: Donald I. Fine, 1988) at numbers 22–23.

Chapter 8

Suppression During the Vietnam Era

Sharon Downey and Karen Rasmussen

As previous chapters of this book have indicated, war magnifies concerns related to the First Amendment because increases in dissent and civil disobedience, as well as restraints on the press, almost invariably accompany war.[1] War demands unity and attention to national security. As a result, collective interests may supersede individual rights if the latter interfere with the nation's defense or its capacity to wage war.[2] Armed conflict, then, produces a volatile context, which strengthens the salience of, but simultaneously sanctions limitations on the First Amendment. Therefore, examining challenges to constitutional freedoms during crisis is both useful and rhetorically intriguing because such a context reveals the inherent tension between making war and preserving rights in a democratic society.

That tension was conspicuous during the Vietnam War, an experience unique among America's armed conflicts. Vietnam was our longest war, spanning four presidencies;[3] it was our most protracted undeclared war, our first "living room" war, and our only military defeat; its aftermath engendered "bewilderment, guilt, and shame" stemming from a "collapse of confidence" in the military, in society in general, and in American leaders.[4] But, although "Vietnam was a real place, with real people, real problems, and real importance, . . . in American eyes it was essentially a bloody backdrop against which people argued about American interests, [character], and . . . the values and ends of their country."[5] Situated within one of the most sociopolitically divisive periods in U.S. history, Vietnam symbolized a crisis in American identity.

Four interdependent factors coalesced during this period to produce conditions jeopardizing constitutional freedoms. First, administrative efforts to justify and execute a *policy* for Vietnam that failed to achieve more than passive public understanding or support generated widespread national frustration and confusion. Second, *protests* against Vietnam intensified, partially because of the war's unclear objectives, but largely because it also triggered a period marked by broad social upheaval and change: the civil rights, Native American, and women's movements, along with campus rebellions, draft resistance, and antiwar opposition, all challenged prevailing social norms. Third, the burgeoning power of the *press*—especially television—to influence policy, along with the concomitant potential for political exploitation of the media, established the foundation for antipathy between press and government. Finally, both *presidents* presiding over the main part of the era were singularly hostile toward both the press and dissent. Collectively, these contextual dimensions created exigencies contributing to the subversion of the First Amendment.

This chapter examines recurrent patterns in the rhetoric and actions of the Johnson and Nixon administrations which served to undermine First Amendment principles. This task is confounded at the outset, however, because the unique relationship between the presidency and the First Amendment affects the assessment of actions that might be labeled suppressions of freedom of expression. Before proceeding, then, some explanation is warranted. As we have seen throughout this book, America's leaders face conflicting responsibilities with regard to freedom of expression. By virtue of oath of office, the president swears to uphold sacred American principles but also has license to suspend rights for the greater good of the nation. Compounding this tension is war because, as commander-in-chief, the president can justify suspending individual rights under the rubric of national security but, at that same time, cannot extend the rationale to other routine executive activities where no apparent conflict exists between individual and collective needs. Consequently, whether a presidential action infringes on the First Amendment depends on the exigency to which that action is tied and the larger context in which it occurs.

Chief executives also owe their power to constitutional mandates but wield tremendous power over the enactment of many of those same constitutional principles, the First Amendment in particular. Furthermore, while honor-bound to safeguard freedom of expression, the president enjoys the same rights contained in and protected by the First Amendment. This mingling of public and private expressive domains makes identifying constitutional violations problematic. Yet, the complexities indigenous to the president's rights as an individual, responsibilities to the nation, and obligations to oversee the progress of war lie at the heart of evaluating the Johnson and Nixon administrations for actions that violated the spirit of the First Amendment during the Vietnam era.

In light of the above, we argue that unethical if not illegal suppression of the First Amendment occurs when administrative actions, singularly or collectively, result in an *arbitrary denial of the legitimacy of the voice of the opposition*. Neither simple disagreement with an adversary nor an alterative form of advocacy, this denial functions as a failure to honor the integrity or the validity of dissent, a negation of the First Amendment's purpose of respecting competing ideas and facilitating the testing of those ideas, and a subversion of the philosophical grounding of freedom of expression. We use three rhetorical dimensions as the basis from which to assess actions as potential First Amendment infractions: an action is likely suppressive 1) situationally, when it occurs in the absence of a defensible, compelling exigency warranting the act; 2) definitionally, when it actively or blatantly misuses power or when it passively or subtly exploits; and 3) functionally, when its seeming legitimacy as an isolated action is offset when viewed holistically within the context of other actions and/or the sociopolitical context of war.

Given these criteria, we argue that the Johnson and Nixon administrations engaged in systematic, sometimes unethical, sometimes illegal suppression of freedom of expression during the Vietnam era. Our thesis is that, while often protected by the First Amendment, administrative rhetoric undermined national unity because it employed strategies and tactics that functioned rhetorically to subvert public trust, increase dissension, and exacerbate the rift between government and both protesters and the press. Such actions were counterproductive because their divisive nature was antithetical to the national good. We begin this essay with a short history of the Vietnam War and the conditions surrounding it to define the context in which suppression of rights was played out. Subsequently, we identify recurrent strategies and tactics used by the Johnson and Nixon administrations and then address the effects and implications of those maneuvers for the First Amendment.

Rhetorical Context: Chronicling Vietnam

America's commitment to Vietnam prior to 1961 consisted largely of economic aid and military advice to South Vietnamese forces in their efforts to quell internal civil strife and halt Communist incursion from the North. However, in reaction to Communist insurgencies in Laos, which were neutralized by a treaty, President John Kennedy began sending combat troops to Vietnam. Soon, deteriorating political conditions in South Vietnam led to a U.S.-supported overthrow of President Diem in November 1963 and the subsequent installation of a new military regime. Almost immediately afterward, Kennedy was assassinated; his last memo regarding the war ordered another Marine division into Vietnam.

Under President Lyndon Johnson, the failure of American-trained South Vietnamese forces to halt advances from the North led the U.S. to try to "save South Vietnam from a communist takeover" by assuming a more direct combat role in Southeast Asia. The "Americanization of the war in Vietnam" had begun.[6]

Escalation of the War: 1964–1968

Johnson's original plan, which generated "widespread popular and congressional support"[7] for his foreign policy in 1964, was to promote human freedoms and stem Communist infiltration in South Vietnam and simultaneously "maintain Vietnam as a low-profile issue"[8] by "not . . . enlarg[ing] the war."[9] However, the Gulf of Tonkin incident in August 1964, an event that would later prove to be the tragic "turning point in the war,"[10] changed his course significantly. After the allegedly unprovoked North Vietnamese attack on America's destroyer *Maddox*, Johnson ordered retaliatory air strikes. These actions spawned Congressional passage of the Gulf of Tonkin Resolution, a proclamation authorizing Johnson to escalate military involvement without formally declaring war.

Johnson based his policy on the belief that the threat of American military might would force North Vietnam to negotiate and, hence, would deter war. Therefore, the president systematically deployed additional American air and ground forces as a response to each new North Vietnamese offensive or act of noncompliance with U.S. demands; later, he would interrupt and then resume bombing contingent on North Vietnam's willingness to talk peace. In December 1964, after his landslide victory in the presidential election, Johnson ordered the first air attacks on the North and then accelerated them in February 1965 after a Vietcong assault on an American military advisers' compound at Pleiku. In March, ground troops arrived in Vietnam only to aid America's sustained air war; by June, however, they participated in the first major "search and destroy" missions.[11] Hoping for an end to stalemate, Johnson suspended air strikes during a Christmas truce only to resume bombing in full force a month later.

This pattern of deployment-escalation-de-escalation characterized administrative actions throughout 1965, 1966, and 1967. By the end of 1965, 184,300 American military personnel were serving in Vietnam to support ongoing air and ground missions; this figure climbed to 385,300 by the end of 1966, during which time U.S. and South Vietnamese forces completed plans for the invasion of North Vietnam and engaged in a continuous agenda of air raids against oil installations, power plants, and transportation depots adjacent to Hanoi. By early 1967, raids came within one mile of Hanoi, hitting Haiphong harbor and its shipyards; by Christmas, American troops topped 485,600.[12] Negotiations, however, remained at an impasse.

Events in 1968 symbolized the frustrations of the Vietnam campaign. In January, the North began the TET offensive, which produced the war's heaviest fighting to date. Although successfully repelled by April (allied victory was instrumental in initiating formal peace talks in Paris in May), TET was pivotal, not only because of its carnage, but because it marked the anguish and futility of America's policy: it validated North Vietnamese tenacity; it confirmed the inadequacy of the air war, the linchpin of U.S. military strategy;[13] and, because of the atrocities attending the March massacre at My Lai, it unmasked the moral uncertainties of Vietnam. Ironically, despite the Paris negotiations and the gradual realization of the failure of U.S military intervention, American forces swelled to 536,100 by year's end, a year marked by the loss of the presidential election by Johnson's hand-picked successor.

At home, meanwhile, strained relations with the press exacerbated Johnson's problems abroad. Although the president's relationship with the media had never been cooperative, that association turned hostile because of allegations deploring censorship and control of information as well as condemnation by the press of the administration's handling of Vietnam. Moreover, daily reports from the battlefields that saturated American television and newspapers bore witness to war's slaughter and amplified uncertainty about American presence in Vietnam. "It was this antagonism," notes Turner "that . . . ultimately led Lyndon Johnson to decide not to seek a second full term in office."[14]

In addition, growing public opposition to the war began to threaten Johnson's foreign policy. Throughout his term in office, he repeatedly faced antiwar factions that grew increasingly confrontational and violent. Soon after the Gulf of Tonkin resolution, for example, regional antiwar demonstrations and "teach-ins" designed to educate the public about Vietnam occurred with regularity. The assault on Defense Secretary Robert McNamara at Harvard in November 1966 capped a series of protests and sit-ins spanning late 1965 to spring 1966. University campuses became frequent sites of violent dissent: most significant were at Berkeley, along with the Pentagon March, and the siege at Columbia University in April 1968. The Democratic National Convention in August 1968 in Chicago marked the low point of Johnson's administration for the tension that erupted between the establishment and an aggregate of student demonstrators, civil rights advocates, and antiwar protesters affirmed the president's inability to contain the powerful sociopolitical forces opposing his policies.

Johnson's last decision regarding Vietnam—another recess in bombing in October of 1968—stood in stark contrast to his concomitant escalation of American troops, a figure that crested by Christmas 1968. Such contradictions affected his administration's policies on both foreign and domestic fronts: it undermined the credibility of his vision of the "Great American Society"; it exacerbated his alienation from the press; and it eroded public confidence.[15] Disillusioned, and with his worst fear realized, Lyndon Baines Johnson left office.

De-Escalation of the War: 1969–1975

In effect, the failure of LBJ's Vietnam policy negated the possibility of military victory in Vietnam. Richard Nixon, therefore, grounded his bid for the presidency on two promises: an end to the war and a "peaceful and honorable" withdrawal from Vietnam. The resulting policy of "Vietnamization" would remain largely unchanged throughout his presidency; for example, Nixon never deviated from his promised troop reductions beginning with his speech to the nation in May 1969. However, Nixon frequently took action inconsistent with de-escalation.

Although Nixon's policy resonated with the American public—especially the audience he constituted as the "silent majority"—its implementation proved to be a nightmare. Escalating attacks by the North along with strife and corruption within South Vietnam itself mitigated against the transition to an all–South Vietnamese army.[16] Nixon endured intense domestic criticism because he simultaneously engaged in retaliation against the North Vietnamese while he reduced troop levels. Hence, at the height of the fighting during Nixon's incumbency—from June 1969 to December 1971—troop strength decreased from 538,700 to 156,800.[17]

Complicating these contradictory impulses were the Paris peace talks. For over four years, negotiators Henry Cabot Lodge and Henry Kissinger held both open and secret meetings with delegates from South Vietnam, North Vietnam, and the Vietcong. Although these sessions eventually culminated in a cease-fire in January 1973, they were plagued by stalemates, stalls, stoppages, and strategic posturing triggered by events on Vietnam's frontlines. The war's intrusion on these delicate meetings, then, frequently held negotiators hostage.

This policy of de-escalation, reprisal, and negotiation created public confusion. For example, as we have seen, during his first year in office, Nixon announced plans for significant reductions in combat troops. At the same time, he issued the ultimatum that North Vietnam halt its most recent offensive or else expect retribution. However, he let his own November deadline pass without incident, but then, in a surprise attack, invaded Cambodia to destroy supplies and enemy sanctuaries in April 1970.[18] A month later U.S. forces raided supply depots in North Vietnam, but soon after, the administration announced withdrawal of additional American forces. During a period of progress in

Paris, Nixon sanctioned an unsuccessful surprise raid in November 1970 to rescue American POWs held in Son Tay prison on the outskirts of Hanoi; in February 1971, allied forces launched an ill-fated excursion into Laos, which though neutral, had allowed North Vietnamese troops to use trails through its jungles. During the latter half of 1971, discussions in Paris dominated the administrative agenda, and troop withdrawals continued on schedule.

The pivotal year of the war for Nixon was 1972. Nixon's charge that North Vietnam was refusing to negotiate seriously ultimately led to a complete halt in the talks. While meetings did resume in late April, culminating in a fragile peace proposal by year's end, in the interim, the president dramatically escalated fighting. Because in April, North Vietnam seized control of Quang Tri, South Vietnam's northernmost province, the United States countered with sweeping raids near Hanoi, the mining of Haiphong Harbor and other major ports, and the blockading of supplies to North Vietnam. Fighting ebbed in September after the recapture of Quang Tri but resumed full-scale in December and then ceased completely in January, coinciding with the formal peace agreement on the 23rd that Nixon labeled "peace with honor."

Nixon's Domestic Battle

After his first election to the presidency, Nixon's charge was "not only to end the war but also to deal with the unprecedented wave of civil disturbances and the fragmentation of American society."[19] Those goals were inextricably tied, for the rise and decline of the antiwar movement and related dissent paralleled events in Vietnam. A respite in protest activities followed Nixon's inauguration in January 1969. However, from 1969 through 1971, opposition mobilized in full force. Antiwar activities generated 11,000 arrests for political violence and 8,000 threats and/or bombings.[20] In June 1969, Brown University graduates turned their backs on Henry Kissinger as he received an honorary degree during commencement ceremonies; protesters picketed Nixon's San Clemente, California compound on August 17.

These incidents presaged the nationwide Moratorium on October 15. Echoing the sentiment reflected in an unprecedented Harvard University faculty vote against U.S. involvement in Vietnam, millions of citizens at more than 200 sites across America voiced their outrage. The Moratorium, and the Washington Mobilization a month later, became "the single most important . . . demonstration[s] of the entire war":[21] they solidified opposition to Vietnam in the press and by the public; and they inspired Nixon's vow never to permit mass assembly to dictate government policy.

Reactions to Nixon's decision to invade Cambodia the following April would test the President's resolve dramatically. Nationwide demonstrations ignited a monthlong reign of terror: four students were killed by the National Guard at Kent State University on May 4; during the next week, an average of more than 100 demonstrations occurred daily on college campuses and in Washington, D.C.; more than 430 colleges shut down; and the National Guard was called in "at least 24 times."[22] Although these protests failed to deter administrative policy, they were instrumental in the Senate's June decision to revoke the Gulf of Tonkin Resolution.

After May 1970, various factors caused antiwar activities to wane: the movement's internal strife, its growing gratuitous violence, fatigue among protesters, decreased media coverage, Justice Department restrictions on demonstrations, the end of the draft and, naturally, the winding down of the war all took the steam out of protest. Nixon's sanctioning of military forays into Laos sparked but a moderate revival of dissent in April and May 1972, precipitated largely by Vietnam Veterans Against the War.

Sympathy by news people with antiwar factions intensified the long-standing animosity between Nixon and the press. This adversarial relationship was the product of confrontations related to the Alger Hiss case, Nixon's campaign for Senate in 1950, his campaign slush fund in 1952, and his unsuccessful bids for the presidency in 1960 and California's governorship in 1962. Vietnam triggered a new set of charges that the media engaged in distorted, emotional, and speculative reporting; the press responded with unrelenting attacks on Nixon's credibility, his penchant for secrecy, and his alleged abuse of power. This friction between the president and the press exacerbated his difficulties in dealing with Vietnam and, along with Watergate, contributed significantly to his eventual downfall.

After American POWs returned home in February 1973, Nixon again accelerated troop withdrawals; by June 1974, few American personnel remained in Southeast Asia and, despite Nixon's pledge of assistance to allied forces in Cambodia, Laos, and Thailand, Congress drastically cut financial aid to the still-beleaguered countries. Soon after Nixon's resignation in August 1974, momentous internal conflicts in South Vietnam, coupled with continued North Vietnamese aggression, reignited the war. By May 1975, all American military and civilian personnel were airlifted from South Vietnam, the Khmer Rouge overran Cambodia, and North Vietnam seized control of Saigon. The war's quick, brutal end bore witness to the painful legacy of American intervention in Southeast Asia.

During Johnson's and Nixon's terms in office, the Vietnam War formed a formidable backdrop for sustained volatile relationships between the administration on one side and the protestors and press on the other. The era's uncertainty and turmoil thus created a context antithetical to national unity. This did not stop either president from engaging in conventional strategies to rally the public behind administrative policies. Collectively, however, these strategies often digressed into suppressive tactics undermining First Amendment freedoms.

Analysis: Strategies of Suppression

Four strategies characterizing Johnson's and Nixon's actions during the Vietnam era are relevant to the First Amendment. Together they effect the *assertion of power* over persons or groups opposed to administrative policies for the purpose of creating national unity and achieving victory in war. Although not illegal, *co-optation* appropriates the goals of protest and the role of the press to appease and deflect criticism; *condemnation* shifts responsibility to media and demonstrators through marginalizing and demonizing. *Coercion* features harassing and sanctioning to thwart dissent and criticism; and *circumvention* entails avoiding and preempting adversaries of the administration to maintain control, both of which used extra-constitutional tactics.

Co-optation

Co-optation, the strategic incorporation of an adversary's goals, functions, or beliefs into one's own framework, alters the meaning of ideas so that they serve the interests of the appropriator and diminish the force of opposing positions. Johnson and Nixon utilized co-optation to respond to antiwar resistance and, importantly, to justify policy regarding Vietnam through tactics of *appropriation* and *deflection*. Appropriation by both presidents involved usurping and redefining the disparate positions, ideologies, and fears of their critics; in turn, these moves enabled the rhetors to deflect criticism by opponents.

   Appropriation. In hindsight, Johnson's decisions with respect to Vietnam were escalatory, erratic, and ineffectual. Obviously, such outcomes were not what he had in mind when inaugurating his foreign policy program in 1964. At that time, Johnson viewed Vietnam as a minor foreign obstacle in the path of his greater domestic aims. Consequently, he needed a policy that simultaneously would contain war, garner public support, and offset criticism by the political left and right. DeBenedetti summarizes the exigence he faced:

> On the Right, a powerful constellation of critics urged the president to unleash the U.S. military to conduct more massive bombing campaigns throughout Indochina, a blockage of North Vietnam, an invasion of the North, and, if necessary, war against China and Russia. On the Left, a less powerful but surprisingly

vocal combination of critics called for decreased U.S. military involvement and a greater effort toward a negotiated peace, if not immediate U.S. withdrawal, on the grounds that the American intervention was morally unjustifiable, corrupting of American democracy, and grossly disproportionate in costs to the peoples of Indochina and to America's broader security interests.[23]

The president's response was to try to appease both sides by opting for a "limited war," a position falling between engagement and withdrawal. This policy was to "minimize the significance"[24] of Vietnam through a series of temporary, reactive military operations demonstrating American strength and resolve but stopping short of full-scale war. Hence, the limited war appropriated vestiges of the preferred *positions* of both hawks and doves.

Not long after the Gulf of Tonkin incident, however, events intimated that this policy was untenable both militarily and politically. Nevertheless, Johnson's resolve to pursue his position created a situation which quickly degenerated into a "rhetorical nightmare"[25] marked by inconsistency, secrecy, and misrepresentation stemming from contradictions between stated policy and subsequent actions required to manage the conflict.[26] In essence, then, because Johnson adopted an unworkable policy based on incompatible goals, his efforts to appear to adhere to that policy generated dysfunctional contradictions that eventually produced a credibility gap from which he would not recover.

The intrinsic difficulties posed by the limited war heightened the need for its justification. Therefore, Johnson warranted the actions of his administration by linking them to traditional American *ideology*. Perplexed by Vietnam, but impassioned by his commitment to enduring American principles, Johnson consistently justified military intervention by reminding Americans of their nation's strengths and duties. In major addresses from 1964 through 1967,[27] he depicted Vietnam as the scene of confrontation over the "indivisibility of freedom," and a sovereignty's "choice of destiny." He emphasized the sacredness of American commitment, repeatedly contending that because our nation "keeps her word," we cannot "abandon Vietnam." In addition, he often linked his struggles with the trials of other American presidents in times of crisis, especially those of Franklin Roosevelt prior to World War II. America's burden, he reiterated, was to promote peace, stability, and fundamental human rights for the oppressed people of the world.

As the president noted on February 7, 1966, "unity [is] the bedrock" of democracy.[28] The desire to ensure that unity was complicated by his belief in the right to dissent. His genuine affection for young people and college students, those comprising the majority of antiwar protesters, predisposed him toward kind treatment of them.[29] Furthermore, he often publicly articulated his belief in freedom of speech and assembly: "Debate's healthy," stated Johnson on March 20, 1965, "it's good for us"; on August 26, 1966, he reiterated, "we defend, and we intend to defend, the right of everyone to disagree with what we urge or do." But, rightly claiming that he too was entitled to the benefits of freedom of expression, he "saw nothing wrong" with exercising this right by "directing the directors under the table" to influence opinion on college campuses.[30] Through subtle machinations, Johnson upheld the legitimacy of opposition yet tried to undercut the legitimacy of views contrary to his own.

Johnson complimented his ideological arguments with appeals to Americans' *fear* of a totalitarian enemy who threatened not only South Vietnam but the nation's security. His early speeches repeatedly painted "Communist aggression" as an insidious foe whose actions demanded a decisive response in Southeast Asia. Indeed, Johnson's rhetoric took on direct, emotional, and "electric" qualities when portraying Communism as a global menace.[31] Because the fate of Vietnam affected that of the United States, Johnson frequently asserted that "[w]e fight because we must fight if we are to live in a world where every country can shape its own destiny. And only in such a world will our own freedom be finally secure."[32] Later addresses vilified North Vietnam through analogies to events involving Nazi Germany, Korea, and Cuba, as well as through dyslogistic descriptions of North Vietnamese guerrillas as "murderers," "assassins," and "invaders."[33]

Unlike Johnson, Richard Nixon did not subscribe to superordinate domestic priorities like those embodied in his predecessor's dream of the Great Society. Furthermore, by the time he took office, an easy victory in Vietnam clearly was out of reach. Thus, his task was to find a palatable way to wind down the war. The urgency associated with ending the conflict in 1969 and then later with achieving peace in 1972 was evident in the obfuscation practiced by the Nixon team in both campaigns. Shortly before the 1969 election, Republicans sent out the word that their candidate had a "secret plan" to end the war. Among those taken in was the venerable Senator William Fulbright (D-Arkansas), who later lamented that he had been "hoodwinked and misled" by Kissinger into believing in the existence of the "plan." Similarly, on the eve of the 1972 election, Kissinger claimed to have negotiated peace with the Communists. Later the accord fell apart, largely because Kissinger had not secured agreement from the South Vietnamese. Even so, Nixon publicly blamed the North for the failure to achieve peace.[34]

In short, Nixon's task was to achieve an acceptable end to the war *sans* military victory. Like Johnson, his solution was an appropriation of politically disparate positions through use of the phrase "peace with honor," an objective grounded in American *ideology* and implemented through what would variously be termed "the Nixon Doctrine" and "Vietnamization." At his initial press conference on January 27, 1969, Nixon outlined his mysterious "peace plan": "restoration" of the DMZ defined at Geneva in 1954, "mutual withdrawal" by both sides, and "the exchange of prisoners."[35] In his first nationally televised address on Vietnam in May, he revised his plan to add "free choice" for the South Vietnamese and staged, internationally supervised withdrawal of all "non-South Vietnamese forces."[36] Similarly, on November 3, 1969, the president addressed the nation, appealing to the soon-to-be-famous Silent Majority to support Vietnamization. Vietnamization entailed "complete withdrawal of all United States combat ground forces and their replacement by South Vietnamese forces on an orderly scheduled timetable." Such a timetable was to remain flexible to provide motivation for the North to negotiate and to allow for adjustment given "the level of enemy activity" as well as the "progress of the training programs" for South Vietnamese troops.[37] The policy, argued Nixon, would achieve peace and protect lives, reinforce American credibility, and promote South Vietnam's independence. Moreover, such proposals upheld the values of honoring another nation's sovereignty, adhering to international law, and maintaining national security.

Like those of Johnson, then, Nixon's policies promoted values ostensibly appealing to both hawk and dove. He could not offer victory to the right, but he could argue that he was protecting American prestige and security while simultaneously deterring aggression. Although he would not disengage as quickly as those on the left advocated, he did contend that his policies pursued peace while protecting human life and promoting free choice. This co-optation of goals of various segments of the electorate also characterized his stance toward the press.

The Nixon Administration worked diligently to usurp the informative function of the press by devising numerous measures to convey the president's message directly to the people without filtering by the media. Shunning the more confrontational press conference, the president gave numerous national addresses, turned mundane actions such as the vetoing of an HEW appropriations bill into televised events, appeared on talk shows and in exclusive televised interviews, and sent forth surrogates to spread his message. In addition, he appropriated the mandate that the press function to test ideas by arguing that his administration already performed that function internally. At a June 19, 1969 press conference, for example, he asserted that he "allow[ed] more controversy and . . . open dissent . . . within [his] administration than any in recent years."[38]

Like Johnson, Nixon also appealed to Americans' common *fears*. Although he too played on uneasiness inspired by the specter of Communist aggression, he targeted the fears of the young associated with the draft and the potential of dying in Vietnam. By 1970, the old means of drafting soldiers, a system that readily lent itself to abuse by the more fortunate, had given way to a national lottery. At the same time, troops were coming home from Vietnam, thereby defusing a second concern of protesters. As Nixon indicated in his memoirs, the recalling of an additional 150,000 troops in April of that year was to serve to "drop a bombshell on the gathering spring storm of antiwar protests" that likely would mushroom once the public learned of the invasion of Cambodia planned for later that month.[39] Based on that and other evidence, Smith argues that Nixon timed troop withdrawals to ensure "political payoff[s]."[40]

Deflection. The appropriation by both administrations of the positions, ideologies, and fears of various segments of the American public formed the foundation for subsequent efforts to deflect and thereby reduce the effectiveness of criticism. The ideological grounding of their respective policies constituted a formidable persuasive base from which Johnson and Nixon could arouse American public opinion. Their rhetorical choices, then, embodied elements of *distortion* and *diffusion* to depict disagreement as unreasonable at best and, at worst, un-American.

The righteousness born of ideological conviction likely prompted both presidents to resort to *distortion* either to placate their critics or throw them off guard. Nixon repeatedly denied the existence of an American presence in Laos and Cambodia, where he engaged in secret bombings; in 1972 he allowed Kissinger to advertise success in securing an accord that did not exist. Furthermore, he downplayed the seriousness of incidents such as My Lai[41] and tried to blame the tragedy at Kent State at least partially on the actions of protesters.[42]

Similarly, Johnson frequently misrepresented events to shape public opinion. This took a variety of forms, beginning with his manipulation of the Gulf of Tonkin incident to depict the United States as the reluctant victim of North Vietnamese aggression.[43] Later, it extended to exaggerating American military successes, downplaying American casualties, and overstating the strength of the enemy.[44] To quell potential criticism of the contradiction indigenous to escalating a limited war, Johnson "kept his decisions secret until the last minute"[45] and then treated decisions to intensify the war "in a routine manner" so as not to call attention to them.[46]

Conducting the limited war also led Johnson to engage in rhetorical "doubletalk" that cloaked the degree of American involvement in Vietnam. At times Johnson simply was dishonest;[47] more often he was confusing and obscure. For instance, he euphemistically labeled combat troops as "advisors" and "assistants" for noncombat personnel already in Vietnam;[48] accelerated bombing inexplicably was "not a change in [the limited war] policy but in what policy requires."[49] To avoid charges of inconsistency and obfuscation, he relabeled escalatory actions so that they seemed to conform to his publicly stated policy.

Grounding intervention policy in an appropriated American ideology also allowed both presidents to *defuse* criticism. Nixon's co-optation of the aims of protesters and the press is instructive. As far back as 1965, he observed that the goals motivating protesters were "the very objective for which Americans . . . [were] fighting in Vietnam."[50] Similarly, in his May 8, 1970, press conference, Nixon expressed confusion at the vehemence of protest since he "agree[d] with everything that they were trying to accomplish"—attaining "peace," stopping the "killing," "end[ing] the draft," and "get[ting] out of Vietnam."[51] The implication was, of course, that agreement over ends should eclipse disagreement regarding means. Hence, his argument took the wind out of dissent, provided that a significant portion of the population bought his position. His landslide victory in 1972 indicates that they did.

Johnson engaged in similar practices of diffusing and co-opting press and protesters' sentiments through commiseration with them. He expressed sympathy with reporters who were agitated about this unavailability; yet he simultaneously countered their criticism by arguing that the scope and pressures attending presidential duties necessitated that he dictate "the timing and the setting of that availability."[52] Likewise, he appropriated the emotional fervor of protesters by aligning his own frustrations about the war with theirs. He empathized with their plight by voicing like-minded distaste for armed conflict; he offered assurances that, despite dissimilar means, his and their goals were the same; and he stressed that his commitment to war was equally as ardent as their opposition to it. This diffusion through identification, then, enabled the president to chastise his adversaries for unwarranted antipathy toward a leader who possessed convictions identical to theirs, but who—unlike they—had to shoulder responsibility for the repercussions of his actions. Thus, Johnson appropriated the affective grounding of protest to diffuse its effects.

Taken holistically, co-optation functioned as a legal, but suppressive strategy. Both presidents commandeered the functions and goals of press and dissent, moves that enabled them to promote administrative policy and diffuse criticism by appearing to accommodate the wishes of their adversaries. However, appropriation also fundamentally distorts and misrepresents the position of both groups, disavowing their respective rights to unabridged expression. Hence, it reflected administrative motives designed to stifle anticipated criticism rather than to find legitimate, workable policy compromises. Co-optation accomplished the feat of undermining First Amendment principles; furthermore, it served to ground justification for both administrations' systematic and trenchant condemnation of the opposition.

Condemnation

Condemnation is designed to denounce and to place blame on an individual or group. Both presidents utilized this strategy incessantly and with enthusiasm to assign responsibility for both domestic and international difficulties to their adversaries. Two recurrent tactics dominated their rhetorical choices: *marginalizing* discredits press and protest by circumscribing and trivializing their respective missions and voices; *demonizing* censures press and protesters by depicting their activities as subversive of American principles and as aiding the enemy. The tactics allowed the chief executives to undermine their opposition and simultaneously enhance their own arguments. Hence, they coupled condemnation with bolstering, a strategy of reaffirmation which is a natural counterpart to subversion.[53]

Marginalizing. During a news conference on November 17, 1967, Johnson observed: "If I have done a good job of anything since I have been president, it is to insure that there are plenty of dissenters."[54] This acknowledgment aside, little of that struggle found its way into Johnson's public discourses. His major addresses are conspicuously void of references either to press coverage of or protest directed at his policies; when probed during press conferences, even his more spontaneous remarks were guarded and ambiguous but rarely provocative. Instead, the president chose to condemn through dis-confirmation designed to render the opposition impotent.

However, this calculated avoidance was short-lived, partly because of the persistence of antiwar opposition, and largely because of the president's predilection for direct confrontation. Thus, Johnson shifted to more overt methods of combating his detractors. One recurrent ploy involved coupling his depiction of the opposition as a distinct minority—or, as one congressional supporter termed, "an infinitesimal fraction of American public opinion"[55]—with indictments against the media for pandering to the small but vocal group. For example, during an interview with journalists on December 19, 1967, Johnson accused "television people" of encouraging dissent by granting undue voice and attention to "exhibitionists." Inevitably, such criticism would be followed by reiterating the support his administration enjoyed from the majority of Americans.[56]

The Johnson Administration also waged a war of words through invective targeted at students, professors, and lawbreakers. Students enjoyed the dubious distinction of receiving the administration's mildest condemnation. Depicted as "naysayers"[57] who were also misguided, Johnson called their voices "irrelevant"[58] and "a concoction of wishful thinking and false hopes."[59] But whereas students' naïveté was excusable, their mentors' ignorance and irresponsibility were not. Administration figures freely lambasted college professors for their lack of knowledge about foreign affairs and the dangers of Communism. Secretary of State Dean Rusk's remarks on October 12, 1967 are illustrative: he lamented that "an idea stands or falls on its own merits and the fact that a man knows everything there is to know about enzymes doesn't mean that he knows very much about Vietnam or how to organize a peace or the life and death of nations."[60] Johnson also condemned professors' unwillingness to face the consequences of their actions. At his November 1, 1967, news conference, the president chastised them for not making "any great contribution to solving"[61] America's problem with Vietnam and urged introspection and prudence as antidotes to misdirected sentiments that simply incited young collegians.

Johnson emphatically disapproved of civil disobedience that, even for the noblest of purposes, resulted in illegal acts or violence. He expressed particular disdain for rude, noisy demonstrators, "exhibitionists . . . that have nothing to do but carry a sign around on their shoulders and try to obstruct someone else from getting to a place or try to howl them down after they get here."[62] Antiwar protesters were hooligans, storm troopers, and violent hippies; none could be tolerated because their actions reflected "unreasoned" not reasoned dissent. Such irrationality led Vice President Hubert Humphrey to remark on August 23, 1965, that "the right to be heard does not automatically include the right to be taken seriously."[63] The Johnson Administration's approach to handling antiwar protest, then, consisted of a recurrent pattern of name-calling and derision designed to diminish the credibility and the frequency of discourse critical of government.

Richard Nixon's diatribes against protest perpetuated the pattern Johnson began. However, whereas Johnson was relatively restrained in his criticisms, Nixon pursued his detractors with a vengeance. Stemming from the "visceral nature" of his "antagonism" toward agitators, the president alternatively blamed "faculty leaders and professional agitators"—whom he characterized as "sanctimonious frauds"—and the "pampered kids"[64] who engaged in "juvenile chanting"[65] merely "to keep from getting their asses shot off."[66] His antipathy toward such critics was evident in his actions in San Jose, California before the 1970 midterm election as he actively encouraged "heckling and stone throwing" to create damning television footage demonstrating "how radicals treated his office."[67]

Spearheading the attack on the protesters, however, was the ever-intrepid Vice President Spiro T. Agnew. In spring 1969, the vice president lamented the "continuous carnival" on America's "streets" and "campuses," which had "create[d] first chaos, then repressive reaction."[68] Perhaps most famous of the Agnew onslaughts were his "Ten Commandments of Protest" presented in an address to the nation's governors and their families in December of the same year:

Thou Shalt Not Allow Thy Opponent to Speak.
Thou Shalt Not Set Forth a Program of Thine Own.
Thou Shalt Not Trust Anybody Over Thirty.
Thou Shalt Not Honor Thy Father or Thy Mother.

Thou Shalt Not Heed the Lessons of History.
Thou Shalt Not Write Anything Longer than a Slogan.
Thou Shalt Not Present a Negotiable Demand.
Thou Shalt Not Accept Any Establishment Idea.
Thou Shalt Not Revere Any But Totalitarian Heroes.
Thou Shalt Not Ask Forgiveness for Thy Transgressions.[69]

Along with the president and other spokespersons for the administration, Agnew marginalized demonstrators and other protesters by portraying them as an unrepresentative, incompetent minority who employed repressive, irrational, destructive means.

Like Johnson, Nixon depicted protests against the war as the efforts of an unrepresentative minority.[70] On December 3, 1969, he launched his administration's attack on dissidents by appealing to "the great silent majority" to stand firm in the face of the "vocal minority" who strove to make policy by "mounting demonstrations in the streets."[71] Dissenters' sins, however, exceeded merely assailing the principle of majority rule; Nixon and Agnew also demeaned their competence. Agnew accused them of "arrogat[ing] unto themselves voice, virtue and power out of proportion to their numbers and even more out of proportion to their abilities."[72] Nixon described students "intoxicated with the romance of violent revolution" who found the "continuing revolution of democracy . . . unexciting."[73] Similarly, Agnew castigated "arrogant, reckless, inexperienced elements" of society who engaged in the "tantrums" of "unbridled protest."[74]

The incompetence of protesters and other critics led the Nixon Administration, in turn, to decry the use of irrational, destructive methods. Deploring illegal conduct such as marches that stopped traffic, and violence that destroyed public property on campuses[75] and elsewhere, Mr. Nixon pledged that "policy in this country" would not be "made by protests."[76] The vice president extended these themes by arguing against the viability of protest itself. He described "the Mob, the Mobilization, [and] the Moratorium" as "negative in content [and] disruptive in effect" because they "inflame the emotions rather than stimulate solutions,"[77] and because they involved the assertion of "rights without commensurate responsibilities."[78] During one of his less restrained moments, Agnew depicted critics of the administration as "merchants of hate" and "parasites of passion," "ideological eunuchs" leading an "effete society" down "tortuous paths of delusion and self-destruction."[79]

By comparison, the Nixon Administration assumed a considerably more passive role in undermining the press. With few exceptions, during much of his first term, Mr. Nixon's acrimonious, personal confrontation with the fourth estate was on hiatus. After his reelection, however, he let it be known that he "would no longer uncomplainingly accept their barbs or allow their unaccountable power to go unchecked."[80] True to his word, he lashed out at reporters on various occasions. For example, in October 1973, during a press conference, he disabused CBS's Robert C. Pierpoint of the "impression" that the columnist had "arouse[d]" his "anger," for such arousal was impossible because "one can only be angry with those he respects."[81]

Nixon gave little credence to the notion that the press as watchdog served to confront government, thereby contributing to the healthy testing of ideas and preventing abuses of power. Rather, he defined its legitimate function as informative, not confrontational. His administration's condemnation of the media consisted of a pattern that circumscribed, hence trivialized, the mission of the press. However, since Nixon was not wont to enter the political fray personally, he left the brunt of that task to a group of surrogates led by the colorful and chloric Agnew.

Nixon's wrath was stirred by negative press commentary after his November 3, 1969 Vietnamization speech. He approved an attack on the press to be initiated by his vice president.[82] Agnew pummeled the media in two speeches: a nationally televised address on November 13 in Des Moines decrying what he termed "network censorship,"[83] and a speech lamenting the power of the press before the Montgomery Chamber of Commerce on the 29th of the month. He indicted the media on two counts. First, echoing a long-held Nixon belief, the vice president accused the press of promulgating their entrenched, unreasonable bias against the president. Especially galling was that an address "weeks in the preparation" was "subjected to instant analysis and querulous criticism:"

> One commentator twice contradicted the President's statement about the exchange of correspondence with Ho Chi Minh. Another challenged the President's abilities as a politician. A third asserted that the President was following a Pentagon line. Others, by the expression on their faces, the tones of their questions, and the sarcasm of their responses, made clear their sharp disapproval.

"[O]bvious[ly]," Agnew continued, "their minds were made up in advance."[84] The press failed to engage in "objective" transmission of the details of Nixon's proposal, thus overstepping their bounds by challenging and contradicting the president.

Second, Agnew described an unrestrained, insular press whose limited viewpoint created an insidious censorship. Rebuking that "little group of men" who "wield[ed] a free hand in selecting, presenting, and interpreting the great issues . . . [of our] nation,"[85] he attributed their insularity to a system suspect because a single company in Washington, D.C. could "control" a large newspaper, four television stations, an "all-news radio station," as well as "three major news magazines."[86] The resulting censorship of the administration was particularly dangerous because of the "profound influence" of television "over public opinion" and because it masqueraded as informed, impartial reportage and commentary. Consequently, he argued that because of television's "monopoly" over the airwaves, its defenders were wrong in claiming the same First Amendment privilege to "the . . . unlimited freedom held by the great newspapers of America."[87]

Demonizing. Both administrations characterized protest and press as subversive of and therefore harmful to America's war effort in Vietnam: protesters were violent, negative, destructive, and lawless; the media was culpable because it challenged national policy. Although these administrations had a right to express their opinion, it is fair to note that each utilized invective to damn and marginalize the force of opposition. At the same time, both negated the potential constructiveness of confrontation: while Johnson essentially disregarded the press and disconfirmed protest, Nixon and Agnew ignored more thoughtful press critiques and more peaceful manifestations of dissent, such as sit-ins, teach-ins, and the tens of thousands who marched calmly. Painting *all* protest as violent, *all* criticism as destructive, they created a demonic portrait of dissent by arguing that the actions of their adversaries functioned to undermine American society and to aid and abet the enemy.

Johnson's public discourses demonized press and protest through the construction of two competing narratives. In one, heroes were valiant leaders and soldiers whose patriotism and sacrifices deserved America's gratitude. That gratitude, however, was not forthcoming because of dishonorable, frivolous protesters and like-minded critics in the press. While their antics sometimes left Johnson feeling betrayed personally, what he perceived to be an anti-American spirit sickened him. His second story identified these two as villains who shared responsibility for promoting social unrest, undermining American power, and prolonging the war.

Johnson repeatedly held the media accountable for creating misleading impressions that thwarted America's efforts in Vietnam. He blasted the press for selective coverage of the war's atrocities because that coverage censured American actions while essentially ignoring deeds by the Vietcong that were far more horrendous. On the Ides of March, 1967, Johnson referred to this hypocrisy, describing it as "moral double bookkeeping."[88] His judgment of the media never wavered in this respect for he charged them with "creat[ing] a climate of dissent and opposition . . . that was a tremendous distortion of the way the country felt." The net effect "weaken[ed]" and "diminish[ed]" the chance to negotiate peace.[89] More importantly, however, the media was guilty of aiding and abetting the enemy. For example, Ambassador Averill Harriman scolded The New York *Times* for promoting the view that America lacked will and dedication to the Vietnam cause; and Johnson alleged that media coverage of the TET offensive erroneously contributed to the impression that the Communists had won that campaign.[90]

Yet, Johnson had to be careful in his dealings with the press because such explicit public accusations came dangerously close to denying the press its constitutional function. Thus, he legitimated his demonization of the press by merging criticism of the media with that of protest and defining the conglomerate as dissidents through guilt by association. Demonstrators induced the enemy "to persist [with] aggression, postponing rather than advancing the progress toward peace"; moreover, they "demoraliz[ed] the American forces in combat."[91] Ambassador Henry Cabot Lodge echoed that criticism on April 26, 1967, proclaiming that "disunity in America prolongs the war. . . . [It makes] Hanoi thinks all they have to do is hang on and we'll fall apart."[92]

Protesters' self-absorption drew Johnson's ire and he played on that weakness, parlaying it into public anger directed at dissidents. The president portrayed himself as the combat soldier's guardian angel. While protesters voiced insipid rhetoric, American "boys" were spending holidays away from their families "in a lonely and dangerous land";[93] while opposition forces philosophized about the meaning of war, the experience of Vietnam was "no academic question" for combatants whose lives were "tied by flesh and blood to Vietnam." For them talk of Vietnam did not "come cheap."[94] To the end, Johnson defended American ideology and the preeminence of soldiers' concerns over those of protesters.

The Nixon administration was equally unyielding in its vilification of press and protest, America's internal enemies. For instance, protest marches did not bring issues to light, they stopped government;[95] resisters did not act on conscience, they deserted their country;[96] students did not question the principles guiding American policy, they "assault[ed] the processes of free inquiry which are the very life of learning."[97] Moreover, criticism of the war in the media and dissent against it on campuses and in the streets constituted a betrayal of American service personnel fighting and dying in Southeast Asia. The president thus portrayed critics of the war, whether the press, protesters, or politicians, as a snobbish minority who not only demeaned the American soldier but in effect promulgated disloyalty.[98]

Besides attacking the foundations of American society, the administration argued, the antics of the press and protesters either consciously or unconsciously gave aid to an evil enemy. Nixon believed that the destructive dissension permeating American society sent signals to Hanoi that it could well afford to remain intractable at the Paris peace talks. Conversely, support of the administration would lead to peace because "nothing could have a greater effect in convincing the enemy that he should negotiate in good faith than to see the American people united behind a generous and reasonable peace offer."[99] Similarly, dissent served to prolong, not shorten, the war, because it gave the North hope that if they just waited long enough they would win the "victory" they could not "win among the people of South Vietnam or on the battlefield."[100]

Condemnation functioned as a legal but insidious form of suppression. Both chief executives used the power of the presidential office to embark on a vigorous program undercutting the force and legitimacy of dissension that emanated from press and protest. Their tactics of marginalizing and demonizing subverted First Amendment principles because by enacting a rhetorical transformation of disagreement into, by turns, a trifling nuisance and an ominous threat, they advanced the argument that dissension was undeserving of voice. Hence, by implication, they should be dismissed. This categorical denunciation, together with the effects of redefining opposition through co-optive tactics, established the foundation for both presidents to justify widespread actions that circumvented protesters and the press.

Circumvention

Circumvention entails evading and bypassing conventional or appropriate communication channels to direct and control the flow of information. Presidents Johnson and Nixon, relying heavily on such tactics in their dealings with press and protest, sought to avert mediation of their messages and to diminish confrontation. Their actions involved two dominant tactics: *preemption* of the function of the press and *avoidance* of protest and the media.

Preemption. President Johnson directed his preemption tactics at the press. He described his association with the media as a "lover's quarrel" turned nasty; metaphorically, the press personified the shotgun and Johnson operated from "the open end of the gun barrel."[101] Johnson justified avoiding that barrel in two ways.

First, he believed that it was the business of government to govern, and the business of the press to simply convey that governance to the people, preferably in a manner that would generate support for the president. This conviction led him to regard secrecy and other like maneuvers as presidential prerogatives and "essential components of good government." But, because the media saw those same actions as "antithetical to the concept of democracy," their scrutiny of the Johnson administration intensified dramatically.[102] Second, although this scrutiny took a variety of forms, it was most prevalent in assessments of his Vietnam program. As Turner observes, "the national press gravitated from an initial position of . . . disinterest concerning Vietnam to one that was . . . actively hostile to presidential policy."[103] Consequently, Johnson grew increasingly skeptical of the press's ability to cover his administration fairly. On a personal level, he desired both understanding and support from the media, but he was also "determined to prove that the press was not going to be allowed to lead him around by the nose."[104]

Therefore, Johnson's dismay at "difficulties . . . communicating with and through the press"[105] prompted him to develop alternate methods of delivering his messages "directly" to the American public. For example, he frequently made himself available for interviews with small town newspaper reporters and talk show hosts while declining interviews on national networks and with what he called the "elitist" Eastern newspapers such as the New York *Times*. In addition, because of his disdain for live press conferences, he would conduct informal conferences in the Oval Office, while walking his dogs around the White House lawn, during barbeques at his Texas ranch, early on Saturday mornings, or in his automobile while riding around the ranch—all to the consternation and inconvenience of reporters.[106] Moreover, because he spent so much time talking during these meetings, he effectively preempted reporters' questions, delivered cutting, dismissive replies, and fed them more information than could be adequately digested.[107] He also called press conferences or delivered televised addresses with little advanced notice to the print and broadcast media. Numerous instances of this kind of preemption contributed to the suppression of the critical, informational, and evaluative functions of the press for his "unorthodox" methods left reporters little time to prepare, investigate background issues, contact experts, or even "leave the White House for fear of missing some spontaneous presidential announcement."[108]

The president's need to control the time, setting, and content of his interactions with reporters often was interpreted by them as insensitive. To counter this criticism, he engaged in favoritism with select press members, going so far as to cultivate personal relationships with those he found responsive to or approving of his administration. For example, he wrote personal notes of thanks to editors when supportive articles appeared in their papers; he enhanced the careers of sympathetic reporters by granting them exclusive interviews; and he interacted socially with favored journalists and their families. The upshot of these "crony-like" actions was to place reporters "under obligation,"[109] thereby generating more positive media coverage.

This orchestration of the media extended to live press conferences. Although he disliked their formality, unpredictability, and potential for embarrassment, he did not hide from them. In fact, MacDonald reports that Johnson held "126 news conferences, . . . 17 [of which] were on live TV during his first 22 months."[110] However, the president minimized his vulnerability by using various evasive procedures. For instance, he perfected ambiguous and indirect responses to questions; he "cut into the time allotted for reporters' questions" by preparing lengthy opening policy statements and announcements; and he "had questions planted in his news conferences."[111]

Because the substance of press conferences inevitably revolved around the "bad news" of Vietnam, Johnson soon discovered that the structure of press conferences left him relatively unprotected. Therefore, he began to circumvent and distance himself from potential traps by delegating to surrogates the responsibility of publicizing such news prior to press meetings. He routinely assigned Defense Secretary Robert McNamara the task of informing the public about raising troop ceilings.[112] In addition, since coverage of the war adopted a tone increasingly critical of American policy, particularly around the time of TET, Johnson ordered General Westmoreland to conduct authoritative briefings with the press daily.[113] Journalists' reactions to surrogates enabled the president to predict the questions he would face and prepare accordingly.

Johnson's quarrel with the press over what he perceived as distorted and untruthful reporting prompted him to take the stance that "forewarned is forearmed." Thus, he had his staff carefully monitor major publications and correspondents. What he accumulated became grist for launching both overt and surreptitious counterattacks. For example, in addition to submitting stories for inclusion in the *Congressional Record* each week, his staff wrote prolific refutations of critic's charges: after a trenchant attack on Johnson's Vietnam policy by Senator Edward Kennedy (D-Massachusetts) and later Senator Clifford Case (R-New Jersey), LBJ's staff responded with two lengthy rebuttals.[114] He also created the White House Vietnam Information Group composed of elitists known as the "Wise Men" to aid him in devising messages for dissemination to the American public.

Preempting the press took various forms for Nixon's Administration. Both Nixon and Agnew frequented talk shows—Nixon appearing with Art Linkletter, Agnew on Johnny Carson and with David Frost.[115] The president also joined various television journalists in special interviews: an informal conversation by the fireplace in the White House with John Chancellor, Howard K. Smith, Nancy Dickerson, and Eric Sevareid allowed him to enhance his personal image by appearing warm, confident, and presidential.[116] Most of his television appearances, however, were in national addresses and at the occasional press conference. As CBS's Frank Stanton remarked, Nixon had, by the middle of his first term, "appeared on network prime-time television as many times as Presidents Eisenhower, Kennedy, and Johnson combined."[117] As the president noted, his objective was to "go over the heads of the columnists."[118] Although frequent, his speeches tended to be short to avoid trying viewer patience. In 1970 he even delayed a press conference to avoid conflict with a basketball game aired on ABC.[119]

Buttressing these direct appeals to the public were several more covert techniques designed to bypass the national press. To disseminate Nixon's ideas, his staff mailed out hundreds, and in some cases thousands, of press kits to local editors and writers. At times the content was general, at others targeted toward specific interests. These missives typically contained articles favorable to the administration, poll results, and excerpts from press conferences and presidential addresses.[120]

A second mode of preemption was to take action, to *make* news by creating events that would dominate the public eye. Given any chief executive's access to the media, such a task was not difficult. Nixon, however, was a master of the art for he turned mundane occurrences into dramatic phenomena. In December 1969, for example, the president-elect presented his newly selected cabinet on national television.[121] Later that year, he preempted network programming to justify and then veto an HEW appropriations bill, an act that generated 55,000 telegrams supporting his decision and mail to Congress favoring his position by four to one.[122]

Making news rather than submitting to confrontation by adversaries also dominated his bid for reelection. During the 1972 contest with George McGovern, he remained secluded as much as possible, emerging only occasionally to do token campaigning and to take "presidential" action. On radio, he gave 16 campaign speeches on 16 different issues. The major event of the primaries was his historic trip to China. The presidential jet landed in China at 10:30 A.M. EST, an event a writer for *Time* termed "an excellent hour for a presidential candidate seeking reelection to make a television appearance."[123]

Avoidance. Johnson rarely evaded the press directly; with protesters, however, he perfected the art of avoidance. Privately, he had mixed feelings about antiwar resistance: on the one hand, he sympathized with their plight, telling a colleague "I don't blame them. They didn't want to be killed in a war, and that's easy to understand";[124] on the other, he resented "open and serious dissent over policy," failing to "understand why Americans who dissent can't do their dissenting in private."[125] However, Johnson's actions reflected a preoccupation with and calculated avoidance of dissension. For example, he stopped answering protest mail even though early in his presidency he had done so routinely, corresponding in a "genteel" fashion with protesters.[126] He also made spontaneous travel plans to prevent demonstrators from mobilizing quickly enough to greet him at his destination. Because most protest originated on college campuses, he made decisions about Vietnam—particularly those related to the war's escalation—during the summer months when students were not in school.[127]

His avoidance extended to members of his own political party and cabinet. He distanced himself from Senate foreign relations committee head

J. William Fulbright, as well as from Senators Frank Church and George McGovern, two prominent critics of his policy;[128] Secretary of Defense Robert McNamara became a political pariah when he, in the president's estimation, defected from the party line; and Johnson eventually retreated from cabinet meetings because of disagreements with Ramsey Clark and Stewart Udall, among others.[129] While the president's more politically motivated evasion enabled him to thwart candid and personal criticism, it also undermined substantive appraisal of administration policy. Coupled with concerted efforts to minimize public antiwar protest, Johnson's circumvention strategies suppressed the critical function of argument.

Nixon's circumvention of the press was more unconditional. Given his previous history with them during the Alger Hiss case, as well as his gubernatorial and presidential campaigns, Nixon held a degree of animosity toward the media—a sentiment Crouse describes as a "deep, abiding, and vindictive hatred"[130]—likely unique among chief executives. Hence, he carried into his presidency the conviction that he needed to avoid situations potentially exposing him to attack from a hostile adversary.

This avoidance led to his violation of the then well-established expectation that the chief executive would hold frequent press conferences. His average of less than one per month, a figure that included informal nontelevised sessions held in the Oval Office or press briefing room, was dramatically smaller than his predecessors.[131] Nixon argued that he met his obligation to "inform the American people"[132] by engaging in such encounters when they served the "public interest,"[133] but that interest could be served equally well through other formats. Various journalists, however, questioned the worth of the press conference in light of what David Broder argues is the critical factor making the press conference format valuable:

> The key thing is frequency. If you have them weekly . . . it doesn't make any difference if you blow ten minutes on some trivial thing or if you don't get to follow up on a question, because the president is going to be back there the next week and you'll have another chance. . . . Now obviously, if you're down to three or four a year, the press conference doesn't serve that function at all.[134]

In essence, then, a functional press conference goes beyond merely *informing* the public through creating a forum designed to *test* the ideas of the president. Given Nixon's distrust of the press, that he should avoid such a situation hardly is surprising. Consequently, even when he did hold press conferences, he employed tactics facilitating his control of the interaction.

Preparing for, staging of, and performing at the press conference was a complex undertaking. Advisors first gathered information utilizing the considerable resources available to the executive. Next followed analysis and integration designed to identify probable questions; these formed the basis for the information sheets Nixon used in his own thorough rehearsal.[135] This staging deemphasized the importance of the press in two ways. First, Nixon gave *news*, not press conferences, thereby defining the event as one designed to inform, not test presidential positions.[136] Second, he disdained notes and spoke from a sparse stage using only a single microphone; such a setting allowed him to face television cameras directly, thus addressing the television audience, not the reporter asking questions.[137] Nixon's responses were clearly structured answers that foregrounded those aspects of administration policy he wished to emphasize. When faced with difficult questions, he typically evaded direct response and at times declared a "moratorium" on sensitive subjects.[138] In addition, he always had the option of turning to a reporter likely sympathetic to him because he routinely memorized the press seating chart.[139] Even the infrequency of the conferences augmented his ability to avoid direct confrontation because the multiplicity of salient issues that accumulated since his last conference meant that any in-depth exploration was unlikely.

Averting confrontation is easier, of course, if antagonists remain distanced from each other. By nature a private person, Nixon made frequent trips to various retreats: 42 to Camp David, referred to by aides as "Mount Sinai," in the first 18 months of his presidency, as well as excursions to both Key Biscayne and the Western White House at San Clemente. The advantage of each locale was that facilities for reporters were far from adequate, a condition the Nixon people assiduously avoided improving. They went so far as to pipe daily briefings from Camp David into the pressroom at the White House, thereby encouraging reporters to stay in Washington rather than accompany the president.[140]

Guaranteeing Nixon's privacy was the task of his chief staffers, notably H. R. "Bob" Haldeman, John Ehrlichman, and press secretary Ronald Ziegler. Haldeman and Ehrlichman together formed a "Berlin Wall,"[141] a nearly impenetrable barrier protecting the president. To Ziegler fell the task of diverting the press on a regular basis. Generally choosing to brief correspondents twice daily—once during Watergate—he became skilled at inundating his audience with endless announcements, avoiding giving specific data, refusing to respond to questions, and presenting incomplete or inaccurate information.[142] If a briefing was likely to be stormy, he would execute what the press termed the "old Squeeze Play," arriving late so that journalists would not extend the briefing because they needed to meet filing deadlines.[143]

The Nixon team also sequestered the press, functionally removing them from many news-making events. Nixon oversaw the creation of the West Terrace Press Center, a well-appointed facility that replaced the old pressroom off the White House's main entrance. Because reporters no longer could observe the arrival of visitors to the executive mansion, Helen Thomas dubbed the new quarters as "a subtle part of the Nixon war against the press."[144] Aboard the presidential aircraft, reporters were confined to their own section of the plane.[145] And, on presidential motorcades, a small contingent of reporters, camera persons, and sound technicians rode in cars directly behind the president, with the rest following in busses well to the rear.

In addition to sequestration, the Nixon team took pains to limit their access to key sources. With the president setting the tone, Henry Kissinger echoed his boss's distrust of the press. He instructed members of the National Security Council to "sever . . . [their] relations with the press. . . . The penalty [for talking with reporters] is being fired. If anybody leaks in this administration, I will be the one to leak."[146] As a result, White House staffers tended to avoid writing memos that could become the source of leaks.[147] The administration's paranoia about leaks was, of course, the motive for forming the infamous "Plumbers" unit. As William Safire observed, "a need to 'stop the leaks' and to teach the leakers a lesson" led Nixon to "defend his privacy at the expense of everyone else's right . . . and to create the climate that led to Watergate."[148]

Like co-optation and condemnation, circumvention subverted First Amendment principles. Through tactics of preemption and avoidance, Johnson and Nixon exerted almost unilateral control over dissenters' access to the president and other administration figures as well as press access to information. Their actions both passively and blatantly obstructed the media's informational and critical functions; moreover, they were responsible for undermining free speech and assembly because their actions disavowed dissenters' rights to be heard. If circumvention enabled both presidents to stifle opposition through largely legal and symbolic means, coercion tactics enabled them to achieve the same goal through nonsymbolic, sometimes illegitimate control.

Coercion

Coercion involves the use of sources of power by the president and administration. Presidential powers entail accessing information unavailable to others, mobilizing the FBI, CIA, and the National Guard, and pursuing avenues to restrict others' actions. Both presidents—Nixon more so than Johnson—availed themselves of these mechanisms to manipulate and constrain their critics in two ways: *harassment* includes surveillance, intimidation, and related means to obstruct the "other," while *sanctioning* exacts more formal retribution by marshaling the resources of the judicial system and various regulatory agencies.

Harassment. Because Johnson believed that press coverage of his administration was fundamentally biased and distorted, he dogged the media. However, he chose mainly private and covert methods of harassment to avoid the charge of violating the spirit of the First Amendment. These ploys consisted of monitoring press activities and systematically countering their interpretations of events. The key to Johnson's power lay in the extensive network of information he accrued, a tactic honed during his days in the U.S. Senate: as one reporter noted, "he knows more about individual newsmen and their publications than any president I have ever known."[149]

His surveillance of media personnel began early in his presidency when he charged staff members with the responsibility of compiling dossiers on individual correspondents and their organizations. This knowledge enabled him to distinguish supporters from critics and to tailor information passed from the White House to reporters.[150]

In addition, Johnson used his role as commander-in-chief to intimidate newspeople covering the Vietnam War. To complain about unflattering news reports, he would contact network presidents and publishing heads. Such was the case during the TET offensive in 1968. His perception of press "negativism" prompted him to chastise the media publicly, asserting that competition among various organizations created a sensationalism resulting in the dissemination of incessantly "lurid and depressing accounts" of that event.[151] At other times Johnson resorted to more blatant coercion. For example, when a segment of *60 Minutes* featured a U.S. soldier setting a fire in Southeast Asia with a Zippo lighter, Johnson ordered an FBI investigation and security check on Morley Safer, the reporter responsible for the story.[152]

Johnson supplemented his covert form of harassment of the press with more public counterattacks. Some of the most vehement criticism of his handling of Vietnam occurred during TET. After publication of firsthand accounts of the war by Harrison Salisbury, a New York *Times* correspondent working out of Hanoi, Johnson counterattacked by encouraging sympathetic reporters to interview military commanders, by deploying his cabinet members on a variety of television news programs, and by reprimanding the press pool.[153] This effort to either overshadow or silence opposing views through an organized rebuttal of coverage counter to his position was Johnson's dominant rhetorical response to criticism in the media.

His approach to countering civil strife was more aggressive. Spurred by his conviction that protesters were both misguided and vulnerable to scare tactics, the president and his staff monitored the activities of antiwar movement leaders and scoured newspapers for advertisements and open letters listing persons opposed to the war. Johnson planned to use such information to investigate and otherwise squelch those hostile to him; typically, though, the information grounded countermeasures. For example, immediately following any printing of a public letter naming well-known antiwar activists,

Johnson would publish a list of "notables" supporting administrative policy;[154] similarly, he dispatched "truth squads" to college campuses to offset demonstrators' effects.[155]

Johnson also attempted to intimidate protesters. Because he could not legally ban picketers who frequented the White House, he obstructed them by "limiting their numbers in certain venues and demanding letter-perfect permits for every activity."[156] Draft card burners were threatened with prosecution; and when Martin Luther King joined with the antiwar movement, administration representatives circulated rumors of Communist infiltration into the core of the civil rights organization.[157]

Johnson was particularly vindictive with former political cohorts he thought to be "traitors." McGeorge Bundy, for example, incurred the president's wrath when he agreed to meet with protesters without executive approval. Johnson got him out of the way by dispatching him to the Dominican Republic to plan meetings there. Similarly, the president chastised Senator Robert Kennedy (D–New York) repeatedly and would vent anger at members of Congress and university presidents who made public their disapproval of his actions with respect to Vietnam.[158] In essence, Johnson's monitoring of his opponents turned into counterattacks involving both rebuttal and intimidation.

Nixon followed a similar pattern in scope and function despite the fact that, unlike Johnson, he and his administration were well-prepared to deal with dissent in its myriad forms by the time he assumed the presidency. Not surprisingly, then, both harassment and sanctioning during the Nixon years were more pronounced than during Johnson's tenure. Like his predecessor, Nixon's censorship started with the acquisition of information; unlike Johnson, he regularly moved beyond threats to actions employing the machinery of government.

Indicative of its penchant for tracking the activities of the press in general are recommendations made by Jeb Magruder in a memo to Haldeman in October 1969. Spear explains that after highlighting the need to target anti-administration spokespersons, "Magruder recommended that the Federal Communications Commission set up an official monitoring system to keep track of network news coverage; that the Justice Department's antitrust division 'investigate various media'; that the [IRS] 'look into the various organizations that we are most concerned about'; and that the White House 'begin to show favorites within the media.' "[159]

In other words, even in the administration's early days, the bent toward monitoring protesters, the output of news organizations, and specific news people was well developed. For example, in 1972 the CIA initiated "Project Mudhen," a systematic program of surveillance of columnist Jack Anderson and his staff.[160] Others targeted for investigation by federal agencies were Daniel Schorr and Cassie Mackin. The FBI installed wiretaps, not only on the telephones of newspeople, but also as a way of monitoring the communication of members of the State and Defense departments. By early 1971 the Bureau had tapped members of Henry Kissinger's staff, officials at both Defense and State, and personnel on the White House staff.[161]

The latter was emblematic of Nixon's concern with leaks, a concern that manifested itself in the formation of the infamous "Plumbers" unit in 1971. The precipitous event was the leaking of classified documents by Daniel Ellsberg, a Rand employee who in 1969 discovered a report to Secretary of Defense McNamara during the Johnson Administration. The report indicated that the Gulf of Tonkin incident that led to a major escalation in the war may have been faked. In March 1971, Ellsberg gave the papers to Neil Sheehan of the New York *Times*, which then published the first installment of the "Pentagon Papers" in June 1971. Ellsberg was soon arrested and the Nixon administration got a restraining order placed on the *Times*. In late December 1971, Ellsberg along with a colleague, Anthony Russo, were charged with conspiracy, theft, and espionage; however, the courts ruled that the papers did not contain anything that would damage current American security and allowed the New York *Times* to continue publishing. The case against Ellsberg and Russo was not dismissed until May 1973 when it was discovered that a team of covert agents had broken into Ellsburg's psychiatrist's office attempting to find evidence to discredit Ellsburg. These same "plumbers" would enter the Watergate Hotel in June 1972.

How were they formed? Alarmed by the publication of the *Pentagon Papers*, Nixon dubbed Haldeman "Lord High Executioner," directing him to chastise and threaten employees suspected of indiscretions in their dealings with the press. He instructed Ehrlichman to create a special unit to figure out how to stop administrative leaks. According to Haldeman, "the Vietnam war had created almost unbearable pressures which caused . . . [Nixon] to order wiretaps and activate the plumbers in response to antiwar moves."[162] "Plumbing" was not just reactive, however, it also was proactive. As Deep Throat (Mark Felt) told Bob Woodward, the Plumbers both tried to stop leaks and to manufacture them. For example, the reporter's source said, "[t]he business of [Democratic Vice-Presidential candidate] Eagleton's drunk-driving record or his health records . . . involve[d] the White House. . . . Total manipulation—that was their goal."[163]

The information collected by the Nixon Administration was used to harass its opponents. Newspeople drew special attention; Jack Anderson was a favorite target. Cassie Mackin of NBC aired a report during the 1972 campaign that challenged the legitimacy of Nixon's charges against McGovern. After calls from Herb Klein and Kenneth Clawson to network bosses, Mackin found herself in Los Angeles to receive "film training."[164] CBS's Morley Safer also discovered the disadvantages of being *persona non grata* at the White House: on a trip to Vietnam to report on Vietnamization, he found himself refused the transportation necessary to develop a story.[165] The Nixon team also used more direct threats at times. In 1972, Clay Whitehead, the White House's director of the Office of Telecommunications Policy, delivered an attack on the First Amendment worthy of Agnew. Speaking in Indianapolis, he warned television stations around the nation that were they to persist in airing the "biased" stories produced by national networks their licenses could be in jeopardy.[166]

Sanctioning. Intervention in Vietnam followed a course that Johnson had never anticipated; consequently, he was ill-prepared for the onslaught of opposition that ensued. He sought advice from close ally and FBI chief, J. Edgar Hoover, and subsequently authorized the FBI and CIA to probe the possibility of outside influence within the antiwar movement. In essence, Johnson sent the CIA on an unsuccessful mission to link the civil rights and antiwar movements to a covert Communist conspiracy. His legal machinations reflected a similar pattern of investigation leading to threat but stopping short of overt action. For instance, although Johnson publicized his intent to prosecute draft card burners, few landed in court.[167] Moreover, he readied, but did not consummate, plans to obstruct demonstrators who promised to disrupt his public appearances.[168]

Johnson did encourage activities designed to discourage dissent. The CIA inaugurated "Operation CHAOS," a campaign that involved infiltrating dissident groups to gather information that would make it more difficult for protesters to receive a fair public hearing. The IRS also created a Special Service Staff to probe political organizations, and the Justice Department delegated responsibility for coordinating riot control to a newly formed Interdivision Information Unit.[169] The Johnson Administration thus endeavored to suppress dissent through legal means. The efforts of all of these regulatory agencies, however, produced considerable data but otherwise had marginal impact on dissidents or the progression of the antiwar movement.

Unlike the Johnson Administration, many of the Nixon Administration's actions exceeded simple harassment or surveillance. Burgeoning unrest in the cities and on the nation's campuses was a key problem faced by both local and federal authorities. As frustration among the disaffected increased, protest degenerated into gratuitous violence that required a series of interventions by police and the National Guard. Arrests on university campuses for political violence totaled better than 4,000 in 1968–1969, a number that rose to 7,200 the following year.[170] The pivotal event in the escalation of violence was the tragedy at Kent State. Dissent flared across the nation after the president's announcement of the invasion of Cambodia. On May 4, 1970, after Ohio's governor called in the National Guard to stop damage at both the Kent State campus and the town itself, four students who charged the Guard were killed. The incident inflamed the already strident protest, closed down better than 450 campuses, if only briefly, and required intervention by the National Guard at least 24 times. The following spring in Washington, D.C., the last of the Vietnam protests in the nation's Capitol, resulted in nearly 10,000 arrests. In 1975, with the war over, the courts declared most of the mass arrests illegal and awarded damages to 1,200 of those thus detained.[171]

The Nixon Administration was adept at using regulatory agencies and the justice system to coerce opponents. At times, intimations that broadcasting licenses could be in jeopardy unless stations took steps to air news favorable to the administration went beyond simple threats. The administration's targeting of national television networks is illustrative. In April 1972, NBC, CBS, and ABC faced antitrust suits filed by the Justice Department, charging that their monopoly of prime-time television denied the American people programming resulting from open competition. Whatever the merit of the suits, their timing made them highly coercive. They could well have been designed to serve as a ploy to offset the impression that the administration unfairly favored big business because of its lax approach to a controversy involving International Telephone and Telegraph (ITT); and because they were filed just prior to the 1972 campaign, that filing sent a clear message to the networks that the tenor of coverage during the campaign could have an impact on the fervor with which the government pursued the lawsuits.[172]

The president also tried to initiate revisions of the criminal code to strengthen regulations designed to deter the leaking and receiving of government documents. For example, under the leadership of Attorney General John Mitchell, the Department of Justice was involved in one of the era's more sensational attacks on the press, the imposition of prior restraint to block publication of the Pentagon Papers. Those documents were an intricate chronicle of the escalation of U.S. involvement in Southeast Asia that was especially critical of the Kennedy and Johnson Administrations. For that reason, Nixon was not particularly concerned initially. However, Henry Kissinger convinced him that such leakage could hamper the administration's ability to conduct international affairs and, furthermore, would create the image of a weak Nixon.[173] Consequently, the president ordered Mitchell to take measures to halt the papers' publication and also indict Daniel Ellsberg because "it is the role of government, not the New York *Times*, to judge the impact of a secret document."[174] Through a series of court orders and injunctions against a large sample of major newspapers, the Nixon administration achieved what no other had before: stopping national presses for 15 days. And, although the Supreme Court ruled in favor of the newspapers by a vote of 6 to 3, some of the Court's opinions had the potential for eroding the First Amendment.[175]

Presidents rely on regulatory agencies and legitimate sources of power to maintain control and social order. Thus, utilizing such resources judiciously is well within the purview of a leader's responsibilities. However, the sanctioning and harassment tactics employed by Johnson and Nixon too often reflected motives designed solely to intimidate and obstruct in situations where the rationale for such actively suppressive measures was negligible. For this reason, their actions constituted a campaign of suppression on First Amendment rights.

Conclusions and Implications

As we noted at the beginning of this essay, war heightens the inherent tensions between freedoms guaranteed by the First Amendment and needs related to national security and unity. In such times, our nation's leaders face the difficult task of striking a balance between these potentially conflicting interests so that neither the individual nor the exigencies of war jeopardize the integrity of the other. Presumably, Johnson and Nixon were guided at least in principle by this rule of governance as they confronted the dilemmas of Vietnam. Yet, as our analysis indicates, both administrations upset that balance and succumbed to practices damaging to the First Amendment. In what follows, we address the implications and effects of the era's threats to that Amendment.

Our analysis reveals four recurrent patterns of suppression marking administrative discourses during Vietnam: co-optation, condemnation, circumvention, and coercion. In deriving these strategies, we submerged differences in the rhetoric of the two administrations to focus on commonalities evident in responses to challenges from press and protest. However, two key differences did emerge. First, the divergent *characters* of the two presidents appear to account for varied tactical choices. For instance, because of an ideological idealism intrinsic to his vision of the Great Society, Johnson's commitment to the principles grounding the First Amendment likely resulted in his downplaying of condemnation, especially that directed toward young protesters; in like manner, his version of co-optation rested heavily on ideology. By contrast, Nixon's pragmatism explains his comparably greater reliance on coercion and circumvention to thwart threats from critics. In addition, Johnson's confrontational style contrasted sharply with Nixon's penchant for privacy and his resulting aloofness. Not surprisingly, then, whereas virtually all of Johnson's tactics employed some kind of direct, interpersonal engagement with detractors—"pressing the flesh" in true Texas-style persuasion—Nixon kept his distance from the fray by perfecting tactics of circumvention and utilizing the legitimate power of legal mechanisms and agencies to coerce his adversaries.

Second, because Johnson presided over escalation and Nixon over de-escalation of the war, the presidents faced different *contextual* constraints. Thus, Johnson's strategic choices reflected the need to garner public support and create the unity paramount to the successful enactment of war. He emphasized tactics of co-optation, condemnation, and circumvention associated with traditional American justifications for war; that is, the sanctity of national ideology, the diabolical nature of the enemy, and the adverse effects of press coverage and dissension on the war effort. By contrast, Nixon faced the difficulties inherent in ending the war, difficulties exacerbated by a society fractured by ever-increasing social strife. Consequently, he resorted to a program of damage control through tactics of circumvention, condemnation, and coercion designed to contain opposition and simultaneously promulgate his administration's policy.

In spite of these characterological and contextual variations, Johnson and Nixon pursued suppressive strategies remarkably similar in theme and function. Both presidents targeted their appeals to America's "silent majority," a move that enabled them to justify dismissing dissent as nonrepresentative and subversive because it ran counter to the sentiment of the majority. Likewise, both leaders embraced a narrow definition of the role of the press, one in which the media performed an informative but not an evaluative function. This redefinition allowed them to condemn criticism by the press as unfair and misplaced and to rationalize circumventing the media. Additionally, both chief executives depended on counterattacks to promote policy and simultaneously undermine opposition; they alleged that protest activities and criticism in the press aided the enemy; and they were equally guilty of failing to level with the American public.

Because of the scope and pervasiveness of these patterns, both administrations clearly deserve indictment for employing suppressive tactics. But obviously not all of Johnson's and Nixon's actions violated the First Amendment. What mitigates a categorical denunciation of both leaders are two factors indigenous to a democratic society: the need to balance conflicting interests and the right of *all* citizens, including the *president*, to freedom of expression. Those factors imply a number of questions relevant to the assessment of both chief executives' actions. Is condemnation, for example, intrinsically suppressive or is it the exercise of a rhetor's right to alert the public to dangerous ideas? Does co-optation automatically render another's position powerless in an unfair and unacceptable way, or might it ground a workable compromise leading to the resolution of conflict? To what degree is circumvention a suppression of the freedom of the press or simply the use of alternate avenues for a speaker to convey information? What is the difference between coercive actions that fall legitimately within the purview of a leader's responsibilities and those that abuse power? The central issue, then, is not whether Johnson and Nixon undermined the press and protest related to the Vietnam War but the degree to which those actions violated the constitutional principles they swore to uphold.

As we indicated in the essay's introduction, we argue that suppression of the First Amendment occurs when administrative actions effect an arbitrary denial of the legitimacy of the voice of opposition. Our analysis reveals that independently and collectively, co-optation, circumvention, coercion, and condemnation function to deny voice by subverting the *position*, *person*, and *purpose* of protesters and the press.

Denial of *position* occurred primarily through co-optation. Johnson's and Nixon's advocacy of the "limited war" and "Vietnamization," respectively, rested in large part on redefining the nature of the challenge to their policies. Hence, they relied on advocacy based in distortion and misrepresentation of opposition views. Driven by the need to garner public and political support, both men settled on courses of actions designed to mediate between and ostensibly appease those holding disparate political convictions. But their commandeering of the positions, ideology, and fears of their adversaries was deceptive: although Johnson and Nixon *appeared* to acknowledge, affirm, and incorporate difference, they actually reframed and altered its meaning to serve their own interests. Consequently, appropriation not only accomplished the feat of distorting the nature of opposition, but, in effect, manipulated disagreement *and* rendered it harmless. In this sense, co-optation functioned to quell criticism in a disarming and exploitive way because it undercut the nature, value, and force of dissenting opinion.

Johnson and Nixon undermined the *purpose* or function of the press and protest in two ways. First, they rationalized circumventing both sources of criticism by affirming their right and need to communicate directly to the American public and therefore defining the role of the press as essentially informative and that of protest to simply convey opinion. In effect, they denied the legitimacy of critical evaluation, thereby subverting the mission of both press and protest.

Second, through both circumvention and coercion, they restricted access to channels of communication, thereby limiting the means available to their critics for achieving the purpose of evaluation. Coercion probably was the most overtly suppressive of the strategies utilized by the two administrations. After all, the goal of coercion *is* to constrain action through the threat of punishment, whether real or implied. Johnson employed such tactics sparingly while Nixon perfected the art; both specialized in compiling information for potential use against dissidents, demonstrators, and members of the press. If judiciously applied, that is, deploying law enforcement to stem violence or illegal activities, coercion constitutes no threat to the First Amendment. However, if designed solely to silence criticism or intimidate opposition, as

Nixon was especially prone to do, then coercion is fundamentally antithetical to principles governing freedom of expression. Since both administrations exhibited tendencies toward the latter, their efforts served to deny their critics access to legitimate channels through which to promulgate criticism.

Denial of *personhood*, the attack on the competence and integrity of an adversary through condemnation, was perhaps the most insidious of the assaults on the First Amendment during Vietnam. Various modes of marginalizing served to undermine the legitimacy of opponents: by depicting opponents as a vocal minority or as elitist, both administrations subverted the persuasiveness of their critics effectively by undercutting the bases on which the larger population could identify with them. Demonizing redefined and transformed opponents into a malevolent threat by questioning their competence and portraying their actions as antithetical—either inadvertently or consciously—to American interests. Both administrations depicted their adversaries as naïve but, more importantly, dangerous, hence undeserving of voice. Condemnation, then, functioned as suppression of personhood because it denied the inherent legitimacy of any and all parties who questioned national policy.

If denial of the legitimacy of an adversary's position, personhood, and purpose signifies a threat to the First Amendment, then both administrations of the Vietnam era were culpable for widespread suppressive practices. Johnson and Nixon systematically distorted and manipulated protesters' positions, frustrated their rights and ability to be heard, and thwarted the press's capacity to perform its constitutional functions. Ironically, despite their pervasiveness, it is unclear whether these suppressive activities had any demonstrable impact on either press coverage or protest of the war, or on the war's outcome. Thus, we turn to a consideration of the effects of administrative subversion of the First Amendment on protest, press, and public opinion.

The Johnson and Nixon Administrations patently failed in their efforts to halt *protest* of the war. Of course, obstructionist tactics did impede demonstrators' activities at times; over the long term, however, protest intensified rather than ebbed. Moreover, it apparently wielded greater impact on presidential decision-making than did administrative efforts to short-circuit protest. Thus, while suppressive strategies marginally influenced the scope and direction of dissension, by contrast, antiwar opposition ultimately changed the way Johnson and Nixon managed the Vietnam conflict.[176] The relative ineffectiveness of strategies waged against protesters may be due in part to the normal growth of dissent during times of war, and in part to the atypical nature of the Vietnam conflict as well as the sociopolitical context of its occurrence. More importantly, however, the inability of both administrations to stifle dissent attests to the power and preeminence of the First Amendment to survive even in the face of significant subversion by America's leaders.

Administration efforts to suppress *press* freedoms resulted in comparably more mixed effects. On the one hand, both presidents, exercising the same powers granted to all American leaders during war, controlled information and maintained secrecy for purposes of national security. They also achieved temporal success in inhibiting individual reporters and media outlets regarding coverage of the war. In fact, the repercussions of Johnson's and Nixon's treatment of the press on the relationship between government and media has extended from Vietnam to more recent armed conflicts.[177] On the other hand, neither president made significant inroads in containing the freedoms of the press. Critiques of administration policy in Vietnam continued unabated as did uncensored coverage of the war on the battlefields. More importantly, attempts to suppress the press merely accomplished the reverse effect of intensifying press scrutiny of administration actions. Eventually, that monitoring contributed to the downfall of both presidents, in effect, just retribution for trying to subvert First Amendment rights.

Both administrations enjoyed considerably more influence with *public opinion*. Regardless of whether their suppressive strategies worked against press or protest, in the public arena, Johnson and Nixon secured enough popular support to sustain their respective intervention policies in Vietnam. Part of that success can be attributed to their manipulation of the media, particularly television. MacDonald notes, for example, that in Johnson's case, "television was crucial in persuading the American public to accept Johnson's radical change in policies after the Gulf of Tonkin [incident]. . . . It was television that made protracted, undeclared war acceptable."[178] Similarly, television coverage of antiwar demonstrations often benefitted administration policy, for visual portraits of rude, unruly, or inappropriate actions by protesters garnered sympathy votes for the presidents.[179] Part of their success, however, must also be attributed to public trust in elected officials, and at least initially the public's willingness to condone actions—even if sometimes questionable—by leaders because of the inherent complexities in conducting war. As late as August 1968, the public was evenly divided on whether to withdraw from Vietnam or escalate the war.

In the final analysis, however, suppressive strategies during the Vietnam era are indefensible. Such strategies succeeded only in undermining the principles of the First Amendment, the processes of democracy, and trust in our nation's leaders. These actions not only failed to meet the goal of uniting the country to achieve victory in war, but they exacerbated the divisiveness already permeating the nation. In the years since Vietnam, the American public has made it clear that it deserves far more from its leaders.

Notes

1. Margaret A. Blanchard, "Free Expression and Wartime: Lessons from the Past, Hopes for the Future," *Journalism Quarterly* 69 (1992): 5–17.

2. Abe Fortas, *Concerning Dissent and Civil Disobedience* (New York: New American Library, 1968).

3. John Kennedy committed the first combat troops; Gerald Ford watched the North Vietnamese invasion of the South, powerless to intervene because Congress would not fund any effort to rescue the South Vietnamese government.

4. Fred Bruning, "The Vietnam Lessons George Bush Forgot," *MacLean's* February 18, 1991, 13.

5. Charles DeBenedetti, "Lyndon Johnson and the Antiwar Opposition," in *The Johnson Years, Vol. II: Vietnam, the Environment, and Science*, ed., Robert A. Divine (Lawrence, KA: University Press of Kansas, 1987), 48.

6. Melvin Small, *Johnson, Nixon, and the Doves* (New Brunswick, NJ: Rutgers University Press, 1988), 25.

7. Small, *Johnson, Nixon*, 28.

8. Kathleen J. Turner, *Lyndon Johnson's Dual War: Vietnam and the Press* (Chicago: University of Chicago Press, 1985), 72.

9. Theodore Draper, *Abuse of Power* (New York: Viking, 1967), 67.

10. Turner, *Lyndon Johnson's Dual War*, 83.

11. Allan R. Millett, "Chronology of the War for Vietnam," in *A Short History of the Vietnam War*, ed. Allan R. Millett (Bloomington, IN: Indiana University Press, 1978), 144–145.

12. For a series of tables charting U.S. involvement during this time, see Small, *Johnson, Nixon*, 26, 76, and 94.

13. The ineffectiveness of the airwar campaign had been a concern of military strategists and Defense Secretary Robert McNamara from as early as 1966.

14. Turner, *Lyndon Johnson's Dual War*, 2.

15. Polls reflected this decline: in 1964, 24 percent of Americans disapproved of the war, but by late 1968, that figure rose to 58 percent. Small, *Johnson, Nixon*, 26, 130.

16. Nixon was inundated at every press conference he held with questions pertaining to troop withdrawal schedules.

17. Small, *Johnson, Nixon*, 164, 194, and 214. In essence, the mathematics of troop strength or withdrawal became the measure of the efficacy of Nixon's Vietnamization program for the American public.

18. As a result of the Cambodian invasion, the Senate repealed the Gulf of Tonkin resolution, significantly limiting the president's power to make war-related decisions without congressional approval.

19. Small, *Johnson, Nixon*, 166.

20. Scranton Commission, *Report of the President's Commission on Campus Unrest* (New York: Arno, 1970), 38–39.

21. Small, *Johnson, Nixon*, 183.

22. Small, *Johnson, Nixon*, 202.

23. DeBenedetti, "Lyndon Johnson," 24.

24. F. M. Kail, *What Washington Said: Administration Rhetoric and the Vietnam War: 1949–1969* (New York: Harper & Row, 1973), 233; see also Nicholas de B. Katzenbach, "Foreign Policy, Public Opinion, and Secrecy," *Foreign Affairs* 52 (1973): 1–19.

25. Turner, *Lyndon Johnson's Dual War*, 4. George C. Herring ("The Reluctant Warrior: Lyndon Johnson as Commander in Chief," in *Shadow on the White House: Presidents & the Vietnam War, 1945–1975*, ed. David L. Anderson [Lawrence, KA: University Press of Kansas, 1993]: 88) notes that "the president's role in a limited war is ... difficult. ... [I]t should be waged without too much intrusion into the life of a nation." Further, the president "cannot appear preoccupied with the war to the exclusion of other things; ... [but] cannot appear indifferent either."

26. Kail identifies three contradictions pervading Johnson's Vietnam rhetoric: "the establishment of limits on operational strategy and their summary abandonment; the insistence that a changing policy remained essentially fixed; [and] the expression of confidence in the face of a defiant reality" (*What Washington Said*, 241).

27. See, in particular, Lyndon B. Johnson, "United States Vietnam Policy: Destroy or Build," speech delivered at the Johns Hopkins University, April 7, 1965, *Vital Speeches of the Day* 31 (1965): 386–388; Lyndon B. Johnson, "Vietnam: The Cause of Human Freedom," speech delivered on the occasion of his receipt of the National Freedom Award, New York, February 23, 1966, *Vital Speeches of the Day* 32 (1966): 579–582; Lyndon B. Johnson, "Vietnam War: World Food Crisis," speech delivered at Omaha, Nebraska, June 30, 1966, *Vital Speeches of the Day* 32 (1966): 321–325; and Lyndon B. Johnson, "Vietnam: Our Position Today," speech delivered before the Tennessee Legislature, Nashville, Tennessee, March 15, 1967, *Vital Speeches of the Day* 33 (1967): 354–357.

28. Lyndon B. Johnson, news conference on February 7, 1966, *Public Papers of the President. Lyndon B. Johnson* (Washington, DC: GPO, 1971). Subsequent references to press conferences will cite the date and page number from this source in the text rather than footnoting this source again.

29. DeBenedetti, "Lyndon Johnson," 34. At times, Johnson even employed humor, beginning a speech on August 4, 1965 to an assembly of students working in Washington with the phrase "my fellow revolutionaries." Quoted in Small, *Johnson, Nixon*, 64.

30. Small, *Johnson, Nixon*, 46.

31. Kail, *What Washington Said*, 187. For an analysis of Johnson's contradictory symbolization of Vietnam, especially his delineation of the enemy, see Cal M. Logue and John H. Patton, "From Ambiguity to Dogma: The Rhetorical Symbols of Lyndon B. Johnson on Vietnam," *Southern Speech Communication Journal*, 47 (1982): 310–329.

32. Lyndon B. Johnson, "United States Vietnam Policy," 387.

33. See, for example, "Vietnam: The Cause of Human Freedom," 580, and "Vietnam: Our Position Today," 355.

34. Small, *Johnson, Nixon*, 166, 197, 222.

35. George W. Johnson, ed., *The Nixon Presidential Press Conferences*, January 27, 1969 (New York: Earl M. Coleman, 1978), 3. Further references to press

conferences will be made in the text by listing the date of the press conference and the page number from this source.

36. Richard M. Nixon, "Address to the Nation of Vietnam, May 14, 1969," *Public Papers of the Presidents. Richard M. Nixon, 1969* (Washington, DC: GPO, 1971), 372.

37. Richard M. Nixon, "A Vietnam Plan: The Silent Majority," nationally televised address, November 3, 1969, *Vital Speeches of the Day* 36 (1969): 68.

38. (56). A little over a year later, while defending his decision to invade Cambodia, he told reporters at a May 8, 1970, press conference that "[e]very one of . . . [his] advisors . . . raised questions about the decision." Furthermore, he "raised the most questions" because he knew the "division" the action "would cause" (106). It should be noted that the press conference was one of Nixon's most successful venues; his poll ratings went up after almost all of them, including those held during the Watergate Crisis.

39. Richard Nixon, *Richard M. Nixon: The Memoirs of Richard Nixon* (New York: Warner, 1978), 448.

40. Similarly, Daniel Henkin, PR officer for the Department of Defense, argued that the lottery itself did much to contribute to the decline in protest. See Curt Smith, *Long Time Gone: The Years of Turmoil Remembered* (South Bend, IN: Icarus, 1982) 199, 219.

41. At a press conference on December 8, 1969, Mr. Nixon told journalists, "I believe that it [My Lai] is an isolated incident. . . . Virtually all of them [U.S. soldiers] have helped the people of Vietnam in one way or another. They built roads and schools. They built churches and pagodas . . . and temples for the people of Vietnam" (71).

42. At a press conference on May 8, 1970, shortly after the Kent State killings, Mr. Nixon told reporters, "I want to know what the facts [about Kent State] are. . . . When I get them, I will have something to say about it. But I do know when you do have a situation of a crowd throwing rocks and the National Guard is called in, that there is always the chance that it will escalate into the kind of tragedy that happened at Kent State" (103).

43. For discussions of the Gulf of Tonkin incident, see J. Fred MacDonald, *Television and the Red Menace: The Video Road to Vietnam* (New York: Praeger, 1985), 209–212; John W. Finney, "The Tonkin Verdict," *The New Republic*, (March 9, 1968): 17–19; and Richard A. Cherwitz, "Masking Inconsistency: The Tonkin Gulf Crisis," *Communication Quarterly* 28 (1980): 27–37.

44. Small, *Johnson, Nixon*, 109.

45. Small, *Johnson, Nixon*, 60.

46. Kail, *What Washington Said*, 235.

47. An example is the June 1966 launching of air raids on Hanoi-Haiphong area depots three days after Undersecretary of State George Ball announced on *Meet the Press* that the U.S. had no plans for any bombing missions.

48. Kail, *What Washington Said*, 233–234.

49. Quotation attributed to Lyndon B. Johnson by McGeorge Bundy during an interview with Small. Cited in Small, *Johnson, Nixon*, 30.

50. Richard M. Nixon, "Hard Lines and Guidelines: The Surrender to Washington," address to the National Association of Manufacturers' Annual Congress

of American Industry, New York, December 3, 1965, *Vital Speeches of the Day* 32 (1966): 194.

51. (99).

52. Turner, *Lyndon Johnson's Dual War*, 78.

53. See Walter R. Fisher, "Reaffirmation and Subversion of the American Dream," *Quarterly Journal of Speech* 59 (1973): 160–167. A similar point about the relationship between condemning and bolstering is made about apologetic discourses. See B. L. Ware and Wil A. Linkugel, "They Spoke in Defense of Themselves: On the Generic Criticism of Apologia," *Quarterly Journal of Speech* 59 (1973): 273–283.

54. (1052).

55. *Congressional Quarterly*, 23, no. 43, (October 22, 1965): 2112.

56. These perceptions apparently were inaccurate and misleading: public attitudes against the war eclipsed those in favor of it. Moreover, as Kail notes, Johnson began rationalizing his actions, arguing that public "support while desirable was not a necessity.... By 1967, the support which the president said he no longer needed, he no longer had" (*What Washington Said*, 228).

57. (November 1, 1967, 970)

58. Lyndon B. Johnson, remarks at a reception at Government House, Melbourne, Australia, (October 21, 1966), *Public Papers*, 1247.

59. Lyndon B. Johnson, remarks to delegates to the National Convention, AFL-CIO, (December 12, 1967), *Public Papers*, 534. Vice President Hubert Humphrey echoed these sentiments but with more vehemence: on April 25, 1966, he dismissed their claims as a "waste of time"; on August 13, 1968, he mused that " 'a lot of the talk we've had on Vietnam is escapism engaged in by those who don't want to go out' and confront the harsh realities of the world." Quoted in Kail, *What Washington Said*, 215.

60. Cited in Kail, *What Washington Said*, 214.

61. (970)

62. (November 1, 1967, 970).

63. Cited in Kail, *What Washington Said*, 215.

64. Smith, *Long Time Gone*, 213, 215.

65. William Safire, *Before the Fall* (Garden City, NY: Doubleday, 1975), 288.

66. Smith, *Long Time Gone*, 217.

67. Small, *Johnson, Nixon*, 212.

68. Spiro T. Agnew, "Radicalism in Our Midst," address before the Young President's Organization in Honolulu, May 2 1969, in *Frankly Speaking: A Collection of Extraordinary Speeches* (Washington, DC: Public Affairs Press, 1970), 9.

69. Spiro T. Agnew, "The Politics of Protest," *Frankly Speaking*, 86.

70. Nixon, "Hardlines," 194.

71. Nixon, "Silent Majority," 69.

72. Spiro T. Agnew, "Striving Toward Workable Democracy," *Frankly Speaking*, 59.

73. Richard M. Nixon, "Address at the Dedication of the Karl E. Mundt Library at General Beadle State College, Madison, South Dakota, June 3, 1969," *Public Papers*, 431, 428.

74. Spiro T. Agnew, "Impudence in the Streets," address at the Pennsylvania Republicans Dinner, Harrisburg, Pennsylvania, (October 30, 1969), *Frankly Speaking*, 44.

75. In February 1970, students at the University of California, Santa Barbara burned down the Bank of America blocks from the campus after William Kunstler, the defender of the Chicago Eight, had spoken on the campus.

76. Nixon, "Hardlines," 194

77. Agnew, "Democracy," 69.

78. Agnew, "Radicalism," 11.

79. Agnew, "Impudence," 49–51.

80. Nixon, *Memoirs*, 762.

81. (October 26, 1973, 373).

82. Spear, *Presidents and the Press*, 114; see also Nixon, *Memoirs*, 411; and Safire, *Before the Fall*, 352.

83. Patrick Buchanan had written the speech for Nixon, but Nixon believed it was "unpresidential" and assigned it to Agnew.

84. Spiro T. Agnew, "Television News Coverage: Network Censorship," speech delivered at the Mid-West Regional Republican Convention, Des Moines, Iowa, (November 13, 1969), *Vital Speeches of the Day* 36 (1969): 98.

85. Agnew, "Censorship," 99.

86. Spiro T. Agnew, "The Power of the Press," address delivered to the Montgomery Chamber of Commerce, (November 29, 1969), *Frankly Speaking*, 80.

87. Agnew, "Censorship," 99, 98, 100.

88. Johnson, "Vietnam: Our Position Today," 356.

89. Lyndon B. Johnson, quoted in interview with Elspeth Rostow, September 28, 1970, cited in Turner, *Lyndon Johnson's Dual War*, 253.

90. Small, *Johnson, Nixon*, 82, 139.

91. Kail, *What Washington Said*, 216.

92. Cited in Kail, *What Washington Said*, 216.

93. Lyndon B. Johnson, "The President's Thanksgiving Day message to members of the Armed Forces," (November 24, 1965), *Public Papers*, 1125.

94. Lyndon B. Johnson, remarks at Doughboy Stadium, Fort Benning, Georgia, November 10, 1967, *Public Papers*, 1013.

95. (June 1, 1971, 186)

96. Agnew, "Power of the Press," 83.

97. Richard M. Nixon, "Statement on Campus Disorders," (March 22, 1969) *Public Papers of the President*, 236.

98. Spiro T. Agnew, "Racism, the South, and the New Left," address at the Mississippi Republican Dinner, Jackson, Mississippi, (October 20, 1969), *Frankly Speaking*, 38.

99. Richard M. Nixon, "Address to the Nation on Vietnam," nationally televised address, (May 14, 1969), *Public Papers*, 374.

100. Richard M. Nixon, "The Situation in Vietnam," nationally televised address, (April 26, 1972), *Vital Speeches of the Day* 38 (1972): 451.

101. Lyndon Baines Johnson, *The Choices We Face* (New York: Bantam Books, 1969), 140.

102. Turner, *Lyndon Johnson's Dual War*, 13.

103. Turner, *Lyndon Johnson's Dual War*, 5.

104. Lyndon B. Johnson, quoted in Jack Valenti, *A Very Human President* (New York: Pocket Books, 1976), 212.

105. Lyndon B. Johnson, remarks made at the National Press Club, (January 17, 1969), *Public Papers*, 51.

106. Turner, *Lyndon Johnson's Dual War*, 10–11.

107. Turner, *Lyndon Johnson's Dual War*, 79.

108. Turner, *Lyndon Johnson's Dual War*, 62.

109. "Johnson and the Press—What the Grumbling is About," *U.S. News & World Report*, (March 22, 1965): 50.

110. MacDonald, *Television and the Red Menace*, 203.

111. MacDonald, *Television and the Red Menace*, 204.

112. Kail, *What Washington Said*, 235.

113. Turner, *Lyndon Johnson's Dual War*, 220–222.

114. Turner, *Lyndon Johnson's Dual War*, 200.

115. Marvin Barrett, ed. *The Alfred I. DuPont-Columbia University Survey of Broadcast Journalism, 1969–1970* (New York: Grosset & Dunlap, 1970), 53–54.

116. "Advantage Mr. President," *Time* (January 18, 1971): 13.

117. Herbert Block, *Herlock's State of the Union* (New York: Simon and Schuster, 1972), 66.

118. Safire, *Before the Fall*, 177.

119. Barrett, *Alfred I. DuPont*, 19.

120. Donn Bonafede, "Commissar of Credibility," *The Nation* (April 6, 1970): 394; Erwin Knoww, "The President and the Press: Eliminating the Middleman," *Progressive* (March, 1970): 16.

121. Spear, *Presidents and the Press*, 86.

122. Barrett, *Alfred I. DuPont*, 46.

123. "A Guide to Nixon's China Journey," *Time* (February 21, 1972): 28.

124. "LBJ Reminisces," *Among Friends of LBJ*, (November 1, 1983): 2–7, cited in Small, *Johnson, Nixon*, 152.

125. Lyndon B. Johnson, quoted in interview with Frank Church, cited in DeBenedetti, "Lyndon Johnson," 35.

126. Small, *Johnson, Nixon*, 35.

127. Small, *Johnson, Nixon*, 63.

128. Rowland Evans and Robert Novak, *Lyndon B. Johnson: The Exercise of Power* (New York: New American Library, 1966), 563.

129. Small, *Johnson, Nixon*, 154.

130. Timothy Crouse, *The Boys on the Bus* (New York: Ballentine, 1972), 191, 192.

131. FDR had two a week, Truman, Eisenhower, Kennedy, and Johnson 14 to 36 a year. Spear, *Presidents and the Press*, 79.

132. (December 10, 1970, 134)

133. (December 8, 1969, 78)

134. David Broder, quoted in Crouse, *Boys on the Bus*, 243.

135. Spear, *Presidents and the Press*, 80–81.

136. Safire, *Before the Fall*, 351.

137. Julius Duscha, "The President and the Press," *Progressive* (May 1969): 26.

138. Crouse, *Boys on the Bus*, 272.

139. Spear, *Presidents and the Press*, 81.

140. "Nixon's Movable White House," *Newsweek* (August 24, 1970): 16–19; Dan Rather and Gary Paul Gates, *The Palace Guard* (New York: Harper & Row, 1974), 27; Safire, *Before the Fall*, 618; Spear, *Presidents and the Press*, 68–69; Jules Witcover, "How Well Does the White House Press Perform?" *Columbia Journalism Review*, (November–December 1973): 41.

141. Spear, *Presidents and the Press*, 72.

142. David Wise, "The President and the Press," *Atlantic* (April, 1974): 57.

143. Crouse, *Boys on the Bus*, 200.

144. Helen Thomas, *Dateline: White House* (New York: Macmillan, 1975), 137.

145. Raymond Price, *With Nixon* (New York: Viking Press, 1977), 293.

146. Ted Szulc, *The Illusion of Peace: Foreign Policy in the Nixon Years* (New York: Viking Press, 1978), 19.

147. "Writing Block," *Time* (March 27, 1972): 20.

148. Safire, *Before the Fall*, 358.

149. *U.S. News & World Report* (March 22, 1965), 51.

150. Turner, *Lyndon Johnson's Dual War*, 175.

151. Lyndon Baines Johnson, *The Vantage Point: Perspectives of the Presidency, 1963–1969* (New York: Holt, Rinehart, and Winston, 1971), 383.

152. Small, *Johnson, Nixon*, 65. CBS learned that Safer had had the soldier stage an event that happened earlier in the day.

153. Turner, *Lyndon Johnson's Dual War*, 222.

154. Small, *Johnson, Nixon*, 70.

155. DeBenedetti, "Lyndon Johnson," 36.

156. Small, *Johnson, Nixon*, 66.

157. Small, *Johnson, Nixon*, 100.

158. Small, *Johnson, Nixon*, 75–78. Small also notes that the President "allegedly refused to allow" certain government personnel to testify at Senate hearings on the war in Southeast Asia.

159. Jeb Stuart Magruder, quoted in Spear, *Presidents and the Press*, 113.

160. Spear, *Presidents and the Press*, 136.

161. Szulc, *Illusions of Peace*, 181–188.

162. H. R. Haldeman with Joseph DiMona, *The Ends of Power* (New York: Times Books, 1978), 121.

163. Carl Bernstein and Bob Woodward, *All the President's Men* (New York: Simon and Schuster, 1974), 133–134.

164. Spear, *Presidents and the Press*, 144–146.

165. Fred Powledge, *The Engineering of Restraint: The Nixon Administration and the Press* (Washington, DC: Public Affairs Press, 1971), 19.

166. Spear, *Presidents and the Press*, 150–151.

167. One who did was a young man named O'Brien who burned his draft card on the steps of the Boston town hall. The Supreme Court upheld his conviction in *U.S. v. O'Brien* (391 U.S. 367 [1968]).

168. Small, *Johnson, Nixon*, 125.

169. Small, *Johnson, Nixon*, 104–105.

170. *President's Commission on Campus Unrest*, 38–39.

171. Smith, *Long Time Gone*, 202, 217–218.

172. Spear, *Presidents and the Press*, 143–144.

173. Haldeman, *Ends of Power*, 110–111.

174. Nixon, *Memoirs*, 509–513.

175. Spear, *Presidents and the Press*, 161–162; Jules Witcover, "Two Weeks That Shook the Press," *Columbia Journalism Review*, 10 (September–October, 1971): 7–15. One of the most thorough treatments of the events involved in the publication of the papers is that of Sanford J. Unger in *The Papers & the Papers* (New York: Dutton, 1972).

176. This is the central argument made by Small in *Johnson, Nixon*.

177. For a discussion of the long term effects of Johnson's and Nixon's handling of the press, see Spear, *Presidents and the Press*.

178. MacDonald, *Television and the Red Menace*, 212.

179. Small, *Johnson, Nixon*, 127.

Chapter 9

Suppressing Political Speech Through Broadcast Regulation and Campaign Reform

Craig R. Smith

On March 24, 2009, the Supreme Court heard *Citizens United v. Federal Elections Commission*, a case regarding campaign persuasion, the kind of political persuasion the founders most wanted to protect. During the 2008 presidential campaign, a "documentary" film, *Hillary: The Movie*, was released that debunked Democratic candidate Hillary Clinton. Because the film was financed by corporate funds through an advocacy group known as Citizens United and because it was going to be shown on on-demand cable within 30 days of various primary elections, injunctions succeeded in stopping the broadcast of the film because it violated federal election laws.[1] A three-judge panel upheld the injunctions under the McCain-Feingold law (see below) ruling that the film was "electioneering communication" directed against a candidate. The judges said the film could not be shown within 30 days of a primary election and it must disclose who its donors were. During oral arguments, Justice Samuel Alito asked the Deputy Solicitor General Malcolm Stewart defending the injunctions if the same rule could be applied to a book that was critical of Clinton and funded by a corporation. Stewart answered in the affirmative, shocking the justices. Alito remarked, "That's pretty incredible." Justice Anthony Kennedy followed up by asking if such a book were distributed through Amazon's Kindle device if it could be banned, and Stewart again answered, "Yes." Chief Justice Roberts joined in the same line of questioning indicating that the conservative majority might strike down this provision of the 2002 law, which in fact they did on January 21, 2010, in *Citizens United v. FEC*.

The question this chapter addresses is how did we get to the point where one of our most basic rights, the freedom to criticize political candidates, got so infringed upon? The answer lies in the reform resulting from the Watergate scandal, and thus provides a natural bridge from the preceding chapter. However, this chapter varies from most of the others in several important ways. First, the implied threat in this case is wholly internal; it is political corruption, which starts with findings of malpractice in the Nixon campaign of 1972 and continues to the abuses of foreign donors and corporate and union "soft money" contributions into 2000. Second, thus, the crisis is carried over many years because politicians are able to subvert the intent of reforms and the Congress is forced to act again to correct these problems. Third, the Supreme Court intervenes not on the side of the First Amendment, but consistently on the side of restrictions, even though there is no external threat and the internal threat has been reduced to the *perception of the possibility* of corruption of the political system.

The Watergate Scandal

While the Vietnam War raged on, the two political parties gathered in the summer of 1972 in Miami Beach, Florida to nominate their candidates. Prior to the conventions, I came to Miami as researcher/writer for the CBS News Special Events Unit for which I had covered the rather peaceful Miami convention of the Republicans and the bloody Chicago convention of the Democrats in 1968. On June 17, 1972, five bells sounded on the Associated Press ticker in the newsroom. I ran to the machine and saw an odd story about a group of men who had been arrested for breaking into the Watergate Hotel in Washington, D.C. Specifically, the men had entered offices of the Democratic National Committee.[2] We were about to learn that the strategies of suppression used by the Nixon administration during the Vietnam War reflected a paranoia inside the administration that generated an enemies list and illegal activities.

When it was discovered that secret and/or classified material was being leaked to the press, Nixon approved the creation of a group of "plumbers" to stop the leaks (see chapter 8). These plumbers had gone so far as to enter the office of the psychiatrist of Daniel Ellsberg, the man who released the infamous Pentagon Papers to the press. Led by former CIA operative Howard Hunt, the "plumbers" became a rogue operation that exceeded its authority—hence the break-in at Ellsberg's psychiatrist's office and the forced entry into the Democratic offices in Watergate Hotel in June 1972. When Nixon met with his advisors on June 23, less than a week after the break-in, he was presented with a number of options regarding the scandal. He elected to cover up the scandal despite his huge lead in the polls over his projected opponent, Senator George McGovern (D–South Dakota), because Nixon had enjoyed large leads before only to see them evaporate. He lost the presidential election of 1960 to John Kennedy by 112,000 votes; he lost the governorship race in 1962 by more than 50,000 after having led in early polls during the campaign; he even lost his lead over Hubert Humphrey in 1968 when it disappeared by election night. Nixon was not declared the winner until early the next morning. So he would not gamble that his campaign could survive telling the truth in June 1972; the election was more than four months away and much could change in that time period. Although Nixon eventually carried 49 states on election night, over the next two years the continuing cover-up would become more egregious than the original crime. The president of the United States engaged in obstruction of justice. He eventually resigned rather than face impeachment in August 1974.

The investigation of the Watergate scandal led to discoveries about how Nixon had conducted his political campaign of 1972. Without disclosure laws, Nixon and many other candidates enjoyed large contributions that were often untraceable. In other cases, such as the donation of $1,000,000 by millionaire, Clement Stone, the campaign contribution cast a shadow of undue influence over the administration. In response, Congress began work on a major campaign reform bill. Though no doubt well intentioned, it would result in restrictions on Americans' most important First Amendment right, freedom of political communication. Thus, this chapter covers one of the subtlest attacks on the First Amendment because many of the reforms had unforeseen consequences, enjoyed broad support, and seemed sensible to a nation reeling from of its worst political scandal.

This chapter examines the post-Watergate reform bill and those that came after it, in an effort to demonstrate once again that even the most well-intentioned legislation can have a chilling effect on free speech. Reformers perceived monied influence to be a serious threat to the electoral system. That threat justified the need to not only regulate campaign contributions and spending but to curtail both. However, the problem here is not confined to the initial action taken by the Congress in response to this threat. Some in Congress and in the national Republican and Democratic Party organs used the reforms to game the system in a way that enhanced the ability of incumbents to retain office, that undermined the anonymity of contributors, that silenced third parties and their candidates, and that further institutionalized the two-party system.

The Context of the Watergate Reforms

Aside from the outcry over Watergate and the campaign scandals of 1972, one of the reasons that reformers believed their legislative effort would succeed was that, with regard to federal campaigns in general, and the media specifically, the Supreme Court upheld restricting broadcasters' speech in the past. This clear violation of the First Amendment rights of broadcasters was linked to political speech from the very beginning. When the Congress passed the Federal Radio Act in 1928, it created the Federal Radio Commission (FRC) to hand out broadcast licenses and make sure that licensees served the "public interest" with a clear signal that did not interfere with another broadcaster's signal. However, in 1929, the FRC used the "public interest" standard to deny an operating license to a radio station owned by the Knights of Labor. Thus, it took only a year for a government agency to convert a noncontent-oriented standard, "serving the public interest," into a way to control and suppress political speech. When the law was rewritten into the Communication Act of 1934 to cover all telecommunications and broadcasting, more control over the content of broadcasts was given the new Federal Communications Commission (FCC).

In an effort to level the playing field between Republicans and Democrats, the new heavily Democratic Congress of 1933–1934 imposed content rules on broadcasters; to this day, they require a broadcaster to provide *"equal opportunities"*[3] for appearances by all bona fide candidates for public office, including write-ins. That is, if a broadcaster makes time available for one candidate running for sheriff, the broadcaster must make comparable time available to all candidates running for sheriff who request it within seven days. However, candidates may speak in support of ballot propositions without triggering the equal opportunities provision. Thus, in California it is normal practice for candidates to link themselves to ballot measures in order to get more airtime than their opponents.

The 1934 Communication Act also required that *"reasonable access"*[4] be provided for any *federal* candidates who sought to purchase it, and that they be billed at the lowest unit rate available for advertising at the station during the 45 days prior to a primary and 60 days prior to the general election. More recently, the FCC has ruled that such access must be provided to presidential candidates 11 months prior to the election.

For a while this meant that if a station wished to sponsor a debate between the Democrat and Republican running for federal office, it had to provide comparable time for others who had filed for the office, no matter how small their following. In 1975 with the Aspen Rules, and again in 1983, the FCC made it easier for major candidates to debate without lesser candidates in the forum by allowing a station to cover a debate, no matter who participated, as long as the debate was put on the air live and in its entirety.

In 1984, half the television stations in the country offered time for debates, a major increase over the number offering to cover debates in years when the FCC did not suspend the rules. However, the rule clearly marginalized third-party candidates, a problem that continues to this day. Even major party candidates with small followings can be eliminated from these live debates as former Senator Mike Gravel found out in 2008 when he ran for president as a Democrat and was excluded from some primary debates.

The regulations of how broadcasters treated candidates was soon followed by rules to control all editorializing by broadcasters. During World War II, the FCC ruled that broadcasters would no longer be allowed to editorialize. The Supreme Court upheld the rule in 1943 arguing that NBC so dominated the radio airwaves that it was a virtual monopoly and therefore could be restricted.[5] In 1949, the Federal Communications Commission promulgated a rule that came to be known as the "Fairness Doctrine," which was an attempt to modify the 1943 ruling. It required broadcasters to comment on important issues of the day and to present contrasting views to those of the station. No such rules had ever succeeded in being imposed on the press because of the wording of the First Amendment.[6] Basically, the Supreme Court held that in most cases, the government cannot compel print media to publish a message. However, as we shall see, the Court did not apply the same rationale when it came to broadcasters.[7] Despite the availability of libel and slander laws to prevent or correct errors, the FCC decided that further restrictions were required of the electronic media. Over the years, the FCC developed several "corollaries" to the "Fairness Doctrine," which further infringed on the rights of broadcasters to carry political speech.

The first was the *Personal Attack Rule*, which required that the person attacked be allowed to respond when the honesty, integrity, or like characteristic of any identified group or individual was attacked. The individual or group was to be notified of the attack and provided with a script or tape of the attack. The second corollary was the *Political Editorial Rule*, which had similar requirements: candidates who were opposed by a station were to be notified of the date and time of the broadcast, be provided with a script or tape, and be given a "reasonable" opportunity to respond. The third corollary, the *Zapple Rule*, referred to announcements by political parties. If a spokesperson for a group was allowed on the air to endorse or oppose a candidate, the broadcaster was required to afford "equal" opportunities to a spokesperson of the opponent.

In 1969 with the *Red Lion Broadcasting* ruling, the Supreme Court addressed the constitutionality of the application of the *Personal Attack Rule*.[8] The precedent set in the unanimous ruling was generally held to apply to the other corollaries mentioned above. Red Lion Broadcasting owned radio station WGCB in Red Lion, Pennsylvania, a town of less than 6,000 persons. Listeners in the small suburb of Philadelphia had access to more than 20 radio stations in 1964 at the time of this incident. They also had access to cable television, of which about half the households took advantage. During the election of 1964, WGCB aired a five minute syndicated editorial by the Reverend Billy James Hargis of the "Christian Crusade." In the editorial, Hargis attacked Fred Cook, a liberal writer who was a consultant with the Democratic National Committee. Singling out Red Lion in an apparent attempt to coerce small broadcasters into not airing the Hargis tirade, Cook demanded time for a response under the "personal attack rule." WGCB said that Cook would have to pay five dollars for his response time. Cook refused and took the case to court. In 1969 the Supreme Court ruled unanimously in favor of Cook, arguing that the electromagnetic spectrum is scarce, that licensees are public fiduciaries, and therefore, subject to government control to insure "fairness."[9] Many who believed broadcasters fell under the protection of the free press clause of the First Amendment were appalled. The Fairness Doctrine was not suspended until 1987; its corollaries were not ended until 2001. However, the access and equal time rules are still in effect.

There is another aspect of this context that is also important. As we have seen in this volume, discourse that attacks the policy of a government at war is a serious matter, as is specifically advocating ways by which such a government can be overthrown. Traditionally, however, Americans have not accorded the same importance to political rhetoric. From colonial times to the present, campaign communication has been filled with innuendo, promises, half-truths, and the like. In the 1952 presidential campaign, the first political advertisements were televised; they were amateurish cartoons and short on specifics. In 1964, the first "negative" political advertisement in a presidential campaign was put on the air. It depicted a small girl picking petals from a daisy as the narrator called out a count down to nuclear war. Run only once because of protests, the advertisement was clearly an attack on the policies of Republican candidate Barry Goldwater by the sitting President Lyndon Johnson. Negative or attack advertising has been with us ever since.

Many states now have campaign fair practices commissions, which can fine and/or censor candidates for distorting the record or defaming their opponents, among other offenses. The Federal Communication Commission has also ruled that campaign advertisements that are obscene, indecent, or tasteless may be refused by broadcast stations even though they are required to take commercials from federal candidates.

Attempts at Reform

United States citizens live in an atmosphere where regulation of political speech over the airwaves is common. That is the context in which the

Watergate reforms began to surface. In the wake of the scandal, a passel of requirements were added to the Federal Corrupt Practices Act of 1925 (passed in reaction to the Tea Pot Dome scandal of the Harding Administration) and the Federal Election Campaign Act of 1971. Citing the threat of corruption, the reforms required that any contributor giving $10 or more to a federal campaign had to be included in the campaign's next quarterly report to the Federal Elections Commission (FEC); the name and address of the contributor must be listed.[10] The new rules limited individual contributions to $1,000 per candidate per election, prohibited corporate contributions,[11] but allowed employees to contribute to a campaign by forming political action committees (PACs), which could make maximum contributions of $5,000 per candidate per election. No individual would be allowed to give more than $5,000 to a PAC or $25,000 overall to federal candidates during a single election cycle. The new law also carefully monitored and limited what corporations or unions could "contribute in kind"—equipment, services, travel, and the like. However, for-profit (501c6) and nonprofit (501c4, 501c3) organizations could provide advocacy advertisements favoring federal candidates or their issue-positions as long as such activity was not "coordinated" with that campaign. This provision opened a loophole in the law, which allowed religious, environmental, and other groups to campaign against candidates who did not endorse their agendas. It also allowed for the creation of independent action groups—designated as 527s—which are tax-exempt and can raise unlimited amounts of money for political activity and issue advocacy. The most infamous of these action groups may have been the "Swiftboat" advocacy group attacking presidential candidate John Kerry during the 2004 election. Loopholes in the law continued to allow for disguised candidate advertisements in the form of issue advocacy. In 2000, for example, more than $500 million was spent by 130 "independent" groups on such ads.

Political parties were forced to allocate their contributions based on population formulas, but they could provide unlimited money to and in states for the purpose of "party-building activities." This provision opened the law to what is called "soft money": unlimited contributions given to the party for grassroots and party-building activities were allowed under amendments to the Federal Election Campaign Act (FECA) passed in 1979. These activities were not subject to the limitations of the FECA or the regulations of the FEC. Nor were certain activities of corporations and unions including corporate communication to stockholders, labor communications to its members or their families, nonpartisan voter registrations and get-out-the-vote activities, and creation of political action committees. Further, the law provided for public financing of presidential nominating conventions and for matching funds to help pay for presidential primary and general election campaigns. In return for accepting matching funds, presidential candidates were limited in how much they could spend overall. If they refused matching funds, they could spend all the money they could raise under the rules. Senator Barack Obama chose this latter course in the 2008 presidential campaign, while Senator John McCain accepted federal funding. Thus, following his convention, McCain was limited to spending only the $84.1 million the federal government provided to him, while Obama could spend all he raised and, thus, vastly outspent McCain.

There were other problems with the law. First, the distribution of federal funds favored the two-party system thereby quashing the voices of third-party candidates. Full matching funds were provided *only* to those parties that scored 25 percent of the vote or more in the previous presidential election. Worse yet, the law funded the two parties' primary candidates, conventions, and election campaigns, while marginalizing third parties and their candidates. On top of that, by creating joint committees and joint fund-raisers, candidates could raise nearly $100,000 for their campaigns. Thus, candidates with a large party apparatus behind them had an advantage. The developer Alex Spanos, who owns the San Diego Charger football team, provided more than $85,000 to the McCain campaign using this tactic prior to the Republican convention. The family of Carl Pohlad, the owner of the Minnesota Twins, gave $170,000 to the Obama campaign under the same scheme.

Second, each congressional district and state was treated equally under the law when it came to providing funds to buy advertising in media markets. Though it is much more expensive to buy advertising time in New Jersey than it is in New Mexico, candidates from each state are under the same funding limits.

Third, to require disclosure of the membership in an organization is a violation of the rights of privacy and assembly.[12] When the state of Alabama upheld the right of employers to fire employees who were found to be members of the NAACP or who had not disclosed their memberships, the Supreme Court overruled the state on the grounds that membership in the NAACP was a form of free assembly that should not be penalized. The Watergate reforms flew in the face of this precedent. Ironically, as recently as 1995, the Supreme Court reinforced this right of private assembly and did so in the political context. In *McIntyre v. Ohio Elections Commission*,[13] the Court held in a 6–3 decision that an Ohio law prohibiting the distribution of anonymous tracts was unconstitutional. Mrs. McIntyre had been fined $100 for violating the law; the conviction was upheld by the Ohio Supreme Court, which relied on the disclosure provisions of federal law. However, in his majority opinion, Justice John Paul Stevens referred to the long tradition of anonymous political dissent going back to the American Revolution. For example, in the debate over ratification of the Constitution, Federalists and Anti-federalists used pseudonyms when publishing their editorials. Stevens claimed that anonymity is a "shield from the tyranny of the majority." This argument clearly implies the right to contribute anonymously to a political campaign.

Fourth, the reform favors incumbents since they don't need to spend money to attain name identification with voters and their opponents usually do. The less money available to candidates, the more incumbents have an advantage. By equalizing contributions and expenditures through arbitrary limits, the law virtually institutionalizes incumbents and marginalizes their opponents.

Appealing for Relief

Senator James L. Buckley, a conservative Republican Senator from New York and Eugene J. McCarthy, a liberal Democrat and former Senator from Minnesota, brought suit against the Watergate reforms. They argued that the rules infringed on freedom of expression because money is tantamount to speech; the more media time a campaign can buy, the more it can communicate its message. Limiting campaign funds limits campaign communication and thereby, violates the First Amendment. They also argued that campaign contributions were tantamount to symbolic speech, the contributed money being the same as an endorsement. Thus, limiting the collection of funds chilled political speech. Remember that the nation's founders believed political speech had the highest value in a democratic republic. Buckley and McCarthy lost at the appellate level when the court found that preventing the "appearance of corruption" in federal elections was more important than First Amendment concerns. The case then went to the Court of Appeals of the District of Columbia, which affirmed the lower court ruling and added that contributions and spending were conduct, not speech, and therefore, not protected under the First Amendment. This ruling was appealed to the Supreme Court.

The Supreme Court, in a curious decision in 1976, ruled that the restrictions on contributions were constitutional but that the spending limitations were not. The former, said the Court, were appropriate ways of controlling undue influence in a campaign; the latter, however, restricted freedom of expression. The majority also used the "undue influence" argument to allow full disclosure of membership in organizations that become involved in political campaigns. The Court upheld the unfair treatment of third parties, those candidates who were not incumbents, and those candidates running against candidates with larger personal fortunes.

No wonder the majority was so fragmented and fragile. Only Justices William Brennan, Potter Stewart, and Lewis Powell concurred in all parts of the decision; other justices endorsed different parts of the ruling creating pluralities for one part or another. Basically, the Court was divided between those who believed in a need to reform in light of the Watergate scandal and those who believed the First Amendment afforded protection to political speech including anonymous association. Thus, a plurality claimed that contributions could be restricted and a different plurality claimed that expenditures should not be restricted. (Money does not equal speech in the former case; but it does equal speech in the latter.)

In his dissent in *Buckley v. Valeo*, Justice Harry Blackmun wrote that the Court could not make a distinction between contributions and expenditures on the basis of which was more vital to freedom of expression. Joined by then Associate Justice Rehnquist, Chief Justice Burger said in his dissent: "Contributions and expenditures are two sides of the same First Amendment coin. . . ."[14] One person's contribution is another person's expenditure. Burger also objected to disclosing small donors who might be retaliated against by employers. He opposed the public funding of elections because such funding favors the two major parties and undercuts representative democracy. Joined by Associate Justice Byron White, Burger also pointed out how the reform vastly favored rich candidates, who can rely on their own funds, over poor candidates, who had no choice but to raise funds from the public in small amounts.

While the *Buckley* decision was widely criticized for labeling money as speech when it was spent, but not as speech when it was donated, the Court did not overturn the decision when it had a chance and often supported the contradictory ruling with contradictory decisions. In *FEC v. Massachusetts Citizens for Life* in 1986, for example, the Supreme Court closed down a vital right in any political system.[15] It ruled that the federal government could limit speech by organizations that "expressly" advocated *for* one candidate or *for* the defeat of another in federal elections, though these groups were still free to enter into issue advocacy.

In 1987, the Supreme Court denied *certiorari* in a Ninth Circuit case, *FEC v. Furgatch*, which established a three-part test to determine what constituted legitimate issue advocacy. To fall under the FEC's jurisdiction the speech must be "unmistakable and unambiguous" in its meaning. Second, it must include a "plea for action" not be merely informative. Third, the speech must be "express advocacy of the election or defeat of a candidate."[16]

The Supreme Court clarified the *Furgatch* standard in two cases. In *Colorado Republican Committee v. FEC*,[17] in 1996, the Supreme Court ruled that First Amendment prohibited the application of any provision of the FECA (1971, as amended 1979) to political party expenditures made independently. The majority argued that party advocacy was a core democratic value.[18] Not surprisingly then, in only the first 15 months of the 1997–1998 cycle, the national Democratic and Republican Parties had raised a total of $90 million.[19] In that cycle, because of overseas contributions—some of which were laundered through subsidiaries—the Democrats caught up with the Republicans in terms of fundraising, but also faced serious ethical and legal questioning. Thus, the Supreme Court took up *FEC v. Colorado Republican Party* in 2001; a five-to-four ruling reaffirmed the prohibition on coordination between party organs and campaigns in federal elections.[20]

However, while the Court moved to protect issue advertising, it also gave the states the right to issue the same restrictions the Court had upheld on the federal level with regard to contribution limits. In *Nixon v. Shrink Missouri Government PAC*, which was decided on January 24, 2000,[21] the Supreme Court argued that *Buckley* is the authority for comparable state limits on contributions and those limits need not be pegged to the precise dollar amounts approved in *Buckley*. Justice David Souter, writing for the majority, claimed that the possibility of the appearance of corruption was enough of a compelling interest for the state of Missouri to restrict contributions in this case. That interest combined with states' rights overwhelmed, in Souter's opinion, concerns about restricting freedom of speech and association. The decision was a clear endorsement of efforts at reform on the state level but it also restricted the First Amendment rights of candidates at that level making the *Buckley* context and restrictions all the more pervasive.

Continuing Problems

Buckley v. Valeo and the decisions that followed created many problems. The provisions that were retained often proved unworkable, circumventable, and/or unconstitutional. Remember that the contribution limits were not indexed for inflation. One thousand dollars in 2009 would buy a lot less than it was in 1975, when the law did pass. Furthermore, with regard to ending political action committee contributions, one could argue that dollars given to political campaigns no longer represent corporations and unions; they represent individuals who associate in campaigns by giving to their favorite candidates through PACs to increase their influence. In 1996, the average contribution to a PAC was only $120 a year.[22] However, political action committees provide a way for citizens to participate in the political process and give clout to that participation by joining together those with similar interests. Millions of people contribute to PACs. As long as contributions must be fully, promptly, and publicly disclosed, as they are now, it seems anti-democratic to limit them.

The decision in *Buckley* sent politicians scrambling for ways by which they could raise money in small amounts, but gather enough contributions to meet their campaign needs. The loopholes created by the Supreme Court had several weird consequences. First, those running for office could spend their own money in unlimited ways, a loophole through which John Connolly, Ross Perot, and Steve Forbes, among others, have driven their self-funded campaign wagons.

Second, the Republican Party became the party of the small donor by using sophisticated direct mail campaigns to build long lists of supporters. The result was that in first 18 months of the 1986 election cycle, for example, the National Republican Senatorial Campaign Committee raised $59.6 million compared to $6.8 million raised by its Democratic counterpart. But the Republican donations were much smaller than the Democratic donations.

Third, the "soft money" loophole meant that rich donors, corporations, and unions could give a great deal of money directly to political parties and with a wink and a nudge, it would wind up in the pocket of their preferred candidate. In 1984 the National Republican Party placed money in the coffers of the Colorado Republican Party, which then paid for advertisements attacking the Democratic candidate. As we have seen, this practice was upheld by the Supreme Court when the FEC tried to stop it.[23]

The bottom line on the soft money loophole was that it further disempowered third parties, individual voters and the poor, while ratcheting up the influence of big labor and corporations and their PACs. From 1993 to 1997, campaign contributions by the 544 largest public and private companies in America jumped 75 percent to $129 million.[24] Soft money was the fastest growing component of this sum.[25] For example, in the 1996 election cycle, Philip Morris contributed $3.9 million and AT&T contributed $2.2 million in PAC money to the two major parties. From January 1, 1995, to November 25, 1996, the Republican national committees reported raising $141 million in soft money, an increase of 183 percent over the previous cycle. The Democratic national committees raised $122 million, an increase of 237 percent. In the round of "soft money" donations reported by *Time* magazine in September 1999, the Democratic National Party received $525,000 from the Communication Workers of America, $460,000 from the American Federation of State, County and Municipal Employees, $315,000 from commercial realtor Walter H. Shorenstein, $315,000 from Williams Bailey Law Firm, and $305,350 from AT&T. Each of these donors had lobbied extensively for legislation that was then supported by the Democratic Party.[26] For example, Williams Bailey Law Firm opposed personal-injury tort reform and most Democrats supported the firm's position.

The givers in the same time period to the Republican National Party were AT&T with $527,000, American Financial Group with $500,000, Philip Morris with $378,467, United Parcel Service with $363,550, and Kojaian

Management with $300,000. Again, each of these companies lobbied extensively for legislation that was supported by the Republican Party.[27]

How does the lobbying work? Let's examine one case study reported by *Time*. On the night of October 17, 1994, the head of American Financial Group had dinner at the White House. Soon after, the United States Trade Representative, Mickey Kantor, launched a major investigation of European companies opposing American Financial Group in various markets. A week later, Vice President Gore called the head of American Financial Group and requested more contributions to the Democratic Party. On November 3, 1994, AFG sent a check for $50,000 to the Democratic National Committee; and $50,000 followed from the other companies that AFG controlled.[28]

Finally, with regard to soft money, the 2000 presidential campaign led to an influx of foreign money into campaign coffers. Although foreigners are prohibited from contributing to federal campaigns, green card holders are not.[29] Furthermore, foreign groups, particularly Asian ones, attempted to circumvent the law by passing money through American citizens or American subsidiaries. Both tactics are illegal if the money is spent directly on candidates; however, if the money is given to parties as soft money, it may not be covered under the statutes. John Huang, a representative of the Indonesian based Lippo Group, an official at the DNC and the Commerce Department, raised more than $4 million for the Democratic Party primarily from Asian-Americans, some of whom were used as conduits for foreign funds.[30] Cheong Am America's $250,000 was returned when it was pointed out to the DNC that the money was from a subsidiary of a South Korean firm that had not yet generated revenues in the United States. Resident aliens Arief and Soroya Wiriadinata donated $452,000 in 23 separate contributions to the DNC of which $320,000 was donated after they returned to Indonesia. Since the couple did not file 1995 income tax returns, the DNC returned the money. Many of the agents involved in these transfers, including Huang, have pled guilty to violating the law.

None of these scandals stanched the flow of funds to the coffers of the two major parties. In the 2000 election cycle, the two major parties raised $500,000,000 in soft money. No third party raised anywhere close to 10 percent of that amount.

Fourth, PACs through which employees can shift money to campaigns grew to more than 4,000 in 1986. PAC contributors, including union and corporate members, number more than 4 million, and total donations to House and Senate campaigns in 1996 reached more than $200 million. Cantor reports that "Twenty-nine percent of House and Senate general election candidates' funds came from PACs in 1996, up from less than 20% in 1976."[31] However, some in Congress sought to restrict PAC funding since it mainly came from corporation and union employees.

New Reforms

All of these concerns along with the controversial presidential election of 2000, which was decided by the Supreme Court, led to the introduction in 2001 of more than 72 bills to reform the system. These included such unconstitutional content reform proposals as making the openings and closings in federal campaign commercials uniform, requiring candidates to appear in their commercials, and forcing stations that aired "negative ads" to grant free response time to attacked candidates. Emerging from this sea of legislation was a consensus bill, S. 25, authored initially by Senators John McCain (R-Arizona) and Russell Feingold (D-Wisconsin). It became the *Bipartisan Campaign Reform Act* (public law no. 107–155) when signed by President Bush in March 2002.

Like its progenitors, it contained controversial provisions. For example, it raised contribution limits to only $2,000 per person per candidate and not to exceed $25,000 for all candidates funded during any calendar year thereby retaining an unrealistically low ceiling on individual contributors, although pegged to inflation.[32] Thus, the average citizen continued to be gagged when it came to expressing enthusiasm for a candidate through the symbolic gesture of giving funds. For example, if you contributed $2,000 to 13 candidates, you would exceed the federal limits.

Reporting to the FEC was now required of those who financed advertising for elections in excess of $10,000. The law also required that no party organ could solicit funds from or make donations to any organization that holds charitable or nonprofit status. This provision was aimed at preventing further collaboration between nonprofits and party organs.

Other provisions required that no candidate for federal office could receive any funds that did not meet FECA requirements. Accepting funding from foreign nationals was forbidden. State parties could create their own grassroots funds. "Express advocacy" was redefined as communication that advocates the election or defeat of a candidate by containing the phrase "vote for," "reelect," or words that in context can have no reasonable meaning other than to advocate the election or defeat of a clearly identified candidate. The law mandated that if a broadcast advertisement appears within 60 days of a federal election and refers to a "clearly identified candidate," it is considered an "electioneering communication" and prohibited because these ads are tantamount to campaign contributions. The law said that union members could not be required to pay full union dues if some of those funds were used for political purposes.

In order to obtain federal funding, the act compelled candidates to say they approved their own ads. However, it cleverly avoided violating the *Miami Herald* precedent against compelled speech[33] by saying that if they did not identify themselves in their advertisements, they would not be allowed to advertise at the lowest unit rate; if candidates admitted that they did "approve" their ads, broadcasters were required to offer them the lowest unit rate on advertising.[34] Furthermore, to protect incumbents, the lowest unit rate was also restricted to positive ads; to receive the rate, the law stated, candidates "shall not make any direct reference to another candidate for the same office." In other words, in such ads, one candidate could not criticize the record of his or her opponent.

One of the most bizarre outcomes of a provision was the so-called "millionaires' amendment," aimed closing a loophole for wealthy candidates. Realizing that the Watergate reform had a huge loophole, which allowed the rich to fund their own campaigns at no limit, McCain-Feingold included a provision that allowed candidates who were opposed by self-funded candidates to receive more funds from their party. If your opponent used more than $350,000 of his or her own money in a campaign for a House seat, you could receive more funds from your party. (The threshold for Senate seats was set on a formula.) However, when a House candidate challenged this provision of the law in 2007, the Supreme Court struck it down.[35]

While meaning to do good, the McCain-Feingold reform was damaging for many of the reasons rehearsed above. Nonetheless, the Supreme Court upheld a good deal of the provisions when it took up the law as a whole in *McConnell v. FEC*.[36] Senator Mitch McConnell (R-Kentucky) was head of the National Republican Senatorial Campaign Committee and sought to weaken the McCain-Feingold law by pointing out its unconstitutional provisions. But for the most part, the Court ruled in favor the law. Congress could bar the collection of soft money by candidates for federal office and even forbid preelection campaign broadcast advertising funded by unions or corporations. The Congress could restrict election cycle ads by special interest groups regarding federal candidates. (In 2007 in *FEC v. Wisconsin Right to Life*, the Supreme Court modified this provision by ruling that "core political speech" is protected by the First Amendment and therefore issue ads are permissible near elections.[37] The division was five to four on the issue.)

Again, the *McConnell* ruling mainly crafted by Justices Stevens and Sandra Day O'Connor was five to four, which weakened its moral authority. The number of concurring comments took the ruling to 275 pages wherein the past arguments regarding *Buckley* again surfaced.[38] In the end, the Court upheld Congress' right to regulate federal elections; the dissenters argued that the First Amendment had been violated and the two parties entrenched. Justice Antonin Scalia pointed out that the same court that afforded protection under the First Amendment to virtual pornography, tobacco advertising, and sexually explicit cable broadcasting had decided to restrict political speech, arguably the most valuable to a fully functioning democratic republic. And hence, in the case of *Hillary: The Movie*, (i.e., *Citizens United v. FEC*) decided on January 21, 2010, Justice Scalia joined the majority and upheld the right of groups to fund speech aimed at federal candidates. Specifically, the 1907 prohibition of corporations spending funds in federal political campaigns was overturned as was the 1947 law barring corporations and unions from spending money independently to elect or defeat federal candidates. The Supreme Court also eliminated the McCain-Feingold restrictions on how much corporations and unions can advertise in federal election campaigns. Thus, coroporations and unions are now freer to make contributions and to campaign for candidates than are individual citizens.

Conclusion

One of the most interesting aspects of these court rulings is that the *imputation of guilt* is used as a warrant for restrictions on free speech. One would like to believe that bribery and influence peddling laws could handle the problem of corruption without having to restrict political communication and where, in such cases, guilt would have to be proved rather than imputed. Further corruption of the system by laundering foreign funds is easily prohibited with laws that do not infringe on the free speech rights of candidates and their legal contributors. "Soft money" abuses can be handled in the same way.

However, a majority of the members of the Supreme Court claimed that the mere appearance of corruption created enough of a compelling government interest to justify limiting speech in federal and state political campaigns by limiting how much money a candidate could raise from single legal donors and legal PACs. Thus, we have a situation in which we have much less freedom of speech than we had in 1970 in American political campaigns. Third parties, challengers, and candidates who cannot afford to fund their own campaigns are disadvantaged. Republican employees of bosses who are Democrats, and vice versa, cannot hide the fact they are contributing to their own party. Employees' rights to private assembly are violated. And a donor's ability to endorse a candidate through the symbolic speech of a campaign contribution is severely restricted.

This last point is critical because restrictions on contributions are limits on endorsements, which are political, symbolic speech normally protected by the First Amendment. The Supreme Court in *Tinker v. Des Moines* and *Texas v. Johnson* ruled that schoolchildren wearing armbands and protestors burning the U.S. flag were engaged in political, symbolic speech that should be afforded First Amendment protection.[39] Keeping order at school and protecting the sanctity of the U.S. flag were not seen as sufficient government interest to overrule First Amendment rights in these cases. However, in the case of the mere "appearance" of impropriety in campaign mechanisms, the Court has restricted the political symbolic speech of citizens who contribute to campaigns. When the Supreme Court revisited *Buckley*, it failed to make it consistent; contributions are not seen as speech, but campaign expenditures are. Furthermore, the Supreme Court failed to work out the inherent contradiction between *Red Lion*, which allows limits to be placed on the speech of broadcasters, and *Miami Herald*, which forbids limits being placed on the speech of the print media. Thus, the communication of political speakers and their supporters remains crimped, chilled, and violated to this day, even though corporations and unions have now been given freedom to advertise in federal campaigns.

Notes

1. *Citizens United v. FEC* (2009). Oral arguments are available at: http://www.oyez.org/cases/2000–2009/2008/2008_08_205

2. Some of the operatives were ex-CIA agents but so bungled the entry that security guard Frank Wills was able to discover their presence and notify the police.

3. Section 315 of the Communications Act. There are four exemptions to the rule: when a candidate appears on a newscast, a news interview program, a documentary, or on the spot news coverage.

4. Section 312 (a) (7) of Communications Act.

5. Known as the Mayflower rule upheld in *NBC v. United States*, 319 U.S. 190 (1943).

6. See *Miami Herald v. Tornillo*, 418 U.S. 241 (1974). One cannot force a newspaper to print opposing views to its own.

7. *Red Lion Broadcasting v. FCC*, 395 U.S. 367 (1969).

8. 395 U.S. 367 (1969).

9. Later Fred Friendly, Edward R. Murrow's producer, discovered that while on the payroll of the Democratic National Committee, Cook had written a book called *Barry Goldwater: Extremist on the Right*, an article in *Nation* magazine attacking the right, and was coordinating an effort to suppress right wing attacks on the Johnson administration (1976, 32–42). The overall strategy of the DNC under the direction of Martin Firestone, a former FCC Commissioner, was to intimidate stations into dropping rightist editorials. L. Powe in *American Broadcasting and the First Amendment* (Berkeley: University of California Press, 1987) has chronicled a long list of cases dating back to Franklin Roosevelt's press secretary in which the public interest standard in general and the Fairness Doctrine in particular were used to threaten broadcasters. See also, L. M. Benjamin, "Herbert Hoover, Issues of Free Speech, and Radio Regulation in the 1920s," (28–29) and R. W. McChesney, "Constant Retreat: The American Civil Liberties Union and the Debate Over the Meaning of Free

Speech for Radio Broadcasting in the 30s," (40–59) *Free Speech Yearbook*, ed. Stephen Smith, vol. 26 (Carbondale: Southern Illinois University Press, 1988).

10. A contribution of $10 or more must be reported by the campaign as received; the name and address of the donor must be provided if he or she gives $100 or more.

11. These were first banned in 1907.

12. *NAACP v. Alabama*, 357 U.S. 449 (1958) established that the right to assembly includes the right to assemble privately without disclosure.

13. *McIntyre v. Ohio Elections Commission*, 514 U.S. 334 (1995).

14. *Buckley v. Valeo*, 424 U.S. 1, 241 (1976).

15. *FEC v. Massachusetts Citizens for Life*, 479 U.S. 238 (1986).

16. *FEC v. Furgatch*, 484 U.S. 850, 864 (1987).

17. *Colorado Republican Committee v. FEC*, 116 S. Ct. 2309 (1996).

18. R. Briffault, "Campaign Finance, the Parties and the Court: A Comment on *Colorado Republican Campaign Committee v. FEC*," *Constitutional Commentary* 14 (1997): 102–103.

19. This statistic is from Common Cause, which claimed that the Republicans had raised $55.7 million in soft money and the Democrats had raised $34.3 million. "Money: More than Ever," Los Angeles *Times*, May 16, 1998, A6.

20. Justice Souter wrote the majority opinion. 533 U.S. 431 (2001).

21. *Nixon v. Shrink Missouri Government PAC*, 528 U.S. 377 (2000).

22. "Donors: Survey Sheds Light on Firms that Play Politics," Los Angeles *Times*, September 21, 1997, A24.

23. See *Colorado Republican Committee v. FEC*, 518 U. S. 604 (1996); 533 U. S. 431 (2001).

24. "Donors . . . ," Los Angeles *Times*, September 21, 1997, A22.

25. PAC contributions constitute about the same amount; but are slower in growth.

26. "Soft Money Dollars," *Time*, September 9, 1999, 42–44.

27. "Soft Money Dollars," *Time*, September 9, 1999, 42–44.

28. In 2000, a federal jury convicted Maria Hsia of funneling $109,000 in illegal donations to Democrats including the 1996 Clinton-Gore campaign. Prosecutors claimed that Hsia used a Buddhist temple event as a cover to reimburse straw donors who were listed as contributors. Gore had called Hsia a political ally and later admitted that he knew the temple event was a fundraiser. Officials in the Justice Department sought to investigate Gore, but Attorney General Reno stopped the investigation.

29. See Sec. 441e, FECA.

30. Ruth Marcus, "DNC Official Concedes 'Mistakes of Process,'" Washington *Post*, November 13, 1996, A4.

31. Joseph E. Cantor, *Campaign Financing: Updated* (Washington, DC: Congressional Research Service: Library of Congress, December 17, 1997), 1.

32. By 2008, the limit on individual giving per person per election had risen to only $2,300.

33. *Miami Herald Co. v. Tornillo*, 418 U.S. 241 (1974).

34. *Miami Herald Co. v. Tornillo*, 418 U.S. 241 (1974). See also *Hurley v. Irish-American Gay, Lesbian and Bisexual Group*, 515 U.S. 577 (1995); *Wooley v. Maynard*, 430 U.S. 705 (1977).

35. *Davis v. FEC* (2007). Sections 319 a&b of the law were held to violate Davis' First Amendment rights and to treat candidates unequally by placing different fundraising limits on the self-funded candidate.

36. 540 U.S. 93 (2003).

37. 551 U.S. 449 (2007).

38. The prior D.C. Court of Appeals ruling in this case ran 1,600 pages and failed to arrive at a consensus on the issues involved!

39. *Texas v. Johnson*, 491 U.S. 397 (1989); *Tinker v. Des Moines School District*, 393 U.S. 503 (1969).

Chapter 10

9/11 and the Ensuing Restrictions on Civil Liberties

Craig R. Smith and R. Brandon Anderson

As Americans watched their early news programs on September 11, 2001, they witnessed the most frightening attack on their mainland since the British invaded Washington, D.C., in 1812 and burned the Capitol and the Executive Mansion. However, this was no invasion by a national army. It was an entirely different kind of attack; it was terrorism. Of the various threats that started a First Amendment crisis in America, none was so vivid as this one. Of the legislative initiatives generated in a crisis, none came so quickly as the USA PATRIOT Act and none was so unanimously supported or so little debated. Of the restrictions on freedom of expression, none lasted as long though many in the previous crises examined in this book were more severe.

Inception of a Crisis

Reports began with what seemed like a tragic accident: a plane had flown into one of the towers at the World Trade Center in lower Manhattan. As cameras focused on the burning tower, they caught a second plane as it flew into the other tower. Suddenly, it was clear that this was no accident; it was a coordinated attack on the United States. Word soon arrived of an attack on the Pentagon across the Potomac from the Capitol; a plane had crashed into its side. A fourth plane headed for the White House, United Flight 93, had crashed into a field in Pennsylvania when passengers overwhelmed the hijackers. Each of the towers of the World Trade Center collapsed, taking lives and spewing dust and debris across lower Manhattan. More than 2,500 Americans died in these attacks.

Following the tragedy of September 11, 2001, President George W. Bush seemed ill at ease in his address from the White House's Oval Office. It was only when he visited the site of the tragedy and yelled back to those who could not hear him, "But I hear you," that he seemed to catch the spirit of the country. A few days later, he delivered the most effective speech of his presidency to a joint session of Congress on September 20.

One of the most remarkable characteristics of that speech was its Manichaean nature. This rhetorical style eliminated middle ground and defined an enemy to which the fight must be taken. For the first time during the crisis, the president concretized the enemy and linked that enemy with the forces of darkness. Democracy was allied with the forces of light. Other nations around the world were either for or against the U.S. There was no middle ground. If a nation harbored terrorists, it was at war with the United States and preemptive attacks on such sanctuaries were warranted.

It was not the first time a president had resorted to Manichaean rhetoric. Ronald Reagan defined the Soviet Union as an evil empire; Franklin Roosevelt demonized the Japanese and the Germans during World War II; and though reluctant to go to war, from 1917 through 1918, Woodrow Wilson painted ugly pictures of those who opposed the allied effort. Bush would also return to the Manichaean style as when he characterized North Korea, Iran, and Iraq as an "axis of evil."[1]

However, in his address before the House and Senate on September 20, 2001, Bush argued that the Al Qaeda network was run from Afghanistan, headed by Osama Bin Laden, a known international outlaw of Saudi descent, and protected by the reigning Taliban government. In his indictment of these terrorists, President Bush announced that the United States was in a new kind of war in which terrorists were using American freedoms against Americans. Thus, the president took the initiative in forming a perception of the crisis, converting it into a "war" and then extending it into an internal threat. Only the Congress can declare war, but the president's rhetorical take went unchallenged and it allowed him to act as if the nation were at war. And that meant that he could restrict First Amendment rights as if we were at war. Six days after the 9/11 attack, Bush returned to the White House from Camp David after meeting with his national security advisors. On this particular Sunday, he told awaiting reporters that, "This crusade, this war on terrorism . . . would rid the world of evil doers."[2] The phrase "war on terror" would not be dropped from the administration's rhetoric until the accession of Barack Obama to the presidency in 2009. What Congress did authorize in the fall of 2001 was about as close to a declaration as they could come without making one. They passed an *Authorization for the Use of Military Force*, which had open-ended targets and no concluding date.

Bush's September 20, 2001, speech before a joint session of Congress is a masterful example of reducing a complex, baffling problem to a simple dialectic between good and evil:[3]

> Tonight, we are a country awakening to danger. . . . [E]nemies of freedom committed an act of war against our country. . . . There are thousands of these terrorists in more than 60 countries. . . . Our enemy is a radical network of terrorists and every government that supports them. . . . These terrorists kill not merely to end lives but to disrupt and end a way of life. . . . They're the heirs of all the murderous ideologies of the 20th century. . . . Today, dozens of federal departments and agencies, as well as state and local governments, have responsibilities affecting homeland security. . . . Many will be involved in this effort, from FBI agents to intelligence operatives to the reservists we have called to active duty.

Soon after his speech, the president sought and received authorization for military action in Afghanistan against Al Qaeda, the Taliban government, and Osama Bin Laden. Action against this external threat to the United States began in October 2001.

At the same time, the president called for new legislation that would deal with the internal threat of secret terrorist cells. Only a handful of members of the Congress and some civil libertarians were ready to make sure that such laws did not curtail civil liberties. They noted that within weeks of the attack on Pearl Harbor, a congressional committee investigated the event not only in terms of the Japanese attack but in terms of the security breach on the part of the U.S. military. Similarly, within days of the assassination of President John Kennedy, the Warren Commission convened to investigate the possibility of a conspiracy. However, no such public investigation was called together regarding the attacks of September 11 until evidence was discovered that the administration might have overlooked signals that an attack was coming.[4] When formal congressional investigations were finally held in the fall of 2002, the Congress considered whether the whole issue should be turned over to an independent commission.

Legislative Response

The USA PATRIOT Act was drafted by the White House with the help of Attorney General John Ashcroft. In the Congress, it was considered by the members of House Judiciary Committee, who favored it 36 to 0. In the

Senate, it was also favorably reported to the floor as a 187-page document; the Senate voted for it 96 to one.[5] That lone dissent came from Senator Russell Feingold (D-Wisconsin) who had presented amendments to protect the rights of "innocent" people. Each had gone down to massive defeat. During the debate over these amendments, Senator Orrin Hatch (R-Utah) argued that the government cannot guarantee total protection of the public "when you have people willing to commit suicide to do us harm. . . . [Those who argue for weakening this law should consider] the loss of civil liberties of those who died" on September 11.[6] A conference committee quickly worked out the minor difference between the House and Senate bills. The compromise bill was briefly stalled over a sunset provision inserted by the House; its negotiators agreed to a four-year life span for the key provisions of the bill. The House then decided not to take up its own version of the bill but to accept the Senate-passed measure for debate. It carried 337 to 79.

With less debate over legislation than in any other crisis examined in this book, the Congress had passed the legislation requested by the Bush Administration to deal with the national security debacle. It allowed a single federal district court to authorize the tapping of phone numbers anywhere in the United States.[7] These "roving taps" allowed interception of electronic evidence such as e-mail and a history of numbers called from or to tapped phones. Moreover, the legislation gave wider latitude to the special court that authorizes wiretaps on suspected agents of foreign powers.[8] Under the new law, information concerning foreign agents in the United States would be shared among government agencies, particularly between the Federal Bureau of Investigation (FBI) and the Central Intelligence Agency (CIA).[9] The legislation allowed the Immigration and Naturalization Service (INS) to detain aliens up to seven days.[10] Moreover, it permitted the Attorney General to detain "terrorist aliens" and expanded the definition of terrorist activity. The district court of the District of Columbia was given exclusive jurisdiction over such cases. The legislation ended the statute of limitations on the newly defined terrorist activities and increased the maximum sentence to life imprisonment.[11] Finally, the new law banned possession of biological agents that pose a threat to national security unless that possession would serve peaceful purposes.

After the president signed the legislation, INS Commissioner James Ziglar and Attorney General Ashcroft outlined the new rules. The federal government's ability to deny visas to and deport immigrants who "endorse" terrorism was stressed. The Attorney General designated 46 "terrorist organizations" around the world. A link to any of these organizations could be used as a justification to deny a visa or to deport an immigrant or visitor. Records of any American traveling or calling abroad were open to review by the FBI and CIA. The Attorney General also established a task force to track foreign terrorists.

In order to assess the strength of the administration's actions, it is important to realize that First Amendment restrictions were couched among restrictions on other civil rights. Fourth Amendment concerns over the right to privacy were raised because the new rules gave the FBI broad latitude to conduct surveillance and information gathering. Although these methods are not prohibited by the Constitution, any evidence obtained in violation of the Constitution may not be used in court. For example, the Fifth Amendment provides a right to avoid self-incrimination. However, there is no prohibition *per se* of the FBI obtaining a confession, for example, to apprehend other terrorists; the confession would be inadmissible in court against the one who confessed but the evidence found based on the confession could be used against other conspirators. It could also be used in a noncriminal case such as a deportation hearing. Furthermore, it should be noted that if a witness were granted "use immunity," nothing confessed could be used against that witness; however, the witness could be compelled to answer questions pertaining to a crime and those linked to it. The due process clause of the Constitution only precludes coercion that shocks the conscience of the court. Thus, if the injection of truth serum could lead to the prevention of a terrorist act, it likely would be upheld by the courts, just as extracting blood from a drunk driver has been upheld.

Perhaps the most controversial interpretation of the new legislation came on November 9, 2001, when Ashcroft announced that federal prison officials would be allowed to eavesdrop on conversations between inmates and their lawyers. According to Ashcroft, as long as officials had a "reasonable suspicion" that useful information was being passed on to an attorney, they could listen in. Senator Patrick Leahy (D-Vermont) sent a letter to the Attorney General arguing that the rule violated the Sixth Amendment right to "assistance of counsel" for one's defense.

We now know that some of these controversial interpretations of the legislation and the constitutional powers of the president came from Ashcroft's Office of Legal Counsel, mostly from John Yoo, a U.C. Berkeley law professor who was serving as Deputy Assistant Attorney General at the time. Most relevant to this chapter is a memo dated October 23, 2001; it claimed that First Amendment "speech and press rights may also be subordinated to the overriding need to wage war successfully. . . . The current campaign against terrorism may require even broader exercises of federal power domestically." Using a D.C. Court of Appeals ruling, *Harbury v. Deutch* (2000), Yoo argued that the Bill of Rights does not extend beyond the borders of the United States. Other memos endorsed the violation of the right to privacy in the United States by stating that search and seizures were allowed during the current crisis.[12] A memo of March 2002 claims that holding prisoners in wartime "is an area in which the president appears to enjoy exclusive authority, as the power . . . is not reserved by the Constitution in whole or in part to any other branch of government."[13]

Relying on some of these opinions, the president further reduced civil liberties on November 13, 2001, in *Executive Order 13234*, which allowed military tribunals to try alleged terrorists. The president warned that these terrorists were capable of "mass deaths" and threatened the orderly operation of the government. Therefore, "it is not practicable to apply . . . the principles of law and the rules of evidence generally recognized in the trial of criminal cases in the United States district courts."[14] The order from Bush said that those that he designates as terrorists will be "placed under the control of the secretary of Defense," who shall have "exclusive jurisdiction" in these matters. These agents of terror may not appeal to "any court of the United States," nor "any court of any foreign nation or any international tribunal." Aside from the infringement on foreign sovereignty implied by this order, it was the starkest restriction of habeas corpus rights during wartime since the Civil War.

The Bush Administration claimed it had a precedent for taking such action with the *Quirin* case of World War II, the last instance of the government's use of a military tribunal in the United States. Nazi saboteurs, who had landed from submarines and then changed into civilian clothes in Amagansett, New York and Ponte Vedra Beach, Florida, were apprehended in the Mayflower Hotel in Washington, D.C., in June 1942 after two of their members defected to the U.S.[15] Ten prosecutors tried the saboteurs in the Justice Department building before a military tribunal. Six of the saboteurs were executed on August 8, 1942, and the defectors were sent to prison.[16] The Supreme Court later upheld the procedure. Thus, when terrorists were apprehended during the 9/11 crisis, government prosecutors often argued that circumstances were analogous to those of the Nazi saboteurs and their military trial on American soil.

The Internal Threat

In other crises, particularly the Red Scare of 1918–1919, we saw that citizens and others persons within U.S. borders were apprehended by the FBI in wide-ranging dragnets. By November 10, 2001, nearly 1,200 persons had been arrested inside the United States on suspicion of helping the conspirators, committing related crimes, or being material witnesses to terrorist activities.[17] A year after the attack, many Arab Americans were still held in jail without charges filed against them. Soon after the apprehension of suspected terrorists and those who worked to support them, stories of abuse of detainees began to emerge. A Pakistani student was beaten by cellmates in Mississippi.[18] The

Israeli consulate complained that six of its citizens had been handcuffed and forced to take polygraph tests.[19] U.S. immigration officials prevented detainees in Wisconsin, Illinois, and Indiana from visiting with lawyers.[20] The INS reported that 26 jails across the country had misapplied INS procedures; the Service began speeding up processing on October 26.

The rampant paranoia often spilled over to college campuses where Muslim students and others of Middle Eastern dissent were persecuted. Campus police were required to work with the FBI and the INS and report any suspicions they might have. In fact, campuses were required to provide confidential information to the INS about students from Muslim countries. By the spring semester of 2003, many of these students had been fingerprinted. All exchange and/or foreign students were also required to register with the new Student Exchange and Visitor Information Service (SEVIS). Renewal of visas became difficult and deportations were common.

The State Department also intensified the crisis by announcing in September 2002 that more than 70,000 names of terrorist operatives had been compiled by various international agencies. The State Department claimed that Al Qaeda agents remained a threat inside the United States;[21] however, other terrorist groups were also targeted. For example, Professor Sami Al-Arian of South Florida University was arrested on February 20, 2003, on conspiracy charges that associated him with the Palestinian Islamic Jihad (PIJ) organization, which has terrorist cells around the world.[22] Professor Al-Arian was directly linked to seven terrorists of the PIJ when, under the auspices of the PATRIOT Act, agencies that had been monitoring his activities were allowed to share information. In 2006, he agreed to plead guilty to a conspiracy charge and was sentenced to 57 months in jail, but was given credit for the time he had already been held, so the sentence was 19 months in prison and then possible deportation. In June 2008, he was found in contempt of court when he refused to answer questions regarding Palestinian activities. While the lawyers on both sides continue to battle, the professor has been placed under house arrest.

On the other side of the coin, Political Science Professor Kenneth Hearlson at Orange Coast Community College was only one of many teachers to fall victim to false claims. In his case, students accused him comparing Islamic students to Nazis. Hearlson was summarily suspended but eventually vindicated when a recording of his actual lecture was discovered.

In the meantime, Attorney General Ashcroft proceeded to employ the Foreign Intelligence Surveillance Act (FISA). The Act had originally been passed in 1978 to prevent the government from conducting surveillance of political enemies and establish a wall between surveillance of foreign and domestic criminals. The Act establishes a seven-judge secret panel to rule on requests regarding national security matters. Any evidence gathered can be used in court but it cannot be passed on to local or state authorities. That rule pertains because the secret court, which operates much like a grand jury, can approve search warrants on a lower threshold of suspicion than the "probable cause" standard imposed on the states and other federal agencies. Thus, if during a surveillance, the FBI discovered that someone was in possession of obscene material by the standards imposed by their state, that evidence could not be used in any state prosecution against the individual. The fruits of the surveillance could only be used to prove a national security threat. However, under the PATRIOT Act, investigators may be granted a warrant even if there is no evidence of wrongdoing.

Reaction

By invoking this provision, Ashcroft overstepped his bounds according to the secret court, which was the first one to raise a red flag regarding restrictions on civil liberties. It rebuked Ashcroft in May 2002 for letting his criminal investigations pursue too many secret searches. Ashcroft appealed this ruling in September 2002 to a three-judge panel that reviews the use of FISA. The panel, appointed by Chief Justice William Rehnquist, was composed of three Reagan-appointed judges from different Federal Circuit Courts of Appeals. The panel had never been convened before. On November 18, 2002, the three judges, Ralph B. Guy of the 6th Circuit, Edward Leavy of the 9th Circuit, and Laurence Silberman of the D.C. Circuit, upheld Ashcroft's appeal and overruled the Foreign Intelligence Surveillance Court. Ashcroft immediately claimed that the decision would revolutionize his ability to investigate and prosecute terrorists. Despite the fears of some civil libertarians, the three-judge panel lowered the wall between intelligence agencies and the FBI, thereby strengthening the authority of the PATRIOT Act.

At the end of the summer of 2002, the U.S. Court of Appeals for the 6th Circuit was the first to warn about improper restrictions on First Amendment rights. The government used a number of procedures to silence defendants and their attorneys. They relied on the *Classified Information Procedures Act* to keep important evidence from defense teams. They invoked sweeping "protective orders" to prevent revealing various materials, which sometimes included such public items as newspaper clippings and such innocuous records as college transcripts. In the name of national security, the government often demanded that hearings be closed.

The Court of Appeals ruled *unanimously that closed hearings violated the First Amendment rights of the press and of detainees on U.S. soil.* In order to hold a closed trial, the INS must demonstrate, and judges must certify, that information in the case would harm national security if an open trial was held. This decision was reinforced on September 17, 2002, by U.S. District Judge Nancy Edmunds, who wrote, "An open detention and removal hearing will assure the public that the government itself is honoring the very democratic principles that the terrorists who committed the atrocities of 9/11 sought to destroy."[23]

The Bush Administration faced other problems. The *Milligan* case, examined in chapter 2 of this book, should protect American citizens and "others on U.S. soil" who are not in war zones from military tribunals. It makes clear that a president must demonstrate that military tribunals are essential because the current system does not allow for the timely prosecution of terrorists. However, the administration claimed that open hearings would compromise national security. They suppressed the speech of their prisoners by refusing to bring them to trial. As we shall see, the courts had great difficulty sorting out these legalities.

Secondly, the U.S. Constitution applies to "persons" not just citizens who inhabit the country. Almost anyone in the country, as illegal aliens have learned, can file a writ of habeas corpus unless they inhabit an area that has been declared under martial law or unless they are "military combatants." Others, relying on Taney's ruling in the *Merryman* case (see chapter 2), claim that Congress must legislate the procedure before the president can implement a suspension. In light of these and other arguments, President Bush eventually restricted his tribunal policy to areas of actual conflict overseas and to foreign areas where prisoners were held, such as the U.S. Navy Base in Guantanamo Bay, Cuba.

The Attorney General faced more criticism on August 22, 2002, when it was revealed that federal judges had grave misgivings about the way the Justice Department had handled some of its cases: "The FBI gave false information in more than 75 requests for top-secret warrants brought before the secret surveillance panel."[24] It was the first time in the 23-year history of the court that it released information about its proceedings.

To this point, we have seen that Congress was complicit in fighting terrorism and supporting internal security measures. Even when in July 2003, the House voted 309 to 118 to repeal parts of the PATRIOT Act that allowed for unannounced "sneak and peak" searches, the bill was not taken up in the Senate. Only when the American Civil Liberties Union (ACLU) launched a series of advertisements in favor of the House Amendment did the Justice Department abandon its plan to introduce PATRIOT Act II.

The Supreme Court Intervenes

The question of post–9/11 arrests of Middle Eastern men and women was ultimately resolved on January 12, 2004, when the Supreme Court refused to take up a challenge to the practice of keeping the names of the arrested secret. The justices did not comment on the denial of *certiorari*. Of the 750 people who were arrested in this category, most had been deported or released by June 2002. The order in *Center for National Security Studies v. Justice Department*[25] narrowed the rights of immigrants, allowing them to be deported for minor violations. According to the ruling, immigrant hearings may be closed to the public. Neither the public nor the media have a right to know who is being detained for questioning in a national security matter.

The Supreme Court combined two other cases to examine the issue of retention of "unlawful enemy combatants." Yaser Essam Hamdi of Louisiana was picked up on a battlefield in Afghanistan in the fall of 2001 and incarcerated at Guantanamo Bay, Cuba. His case was appealed to the Supreme Court for hearing in spring of 2004.[26] José Padilla of the Bronx was arrested at O'Hare Airport on May 8, 2002, where he arrived on a flight from Pakistan. He was suspected of aiding Al Qaeda terrorists to create radioactive bombs. Padilla was incarcerated as an "enemy combatant" subject to a military tribunal. Padilla appealed the arrest and sought his habeas corpus rights. The Second Circuit Court of Appeals ruled 2–1 in Padilla's favor and ordered his release to civilian authorities.

The Pentagon appealed the ruling to the Supreme Court, which agreed to hear the case in April 2004. In 2006, without ruling on the specific individuals, the Supreme Court required the Bush Administration to bring its military commissions into better conformance with common law and habeas corpus rights and to seek congressional guidance on the matter. The Congress then addressed the issue and passed guidelines in this regard. The Supreme Court in June 2008 finally opened the door to detainees in Guantanamo, Cuba to have their day in court. It ruled that the 265 remaining foreign fighters being detained had a right to a trial in which they would be allowed to assert their innocence. By this time, the government had dropped charges against 20 percent of these detainees and was looking for a country to send them. On June 12, 2008, the Supreme Court ruled in *Boumediene v. Bush* (553 U.S. 723 [2008]) that prisoners at Guantanamo Bay have the right to appeal to federal courts to certify the validity of their detention. The majority found that the constitutionally guaranteed right of habeas corpus review applies to persons held in Guantanamo Bay and to persons designated as enemy combatants on that territory. Moreover, the Court contended that if Congress intends to suspend the right, an adequate substitute must offer the prisoner a meaningful opportunity to demonstrate that he or she is held pursuant to an erroneous application or interpretation of relevant law.

In his majority opinion, Justice Anthony Kennedy argued that early English cases in common law applied English laws to Spanish sailors and African slaves on English soil or territory. Thus, habeas corpus is not limited to citizens, but extends to all who inhabit the nation. Whereas Justice Antonin Scalia, in his dissent, took exactly the opposite position, giving examples of where English rights were applied only to English citizens. Scalia complained that the Court's majority "admits that [the courts] cannot determine whether the writ historically extended to aliens held abroad, and it concedes that Guantanamo Bay lies outside the sovereign territory of the United States." Furthermore, Justice Scalia referred to *Johnson v. Eisentrager* (339 U. S. 763 [1950]), which held that U.S. courts had no jurisdiction over German war criminals held in a U.S.-administered German prison; "the Constitution does not ensure habeas corpus for aliens held by the United States in areas over which our Government is not sovereign." Therefore, those held at Guantanamo Bay should not receive equal protection under the guise of habeas corpus. Despite Scalia's dissent and based on the majority's ruling, a judge ruled in November 2008 that five Bosnians held in Guantanamo Bay were not "enemy combatants" and three were flown home to Bosnia in December of that year.

The Bush Administration suffered another reversal when presiding Judge Thomas F. Hogan, who oversees the lawsuits brought by the administration, ruled in July 2008 that detainees deserved their day in court. These would be the first U.S. war crime trials since World War II. Ironically, once the Bush Administration began the first trial, which took up the case of Salim Ahmed Hamdan, his lawyers asked for a delay in the proceedings. Of Yemeni descent, Hamdan was a former driver for Osama Bin Laden. The U.S. District Judge James Robertson ruled against his lawyers and the trial before Navy Captain Keith J. Allred and a panel of at least seven more senior officers began in the summer of 2008. Hamdan was charged with conspiracy and material support for terrorism. He had been held in Guantanamo Bay for six years. During the trial, both major presidential candidates vowed to close the Guantanamo Bay facility should they be elected. In August 2008, Hamdan was convicted of supporting terrorism, but was acquitted of the more serious counts of conspiring to commit terrorism.

Citizen Involvement

In the historic crises examined in this book, we have seen that citizens often took action on their own when they felt threatened. French Jacobins were regularly beaten and run out of town during the Alien and Sedition crisis. During the McCarthy era, the citizens of Boston, among other communities, tried to rid their libraries of controversial books. But most common to a crisis is the citizen as informer. After the attack of 9/11, the administration attempted to enhance a citizen's ability to inform on others with its

Terrorism Information and Prevention Systems, known as TIPS. TIPS was part of the proposed Homeland Security Bill and would have recruited a million volunteers in 10 test cities to check on deliveries, e-mail, Internet use, telephone conversations, texting, and the like. The volunteers would report what they found to a central database in the Justice Department. The Attorney General would then make the information available to appropriate state and local agencies.

Many civil libertarians argued that these practices would severely curtail freedom of expression while enhancing an aura of paranoia. When House Majority Leader Dick Armey (R-Texas) opposed the provision, it was dropped from consideration. However, it was revived after the 2002 midterm elections as the Total Information Awareness program to be conducted in the Pentagon under the guidance of Admiral John Poindexter, who had been implicated in the Iran-Contra scandal. The system had access to all computerized information including what people buy, watch, and who they talk to. The program monitored e-mails, phone calls, and other forms of communication through the National Security Agency. Moreover, the program may have circumvented FISA, which, as we have seen, created a secret court to approve government requests for surveillance in cases of terrorism or espionage.

Escalating the Crisis: War in Iraq

The program was developed not only against the backdrop of the war on terrorism in Afghanistan, but the war in Iraq. In late 2002, large majorities in both houses of Congress passed resolutions giving the president power to invade Iraq. By January 2003, according to CBS polling, 63 percent of Americans supported an invasion of Iraq.[27] The United States led a coalition of allies, including Great Britain, Spain, Denmark, Poland, and Australia, into Iraq on March 20, 2003. The war had been justified—most notably in a speech to the U.N. Security Council by Secretary of State Colin Powell on February 5, 2003—on the grounds that Iraq had failed to abide by the U.N. Resolution 1441 calling for thorough inspections of Iraq to seek out weapons of mass destruction, instigated a war of genocide against the Kurds, and used biological weapons in its war with Iran. The administration had relied on CIA reports and several other authoritative sources to assert that there were weapons of mass destruction in Iraq. President Hosni Mubarak of Egypt and King Hussein of Jordan assured President Bush that Sadam Hussein had such weapons, not to mention the fact that Sadam Hussein himself made such a claim.[28]

In the war, the United States provided the vast majority of the allied troops, numbering almost 250,000, which basically defeated the Iraqi army by May of that year. The easy victory that followed the attack of "shock and awe" was undermined by a civil war among the various Iraqi sects, which often turned on U.S. soldiers. In the meantime, on May 1, 2003, Bush flew to an aircraft carrier and declared "mission accomplished." It would prove the high point of his presidency and his influence. With few exceptions, up to that point the news media remained silent or continued to support the president, his war, and his restrictions on freedom of expression.

The Media

During World War II and the Korean conflict, reporters were allowed to accompany army combat units but had to submit their copy for military censorship. During the Vietnam War, much less censorship was employed. However, with the invasion of Grenada during the Reagan Administration and the War in the Gulf during the Bush Administration, new restrictions were imposed that prevented reporters from traveling with American forces. Instead the media was forced to use pool reporters, thus, information was shared from a single source. The same policy was followed in the war in Afghanistan. American reporters were forced to rely on the Secretary of Defense or his spokespersons plus any foreign sources the reporters could contact. The administration justified this policy on a number of grounds. First, the use of Internet and satellite communications by reporters might jeopardize U.S. ground troops. Second, the precedent established in the Gulf War worked well and would be followed.

It should also be noted that some members of the Bush Administration may have created an environment that had a chilling effect on criticism of the "war" on terrorism. Press Secretary Ari Fleisher was openly critical of commentator Bill Maher's remark that the army's use of missiles in wartime was cowardly. Fleisher later had his comments deleted from the official transcript. When she was National Security Advisor, Condoleeza Rice held a conference call with network news presidents and asked them not to rebroadcast Al Jazeera broadcasts of tapes made by terrorists. Although crop dusters were allowed to return to the air, news aircraft were not, which is why when an American Airlines plane crashed in Queens, the news media was only able to show ground shots of the event. The Justice Department abruptly announced in mid-November 2001 that it would no longer regularly update the number of people being held in association with the September 11 attacks. The Defense Department contracted with satellite operators to prevent them from making pictures available to the media. Worst of all may have been the administration's threat to invoke the Espionage Act against reporters who revealed arguably classified information.

In short, once it had the legislation it requested in hand, the Bush Administration, and particularly the Department of Justice, began to issue orders, regulations, and the like that restricted press freedoms to a greater extent than anticipated. After the initial shock, however, the press began to protect its rights. The media was particularly effective, as we have seen, in bringing suits that forced the Justice Department to release the names of detainees and forced judges to hold open hearings unless it could be proved that such hearings were a danger to national security. Members of the judiciary, particularly the 6th Circuit Court of Appeals and the review panel for FISA, were conscientious in holding the Justice Department to constitutional standards.

As the military activity continued in Iraq and casualties rose, the media and the public began to question the efficacy of U.S. efforts while speculating about when it all might end. On May 29, 2003, the Bush administration claimed vindication when the president declared that, "we have found the weapons of mass destruction," while speaking about two mobile "biological laboratories" captured by the allied troops.[29] More favorable news came when Saddam Hussein was found hiding in a shallow hole in northern Iraq. However, the capture of Hussein did not stop the fighting in Iraq from escalating.

Exactly one year after his declaration of victory, President Bush proclaimed, "life for the Iraqi people is a world away from the cruelty and corruption of Saddam's regime. . . . Because the former dictator is in prison, himself. And their daily life is improving."[30] However, the president's statement disregarded the instability that had become apparent in the newly freed country. In late 2004, foreign fighters from around the Middle East, as well as Al Qaeda in Iraq, led by Abu Musab al-Zarqawi, mounted an insurgent movement. The insurgents focused on the newly trained Iraqi Security Forces, as hundreds of Iraqi civilians and police were killed in a series of bombings. Amid the intense fighting, on June 28, 2004, the Coalition Provisional Authority transferred the "sovereignty" of Iraq to a caretaker government whose first act was to begin the trial of Saddam Hussein. Moreover, the new government began the process of moving toward open elections, even though the insurgency had gained strength and the lack of cohesion within the government itself caused major problems.

Early media reports of failures within Iraq came when the CIA issued a report stating possibilities for the future of Iraq through the end of 2005, with the worst being the development of an Iraqi civil war. During the 2004 presidential campaign, the news media reported that the death toll had reached 1,000 American soldiers, which raised concern about the progress of our military actions. Furthermore, a CIA report released on October 7, 2004, concluded that "Saddam Hussein did not possess stockpiles of illicit weapons at the time of the U.S. invasion . . . and had not begun any programs to produce them."[31] Soon after, United Nations Secretary General Kofi Annan began to speak out against the Iraq war, declaring that the war was illegal and did not conform to the U.N. Charter. Even though information was beginning to mount concerning problems in Iraq, Bush retained the presidency in November 2004 and was determined to continue the fight for democracy in Iraq. For example, when the New York *Times* reported the existence of the "Terrorist Surveillance Program" in December 2005, the president claimed that he did not need the approval of the secret court for his surveillance orders since he was the Commander-in-Chief.

By that time, the hopes for a quick end to the insurgency and a withdrawal of U.S. troops had been dashed, when May 2005 became Iraq's bloodiest month since the invasion by U.S. forces. As the insurgents fought coalition forces, it was becoming evident that the U.S. could be in Iraq for an extended period of time. One anonymous U.S. official claimed that "the United States no longer expects to see a model new democracy, a self-supporting oil industry or a society in which the majority of people are free from serious security or economic challenges. . . . What we expected to achieve was never realistic given the timetable or what unfolded on the ground."[32] Nevertheless, those closest to the president contended that the coalition forces were making progress. In November, Vietnam Veteran and Congressman John Murtha (D-Pennsylvania) called for a troop withdrawal from Iraq, stating that "the war in Iraq is not going as advertised. It is a flawed policy wrapped in illusion. [T]he American troops have done all they can . . . our military is suffering and the future of our country is at risk."[33]

The beginning of 2006 saw the creation of a new ruling coalition in Iraq, growing sectarian violence, and continuous anti-coalition attacks. On May 1, 2006, President Bush insisted that Iraq had reached a "turning point" and things were destined to improve in the region.[34] The new Iraqi government took office on May 20, 2006, following approval by the members of the Iraqi National Assembly. As the new government attempted to gain control of their country, they requested that a timeline be established for U.S. troop withdrawal. However, as civilian casualties increased and civil war continued, U.S. officials were intent on standing their ground in Iraq. Bush stated that, "The strategy is to help the Iraqi people achieve the objectives and dreams which is a democratic society. That's the strategy. . . . We're not leaving so long as I'm the president. That would be a huge mistake."

Resolving the Crisis

One of the most potent rhetorical tactics used by the administration to keep its critics at bay was legal delay and diffusion. It should be noted that throughout legal phases of the terrorism crisis the administration's lawyers established legal barriers that often prevented timely trials. For example, when the ACLU sued over the use of improperly warranted or warrantless wiretapping, the courts agreed with the Bush Administration that the ACLU had no legal standing because its members did not prove that their phones were tapped. When the ACLU sought the list of those who were tapped to see if they were on it, the administration refused to release the list, successfully arguing that releasing the list would compromise national security. The same strategy has been used in wrongful apprehensions.

Perhaps the most egregious was the case of Khaled Masri, a German citizen on vacation in the Balkans who was pulled from a tour bus at a border crossing and flown to a CIA detention center in Afghanistan. It took the CIA six months to determine that this Khaled was not the Khalid Masri they were seeking. The innocent Masri was dumped on a road in Albania, found his way home to Germany, and sued. The administration claimed that hearing the case would compromise national security and the Supreme Court dismissed the suit in a one-line order. Prisoners who have been released—for example, four British Muslims in 2008 who sued Pentagon officials because the prisoners claimed they were tortured—have been told by the U.S. Court of Appeals in Washington, D.C., that they have no legal standing. The court claimed they were aliens without property or presence in the United States. (However, on December 15, 2008, the Supreme Court ordered the Court of Appeals to review its ruling in this case.)

A second rhetorical weapon was the claim that those who criticized the administration were aiding America's enemies. We have seen this tactic in previous chapters, and again note that although it is legal, it is of questionable morality. In 2006, more and more Americans, including commentators and members of Congress, began to speak out against the war, calling for an end to the fighting. However, those dissenting from the administration's viewpoint were often chastised and criticized. By characterizing critics of the war as "weak" and "unable to stomach a fight" or as "aiding the terrorists," the rhetoric of Vice President Dick Cheney[35] and Secretary of Defense Donald Rumsfeld[36] in particular sought to characterize criticism of the administration's policies as giving comfort to the enemy. As the fighting continued, the number of citizens who questioned the war, and were unsatisfied with the administration continued to increase. In the congressional election, the Democrats gained control of the Senate and the House.

Following the surprising resignation of the Secretary of Defense just after the congressional elections of 2006, the administration sought to establish a new strategy to regain the support of the nation. On December 6, 2006, a bipartisan report by the Iraq Study Group was released with suggestions of what needed to take place in Iraq. Former Secretary of State James Baker, a Republican, and former Democratic Congressman Lee Hamilton led the group. After months of investigation, the report concluded that "the situation in Iraq is grave and deteriorating" and "U.S. forces seem to be caught in a mission that has no foreseeable end."[37] The report's 79 recommendations included increasing diplomatic overtures to Iran and Syria, intensifying efforts to train Iraqi troops, and avoiding the establishment of permanent military bases within Iraq. As 2006 ended, U.S. officials disagreed about what course of action to take in Iraq while the new Iraqi government completed the trial of its former dictator. Saddam Hussein was hanged on December 30, 2006, after being found guilty of crimes against humanity. In the meantime, Bush chastised the Iraqi government, which he claimed had great strides to take if it was to become a viable democracy.[38]

On January 10, 2007, Bush delivered a televised address to the American public in which he proposed an increase in the number of troops in Iraq. In the speech, he amended the plans of the Iraqi operations to include a "surge" of 21,500 more troops for Iraq, a jobs program for Iraqis, more reconstruction, and $1.2 billion for these programs. Asked why he believed his plan would work this time, Bush said: "Because it has to."[39] The Congress funded his plan.

General David Petraeus officially took control of the U.S. forces in Iraq and the Pentagon increased the surge to 28,500 troops; it subsequently released a report that acknowledged Iraq was immersed in a civil war. The Pentagon reported that Iraq was experiencing the most violent three-month period since 2003, which was "the bleakest assessment of the war to date."[40] Before the troop surge could effectively take hold, the U.S. Senate passed legislation ordering that troops begin coming home from Iraq by October 1, 2007. The president vetoed the bill and his approval rating hit an all-time low.[41] The House and Senate continued to look for ways to wi†hdraw the troops from Iraq. Finally, after the deaths of more than 3,800 U.S. soldiers and countless Iraqi civilians and soldiers, November 21, 2007, saw the first major pullout of American troops from the Iraqi region. However, as the pullout began, the Iraqi government proposed that the U.S. could maintain a long-term presence of up to 50,000 troops on bases surrounding Iraqi cities. Therefore, the situation in Iraq may eventually resemble the American presence in South Korea. After five years of intense fighting, Army Chief of Staff General George Casey stated that the military was "out of balance" and criticized the war effort.[42]

In the spring 2007, the FISA court ruled that warrants were required in all cases of surveillance. In response, the administration sought corrective legislation in August called the Protect America Act. A compromise was finally reached on the legislation in May 2008. In its closing days, the administration saw the passage of a bill that protected telecommunications companies who had cooperated with the administration from being sued and it expanded government eavesdropping powers. However, the bill restricted the FISA court to approving general procedures for spying rather than approving specific warrants in each case. The House passed the bill 293 to 129; the Senate passed it 68 to 28, with Democratic Senator and presidential candidate Barack Obama voting in favor. On July 10, 2008, the president signed the act into law. The ACLU and others challenged the law in court. Reporters argued that the law chills their ability to report on international matters, particularly terrorism because confidentiality is compromised.

Conclusion

As we write, this crisis is not resolved. Though the Republican party suffered one of its worse defeats at the polls in November 2008, and a Democrat who opposed the war in Iraq was sworn in as president in January 2009, many parts of the Bush anti-terrorist program remain in effect. On the international front, President Obama has not accelerated the withdrawal of troops from Iraq but is using the same timetable that President Bush negotiated. It calls for 30,000 to 50,000 troops to remain behind in support roles. In fact, Obama escalated the war in Afghanistan on March 27, 2009, by committing an additional 17,000 troops to it and later calling on allies for more support. On December 1, 2009, he committed another 30,000 troops to the war, with a promise to withdraw troops in 18 months.

President Obama has claimed the same powers as his predecessor with regard to the treatment and definition of "enemy combatants."[43] He has not called for changes in the national security system. His major change in policy has been to suspend the torture of captives, though he did not end the rendition program, which allows the CIA to turn captives over to agents of other countries for torture. In both Iraq and Afghanistan, he continued the policy of supporting surrogates and mercenaries modeled after the infamous Blackwater Group.

While these actions and proposals are debated, responsible voices on each side of the civil liberties divide need to keep America's history in mind. Hopefully, it will temper the debate and assure that, in the name of national security, laws are passed that do as little damage to civil liberties as possible.

Notes

1. When the phrase drew criticism from the media and other sources, the speechwriter responsible was asked to resign.

2. In George W. Bush, *Remarks to Employees at the Pentagon and an Exchange With Reporters in Arlington, Virginia, September 17, 2001*. [Weekly Compilation of Presidential Documents].

3. John Murphy picks up on this approach when he analyzes Bush's use of the epideictic mode in "Our Mission and Our Moment: George W. Bush and September 11," *Rhetoric and Public Affairs* 6 (2003): 607–632. Denise Botsdorf follows in this vein in "George W. Bush's Post-September 11 Rhetoric of Covenant Renewal: Upholding the Faith of the Greatest Generation," *Quarterly Journal of Speech* 89 (2003): 293–319. See also C. D. Riswold, "A Religious Response Veiled in a Presidential Address: A Theological Study of Bush's Speech on 20 September, 2001," *Political Theology* 5 (2004): 39–46.

4. These charges were not unlike those that plagued the Roosevelt Administration during and after the Pujo Hearings into the attack on Pearl Harbor. After September 11, 2001, some congressional hearings on other matters, employees of the Justice Department and the FBI have been questioned with regard to homeland security. However, their answers have been evasive. Floyd Abrams, a leading First Amendment attorney who, for example, defended the New York *Times* in the "Pentagon Papers" Case, claimed that the "American intelligence community" foiled an attempt to hijack 14 planes from Los Angeles Airport and crash them into the Pacific Ocean, but that they claimed to have been unprepared for what happened in New York and Washington, D.C. on September 11, 2001. Abrams, Floyd. "Remarks for the Cornerstone Project," Washington, DC: Media Institute, November 16, 2001. President Clinton, appearing on The David Letterman Show (September 11, 2002), confirmed that many attacks had been foiled by the United States, including the planned attack on Los Angeles Airport.

5. The legislation on money laundering was also ironed out. Only 66 House members and one Senator voted against the bill. The president signed it on October 26, 2001.

6. Robert L. Jackson, "Senate Oks Anti-Terrorism Program," Los Angeles *Times*, October 12, 2001, A13.

7. A "pen register" allows determining who was called by cell or other phones and deciphers the number of the person called by a suspect in a criminal investigation. Before the Congress acted, if the government sought to "trap" numbers, it needed to obtain court permission in the state of origin.

8. The former rules required the government to show that there was probable cause that the suspect was gathering foreign intelligence

9. The supposed firewall between the CIA and FBI is regularly breached *de facto*. The new acts authorized the practice *de jure*.

10. The limit before the legislation was two days.

11. The Internal Security Act of 1950 allowed the Attorney General to detain aliens who were members of the Communist Party. They were not allowed bail.

12. Five days before President Bush left office, his administration disavowed these policy interpretations. See January 15, 2009, "Memorandum to File," Assistant Attorney General Steven G. Bradbury. In David G. Savage, "Memos Are Called 'tip of the iceberg,'" Los Angeles *Times*, March 3, 2009, A14.

13. David G. Savage, "Bush-era Memos Stun Legal Experts," Los Angeles *Times*, March 4, 2009, A13.

14. George W. Bush, "Military Order—Detention, Treatment, and Trial of Certain Non-Citizens in the War Against Terrorism," Weekly Compilation of Presidential Documents, (November 13, 2001), 1665–1668.

15. *Ex Parte Quirin*. For more on this case and other military tribunals, see Marouf Hasian Jr., *Military Tribunals and the Loss of American Civil Liberties* (Tuscaloosa: University of Alabama Press, 2005).

16. Attorney General Francis Biddle claimed that the Nazis could not use the precedent set in the *Milligan* case (see above) because he was an American citizen.

17. This report goes on to point out that "judges are denying bond, closing hearings, and sealing documents." Richard A. Serrano, "Some Held in Terror Probe Report Being Abused," Los Angeles *Times*, October 15, 2001, A4.

18. Richard A. Serrano, "A Swift, Secretive Dragnet after Attacks," Los Angeles *Times*, September 10, 2002, A16.

19. Serrano, "A Swift, Secretive . . . ," A16.

20. Serrano, "Some Held in Terror . . . ," A4.

21. Josh Meyer, "70,000 Terrorist Suspects Worldwide on U.S. List," Los Angeles *Times*, September, 22, 2002, A1.

22. He was charged with operating a racketeering enterprise, conspiracy to kill and maim innocent people, conspiracy to provide material support to a terrorist organization, interstate extortion, perjury and obstruction of justice. See Josh Meyer and John-Thor Dahlburg, "Florida Professor Charged in Terrorism Case," Los Angeles *Times*, February 21, 2003, A5.

23. "Detention Hearing Linked to Release," Los Angeles *Times*, September 18, 2002, A18.

24. Eric Luchtblau and Josh Meyer, "Terror Probe Feuds Revealed by Secret Court," Los Angeles *Times*, August 23, 2002, A1.

25. 540 U.S. 1104 (2004).

26. *Hamdi v. Rumsfeld*, 542 U.S. 507 (2006).

27. www.cbsnews.com/stories/ 2003/01/23/opinion/ polls/ main537739.shtml

28. In 1981, Saddam Hussein attempted to develop nuclear weapons in a plant just outside of Baghdad. The Israeli Air Force destroyed the plant.

29. Transcript at tvnews.vanderbilt.edu/program.pl? ID=825647

30. George W. Bush, *President's Radio Address*. (Washington, DC: The White House, May 1, 2004.)

31. Wayne Drash, "Report: No WMD Stockpiles in Iraq," *CNN.com* (October 7, 2004) World News.

32. Robin Wright and Ellen Knickmeyer, "U.S. Lowers Sights On What Can Be Achieved in Iraq," Washington *Post*, August 15, 2005, A1.

33. Representative John Murtha, "Troop Withdrawal," (Washington, DC: House of Representatives, November 17, 2005). foxnews.com/story/0,2933,175878,00.html

34. George W. Bush, "President Discusses Recent Visit to Iraq by Secretary of State Rice and Defense Secretary Rumsfeld," (Washington DC: The Office of the Press Secretary, May 1, 2006).

35. The Los Angeles *Times* reported on August 29, 2006, that Secretary of Defense Rumsfeld gave a speech in Reno, Nevada, to the Veterans of Foreign Wars. "Rumsfeld could have taken the opportunity to address the critical challenges of the war in Iraq: the security situation in Baghdad, mounting U.S. military and Iraqi civilian casualties and out-of-control costs. Instead, he took the opportunity to repeatedly attack—implicitly and explicitly—anyone who dares to criticize the administration's 'stay the course' policy" (A1).

36. Vice President Cheney, on *Meet the Press* on August, 31 2006, accused critics of the Administration's policies of assisting terrorists. Cheney said that the strategy of the terrorists is "to break our will." According to Cheney, terrorists "are encouraged, obviously, when they see the kind of debate that we've had in the United States, suggestions, for example, that we should withdraw U.S. forces from Iraq." The debate "validates the strategy of the terrorists."

37. *Iraq Study Group Report.* (Washington, DC: United States Institute for Peace, December 6, 2006), 12.

38. Reuters reported on their news wire and the *PBS News Hour* showed on January 16, 2006, President Bush stating that "When it came time to execute him, it looked like it was kind of a revenge killing. And it sent a mixed signal to the American people and the people around the world. And it just goes to show that this is a government that has still got some maturation to do."

39. www.nytimes.com/ 2007/01/11/world/middleeast/ 11prexy.html

40. Helene Cooper and David E. Sanger, "Iraqis' Progress Lags Behind Pace Set by Bush Plan," New York *Times,* March 15, 2007, A1.

41. On May 8, 2007, CNN reported that 54 percent of Americans polled disapproved of President Bush's decision to veto the Iraq funding bill that called for U.S. troops to leave Iraq by 2008. Additionally, "57 percent of Americans said they want Congress to send another spending bill with a timetable for withdrawal back to the White House." www.cnn.com/ 2007/POLITICS/05/08/schneider.iraq. poll/index.html

42. In an interview with *Stars and Stripes* magazine on December 12, 2007, Army Chief of Staff Gen. George Casey said "the U.S. Army is out of balance . . . [W]e're consuming our readiness as fast as we're building it, and so we're not able to build depth for other things. We're running the all-volunteer force at a pace that is not sustainable." www.army.mil/-news/2007/12/12/7147-stars-and-stripes-interview-with-army-chief-of-staff

43. The Center for Constitutional Rights claimed that the new Obama Administration "offers essentially the same definition of 'enemy combatants' without using the term." David G. Savage, "They are 'enemy combatants' no more," Los Angeles *Times*, March 14, 2009, A16.

Chapter 11

Conclusion

Craig R. Smith

My purpose in this conclusion is to synthesize the contributions of the preceding analyses. Comparing their similarities and differences not only expands our understanding of what has gone before, but enables us to cope more constructively with present and future events of a like nature. I hope to accomplish this overview in several steps: first, by arguing that the crises we have examined here linger in varying ways, in some cases embedded deeply in America's diverse civil religion; second, by extracting paradigms of suppression from the crises; third, by examining the role the media played in these crises; fourth, by comparing the threats to national security that engendered each crisis; fifth, by analyzing the roles of various protectors of national interests and First Amendment values; and sixth, by looking at patterns that emerge from the resolution of the various crises.

Clearly echoes of these events still are with us. The Alien and Sedition crisis functions as a justification for contemporary arguments. Some of the nation's founders did not believe that the First Amendment provides absolute guarantees. The crisis also demonstrates that an educated public is crucial for democracy to perform properly and even then it can move slowly to correct abuses of power. A recent president used reverence for Lincoln to rational suspension of habeas corpus even though Lincoln's own action was eventually declared unconstitutional. Radical Republicans are the founders of the Thirteenth, Fourteenth, and Fifteenth Amendments. Arguments about their original intent and tactics to achieve ratification affect cases dealing with due process and the incorporation of doctrine in our own time, particularly amid cries for a new federalism by those opposed to gay rights, gun control, and a woman's right to have an abortion. More than the Civil War itself, these amendments changed the United States into a singular noun thus continuing the steady erosion of states' rights begun with the ratification of the

Constitution. Most importantly, these amendments allowed later Supreme Courts to apply the Bill of Rights, including the First Amendment, against the states.

The impact of Native Americans' treatment certainly persists. Their mass destruction diminishes the credibility of America's injunction that other nations should honor human rights. Furthermore, in jurisprudence, the cases filed by Indian nations have reasserted the promissory rights of other ethnic groups. The union movement encouraged national legislation and more enlightened management to lessen the need to organize workers. The ironic result is that union membership had fallen to only 11 percent of the workforce during the prosperous 1990s and has shown a resurgence only during times of high employment, such as in 2010. And if business and industry fail to cope with burgeoning problems such as sexual harassment and excessive pay to executives, unions may continue to rise up, their return made easier by laws protecting one of the most important parts of the First Amendment, that of assembly. The same can be said for the suffrage movement, which overcame its attachment to such causes as abolition, thereby alienating the South, and temperance, thereby alienating a drinking public. The suffrage movement was a forerunner to, and made possible the great strides for, the feminist movement of the 1970s and 1980s.

Phrases such as "McCarthyism," "witch hunts," and "black listing" attest to the legacy of the McCarthy era. Furthermore, the demand for political correctness on campuses recently has spawned a severe backlash, partly because similar attacks on professors during the early 1950s are still fresh in academic memories. Especially galling were the actions of campus presidents who regularly fired *tenured* and untenured faculty alike if they invoked the Fifth Amendment or admitted to having been members of a communist front organization in the past, regardless of the naïveté of that membership.

In the same way, the sensitivity of the press to efforts to control it remain strong in part because of the contrast between the freedom it had in covering the fighting in Vietnam and the restrictions it faced on the domestic front. As Americans mourned the fall of Saigon in 1975, they remembered that on the one hand, CBS aired the documentary *Charley Company*, an intimate journey chronicling "fragging," ambushes, and other horrors attendant on war; and that on the other hand, the executive branch protested airing of *The Selling of the Pentagon* and tried to block publication of the *Pentagon Papers*. Those events are brought life by former Secretary of Defense Robert McNamara, an architect of the war, claiming American efforts in Vietnam were "Wrong, terribly wrong." Not surprisingly, in our time, the press protested being denied full access to military invasions and activity in Grenada, Panama, the Persian Gulf, Afghanistan and Iraq.

In short, the ghosts of the crises we have examined haunt the nation to this day and two of the crisis, restrictions on campaign persuasion and restrictions justified by 9/11, remain as of this writing. Some of those ghosts plague the courts, while others frequent corporate boardrooms; some trouble campuses, while still others lurk in the halls of Congress and the corridors of the White House. Fortunately, we neither ignore nor treat them as invisible. More often than not, they inspire citizens to defend our constitutional rights by giving voice to what can happen should people fail to guard their freedoms. We retrieve from these haunting visages a sense that we must never accept a definition of sedition that precludes citizens from legitimately challenging a president or a member of Congress. We should not let war justify the questionable suspension of individual freedoms in the name of the collective good. We should never convert the zeal for victory into a venomous revenge that infringes on the rights of those who question the actions of the victors. We should not try to reeducate or repatriate a race or culture at the expense of its indigenous rites or rights. We should never deny freedoms to assemble peaceably and redress grievances from the underpaid, the underprivileged and/or unrepresented. We should not allow a demagogue to effect abuse of a minority by stirring a segment of the public against its members. We should guard against a president's manipulation of the threat of war or of the aegis of national security to unfairly restrict press or demonstrators, or to peer into private lives unnecessarily.

The previous chapters illustrate the variations inherent in the common cycles of history. The sheer number of cases we have cited chronicling deprivation of First Amendment rights argues that such abuses likely will recur. Thus, citizens must be alert to the possibility of renewed suppression of our rights and know how to manage those problems when they surface. Just as Daniel Webster and Henry Clay cited the Alien and Sedition crisis to prevent President Jackson and John C. Calhoun from passing legislation that was unconstitutional, so too must contemporary Americans be knowledgeable of the history of suppression to deal with new crises when they arise, be they universities trying to impose a code of verbal conduct or Congressional legislators attempting to regulate violence on television.

Paradigms of Suppression

Some crises spawn a movement promoted by a radical group seeking to fight a perceived danger. My analysis of the Alien and Sedition imbroglio, reconstruction, and the McCarthy era gives renewed credibility to the thesis Richard Hofstadter established in 1952: The recurrence of the paranoid style over a long span of time and in different places suggests that a mentality disposed to see the world in a paranoid way may always be present in some considerable minority of the population. However, the fact that movements employing the paranoid style are not constant but come in successive episodic waves suggests that the paranoid disposition is mobilized into action chiefly by social conflicts that involve ultimate schemes of values and that bring fundamental fears and hatreds, rather than negotiable interests, into political action.[1]

One persistent model of crises is marked by spreading the word, emergence of opinion leaders, and building of coalitions until a significant number of people perceive the threat, real, exaggerated, or imagined. Those intensely interested join the party segment or become members of the leader's support group, which can be partisan, ideological, geographic, ethnic- and/or gender-based. They are the true believers, the hard-core activists. As more public attention focuses on the issue of concern, the group promotes legislation or institutes legal action that can infringe on First Amendment rights, causing, in turn, the crystallizing of opposition, which may also be partisan, ideological, geographic, ethnic- and/or gender-based. Once the conflict is joined, at least some in the media eventually move beyond the surface perceptions to expose inaccuracies and unethical or illegal tactics, thus heightening feelings of persecution and fears of conspiracy in the initiating group. The ensuing debate engages the public's attention, often leading to a broad spectrum of activities on the part of the instigators of the crisis. They will at least attempt to silence the opposition using various rhetorical strategies from the simple fallacies of the Hamiltonians to the sophisticated manipulation of the media by Richard Nixon or the federal courts by George W. Bush. They may resort to the use of force and even acts of terrorism, such as those that result in killings during union unrest, or the bombing of the Attorney General's home during one of the red scares. The crisis ends when the real threat diminishes and the need for restrictions of First Amendment rights can no longer be justified.

Another model presents itself when governmental crises provoke presidential and/or congressional actions that sometimes undermine constitutional guarantees. The pattern in these instances differs from that involving radical groups or major political party segments. In these cases, the president or the majority party take action designed to combat what they perceive as threats to the nation or to themselves. This move almost always leads to immediate partisan debate. Thus, Lincoln's suspension of habeas corpus met with challenges in the courts and in Congress within days of its announcement. As soon as Radical Republicans articulated their agenda after the Civil War, they faced opposition from President Johnson, the press, and Democrats. When Lyndon Johnson and Richard Nixon sought to quash protest against the war in Vietnam, their actions generated further protest as well as partisan reproach and criticism in the press. More often than not, the conflict escalates that much more quickly when the president or a majority in Congress act than when a radical segment issues constitutional threats because of the inherent partisan nature of the presidency and the Congress. An able, willing, and loyal opposition is usually prepared to fire up partisan mills.

Long-term efforts to suppress the labor, suffrage, and Native American movements are indicative of yet another model. In these cases, a continuing consensus of those in government leads to the use of a full arsenal of tactics ranging from persuasion to armed force to silence opposition that is ideological, gender- or ethnic-based. Often the government engages in suppression-by-proxy, allowing others to silence the opposition by not protecting its First Amendment rights. For Native Americans, a deep cultural gulf with religious overtones helped to rationalize strategies of suppression. For labor, the gulf was ideological, socialist labor versus capitalist business. For Suffragists, the gap was gender-based, the belief that women were weaker, emotional, in need of care, and/or belonged in the home, not in the voting booth. Over time, various presidents, with the support of Congress, the courts and the media, marginalized Native Americans by refusing to recognize them as equals, by moving them to new territories, by isolating them on reservations, by trying to reeducate them, and by portraying them as savages standing in the way of frontier progress. While some members of some administrations protested these actions, the policy in general transcended party lines. It took on a momentum that lasted because of continued public support.

For a shorter time, the same was true of the labor and suffrage movements. Critics at first linked them with alien ideologies such as communism, anarchism, and socialism, and compared their leaders to radicals, who, like the Populists, would tear the system down. After the Civil War, the emergence of Social Darwinism, which supported unfettered business competition, created an environment in which labor unions were depicted as a threat to capitalism rather than as integral to the free enterprise system. The dominant philosophy of industrial leaders had the force of law for the conservative administrations and courts that followed the Civil War. Not until Theodore Roosevelt's "Man with Muckrake" address did a president clearly call for fair and equal competition. Although writers like Henry Demarest Lloyd and Washington Gladden appealed for a Social Gospel as early as the 1880s, only when progressive journalists began telling personal tales of abused men, women, and children did the nation pursue remediation.

Women had to wait until 1920 when the suffrage movement finally overcame government opposition, led by various presidents culminating with Woodrow Wilson. The movement was seen as undermining family values and subversive to the war effort. That some women in the movement were actually jailed and tortured for peacefully demonstrating at the White House during the Wilson administration should give us pause. If Woodrow Wilson could condone such action, almost any president could.

In sum, these cases warrant the founders' imposition of checks on the government, an entity that has at its disposal an incredible array of mechanisms capable of sustaining its own power. First, it can resort to legal and/or legislative means to silence criticism. The Hamiltonians used laws they had rammed through Congress to jail a congressman. Lincoln suspended habeas corpus and authorized the use of military commissions to thwart opponents of the war. Radical Republicans required Southern states to ratify amendments to the Constitution to be readmitted to the Union. A number of presidents used court orders to suppress union members. Richard Nixon employed mass arrests, later deemed illegal, to "maintain the peace." Campaign laws have entrenched incumbents and the two-party system, while limiting the voices of individual campaign contributors. The USA PATRIOT Act and the Homeland Security Act include provisions that allow invasions of privacy approved by secret courts in Washington, D.C.

A second option almost always available to the government is the use of force. This tactic can take the form of military action by the armed forces as in the case of the suppression of Native Americans; or the president can call out the national guard as in the case of labor unions or Vietnam protesters. We should also note that these forces can simply stand back and let protesters be harassed in an effort to silence them. Members of the suffrage movement were spit on, hit, and burned with cigarettes while the police of Washington, D.C. looked on in the midst of World War I when young men and women were serving in Europe to defeat the forces of oppression.

Members of the government as well as members of radical segments are capable of highly sophisticated propaganda techniques. The president has numerous avenues through which to communicate his perceptions to the Congress, his enemies, and/or the public. Speeches, press conferences, talk show appearances, executive orders, and the like facilitate control over various situations. The Congress as well as extremist factions of political parties have similar rhetorical options. Common among the cases studied are such tactics as exaggeration, attribution of guilt by association, co-optation, circumvention, and outright fallacies.

Third, government has recourse to extra-legal actions. Postmaster Kendall withheld the mailing of Abolitionist tracts into the South. President Jackson, among others, broke numerous treaties with Native Americans and then forcefully moved them. Franklin Roosevelt incarcerated innocent American citizens during World War II. Presidents Johnson and Nixon tapped the phones of journalists, employees, and demonstrators. President George W. Bush used executive orders to overextend the letter of the laws passed by Congress and the meaning of the Constitution, ignoring the phrase "and others" behind the word "citizens" when it came to civil rights of suspects in his "war on terror."

Because of this vast power, opponents of government clearly need
the protection of the First Amendment and due process. Only in that way
can they enter the free marketplace of ideas to secure a fair hearing from
the public. Nothing dramatizes this need more vividly than television's role
in unmasking Senator Joseph McCarthy. That medium allowed viewers to
see the man operate in a congressional hearing in a way that appalled the
majority of them. It allowed Edward R. Murrow to attack the senator and
then air an unedited film provided by the senator himself that revealed him
for the demagogue he was.

The Role of the Media

This is not to say that members of the media always behave responsibly.
Murrow and Henry Luce were the exceptions to the rule, not its norm.
More conscious of audience than any other industry in America, the press
and electronic media attend closely to their public's pulse through constant
polling. The media's support for, or at least lack of questioning of, legislation
following the attack of 9/11 provide a contemporary case in point. Another
is their absence of concern over campaign reform laws that restrict voters'
voices.

At the same time, media transmit viable criticism because of their
enormous, amorphous estate. And as we have seen in case after case, some
journalists in this country were instrumental in ending crises, revealing unfair
tactics, and creating sympathy for the marginalized. They often succeed by
examining each case for whom or what is privileged and how the public
or some segment of it is reconstituted to justify an oppressor's position.
For example, advocates sponsoring the Alien and Sedition Acts privileged
national security while painting the public as victims of a foreign and internal conspiracy. The Radical Republicans and McCarthyists used the same
strategy but with considerable more success. The government privileged
settlers over Native Americans while depicting the latter as members of an
alien nation. A similar strategy surfaced in dealings with labor. In that case,
unions infested with subversive ideologies were seen as threats to the free
enterprise system. The suffragists were pictured as threats to the family. In
like manner, Lincoln privileged the Union and it citizens over states' rights
and certain constitutional guarantees. He underscored the rights gained in
America's war for independence while reconstituting his public as supporters
of a government of, by, and for the people as opposed to the government
of the federated states. Viewed in this light, he and his followers became
saviors of the Union and the goals of the Revolution. After Lincoln, Radical
Republicans adopted the same strategy by eschewing the role of savior and

instead adopting the persona of victors of a bloody war, thereby justifying their taking of economic, geographic, and partisan revenge.

Lyndon Johnson, Richard Nixon, and George W. Bush privileged a government at war and reconstituted their public into a patriotic, long-suffering, and silent majority, who had to tolerate a vocal, violent, arrogant, and unpatriotic minority which at best was naive and at worst guilty of aiding the enemy. Using Vice President Agnew as a surrogate, Nixon also was fairly effective at redefining the motives of press and protesters, thereby inoculating himself against criticism even after the Watergate break-in had been traced to him. In the same way, Vice President Cheney, for a time at least, kept critics of the Bush administration at bay.

Of course, media need to get the story straight and that means clearly identifying the differences that mark one case from another. Journalists engage in instant history; they don't have time to check all the facts and create the proper context for their stories. Thus, journalists are prone to error and to missing things. When newspapers are contracting, as they are now, this phenomenon becomes even more pronounced. Foreign bureaus are shut; media tend to rely on other media, such as wire services, instead of investigating stories for themselves. In such an environment, reporters and editorial writers may find it tempting to toe the company line, particularly if the company is owned by a larger conglomerate with an ideological agenda.

Yet, these errors must be tolerated if media are to provide a check on government. Unlike the Radicals who followed him, Lincoln was reluctant to attack newspapers opposing his policies. He anguished over closing or censoring them. Lyndon Johnson, who was used to playing the media like a fiddle, had trouble understanding their lack of support for his policies in Vietnam, whereas Nixon, who lost the trust of the press as early as 1948, seemed to relish painting the media as elitist, unpatriotic, and biased against common sense.

These observations imply a second distinction among the cases we have examined: the comparative sophistication of the media, particularly its sense of history and its technological capabilities. Johnson and Nixon had greater access to the public than did earlier presidents and, hence, more opportunity to manipulate the press by leaking stories and controlling information. At the same time, the modern media have more access to the world and to the various threats that are generated. Hence, they could fan the fires of protest by presenting graphic images of the war in Vietnam or the battlefields of Afghanistan. Had Lincoln had to face televised coverage of the early failures of his generals and the carnage of the battlefields, he might have fared even less well in terms of public support.

A third difference involves the major voices participating in the crises. Alexander Hamilton, Thaddeus Stevens, Joseph McCarthy, and their henchmen led efforts to enhance the status of their respective political parties without much help from the head of their party, the president of the United States. Stevens and McCarthy, in fact, faced active opposition from their chief executives. However, in these instances, as in the ones in which a president takes the lead, their voices still resounded clearly. Less distinct were the voices raised against Native Americans, suffragists, unions, and political campaign restrictions. Although the government acted in each of these cases, specifically who was accountable for the actions taken was not so clear. Sometimes a president was responsible, as with the practice of relocating Native Americans; sometimes the courts that acted were culpable, as with the policy of suppression of unions. Note, however, that where diffusion of responsibility existed, the parties opposing oppression produced neither major speakers nor memorable speeches, at least in the short term. Although rhetorical prowess characterizes advocacy on both sides of crises related to the Alien and Sedition Acts, Reconstruction, and McCarthyism, such is not the case with the unions, suffragists or with Native Americans. Union discourse remains singularly uninspiring, even in retrospect, and the significance of the treatises generated by crises involving Native Americans is understood only with the advantage of time and cultural perspective.

By contrast, when a president leads efforts to silence the opposition, he provokes a response and usually holds sway. Lincoln was the most successful, particularly in dealing with Vallandigham and the Copperheads. Nixon's 49 state landslide in 1972 says something about the ineffectiveness of his critics, although the opposite was true in the case of Lyndon Johnson, who withdrew from the 1968 presidential campaign in March.

The foregoing makes two clear points: First, rhetorical talent is important in these crises whether one is advocate, counteradvocate, or member of the media. Second, the most successful participants tend to be entrenched in the political system rather than persons on the fringes who seek to destroy or radically change it. Although the public may listen to Dr. Benjamin Spock, watch the antics of Jane Fonda on an anti-aircraft gun, and express irritation at the Chicago Seven, serious opposition to the Vietnam War coalesced only under the leadership of Senators Eugene McCarthy and Robert Kennedy. While the oratory of Native American chiefs is evocative, it did not lead to justice in the same way court appeals did in the last century. It was not until the states began granting women the right to vote that the Congress gave any serious consideration to the movement. Perhaps no one understood better the importance of being part of the system than did Samuel Gompers as he steered his Union between the rocks of socialism and the whirlpool of surrender.

One hopes that the vigorous press, which was a major institution from the beginning of nationhood, is populated by persons with a collective consciousness that can guard against future dangers. At minimum, that consciousness should include cognizance of the fundamental patterns embedded in the crises we have studied.

Parallels in Exposing the Perceived Threat

In most of the cases presented in this book, rhetoric functioned to make the public aware of some threat to national security, whether it was a foreign foe or political corruption. Consequently, the threat served as a justification for suspending First Amendment rights. Although the burden of proof clearly fell on those alleging the danger, they were, each in their own way, extremely effective at using contemporary events and circumstances to convince the public that dangers both external and *internal* did in fact exist and that they were serious enough to warrant legal action to restrict the freedoms of at least some citizens or "others" on American soil. Perhaps the most pernicious is characterizing the electoral process as corrupt to justify restricting campaign and broadcast speech.

How exaggerated those threats were differs from case to case. The parallel between the situation facing the Federalists and that confronted by McCarthy is striking. In both cases, the United States engaged in actual conflict with a regime born out of violent revolution, in one case revolutionary France and in the other revolutionary China.[2] In both, great numbers of people had been displaced by political unrest and many of them had recently arrived in the United States. Their presence and uncertainty about their political convictions generated the perception that they and unknown others were bearers of a pestilence that a foreign regime hoped to use to infest, weaken, and eventually conquer the United States. Even McCarthy's allegation that communists had subverted the State Department had its parallel in the late eighteenth century. In the presidential campaign of 1796 between Thomas Jefferson and John Adams, Secretary of State Jefferson was accused of presiding over a State Department infiltrated by Jacobins and Jacobin sympathizers.

Lincoln also faced the threat of internal subversion but it was more above board. The Copperheads were open in their opposition to his policies. Unfortunately for them, the Vallandigham insurrection gave Lincoln the excuse he needed to suspend habeas corpus in Copperhead counties, particularly southern Ohio, Illinois, and Indiana.

Portraying suffragists as harbingers of societal breakdown was remarkably successful for almost a century. Those who sought to portray union members as insurrectionists had a tougher time establishing their burden of proof because leaders like Gompers understood that unions needed to work within the system to achieve their goals. Nonetheless, they encountered tough sledding at their inception because of the strength of the forces of capitalism dominating both government and public debate. The unions were hurt not only because of opposition from those entrenched in power but because the public perceived the socialist and Populist stances as a threat to the nation. When union frustration led to a riot in Haymarket Square in Chicago, their opponents used that event to "prove" that all unions were anarchistic. Unions eventually overcame these disadvantages, but only through protracted struggles within the confines of mainstream politics.

Because of television, the establishment had a hard time convincing the nation that Vietnam demonstrators were a threat to American ascendancy. Their beaded, beflowered, rag-tag groups were no match for the National Guard or local police. However, Johnson's and Nixon's ability to contextualize protest as giving comfort to the enemy in a foreign war helped to persuade the "silent majority" that suppressive tactics were necessary. Nixon was especially effective in dealing with the press. Using a host of surrogates led by his vice president to attack the media as elitist and liberal, Nixon both deflected criticism and inoculated his administration against it until being undone by the Watergate fiasco.

Obviously the attack of 9/11 was dramatic proof that the United States was subject to attack by coordinated terrorists. That threat was then used to justify legislation that tightened security; it also was used to rationalize two wars against nations that allegedly housed these terrorist groups. And yet, from 2001 through 2004, the Bush Administration saw less opposition than any of the others we have examined in this study.

Assuming the Duty of Protection

Another pattern is that radical spokespersons reinforce and compound the sense of danger through *circular support* (sometimes called "milling" by sociologists). Anti-Abolitionists continued to riot in the South even after President Jackson restricted pamphleteering there. Supporters of Thaddeus Stevens warned of Southern plots to overthrow the government even after the South had been divided into five military districts. McCarthyists, including J. Edgar Hoover, carried out a "witch hunt" that decimated the lives of government servants, writers, performers, professors, and members of the press corps long after McCarthy himself had ceased to be an effective force.

Once a public perceives a threat as real and widespread, advocates can heighten fear by linking it to other issues. In these instances, perceived threats are tied to other established fears and the linkage often goes from the concrete example to the abstract threat. That unions were involved in strike actions proved that they were part of the anarchist movement. That local communists opposed American entry into World War I proved that they were part of an international conspiracy; that women seeking the vote demonstrated during World War I proved they were a threat to social values and the war effort. That campaign contributions during various political campaigns resulted in undue influence proved that all campaign contributions are tarred with brush of corruption.

A threat starts the masses milling; a second threat then renews the activity of the herd and spreads throughout the group in waves that return to further excite the leaders. In turn, they augment the intensity of their rhetoric, which again generates waves of excitement. For example, a desire to control the South politically as well as militarily reignited the activities of the Reconstructionists. Once they won the elections of 1866, Northern Republicans were excited about the possibility of further reprisals against the South. Once milling begins, radicals can heighten excitement and give substance to danger by citing new evidence of conspiracy and dramatizing the situation by linking it to other fears common among the people. This tactic provides a rationale for fears in the world, ordering them into a hierarchy that can be used to drum up support.

All of this allows those who perceive and/or exaggerate the threat to justify their seizing power by casting themselves as protectors of the Republic. President Jackson acted in the name of public safety, as did the presidents who attempted to put down union activity. Hamilton, Lincoln, Wilson, FDR, and McCarthy endeavored to shield citizens from internal organizers they painted as the minions of foreign powers or ideologies. Once obtained, this protector status then justifies legal action.

The Response to Proposed Legislation

Once radicals exaggerate a national threat, the next step is to take concrete steps to defeat it. In the United States, radical legislation often borders on or is unconstitutional; declarations of war or military interventions are not uncommon. In fact, one of the best ways to measure the intensity of radicals' zeal is to examine the legislation they propose. Attempts to pass measures, whether by the president or the Congress, naturally attract the attention of the opposition. At least in the cases studied here, passage of legislation by radical segments is requisite if their efforts are to be taken seriously. Introducing bills into Congress or taking other official actions in turn generates opposition to the president or to a congressional or radical segment. In the cases we have examined, concrete action, whether proposed or accomplished, set the stage for a confrontation that spilled out of the Congress to invade the public's consciousness. The media helped by ensuring that the arguments of those opposed to the radicals received significant attention, at least until the crisis caused by campaign reform and the attacks of 9/11.

At this point, the zeal of national radical factions usually fosters more castigating of their opponent's motives and trustworthiness as well as taking more action into their own hands.[3] Radicals often are able to arouse *community actions* on behalf of the causes they so dogmatically embrace. Federalists encouraged the tarring and feathering of "Jacobin sympathizers." Radical Republicans set up puppet governments in the states they readmitted to the Union, installing local sympathizers as officers who also served as informants to the Freedman's Bureau and even to the Congress. Suffragists were surrounded by hostile mobs, as were unionists. And Richard Nixon activated a "silent majority."

The Role of the Supreme Court

Throughout this study, we have seen instances where the Supreme Court has played a major role in resolving a crisis and in other instances where it was complicit in the crisis. During the Alien and Sedition crisis, the Court was mute. During the Civil War, it kept out of Lincoln's way by refusing Chief Justice Taney's call for action. It did not rule on the rights of citizens in wartime until the war was over. It had no choice but to accept the amendments to the Constitution that were initiated by Radical Republicans, but it also chose not to interfere with the Reconstruction and then basically upheld Jim Crow laws and separate but equal provisions well into the twentieth century. The Supreme Court was no help to Native Americans, union organizers, and suffragists. It upheld Woodrow Wilson's and states' attacks on the First Amendment during World War I and the McCarthy crisis, overturning these rulings only in peacetime and in McCarthy's case, well after his fall from grace. The Court was much more heroic during the Nixon administration when it forced the release of the *Pentagon Papers* and then the Nixon tapes. The Court's rulings regarding the rights of prisoners in U.S. territories or prisons are temperate at best, and a violation of habeas corpus at worst. However, its ruling that campaign spending could be curtailed by the states and the federal government and that broadcast media could have content controls imposed by the government contradicts core decisions regarding freedom of the press and the need for robust and open political campaigns. This mixed record gives little comfort to those seeking to protect the First Amendment through the courts in times of crisis.

Denouement

Not surprisingly, the beginning of the decline of restrictive actions by presidents, Congress, or radical movements correlates with increased activity by the opposition. This usually takes the form of responsible persons within the system using freedom of expression to exert authority and to demonstrate leadership in the interest of restraint. As radicals' threats to their opponents increase, the opponents' programs and rhetoric becomes more coherent and systematic.

In the instances we have examined, one or more of three things happened: 1) opinion leaders stepped forward to protect the political system from being damaged by deprivation of First Amendment rights; 2) restrictions no longer were deemed necessary because the problem abated; 3) a national election resolved the crisis. The national media—newspapers, television, or artists—assumed the task of protecting important rights, particularly freedom of expression. They did this not only by exposing radicals' inaccuracies but by revealing their methods—including rhetorical tactics—in such a way that the public could understand the contradiction between their alleged goals and their practices. They also took the arguments of speakers of the various protagonists and made them credible by reprinting them and examining them critically. These steps often were taken at great risk, but such courage was critical to prevent extremists from further infringing on key civil liberties.

A radical party's political influence usually has a tenure of about four years in the United States; the influence of the president on a given issue generally has a shorter life, unless the conflict spawning the issue drags on as with the Iraqi and Afghanistan wars. This pattern also is true of inherited policies. Presidential policies with regard to Native Americans, suffragists, and unions lasted much longer than those associated with other crises because of the continuity and inertia motivated by deep cultural and ideological differences carried forward by successive administrations.

In the case of radical factions, their Achilles heel is their preoccupation with immediate threats rather than with long-term goals. They argue that if Americans fail to cope with the imminent crisis before them, they will have little need to be concerned with their heritage or long-range goals. In the end, however, responsible elements of society usually attack this mind-set. By focusing so intently on the immediate, radicals reveal a nearsightedness that others find pragmatically flawed and/or unconscionable. Radical factions tend to embrace intense political alignments, narrow concerns, and specific targets, which produce cohesion and visibility, but it also renders them vulnerable to broadly based opposition. Moderates have argued successfully that abandoning constitutionally sanctioned methods to manage problems presents a danger far greater than the one described by radicals. Thus, in the name of the Bill of Rights, Jefferson called on his countrymen to resist the Alien and Sedition Acts. In the name of due process and Union, Senator Grimes cast his vote against the removal of President Johnson. In the name of decency and individual freedom, Joseph Welch rebuked Joseph McCarthy; and in the name of freedom of expression and fair play, the Senate censured him. In the name of preserving electoral freedom of expression, many condemn the Supreme Court's rationale for imposing restrictions on campaign contributions and advertisements by independent groups.

The actions and movements we have discussed follow a pattern of birth, growth, and decline. Furthermore, this pattern—with certain variations to be sure—permeates our history. Except where the opposition can be painted as either culturally or ideologically alien, presidential or radical actions that threaten liberty, even in the name of a national danger, mobilizes those who defend constitutional guarantees. Often these defenders of the Constitution are stigmatized, which leads to a firestorm of activity by both sides in the dispute, sometimes stoked by the news media.

Radicals and their opponents tend to see themselves as "protecting" the establishment. Senator Joseph McCarthy was protecting the American way of life against Communist infiltration; his opponents were protecting the Constitution against his emergency measures. As long as the controversy remains within the realm of *debate*, it remains compatible with the traditions of a free society. However, if radicals move to implement policies in ways that could curtail the rights and freedoms of others, particularly their freedom of expression, counterforces begin to coalesce either to protect established freedoms or to reform the establishment so that changes become unattractive or wholly unnecessary. If, as with the Populists, reform occurs before radicals can implement legislation, the movement tends to die because groups working within the system co-opt its reason for being. If, as with the Radical Republicans and to a lesser degree McCarthyists, radicals impose their will through legislative, administrative, and/or other procedural activities, then their opposition must maintain enough pressure to create a rhetorical space more favorable to constitutionalism. A remarkable feature of the American experience is the frequency with which situations favorable to the safeguarding of individual liberties eventually emerge, thereby preserving the original, balanced, constitutional framework. Although an island of suppression, such as controls over "alien speakers," may be left behind for the Supreme Court to consider, eventually the mass of radical legislation is usually swept away. With regard to their amendments to the Constitution, the Radical Republicans were an exception to this rule; however, I suggest that their program endured only because through the amendments, Americans have inherited personal freedom as a legal guarantee *against states* as well as the federal government.

The controversies we analyzed illustrate that even in a democratic republic with a heritage of civil rights that can be traced to the Magna Carta, erosion of civil liberties is always *possible*. The tensions between freedom and "protection" cited in this book are by no means the only ones in our history. On occasion, presidents, the Congress, and even the Supreme Court have circumscribed private citizens' rights to speak out and to live in freedom. In almost all of those instances, just like the cases presented here, the tension between freedom and constraint arose because of conflict pitting a perceived threat against the need to maintain civil liberties. Hence, society will continue to debate *how much* and *what kind* of personal freedom may be exercised *where*. This condition is indigenous to any society whose preeminent social value is freedom of expression.[4]

Fortunately, prudent judgment by the majority tends to settle contests between freedom and "protection." The radicalism of both left and right tends to be shortsighted as does presidential and congressional responses to crises since members of Congress and the president are responsive to voters. Radical ideas are susceptible to weakening 1) because of changing events or by the majority's eventual boredom with the topics radicals tend to discuss; 2) through comparison with appeals that reflect longer and/or broader views and interests; 3) by surfacing compromises and exceptions that mollify the concerns of the majority; 4) because of changing voter sentiment; and/or 5) because of the inherent difficulties radicals have in offering long-ranged outcomes that promise gratification for a full majority of the society.

While congressional and presidential actions fall prey to some of these pitfalls, radical party segments suffered from all of these forces. Moreover, they also face the daunting conceptual and rhetorical task of having to establish some value *above freedom* of expression. The radical Federalists had placed national security above the already enshrined value of freedom of expression. Lincoln advanced survival of the Union above some constitutional guarantees. The Radical Republicans argued that "racial equality" and "revenge" were more important than reconstituting the old Union. The United States government placed a higher value on expansion, mineral wealth, and the security of settlers than on the preservation of Native Americans' cultural expression. Albeit in the name of freedom and the pursuit of happiness, many administrations elevated the capitalistic system over the rights of employees to organize. McCarthy and those who supported him made a case for circumscribing freedom of expression by demonstrating the ubiquity of subversion. Lyndon Johnson and Richard Nixon valued international credibility above the right to protest government policies. However, because laws and traditions clearly support personal freedom, displacing that value for any length of time has proved difficult.

Although the patterns are not exactly alike, they do bear enough resemblance to provide guidelines for future attempts to reduce constitutionally guaranteed rights, particularly freedom of expression. We have learned that suppressing First Amendment rights can take many and very subtle forms. Worse yet, as we have moved through history, ways to subvert First Amendment rights have become more sophisticated rhetorically. During the Alien and Sedition crisis such tactics as guilt by association and logical fallacies were common, but in our lifetimes subtle forms of co-optation, avoidance, coercion, harassment, appropriation, deflection, circumvention, preemption, and marginalization are likely to dominate. Ethical and unethical rhetorical strategies abound in a First Amendment environment.

Unfortunately, we are witness to continuing problems. Extra-legal tactics, particularly by the president, are not uncommon. The institution of the press is being compromised by electronic fragmentation and corporate consolidation. The natural check of partisan politics seems feckless on foreign policy issues. For these reasons, participants in the struggle for rights would be wise to become well versed in the tactics we have analyzed for surely those who wish to suppress freedom will use these methods again. They should understand that it takes effective rhetorical skill to combat propaganda. Whether it be Benjamin Edes writing an editorial in the Boston *Gazette* or Arthur Miller staging a production of *The Crucible*, whether it be Senator Margaret Chase Smith attacking an irresponsible member of her party or Elizabeth Cady Stanton standing up for women's rights, heroes have emerged to use rhetoric in the service of their country. Hopefully, their example will inspire others to perform similar deeds in the future.

Notes

1. *The Paranoid Style in American Politics* (New York: Knopf, 1952).

2. On February 1, 1799, the *Aurora* printed the Insurance Company of North America's figures for the last six months of 1798; American damages inflicted by French vessels were $260,000. Ironically, during the same period, British vessels inflicted damages of $280,000.

3. Often the tone taken is highly moral or puritanical. The rationale for some of these methods is that they are required by the underhanded tactics of the opposition.

4. Notes from the Constitutional Convention in Philadelphia and reports from the ratification debates in the states show that these built-in tensions were recognized by friends and opponents of the new government. To the Federalists, the structural tensions were one of the virtues of the system because they helped provide a "balance of powers."

Bibliography

18 U.S. Code Annotated, section 2385.

Abbott, Shirley. *The National Museum of American History*. New York: Harry N. Abrams, 1981.

Abrams, Floyd. "Remarks for the Cornerstone Project." Washington, DC: Media Institute, November 16, 2001.

Adams, Alexander. *Geronimo: A Biography*. New York: Putnam's Sons, 1971.

Agnew, Spiro T. "Network Censorship." *Vital Speeches of the Day* 36 (1969): 98–101.

———. *Frankly Speaking: A Collection of Extraordinary Speeches*. Washington, DC: Public Affairs Press, 1970.

Alley, Robert S. "Public Education and the Public Good." *William & Mary Bill of Rights Journal* 4 (1995): 277–350.

Anderson, David. "The Origins of the Press Claus." *U.C.L.A. Law Review* 30 (1983): 533–537.

Anderson, Frank Maloy. "The Enforcement of the Alien and Sedition Laws." *American Historical Association Reports* Annual Report of the 1912. Washington, DC: American Historical Association, 1914.

Arnold, Thurman. "Economic Reform and the Sherman Antitrust Act." Ed. John A. Garraty. *The New Commonwealth*. New York: Harper & Row, 1968.

Avrich, Paul. *The Haymarket Tragedy*. Princeton, NJ: Princeton University Press, 1984.

Akwesane Notes. "A License to Kill." (Mohawk Nation: Winter, 1973): 4–5.

———. "A Question of Sovereignty and Freedom." (Mohawk Nation: Summer, 1973): 5.

———. "Goodbye Rapid City, Hello Sioux Falls, St. Paul." (Mohawk Nation: Winter, 1973): 7.

———. "Justice in America." (Mohawk Nation: Winter, 1973): 5.

Barrett, Marvin, ed. *The Alfred I. DuPont-Columbia University Survey of Broadcast Journalism, 1969–1970*. New York: Grosset & Dunlap, 1970.

Barrett, S. M. *Geronimo: His Own Story*. New York: Dutton, 1970.

Barsh, Russell Larrence. "The Nature and Spirit of North American Political Systems." *American Indian Quarterly* 10 (1986): 181–198.

Bartlett, John. *Familiar Quotations*. 15th ed. Boston: Little, Brown, 1980.

Baskerville, Barnet. "The Illusion of Proof." *Western Speech* 35 (1961): 236–242.

Bateson, Gregory. *Steps to Ecology of Mind.* New York: Ballantine, 1972.

Beard, Mary. *A Short History of the American Labor Movement.* New York: Doran, 1924.

Bechtol, Paul. "The 1880 Labor Dispute in Leadville." *Colorado Magazine* 47 (Fall, 1970): 325.

Bell, Daniel. *Marxian Socialism in the United States.* Princeton, NJ: Princeton University Press, 1967.

Benjamin, Louise M. "Herbert Hoover, Issues of Speech and Radio Regulations in the 1920's." *Free Speech Yearbook* 26 (1988): 28–29.

Benson, Thomas W. "Rhetorical Impasse: The Sedition Trials of 1800." *Southern Speech Communication Journal* 31 (1966): 196–206.

Berger, Raoul. *Executive Privilege: A Constitutional Myth.* Cambridge: Harvard University Press, 1974.

Bernstein, Irving. *The Lean Years.* Baltimore: Penguin, 1966.

Bernstein, Carl, and Bob Woodward. *All the President's Men.* New York: Simon and Schuster, 1974.

Binney, Horace. *The Privilege of the Writ of Habeas Corpus Under the Constitution.* Philadelphia: Sherman, 1862.

Bipartisan Campaign Reform Act (public law no. 107–155).

Blackstone, William. *Commentaries on the Laws of England.* Oxford: Clarendon Press, 1765–1769.

Blaeser, Kimberly M. "Pagans Rewriting the Bible: Heterodoxy and the Representation of Spirituality in Native American Literature." *Ariel* 25 (1994): 12–31.

Blaine, James G. *Twenty Years of Congress.* Vols. 1 & 2. Norwich, CT: Henry Bill, 1888.

Blanchard, Margaret A. "Free Expression and Wartime: Lessons from the Past, Hopes for the Future." *Journalism Quarterly* 69 (1992): 5–17.

———. *Revolutionary Sparks: Freedom of Expression in Modern America.* New York: Oxford University Press, 1992.

Block, Herbert. *Herblock's State of the Union.* New York: Simon and Schuster, 1972.

Bonafede, Dom. "Commissar of Credibility." *The Nation* (April 6, 1970): 392–396.

Borda, Jennifer. "The Woman Suffrage Parades of 1910–1913: Possibilities and Limitations of an Early Feminist Rhetorical Strategy." *Western Journal of Communication* 66 (2002): 25–52.

Botsdorf, Denise. "George W. Bush's Post-September 11 Rhetoric of Covenant Renewal: Upholding the Faith of the Greatest Generation." *Quarterly Journal of Speech* 89 (2003): 293–319.

Bosmajian, Haig. "The Abrogation of the Suffragists' First Amendment Rights." *Western Speech* 38 (1974): 218–232.

Bowers, Claude Gernade. *Jefferson and Hamilton.* St. Clair Shores, MI: Scholarly Press, 1925.

Briffault, R. "Campaign Finance, the Parties and the Court: A Comment on Colorado Republican Campaign Committee v. FEC," *Constitutional Commentary* 14 (1997): 102–103.

Brown, Joseph Epes. *The Sacred Pipe*. Norman: University of Oklahoma Press, 1953.

Bruce, Robert V. 1817: *Year of Violence*. Chicago: Quadrangle, 1970.

Bruning, Fred. "The Vietnam Lessons George Bush Forgot." *MacLeans* (February 18, 1991): 13.

Burtt, Everett J. *Labor Markets, Unions, and Government Policies*. New York: St. Martin's Press, 1963.

Bush, George, W. "Military Order—Detention, Treatment, and Trial of Certain Non-Citizens in the War Against Terrorism, Executive Order 13234." *Weekly Compilation of Presidential Documents*. (November 13, 2001), 1665–1668.

———. *President's Radio Address*. (Washington DC: The White House, May 1, 2004).

Cadwalader, Sandra L., and Vine Deloria Jr. *The Aggression of Civilization: Federal Indian Policy Since the 1880's*. Philadelphia: Temple University Press, 1984.

Cantor, Joseph E. *Campaign Financing: Updated*. Washington, DC: Congressional Research Service: Library of Congress, December 17, 1997.

Capps, Benjamin. *The Indians*. New York: Time Life Books, 1973.

Carroll, T. F. "Freedom of Speech and of the Press in the Federalist Period: The Sedition Act." *Michigan Law Review* 18 (1920): 615.

Cathcart, R. S. "Movements: Confrontation as Rhetorical Form." *Southern Speech Communication Journal* 43 (1978): 233–247.

Catt, Carrie Chapman, and Nettie Rogers Shuler. *Woman Suffrage and Politics: The Inner Story of the Suffrage Movement*. Seattle: University of Washington Press, 1969.

Chafee, Zechariah Jr. *Free Speech in the United States*. Cambridge: Harvard University Press, 1946.

Cherwitz, Richard A. "Masking Inconsistency: The Tonkin Gulf Crisis." *Communication Quarterly* 28 (1980): 27–37.

Chronicles of American Indian Protest. New York: Penguin, 1992.

Classified Information Procedures Act.

Cochran, Thomas C. *Railroad Leaders*. Cambridge: Harvard University Press, 1953.

Cohen, Felix. *Handbook of Federal Indian Law*. Albuquerque: University of New Mexico Press, 1942.

Cole, Terry W. "The Right to Speak: The Free Speech Fights of the Industrial Workers of the World," *Perspectives on Freedom of Speech: Selected Essays from the Journals of the Speech Communication Association*. Eds. Thomas L. Tedford, John J. Makay, and David L. Jamison. Carbondale: Southern Illinois University Press, 1987.

Commager, Henry S. *Documents of American History*. 9th edition. Inglewood Cliffs, NJ: Prentice-Hall, 1973.

Commons J. R., et al. *History of Labor in the United States*. Vol. 2. New York: Macmillan, 1921.

Congressional Globe, Thirty-Ninth Congress, 2nd Session, pt. 1, p. 56.

Conrad, Charles. "The Transformation of the 'Old Feminist' Movement." *Quarterly Journal of Speech* 67 (1981): 284–297.

Cook, Fred J. *Barry Goldwater: Extremist on the Right.* New York: Grove Press, 1964.

Cooper, Helene, and David E. Sanger. "Iraqis' Progress Lags Behind Pace Set by Bush Plan." New York *Times,* March 15, 2007, A1.

Cooper, Jerry M. "The Wisconsin National Guard in the Milwaukee Riots of 1886." *Wisconsin Monthly History* 55 (1971): 31–48.

Creel, George. *How We Advertised America: The First Telling of the Amazing Story of the Committee on Public Information that Carried the Gospel of Americanism to Every Corner of the Globe.* New York: Harper and Brothers, 1920.

Crouse, Timothy. *The Boys on the Bus.* New York: Ballentine, 1972.

Current, Richard N. *The Essentials of American History.* New York: Knopf, 1976.

Current, Richard N., T. Harry Williams, and Frank Freidel. *American History: A Survey.* New York: Knopf, 1963.

Curtis, Michael Kent. *Free Speech, "The People's Darling Privilege," Struggles for Freedom of Expression in American History.* Durham, NC: Duke University Press, 2000.

David, Henry. *History of the Haymarket Affair.* New York: Farrar and Rinehart, 1936.

De Antonia, Emile, and Daniel Talbot. *Point of Order.* New York: Norton, 1964.

DeBenedetti, Charles. "Lyndon Johnson and the Antiwar Opposition." *The Johnson Years, Vol. II: Vietnam, the Environment, and Science.* Ed. Robert A. Divine. Lawrence: University Press of Kansas, 1987: 23–53.

Deloria, Vine Jr. "Knowledge and Understanding: Traditional Education in the Modern World." *Winds of Change* 5:1, 1986: 15.

———. "Ethnoscience and Indian Realities." *Winds of Change* 7(1992): 12–18.

———. "Secularism, Civil Religion, and the Religious Freedom of American Indians." *American Indian Culture and Research Journal* 16 (1992): 9–20.

Deloria, Vine Jr., and Clifford M. Lytle. *American Indians, American Justice.* Austin: University of Texas Press, 1983.

Dennett, Tyler. *John Hay: From Poetry to Politics.* New York: Dodd, Mead & Co., 1933.

Destler, Chester McArthur. *American Radicalism 1865–1901, Essays and Documents.* New London: Connecticut College, 1946.

———. *American Radicalism, 1865–1901.* Chicago: Quadrangle, 1966.

"Detention Hearing Linked to Release," Los Angeles *Times,* September 18, 2002, A18.

Dickerson, Donna Lee. *The Course of Tolerance: Freedom of Press in Nineteenth Century America.* Westport, CT: Greenwood Press, 1990.

———. *The Reconstruction Era: Primary Documents on Events from 1865 to 1877.* Westport, CT: Greenwood Press, 2003.

Dickerson, James R. "Nixon: He Denies He's 'Preening,' Wants U.S. to Look Again." *National Observer,* March 22, 1971, 14.

Divine, Robert A. *Since 1945: Politics and Diplomacy in Recent American History.* New York: John Wiley & Sons, 1975.

"Donors: Survey Sheds Light on Firms that Play Politics." Los Angeles *Times,* September 21, 1997, A2.

Dorris, Michael A. "The Grass Still Grows, the Rivers Still Flow: Contemporary Native Americans." *Daedalus* 110 (1981): 43–69.

Draper, Theodore. *Abuse of Power*. New York: Viking, 1967.

Drash, Wayne. "Report: No WMD stockpiles in Iraq." *CNN.com* (October 7, 2004) World News Ed.

Duscha, Julius. "The President and the Press." *Progressive* (May, 1969): 25–28.

Echo-Hawk, Walter R. "Native American Religious Liberty: Five Hundred Years After Columbus." *American Indian Culture and Research Journal* 17 (1993): 33–52.

Eisenhower, Dwight D. "Radio and Television Address to the American People on the State of the Nation, April 5, 1954." *Public Papers of the President, Dwight D. Eisenhower, 1954*. Washington, DC: GPO, 1960: 375–377.

Evans, Rowland, and Robert Novak. *Lyndon B. Johnson: The Exercise of Power*. New York: New American Library, 1966.

Faulk, Odie B. *The Geronimo Campaign*. New York: Oxford University Press, 1969.

Federal Election Campaign Act, 1971.

Federal Election Campaign Act, 1979.

Fehrenbacher, Don E., ed. *Abraham Lincoln: Speeches and Writings, 1859–1865*. New York: Library of America, 1989.

Ferrell, Robert H. *Woodrow Wilson and World War I, 1917–1921*. New York: Harper & Row, 1985.

Flexner, Eleanor, and Ellen Fitzpatrick. *Century of Struggle: The Woman's Rights Movement in the United States*. Cambridge: Harvard University Press, 1975.

Finney, John W. "The Tonkin Verdict." *The New Republic* 9 (March, 1968): 17–19

Fire, John/Lame Deer, and Richard Erdoes. *Lame Deer Seeker of Visions*. New York: Simon and Schuster, 1972.

Fischer, Mark. "The Sacred and the Secular: An Examination of the 'Wall of Separation' and its Implications on the Religious World View." *University of Pittsburgh Law Review* 54 (1992): 340.

Fisher, Sydney G. "Suppression of the Writ of Habeas Corpus During the War of the Rebellion." *Political Science Quarterly* 3 (1888): 454–488.

Fisher, Walter R. "Reaffirmation and Subversion of the American Dream." *Quarterly Journal of Speech* 59 (1973): 160–167.

Fishman, Donald, and Joyce Lindmark. "George Creel and the Strategy of Benign Censorship during World War I." *Annual Meeting of the Western States Communication Association*. San Jose, 1994.

Fleck, Richard. "Black Elk Speaks: A Native American View of Nineteenth-Century American History." *Journal of American Culture* 17 (1994): 67–69.

Fliegel, Rod. "Free Exercise and the Religious Freedom Restoration Act of 1993: Where We Are, Where We Have Been, and Where We Are Going." *Constitutional Law Journal* 5 (1994): 39–101.

Foner, Philips S. *History of the Labor Movement in the United States*. Vol. 2. New York: International, 1947–1965.

Fortas, Abe. *Concerning Dissent and Civil Disobedience*. New York: New American Library, 1968.

Franklin, John Hope. *Reconstruction After the Civil War.* Chicago: University of Chicago Press, 1964.

Furnas, J. C. *The Americans, A Social History of the United States, 1587–1914.* New York: Putnam's Sons, 1969.

Garfield, James A. *James A. Garfield Papers.* Library of Congress, September 11, 1867.

Garraty, John A. *The New Commonwealth.* New York: Harper & Row, 1968.

Gibbs, Christopher C. *The Great Silent Majority: Missouri's Resistance to World War I.* Columbia: University of Missouri Press, 1988.

Ginger, Ray. *Altgeld's America, 1890–1905.* Chicago: Quadrangle, 1965.

Gleason, Timothy L. "19th Century Legal Practice and Freedom of Press: An Introduction to Unfamiliar Terrain." *Journalism History* 14 (1987): 27–33

Goldstein, Richard J. *Political Repression in Modern America from 1870 to the Present.* Cambridge: Schenkman Press, 1918.

Gordon, Michael A. "The Labor Boycott in New York City, 1880–1886." *Labor History* 16 (1975): 184–229.

Graham, Sarah Hunter. "The Suffrage Renaissance: A New Image for a New Century, 1896–1910." *One Woman, One Vote: Rediscovering the Woman Suffrage Movement.* Ed. Marjorie Spruill Wheeler. Troutdale, OR: New Sage, 1995: 157–178.

Gray, Wood. *The Hidden Civil War.* New York: Viking Press, 1942.

Haiman, Franklyn S. *Speech and Law in a Free Society.* Chicago: University of Chicago Press, 1981.

Hair, William Ivy. *Bourbonism and Agrarian Protest.* Baton Rouge: Louisiana State University Press, 1969.

Halderman, H. R., and Joseph DiMona. *The Ends of Power.* New York: Times Books, 1978.

Hasian, Marouf Jr. *Military Tribunals and the Loss of American Civil Liberties.* Tuscaloosa: University of Alabama Press, 2005.

Hasian, Marouf, Celeste Condit, and John Lucaites. "The Rhetorical Boundaries of 'The Law': A Consideration of the Rhetorical Culture of Legal Practice and the Case of the 'Separate but Equal' Doctrine." *Quarterly Journal of Speech* 82 (1996): 323–342.

Heckscher, August. *Woodrow Wilson.* New York: Charles Scribner's Sons, 1991.

Heilbroner, Robert L. "Andrew Carnegie, Captain of Industry." *Historical Viewpoints: Volume Two, Since 1865.* Ed. John A. Garraty. New York: American Heritage Press, 1970.

Hentoff, Nat. *The First Freedom: The Tumultuous History of Free Speech in America.* New York: Delacorte Press, 1980.

Herring, George C. "The Reluctant Warrior: Lyndon Johnson as Commander in Chief." *Shadow on the White House: Presidents & the Vietnam War, 1945–1975.* Ed. David L. Anderson. Lawrence: University Press of Kansas, 1993: 87–112.

Hesseltine, William B. *Lincoln and the War Governors.* New York: Knopf, 1948.

Higman, John. *Strangers in the Land.* New York: Atheneum, 1970.

Hitchcok, Orville A. "McCarthy's Answer: The Strategy of the Defense." *Quarterly Journal of Speech* 41 (1955): 11–15.

Hofstadter, Richard. *Great Issue in American History.* Vol. 2. New York: Random House, 1958.

———. *The Paranoid Style in American Politics and Other Essays.* New York: Random House, 1967.

Hollihan, Thomas A. "Propagandizing in the Interest of War: A Rhetorical Study of the Committee on Public Information." *Southern Speech Communication Journal* 49 (1984): 240–246.

Howat, Gerald Malcolm. *Dictionary of World History.* London: Thomas Nelson, 1973.

Hudon, Eduard Gerard. *Freedom of Speech and Press in America.* Washington, DC: Public Affairs Press, 1963.

Ivie, Robert. "Realism Masking Fear: George Kennan's Political Rhetoric." *Annual Meeting of Speech Communication Association.* Miami, FL, 1993.

Irwin, Inez Haynes. *The Story of Alice Paul and the National Woman's Party.* 1920. Fairfax, VA: Denlinger's, 1977.

Jackson, Robert L. "Senate Oks Anti-Terrorism Program," Los Angeles *Times,* October 12, 2001, A13.

Jaffe, Julian F. *Crusade Against Radicalism: New York during the Red Scare, 1914–24.* Port Washington, NY: Kennikat, 1972.

Johnson, Donald. "Wilson, Burleson, and Censorship in the First World War." *Journal of Southern History* 28 (1962): 46–58.

Johnson, George W., ed. *The Nixon Presidential Press Conferences.* New York: Earl M. Coleman, 1978.

Johnson, Lyndon Baines. *The Choices We Face.* New York: Bantam Books, 1969.

———. *The Vantage Point: Perspectives of the Presidency, 1963–1969.* New York: Holt, Rinehart, and Winston, 1971.

———. "Thanksgiving Day Message to Armed Forces, November 24, 1965." *Public Papers of the President. Lyndon B. Johnson, 1965.* Washington, DC: GPO, 1971: 1125–1126.

———. October 21, 1966. *Public Papers of the President.* Lyndon B. Johnson, 1966. Washington, DC: GPO, 1971: 1247.

———. "Address to the AFL-CIO, December 12, 1967." *Public Papers of the President.* Lyndon B. Johnson, 1967. Washington, DC: GPO, 1971: 1124–1131.

———. "Veteran's Day Tour of Military Instalations, November 10, 1967." *Public Papers of the President.* Lyndon B. Johnson, 1967. Washington, DC: GPO, 1971: 1012–1013.

———. "National Press Club, January 17, 1969." *Public Papers of the President.* Lyndon B. Johnson, 1968–69. Washington, DC: GPO, 1971: 1350–1362.

Kail, F. M. *What Washington Said: Administration Rhetoric and the Vietnam War: 1949–1969.* New York: Harper & Row, 1973.

Karson, Marc. *American Labor Unions and Politics, 1900–1918.* Carbondale: Southern Illinois University Press, 1958.

Katzenbach, Nicholas deB. "Foreign Policy, Public Opinion, and Secrecy." *Foreign Affairs* 52 (1973): 1–19.

Kaufman, Stuart B. *Samuel Gompers and the Origins of the American Federation of Labor, 1848–1896.* Westport, CT: Greenwood Press, 1973.

Keeley. *Lawrence H. War Before Civilization.* New York: Oxford University Press, 1995.

Kennedy, J. C. "Important Labor Injunction in the Bucks' Stove and Range Company Suit." *Journal of Political Economy* 16, 1908: 102–105.

Kerber, Linda K. *Women of the Republic: Intellect and Ideology in Revolutionary America.* Chapel Hill: University of North Carolina Press, 1980.

Kimball, Clark. "Patriots versus Defenders: The Rhetoric of Intimidation in Indiana During the First World War." Eds. Thomas L. Tedford, John J. Makay, and David L. Jamison. *Perspectives on Freedom of Speech.* Carbondale: Southern Illinois University Press, 1987: 53–65.

Knoww, Erwin. "The President and the Press: Eliminating the Middleman." *Progressive* (March, 1970): 13–18.

Kurtz, Stephen G. *The Presidency of John Adams: The Collapse of Federalism, 1975–1800.* Philadelphia: University of Pennsylvania Press, 1957.

Laidler, Harry W. *Boycotts and the Labor Struggle Legal and Economic Aspects.* New York: John Lane, 1914.

Lake, Randall A. "Between Myth and History: Enacting Time in Native American Protest Rhetoric." *Quarterly Journal of Speech* 77 (1991): 123–151.

———. "The Rhetor as Dialectician in 'Last Chance for Survival.'" *Communication Monographs* 53 (1986): 201–220.

Larson, Cedric, and James R. Mock. "The Lost Files of the Creel Committee of 1917–19." *Public Opinion Quarterly* 3 (1939): 5–29.

Lawson, John D., ed. *American State Trials.* St. Louis: Thomas Law Book, 1915.

Lawson, Paul E., and Jennifer Scholes. "Jurisprudence, Peyote and the Native American Chruch." *American Indian Culture and Research Journal* 10 (1986): 13–27.

Layman, Richard. *Shadow Man: The Life of Dashiell Hammett.* New York: Harcourt Brace Jovanovich, 1981.

Lens, Sidney. *Radicalism in America.* New York: Thomas Y. Crowell, 1966.

Lerner, Gerda. *The Grimké Sisters from South Carolina: Pioneers for Women's Rights and Abolition.* New York: Oxford University Press, 1998.

Levy, Leonard. *Emergence of a Free Press.* New York: Oxford University Press, 1985.

———. *Legacy of Suppression: Freedom of Speech and Press in Early America.* Cambridge: Harvard University Press, 1960.

Levy, Leonard, and Merrill D. Peterson, ed. *Major Crises in American History.* Vol. 1. New York: Harcourt, Brace and World, 1962.

Lind, JoEllen. "Women Trailblazers: The Changing Role of Women in American Legal History." *The Amicus* 7 (1994): 12–14.

Lindsay, Almont. *The Pullman Strike: The Story of a Unique Experiment and of a Great Labor Upheaval.* Chicago: University of Chicago Press, 1964.

Litwack, Leon. *The American Labor Movement.* Englewood Cliffs, NJ: Prentice Hall, 1962.

Lodge, Henry Cabot, ed. *The Works of Alexander Hamilton.* New York: G.P. Putnam's Sons, 1979: 340–342.

Loftin, John D. "Anglo-American Jurisprudence and the Native American Tribal Quest for Religious Freedom." *American Indian Culture and Research Journal* 13 (1989): 1–52.

Logue, Cal M., and John H. Patton. "From Ambiguity to Dogma: The Rhetorical Symbols of Lyndon B. Johnson on Vietnam." *Southern Speech Communication Journal* 47 (1982): 310–329.

Lovestone, Jay. *The Government Strikebreaker: A Study of the Role of the Government in the Recent Crisis.* New York: Workers Party of America, 1923.

Lumsden, Linda J. *Rampant Women: Suffragists and the Right of Assembly.* Knoxville: University of Tennessee Press, 1997.

Luchtblau, Eric, and Josh Meyer. "Terror Probe Feuds Revealed by Secret Court," Los Angeles *Times,* August 23, 2002, A1.

MacArthur, Douglas. "Farewell Address: Joint Session of Congress, 1952." www.americanrhetoric.com/douglasmacarthurfarewelladdress.htm

MacDonald, J. Fred. *Television and the Red Menace: The Video Road to Vietnam.* New York: Praeger, 1985.

Malloy, William M. "Annual Report for 1912." American Historical Association *reprinted in* House Document No. 933, 63rd Congress, 2nd Session: 115–116.

Marcus, Ruth. "DNC Official Concedes 'Mistakes of Process,'" Washington *Post,* November 13, 1996, A4.

Marilley, Suzanne M. *Woman Suffrage and the Origins of Liberal Feminism in the United States, 1820–1920.* Cambridge: Harvard University Press, 1996.

Massachusetts Bureau of Statistics of Labor, Tenth Annual Report. Boston, 1879.

Matthews, Glenna. *The Rise of Public Woman: Woman's Power and Woman's Place in the United States, 1630–1970.* New York: Oxford University Press, 1992.

McChesney, Robert W. "Constant Retreat: The American Civil Liberties Union and the Debate Over the Meaning of Freedom of Speech for Radio Broadcasting in the 30s." *Free Speech Yearbook,* 26 (1988): 40–59.

McCulloch, Hugh. *Men and Measures of Half a Century.* New York: Charles Scribner's Sons, 1889.

McKenna, Clare V. Jr. "Murderers All: The Treatment of Indian Defendants in Arizona Territory, 1880–1912." *American Indian Quarterly* 17 (1993): 359–369.

McNickle, Richard M. *Native American Tribalism: Indian Survivals and Renewals.* New York: Oxford University Press, 1973.

McPherson, Edward. *Political History of the United States During the Period of Reconstruction.* Washington, DC: Philip & Solomons, 1871.

McPherson, James. *Battle Cry of Freedom.* New York: Oxford University Press, 1988.

———. *Ordeal by Fire: The Civil War and Reconstruction.* New York: Knopf, 1982.

———. *This Mighty Scourge: Perspectives on the Civil War.* New York: Oxford University Press, 2007.

Medhurst, Martin J., et al. *Cold War Rhetoric: Strategy, Metaphor, and Ideology.* Westport, CT: Greenwood, 1990.

Meyer, Josh "70,000 Terrorist Suspects Worldwide on U.S. List," Los Angeles *Times,* September 22, 2002, A1.

Meyer, Josn and John-Thor Dahlburg, "Florida Professor Charged in Terrorism Case," Los Angeles *Times,* February 21, 2003, A5.

Miller, John Chester. *Crisis in Freedom: The Alien and Sedition Acts.* Boston: Little, Brown, 1951.

Millett, Allan R. "Chronology of the War for Vietnam." *A Short History of the Vietnam War.* Ed. Allan R. Millett. Bloomington: Indiana University Press, 1978: 144–145.

"Miss Malone Quits the Suffragettes." New York *Times,* March 27, 1908, 4.

Mitgang, H. *Dangerous Dossiers.* New York: Donald I. Fine, 1988.

"Money: More than Ever." Los Angeles *Times,* May 16, 1998, C1.

Mooney, James. "The Ghost Dance Religion and the Sioux Outbreak of 1890." *Fourteenth Annual Report of the Bureau of Ethnology.* Washington, DC: Government Printing Office, 1896.

Morgan, James. *The Life Work of Edward A. Moseley in the Service of Humanity.* New York: Macmillan, 1913.

Morison, Samuel Eliot, and Henry Steele Commager. *The Growth of the American Republic.* Vol. 1. New York: Oxford University Press, 1962.

Morris, Richard, and Philip Wander. "Native American Rhetoric: Dancing in the Shadows of the Ghost Dance." *Quarterly Journal of Speech* 76 (1990): 164–191.

Morse Jr., John T., and John Quincy Adams. Boston: Houghton, Mifflin, 1883.

Moses, L. G. " 'The Father Tells Me Sol' Wovoka: The Ghost Dance Prophet." *American Indian Quarterly* 9 (1985): 335–351.

Mott, Frank Luther. *American Journalism: A History of Newspapers in the United States through 250 Years: 1690–1940.* New York: Macmillan, 1949.

Murphy, John. "Our Mission and Our Moment: George W. Bush and September 11," *Rhetoric and Public Affairs* 6 (2003): 607–632

Murphy, Paul. *World War I and the Origins of Civil Liberties in the United States.* New York: Norton, 1979.

Nabokov, Peter. *Native American Testimony.* New York: Penguin, 1992.

Nash, Howard P. *Andrew Johnson: Congress and Reconstruction.* Rutherford, NJ: Fairleigh Dickinson University Press, 1972.

Neihardt, John G. *Black Elk Speaks.* Lincoln: University of Nebraska Press, 1932/New York: Washington Square Press, 1959.

Nelson, Harold. *Freedom of the Press from Hamilton to the Warren Court.* New York: Bobbs-Merrill, 1967.

Newman, Robert P., and Dale R. Newman. *Evidence.* Boston: Houghton Mifflin, 1969.

Newman, Simon P. *Parades and the Politics of the Street: Festive Culture in the Early American Republic.* Philadelphia: University of Pennsylvania Press, 1997.

Nicolay, John G., and John Hay. *Abraham Lincoln: A History.* Vol. 7. New York: Century, 1890.

Nixon, Richard M. "Dedication of the Karl E. Mundt Library, June 3, 1969." *Public Papers of the Presidents.* Richard M. Nixon, 1969. Washington, DC: GPO, 1971: 425–431.

———. "Statement on Campus Disorders, March 22, 1969." *Public Papers of the Presidents.* Richard M. Nixon, 1969. Washington, DC: GPO, 1971: 235–237.

———. Richard M. *Nixon: The Memoirs of Richard Nixon.* New York: Warner, 1978.

Oshinsky, David. *A Conspiracy So Immense.* New York: Macmillan, 1983.

Parmet, Herbert S. *Eisenhower and the American Crusades.* New York: Macmillan, 1972.

"Pastoral Letter." Assumption College (September 1, 2008). www.assumption. edu/users/mcclymer/His130/P-H/Grimke/PastoralLetter.html

Peterson, H. C., and Gilbert C. Fite. *Opponents of the War.* Madison: University of Wisconsin Press, 1957.

Phelps, Glenn A. "Representation Without Taxation: Citizenship and Suffrage in Indian Country." *American Indian Quarterly* 9 (1985): 135–148.

"Platform." *Publications of the American Economic Association.* Vol. 1. Baltimore, 1887: 6–7.

Pollard, James E. *The Presidents and the Press.* New York: Macmillan, 1947.

Powderly, Terrence V. "The Army of the Discontented." *North American Review* (April 1885): 369–377.

Powe, Lucas A. *American Broadcasting and The First Amendment.* Berkeley: University of California Press, 1987.

Powledge, Fred. *The Engineering of Restraint: The Nixon Administration and the Press.* Washington, DC: Public Affairs Press, 1971.

Price, Raymond. *With Nixon.* New York: Viking Press, 1977.

Prucha, Francis Paul. *Indian Policy in the United States.* Lincoln: University of Nebraska Press, 1981.

Rabban, David M. "The Emergence of Modern First Amendment Doctrine." *University of Chicago Law Review* 50 (1983): 1205–1355.

———. "The IWW Free Speech Fights and Popular Conceptions of Free Expression Before World War I." *Virginia Law Review* 80 (1994): 1055–1063.

Randall, James G. *Constitutional Problems Under Lincoln.* Urbana: University of Illinois Press, 1951.

Rarick, David. *Cong. Congressional Record—House,* (1 Session, 90th Congress, 1967) p. 15641.

Rashin, A. H. "What Communists Can and Can't Do." New York *Times,* April, 26 1953, E12.

Rather, Dan, and Gary Paul Gates. *The Palace Guard.* New York: Harper & Row, 1974.

Ray, Angela. "The Rhetorical Ritual of Citizenship: Women's Voting as Public Performance, 1868–1865." *Quarterly Journal of Speech* 93 (2007): 1–26.

Redich, Martin H. *The Logic of Persecution: Free Expression and the McCarthy Era.* Stanford, CA: Stanford University Press, 2005.

Rhodes, John. "An American Tradition: The Religious Persecution of Native Americans." *Montana Law Review* 52 (1991): 14–72.

Richardson, James D. *A Compilation of the Messages and Papers of the Presidents, 1789–1902.* Vols. 2, 3, 6. Washington DC: Bureau of National Literature and Art, 1907, 1987.

———. *A Compilation of the Messages and Papers of the Presidents, 1789–1897.* Vol. 6. Washington, DC: Government Printing Office, 1911.

Ripley, William Z. *Railroads, Rates and Regulation.* New York: Longmans, Green, 1924.

Riswold, C. D. "A Religious Response Veiled in a Presidential Address: A Theological Study of Bush's Speech on 20 September, 2001," *Political Theology* 5 (2004): 39–46.

Roche, John. *Quest for a Dream*. New York: Macmillan, 1963.

Roosevelt, Franklyn D. Memorandum to J. Edgar Hoover, January 21, 1942. President's Secretary's File. Justice Department—J. Edgar Hoover folder, Roosevelt Library, Hyde Park, NY.

Rosteck, Thomas. *"See It Now" Confronts McCarthyism* (Tuscaloosa: University of Alabama Press, 1995).

Ruth, Marcus. "DNC Official Concedes 'Mistakes of Process,'" Washington *Post*, November 13, 1996, A4.

Safire, William. *Before the Fall*. Garden City, NY: Doubleday, 1975.

Sale, Kirkpatrick. *The Conquest of Paradise*. New York: Knopf, 1990.

Savage, David G. "Memos Are Called 'tip of the iceberg,'" Los Angeles *Times*, March 3, 2009, A14.

———. "Bush-era Memos Stun Legal Experts," Los Angeles *Times*, March 4, 2009, A13.

Schaack, Michael J. *Anarchy and Anarchists*. Chicago: Schulte, 1889.

Scheiber, Harry H. *The Wilson Administration and Civil Liberties, 1917–1921*. Ithaca, NY: Cornell University Press, 1960.

Schrecker, Ellen. *No Ivory Tower: McCarthyism and the Universities*. New York: Oxford University Press, 1986.

Scranton Commission. *Report of the President's Commission on Campus Unrest*. New York: Arno, 1970.

Serrano, Richard A. "Some Held in Terror Probe Report Rights Being Abused," Los Angeles *Times*, October 15, 2001, A4.

———. "A Swift, Secretive Dragnet after Attacks," Los Angeles *Times*, September 10, 2002, A16.

Serrill, Michael S. "Struggling to be Themselves." *Time* November 9, 1992, 52–54.

Sexton, Patricia C. *The War on Labor and the Left, Understanding America's Unique Conservatism*. Boulder, CO: Westview Press, 1991.

Silbey, Joel H. *A Respectable Minority: The Democratic Party in the Civil War Era, 1860–1868*. New York: Norton, 1977.

Sklansky, Jeff. "Rock, Reservation and Prison: The Native American Occupation of Alcatraz Island." *American Indian Culture and Research Journal* 13 (1989): 29–68.

Small, Melvin. *Johnson, Nixon, and the Doves*. New Brunswick, NJ: Rutgers University Press, 1988.

Smith, Craig R. "Daniel Webster's July 17th Address as a Mediating Influence in Conflict Situations." *Quarterly Journal of Speech* 71 (1985): 349–361.

———. *Freedom of Expression and Partisan Politics*. Columbia: University of South Carolina Press, 1989.

———. *To Form a More Perfect Union*. Lanham, MD: University Press America, 1993.

Smith, Craig R., and Scott Lybarger. *The Ratification of the Bill of Rights, 1789–91*. Long Beach, CA: Center for First Amendment Studies, 1991.

Smith, Curt. *Long Time Gone: The Years of Turmoil Remembered*. South Bend, IN: Icarus, 1982.

Smith, James Morton. *Freedom's Fetters: The Alien and Sedition Laws and American Civil Liberties*. 2nd edition. Ithaca, NY: Cornell University Press, 1963.

Smith, Steven A. "Freedom of Expression in the Confederate States of America." *Perspectives in Freedom of Speech*. Eds. Thomas L. Tedford, John J. Makay, and David L. Jamison. Carbondale: Southern Illinois University Press, 1987.

"Soft Money Dollars." *Time*, September 9, 1999, 42–44.

Spear, Joseph C. *Presidents and the Press: The Nixon Legacy*. Cambridge, MA: MIT Press, 1984.

Spores, Ronald. "Too Small a Place: The Removal of the Wilamette Valley Indians, 1850–1856." *American Indian Quarterly* 17 (1993): 171–191.

Sprague, Dean. *Freedom Under Lincoln*. Boston: Houghton Mifflin, 1965.

Stanton, Elizabeth C., Susan B. Anthony, Matilda J. Gage, and Ida H. Harper, eds. *History of Woman Suffrage*. New York: Arno, 1969.

Standing Bear, Luther. "Land of the Spotted Eagle." Chronicles of American Indian Protest. Ed. *The Council on Interracial Books for Children*. Greenwich, CT: Fawcett, 1971.

Steimnetz, Paul B. *Pipe, Bible and Peyote Among the Oglala Lakota*. Knoxville: University of Tennessee Press, 1990.

Stevens, Doris. *Jailed for Freedom*. New York: Boni and Liveright, 1920: New York: New Sage, 1995.

Stevens, John D. "Congressional History of the 1798 Sedition Law." *Journalism Quarterly* 43 (1966): 247–256.

Strausfield, David M. "Reformers in Conflict: The Pueblo Dance Controversy." *The Aggression of Civilization: Federal Indian Policy Since the 1880's*. Ed. Sandra L. Cadwalader and Vine Deloria Jr. Philadelphia: Temple University Press, 1984.

Strickland, Rennard. "Implementing the National Policy of Understanding, Preserving, and Safeguarding the Heritage of Indian Peoples and Native Hawaiians: Human rights, sacred Objects, and Cultural Patrimony." *Arizona State Law Journal* 24 (1992): 175–191.

"Suffragists March in Procession To-Day." New York *Times*, May 6, 1911, 13.

"Suffrage Parader Loses Teaching Job." New York *Times*, May 22, 1912, 1.

Suter, Jon M., and Jack A. Samosky. "Uneasy Reading: Censorship in Woodrow Wilson's Wartime Administration." Annual Convention of the Western States Communication Association. San Jose, 1994.

Szulc, Tad. *The Illusion of Peace: Foreign Policy in the Nixon Years*. New York: Viking Press, 1978.

"Tactics and Techniques of the National Woman's Party Suffrage Campaign." *Library of Congress*. (September 1, 2008). http://lcweb2.loc.gov/ammem/collections/suffrage/nwp/tactics.html

Tapahe, Luralene D. "After the Religious Freedom Restoration Act: Still No Equal Protection for First Amendment Worshipers." *New Mexico Law Review* 24 (1994): 331–363.

The Holy Bible. "I Corinthians 14:34–35." King James Version. New York: American Bible Society: 1999; Bartleby.com, 2000. www.bartleby.com/108/

Theodore, Alisse. "'A Right to Speak on the Subject': The U.S. Women's Antiremoval Petition Campaign, 1829–1831." *Rhetoric and Public Affairs* 5 (2002): 601–624.

Thomas, Helen. *Dateline: White House.* New York: Macmillan, 1975.

Thompson, Slason. "Violence in Labor Disputes." *World's Work* (December, 1904): 1–4.

Thrapp, Dan L. *The Conquest of Appacheria.* Oklahoma City: University of Oklahoma Press, 1967.

Trefousse, Hans L. *Andrew Johnson: A Biography.* New York: Norton, 1989.

Turner, Frederick, W. III, ed. *The Portable North American Indian Reader.* New York: Viking Press, 1974.

Turner, Kathleen J. *Lydon Johnson's Dual War: Vietnam and the Press.* Chicago: University of Chicago Press, 1985.

Tyler, Poyntz, ed. *Immigration and the United States.* New York: Wilson, 1956.

Unger, Sanford J. *The Papers & the Papers.* New York: Dutton, 1972.

United States. Congress, Senate Subcommittee on Permanent Investigations. *State Department Information Program—Information Centers.* 83rd Congress, 1st Session, 1953.

United States Institute of Peace. *Iraq Study Group Report.* Washington, DC: United States Institute of Peace, December 6, 2006.

Valenti, Jack. *A Very Human President.* New York: Pocket Books, 1976.

Wall, Steve, and Harvey Arden. *Wisdomkeepers: Meetings with Native American Spiritual Elders.* Hillsboro, OR: Beyond Words Press, 1990.

Ware, B. L., and Wil A. Linkugel. "They Spoke in Defense of Themselves: On the Generic Criticism of Apologia." *Quarterly Journal of Speech* 59 (1973): 273–283.

Washburn, Patrick S. "FDR Versus His Own Attorney General: The Struggles over Sedition, 1914–42." *Journalism Quarterly* 62 (1985): 717–724.

Washburn, Wilcomb E. "Indian Policy Since the 1880's." *The Aggression of Civilization: Federal Indian Policy Since the 1880's.* Eds. Sandra L. Cadwalader and Vine Deloria Jr. Philadelphia: Temple University Press, 1984.

Wells, D. A. *Recent Economic Changes, and Their Effect on the Production and Distribution of Wealth and the Well-Being of Society.* New York: Appleton, 1889.

———. "Economic Disturbances Since 1873, I." *Popular Science Monthly* 31 (July, 1887): 289–304.

———. "Economic Disturbances Since 1873, II." *Popular Science Monthly* 31 (August, 1887): 433–451.

———. "Economic Disturbances Since 1873, III." *Popular Science Monthly* 31 (September, 1887): 577–597.

———. "Economic Disturbances Since 1873, IV." *Popular Science Monthly* 31 (October, 1887): 768–793.

———. "Economic Disturbances Since 1873, V." *Popular Science Monthly* 32 (November, 1887): 1–17.

Welles, Gideon. *Diary of Gideon Welles*. Ed. Howard K. Beale. Vol. 3. New York: 1960.
Welter, Barbara. "The Cult of True Womanhood: 1820–1860." *American Quarterly* 18 (1966): 151–174.
Wheelan, Joseph. *Mr. Adams Last Crusade*. New York: Public Affairs, 2008.
Wills, Gary. *Lead Time: A Journalist's Education*. Garden City, NY: Doubleday, 1983.
Wilson, Woodrow. *The Papers of Woodrow Wilson*. Ed. A. S. Link. Vols. 43, 44, 55. Princeton, NJ: Princeton University Press, 1979–1991.
Wise, David. "The President and the Press." *Atlantic* (April 1973): 55–64.
Witcover, Jules. "Two Weeks That Shook the Press." *Columbia Journalism Review* 10 (1971): 7–15.
———. "How Well Does the White House Press Perform?" *Columbia Journalism Review* 12 (1973): 39–43.
Wood, Lewis. "28 Are Indicted on Sedition Charge." New York *Times*, July 24, 1942, 1, 8.
Wright, Robin, and Ellen Knickmeyer. "U.S. Lowers Sights On What Can Be Achieved in Iraq." Washington *Post*, August 15, 2005, A1.

Court Cases

A. F. of L. v. Buck Stove and Range Co., Ct. of Ap., D. of C., (1909).
Abrams v. U.S., 250 U.S. 616 (1919).
Albertson v. Subversive Activities Control Board, 382 U.S. 70, (1965).
Barr v. Essex Trades Council, 53 N.J. Eq.101 (1894); or 8 Dick. 108, (1894).
Boumediene v. Bush, 553 U.S. 723 (2008).
Bradwell v. Illinois, 83 U.S. 422 (1873).
Buckley v. Valeo, 424 U.S. 1 (1976).
Citizens United v. FEC (2010), slip opinion.
Center for National Security Studies, et al. v. U.S. Justice Department 540 U.S. 1104 (2004).
Church of the Lukumi Babulu Aye, Inc. v. City of Hialeah, 113 S. Ct. 2217, 2233 (1993).
Colorado Republican Committee v. FEC, 518 U. S. 604 (1996).
Colorado Republican Committee v. FEC, 533 U. S. 431 (2001).
Communist Party v. Subversive Activities Control Board, 367 U.S. 1 (1961).
Davis v. FEC, 501 U.S. 22 (2007).
Davis v. Massachusetts, 167 U.S. 43 (1897).
De Jonge v. Oregon, 299 U.S. 353 (1937).
Dennis v. U.S., 341 U.S. 494 (1951).
Employment Div., Dept. of Human Resources v. Smith, 494 U.S. 872 (1990).
Engel v. Vitale, 370 U.S. 421 (1962).
Ex parte Merryman, 17 Fed. Cas. 144.

Ex parte Milligan, 71 U.S. 2 (1866).
Ex parte Quirin, 317 U.S. 1 (1942).
Ex parte Vallandigham, 68 U.S. 243 (1864).
Everson v. Board of Education, 403 U.S. 602 (1971).
FEC v. Furgatch, 484 U.S. 850, 864 (1987).
FEC v. Massachusetts Citizens for Life, 479 U.S. 238 (1986).
FEC v. Wisconsin Right to Life, 551 U.S. 449 (2007).
Frohwerk v. United States, 249 U.S. 204 (1919).
Gitlow v. New York, 268 U.S. 652 (1925).
Goldstein v. United States, 258 Fed. 908 9th Cir., (1919).
Hague v. Committee for Industrial Organization, 307 U.S. 496 (1939).
Hamdi v. Rumsfeld, 542 U.S. 507 (2006).
Harbury v. Deutch, 233 Fed. 3d 596 (2000).
Harrison v. Laveen, 67 Ariz. 337 (1948).
Hurley v. Irish-American Gay, Lesbian and Bisexual Group, 515 U.S. 557 (1995).
In re Debs, 158 U.S. 654, 15 S. Ct. 900 (1895).
Johnson v. Eisentrager, 339 U. S. 763 (1950).
Jordahl v. Hayda, 1 Cal. App. 696 (1905).
Joseph Burstyn, Inc. v. Wilson, 343 U.S. 495 (1952).
Lemon v. Kurtzman, 403 U.S. 602 (1971).
Lyng v. Northwest Indian Cemetery Assn., 485 U.S. 439 (1988).
McConnell v. FEC, 540 U.S. 93 (2003).
McIntyre v. Ohio Elections Commission, 514 U.S. 334 (1995).
Miami Herald v. Tornillo, 418 U.S. 241 (1974).
Minor v. Happersett, 88 U.S. 162 (1874).
Montana v. U.S., 450 U.S. 544 (1981).
Mutual Film Corporation v. Industrial Communication of Ohio, 236 U.S. 230 (1915).
Mutual Film Corporation of Missouri v. Hodges, 236 U.S. 248 (1915).
NAACP v. Alabama, 357 U.S. 449 (1958).
NBC v. United States, 319 U.S. 190 (1943).
New York Times Co. v. Sullivan, 376 U.S. 245, 276 (1962).
Nixon v. Shrink Missouri Government PAC, 528 U.S. 377 (2000).
Porter v. Hall, 34 Ariz. 308, 411 (1928).
Redlion Broadcasting v. FCC, 395 U.S. 367 (1969).
Reed v. Reed, 404 U.S. 71 (1971).
Rider v. Board of Education of Independent School District, 414 U.S. 1097 (1973).
Sioux Nation v. U.S., 448 U.S. 371 (1980).
Schneiderman v. United States, 320 U.S. 118 (1943).
Schenck v. United States, 249 U.S. 47 (1919).
Sherbert v. Verner, 374 U.S. 398 (1963).
Texas v. Johnson, 491 U.S. 397 (1989).
Tinker v. Des Moines School District, 393 U.S. 503 (1969).
United States v. E. C. Knight & Co., 156 U.S. 1 (1896).
United States v. Motion Picture Film "The Spirit of '76," 252 F. Supp. 946, S.D., California (1917).

United States v. Susan B. Anthony 24 Fed. Cases 829–833, (1873); or 11 Blatchford, 200–212 (1873).

Watkins v. United States, 354 U.S. 178–197 (1957).

Wooley v. Maynard, 430 U.S. 705 (1977).

Yates v. United States, 354 U.S. 298 (1957).

Contributors

Senior Author and Editor

CRAIG R. SMITH is professor of Communication Studies at California State University, Long Beach, where he also directs the Center for First Amendment Studies. At CSULB, he has also served as chair of the departments of Communication Studies, Comparative Literature and Classics, Journalism and Film and Electronic Arts. During his 22 years at CSULB, he has won the Distinguished Teaching, Distinguished Scholar, and Outstanding Professor Awards, along with the Nicholas P. Hardeman Award for Outstanding Leadership. He has twice won the Robert O'Neil Award from the National Communication Association for outstanding scholarship on First Amendment issues. He won the Outstanding Professor Award from the National Speakers Association in 2001. From 1996 through 1998, he served on the California Commission on Teacher Credentialing; from 2005 through 2009, he served on the Board of Trustees of the California State University System as the Faculty Trustee.

He received his Ph.D. from Pennsylvania State University in 1969 and began a teaching career that has taken him to San Diego State University, the University of Virginia, and the University of Alabama in Birmingham where he founded and chaired the Communication Arts Division. He also served as a consultant to CBS News convention, election night and inaugural coverage from 1968 to 1984. He served as a full-time speechwriter for President Gerald Ford and Chrysler CEO Lee Iacocca and was a consulting writer for President George H. W. Bush.

He has written more than 60 scholarly articles and 15 books including most recently *The Four Freedoms of the First Amendment* (2004) and *Daniel Webster and the Oratory of Civil Religion* (2005). The third edition of his *Rhetoric and Human Consciousness: A History* was released in 2009.

Contributors

R. BRANDON ANDERSON is a lecturer and forensics director in the Communication Studies Department at California State University, Long Beach, where he received his M.A. in 2007. His research has been featured on several panels at the Western States Communication Association's and the National Communication Association's annual conventions.

SHARON DOWNEY is chair of the Communication Studies Department at California State University, Long Beach, and received her Ph.D. from the University of Colorado in 1983. She has served as editor of *Women's Studies in Communication*. Critical analyses stemming from her scholarly interest in mass media, apologia, popular culture, and the mythology of war have appeared in the leading journals of the field.

KATIE L. GIBSON received her Ph.D. from Pennsylvania State University in 2004 and was recently promoted to associate professor of Communication Studies at California State University, Long Beach, where she teaches courses in rhetoric and public address. Her research has appeared in the *Western Journal of Communication*, *Women's Studies in Communication*, the *Southern Communication Journal*, and *Communication Quarterly*.

AMY L. HEYSE received her Ph.D. from the University of Maryland in 2006. She is an assistant professor of Communication Studies at California State University, Long Beach, where she teaches courses in rhetorical criticism, American public address, and campaign persuasion. Her research in political rhetoric appears in *Rhetoric Society Quarterly*, *Southern Communication Journal*, and *Western Journal of Black Studies*.

STEPHANIE J. HURST received her M.A. in Communication Studies from California State University, Long Beach, in 1992, where she also served as a research fellow at the Center for First Amendment Studies. She teaches at Kirkwood Community College. She has presented papers at the National Communication Association's annual meeting, one of which was a "top five" paper in freedom of expression.

KAREN RASMUSSEN is a professor of Communication Studies at California State University, Long Beach, who received her Ph.D. in 1974 at the University of Colorado. Her research focuses on popular culture and film and feminist studies and can be found in the leading journals of the field.

ANDREW SACHS received his Ph.D. in 1992 from the University of Wisconsin. He served as an assistant professor of Communication Studies at California State University in Long Beach until 1995, when he became involved in community counseling. His interest in close textual analysis of public address led to his work on a volume of collected essays on the rhetoric of imperialism.

Index

College Campuses. *See*
  Berkeley, University of California;
  Brown University; Columbia
  University; Harvard University
*Colorado Republican Committee v.
  FEC*, 260, 261
Columbia University, 186
  See also College Campuses
Command of the Army Act, 74
Commissary General, 32
Committees. *See*
  Committee on Public Information;
  Fish Committee; House Ways
  and Means; House Un-American
  Activities Committee (HUAC);
  Joint Committee on Reconstruction;
  McCormick-Dickstein Committee
Committee on Public Information, 176,
  199, 314, 317
  See also Committees; Creel, George
Communists, 175, 177–180, 183–190,
  191, 193, 195–198, 202, 215, 224,
  302, 304, 321
Communist Party, 172, 178, 181–182,
  186–189, 190, 196
Communist Revolution, 175
  See also Russia; Communist Front
Communist Front Organization/Group,
  187, 190–191
  See also Communists; McCarthy,
  Joseph
Condemnation, 213, 218–219, 222,
  225, 231, 237
  Demonizing, 213, 219, 223, 225
  Marginalizing, 213, 219, 225
  See also Strategies of Suppression
Confederacy, 32, 39, 52, 60–63, 70,
  74, 82
Confiscatory Act of 1862, 70
  See also Acts
Congress of Industrial Organizations
  (CIO), 131
  See also Unions
Congressional Record, 227
Conkling, Roscoe (Congressman), 59,
  84

Conspiracy Act, 144
  See also Acts; Union Suppression
Conspiracy Laws, 134, 141–142
  See also Union Suppression
Constitutional Convention, 2, 309
  See also Conventions
Conventions. *See*
  Constitutional Convention;
  Democratic Convention of 1866;
  Democratic National Convention of
  1968; Franco-American; Hartford
  Convention, Federalist Party;
  Mississippi State; Republican
  Convention of 1864; Republican
  Convention of 1872; Republican
  Convention of 1952
Cook, George (General), 100–101
Cooper, Thomas (Newspaper
  Publisher), 18, 22, 24, 194
Cooper Union, 98
Co-optation, 197, 213, 216–218, 231,
  237–239, 298, 309
  Appropriation, 213, 215–218, 228,
  239, 309
  Deflection, 213, 217
  diffusion, 217–218, 285, 301
  distortion, 217–218
  See also Strategies of Suppression
Copperheads, xi, 38, 39, 52, 58, 69,
  301–302
Corning, Erastus, 31, 34, 56
Court Cases. *See*
  *Abrams v. United States; Barr v. Essex
  Trades Council; Cherokee Nation v. the
  State of Georgia; Employment Div.,
  Dept. of Human Resources of Oregon
  v. Smith; Gitlow v. New York; Jordahl
  v. Hayda; Lyng v. Northwest Indian
  Cemetery Assn.; Merryman Case;
  Milligan Case; Rosebud Sioux Tribe
  v. Kneip; Sequoyah v. Tennessee Valley
  Authority; Schenck v. United States;
  Sherbert v. Vernor; Teso Oath Case;
  Vallandigham Case; Worcester v. Georgia*
Court of Indian Offenses, 105
Crawford, Harvey T., 107

Welch, Joseph, 189, 192, 307
Wells, Gideon (Secretary), 325
West Terrace Press Conference, 230
Westmoreland, William (General), 227
Western Federation of Miners, 131,
140
See also Unions
Western White House, 230
Wheeler-Howard Act, 107
See also Acts; Indian Citizenship Act
Wheeling Speech of 1950, 194
See also Pearson, Drew
Wherry, Kenneth (Senate Minority
Leader), 185
Whig Party, 58
Whitehead, Clay Thomas, Dr., 235
White House Vietnam Information
Group, 227
See also Vietnam War
White Russian Armies, 175
See also Russia
Wilamette Valley, 118
Wilamette Valley People, 118
See also Native American Tribes
Williams, John, 135
Williams, Thomas (Senator), 84
Williams, Robert, 22
Wilson, Jack, 106
See also Wovoka
Wilson, James (Congressman), 77
Wilson, Woodrow (President), xii,
77, 106, 151, 162, 165–166, 168,
175–178, 184, 189, 202, 272, 297,
305, 315–316, 323

Winchell, Walter (Columnist), 186
Wirt, William, 19
Wobbly, 131–132, 145
See also Industrial Workers of the
World (IWW)
Wolfe, Thomas, 198
See also Freedom of Information Act
Women's Suffrage, xi, xiii, 151–153,
155–171, 297, 312–313, 316,
320–323
Parades, 161–163, 166, 172, 312,
320, 323
Woodward, Bob, 234, 248, 312
Worcester v Georgia (1832), 92
See also Court Cases
Wounded Knee, 87, 101, 103, 107,
112–114, 118
See also Military Interaction and
Native Americans
Wovoka, 106, 120, 320
See also Kwotisauq; Wilson, Jack;
Jesus; Juses; Paiute
Wright, Carroll D., 133

XYZ dispatches, 8

Yankee Doodle, 17

Zablodowsky, David, 196
Zenger, John Peter, 11
Ziegler, Ronald, 230, 320
Zigler, James, 274
Zwicker, Ralph W. (General), 188,
197

QM LIBRARY
(MILE END)